Country House Life

FAMILY,
SEXUALITY AND SOCIAL RELATIONS
IN PAST TIMES
GENERAL EDITORS:
Peter Laslett and Michael Anderson

Western Sexuality: Practice and Precept in Past and Present Times **
Edited by Philippe Ariès and André Béjin

The Explanation of Ideology: Family Structures and Social Systems **
Emmanuel Todd

The Causes of Progress: Culture, Authority and Change
Emmanuel Todd

An Ordered Society: Gender and Class in Early Modern England *
Susan Dwyer Amussen

Sexuality and Social Control, Scotland, 1660–1780
Rosalind Mitchison and Leah Leneman

A History of Contraception: From Antiquity to the Present **
Angus McLaren

The Children of the Poor: Representations of Childhood since the Seventeenth Century
Hugh Cunningham

A History of Youth **
Michael Mitterauer

Marriage and the English Reformation
Eric Josef Carlson

Medieval Prostitution *
Jacques Rossiaud

Wet Nursing: A History *
Valerie Fildes

Porneia: On Desire and the Body in Antiquity **
Aline Rousselle

Highley 1550–1880: The Development of a Community *
Gwyneth Nair

The English Noble Household, 1250–1600 *
Kate Mertes

Country House Life: Family and Servants, 1815–1914
Jessica Gerard

FORTHCOMING

Londoners: The Family and Kinship in Early Modern London
Vivien Brodsky

The Rise and Fall of the Servant in the Twentieth Century
Kate Mertes

The Making of a Woman's World
Kate Mertes

Women and Families: An Oral History, 1940–1970
Elizabeth Roberts

* Out of print.
** Available in paperback.

Country House Life
Family and Servants, 1815–1914

Jessica Gerard

BLACKWELL
Oxford UK & Cambridge USA

Copyright © Jessica Gerard 1994

The right of *Jessica Gerard* to be identified as author of this work has been asserted in accordance with the Copyright, Designs and Patents Act 1988.

First published 1994

Blackwell Publishers
108 Cowley Road
Oxford OX4 1JF
UK

238 Main Street
Cambridge, Massachusetts 02142
USA

All rights reserved. Except for the quotation of short passages for the purposes of criticism and review, no part of this publication may be reproduced, stored in a retrieval system, or transmitted, in any form or by any means, electronic, mechanical, photocopying, recording or otherwise, without the prior permission of the publisher.

Except in the United States of America, this book is sold subject to the condition that it shall not, by way of trade or otherwise, be lent, resold, hired out, or otherwise circulated without the publisher's prior consent in any form of binding or cover other than that in which it is published and without a similar condition including this condition being imposed on the subsequent purchaser.

British Library Cataloguing in Publication Data

A CIP catalogue record for this book is available from the British Library.

Library of Congress Cataloging-in-Publication Data

Gerard, Jessica, 1954–
Country house life: family and servants / Jessica Gerard.
  p. cm. – (The Family, sexuality, and social relations in past times)
Includes bibliographical references and index.

ISBN 0–631–15566–X (alk. paper)

1. Rural families–Great Britain–History–19th century. 2. Great Britain–Rural conditions–19th century. 3. Domestics–Great Britain–History–19th century. 4. Households–Great Britain–History–19th century. 5. Country life–Great Britain–History–19th century. I. Title. II. Series.

HQ613.G47 1994   93-36481
306.85'0941–dc20   CIP

Typeset in 11 on 13 pt Garamond by
Pure Tech Corporation, Pondicherry, India
Printed in Great Britain by
Hartnolls Limited, Bodmin, Cornwall

This book is printed on acid-free paper

For David

Contents

List of Plates	viii
Acknowledgements	xi
Introduction	1
1 The Demography of the Landed Family	21
2 The Country House Childhood	38
3 Parents and Children	65
4 Courtship and Marriage	90
5 Country House Women	115
6 Staff Size	142
7 The Demography of Country House Servants	162
8 Gentleman's Service	190
9 Life Below Stairs	220
10 Relations Between Employers and Servants	239
Conclusion	272
Notes	285
Appendix Servants' Wages Records	331
Bibliography	333
Index	361

List of Plates

1 Trentham Hall, remodelled by Sir Charles Barry in 1834–40 for the second Duke of Sutherland. Reproduced by kind permission of the Trustees of the William Salt Library; photograph, Peter Rogers. 14
2 A hunt meeting at Hampton Court; photograph, Susan Wood. 15
3 A bachelor and his heir: Ralph Sneyd with his nephew and namesake. © Sneyd Papers, Keele University Library. 22
4 A large mid-Victorian family: George, ninth Earl of Carlisle, his wife Rosalind and their eleven children. Private collection. 26
5 The nurse and members of the Lyttleton family in the nursery at Hagley Hall in the 1890s. Reproduced by kind permission of Weidenfeld & Nicolson publishers. 47
6 Two daughters of the eighth Viscount Cobham and their governess in the schoolroom at Hagley Hall. Reproduced by kind permission of Weidenfeld & Nicolson publishers. 50
7 The Fitzwilliam children in front of Wentworth Woodhouse, 1908. Reproduced by kind permission of Weidenfeld & Nicolson publishers. 56
8 Reginald Windsor Sackville-West, Baron Buckhurst, later the seventh Earl de la Warr, with his son. Reproduced by kind permission of Weidenfeld & Nicolson publishers. 77
9 George Howard, Viscount Howard, later ninth Earl of Carlisle, playing "race" with his sons. Private collection. 79
10 Louisa Yorke with her sons Phillip and Simon. © The National Trust for North Wales; photograph, Clwyd Record Office. 83
11 Croquet was a popular occasion for flirtation: Bowthorpe Hall, Norwich. © Norwich Library; photograph, C. S. Middleton. 92
12 A suitable match: the wedding in 1909 of Captain Henry Phillips,

LIST OF PLATES ix

eldest son of Sir Charles Phillips, first baronet of Picton Castle, Pembrokeshire, and an heiress, Victoria Gwynne-Hughes, only child of John Gwynne-Hughes of Tregyb, Carmarthenshire. Reproduced by permission of The National Library of Wales. 99

13 A companionate marriage: Mr and Mrs John Sperling of Dynes Hall playing chess. Watercolour painting by their daughter, Diana Sperling, c.1815. © Neville Ollerenshaw. 106

14 Rosalind Howard, Marchioness Howard, with her estate agent. Private collection. 119

15 Mary Ann Dixon entertaining the Market Rasen volunteers in 1862 at Holton. © Lincolnshire Archives. 125

16 Mrs Sperling and her maid swatting flies at Dynes Hall. Watercolour painting by her daughter, Diana Sperling. © Neville Ollerenshaw. 134

17 Lady Elena Wickham out shooting, c.1897. Reproduced by kind permission of Weidenfeld & Nicolson publishers. 138

18 A typical peer's establishment: the Earl of Sandwich's staff at Hinchingbroke, 1906. © Huntingdon County Record Office; photograph, B. R. Jones. 147

19 Mrs Jameson Dixon with menservants and Minnie Mumby at Holton. Reproduced by kind permission of Mr P.H. Dixon. 154

20 The gardeners at Beaulieu. Reproduced by kind permission of The National Motor Museum, Beaulieu. 165

21 A form sent in application for the position of head gardener at Shugborough, 1907. Reproduced by permission of the Staffordshire Record Office; photograph, Peter Rogers. 173

22 The drying and ironing room of the laundry at Petworth. Reproduced by kind permission of Weidenfeld & Nicolson publishers. 184

23 F. D. Hardy, *After the Party*. The Forbes Magazine Collection, New York. 193

24 A typical wages book, Waldershare Park. Centre for Kentish Studies, Kent County Council. 200

25 A servants' menu from Linton Park. Centre for Kentish Studies, Kent County Council. 210

26 The head gardener's house at Keele. © Sneyd Papers, Keele University Library. 214

27 An invitation to a servants' ball at Prestwold Hall, 1889. © Packe Papers, Leicestershire Record Office. 216

28	A detail from a meals book, from Trentham Hall, showing divisions within the household. Reproduced by permission of the Staffordshire Record Office; photograph, Peter Rogers.	222
29	Servants in the kitchen at Beaulieu. Reproduced by kind permission of The National Motor Museum, Beaulieu.	228
30	Cricket outside the gardener's house, King's Bromley Manor. Reproduced by kind permission of Mrs Ivy Butcher, King's Bromley Historians.	236
31	An agreement with a footman, Northwick Park, 1880. © Hereford & Worcester Record Office.	248
32	Emily Mary Osborn, *The Governess*, 1860. Oil on canvas, 34.9 × 29.2 cm, Yale Center for British Art, Paul Mellon Fund.	256
33	Mrs Stevens, retired nurse, in her room at Earlham. Photograph, author.	258
34	Mrs Jameson Dixon, Mrs Sarah Mumby and her daughter with three maidservants, Holton, *c.*1900. © Lincolnshire Archives.	259–1
35	The family and their grooms, Shugborough. Reproduced by permission of the Staffordshire Record Office; photograph, Peter Rogers.	263

Acknowledgements

I should like to thank the many people who have helped me over the years to complete this book. I owe a special debt to Michael Thompson, for his encouragement and guidance. I am indebted to Roderick Floud for permitting me to attend his lectures on quantitative methods, and advising me on sampling techniques. I am grateful for the assistance I have received from virtually every county record office in England and Wales, and especially for the kindness of the staffs at Stafford, Hereford, Lincoln and Hawarden. Among those who assisted me with my research, I should like to mention with particular gratitude the late Miss Joan and Miss Dora Gibbons for their reminiscences and hospitality, the National Trust staff at Erddig, Merlin Waterson, Thomas Woodcock of the Royal College of Arms, and Paul Thompson, who granted me permission to use the oral history archives at the University of Essex. I am grateful for the financial support I received from the New Zealand University Grants Committee, the University of Canterbury and the University of London, and from my father.

I wish to thank the following people for reading the manuscript in different stages, and for their advice and encouragement: Robert McCarron, Carole Shammas, Craig Horle and Diane Worzala. Above all, I am deeply grateful to my husband, David Gutzke, for his support and assistance over the years, not only reading the manuscript as it evolved and giving invaluable advice and criticism, but taking care of our daughter Caitlin, giving me the time to complete this book.

J. G.

Introduction

The cult of the country house has resulted in an outpouring of books. Every year still more glossy coffee-table books depict country houses of every type and period, while popular writers describe yet another aspect of country house life, be it interior decoration, marriage, childhood, servants, or sport. The nineteenth-century landed classes, a hitherto neglected elite, have enjoyed a boom in academia, too. Architectural historians Mark Girouard and Jill Franklin pioneered the field, examining Victorian country house architecture as social history. Historians of the landed classes have recently multiplied, producing several major surveys, notably Lawrence and Jeanne Fawtier Stone's *An Open Elite? England 1540–1880*, J. V. Beckett's *The Aristocracy in England, 1660–1914*, and David Cannadine's *The Decline and Fall of the British Aristocracy*.[1] What more possibly remains to be said?

Too little is known, in fact, about what actually went on inside the nineteenth-century country house. Architectural historians have proved far more interested in this than have historians of the nineteenth-century landed classes, who have given family and domestic life short shrift. Beckett's *Aristocracy in England*, for instance, omits women's roles and activities, even when discussing philanthropy or "Society," the exclusive social elite made up of upper-class families which gathered annually for social functions in the London Season. Nevertheless, one reviewer commends him for covering "all aspects of the history of the English landed classes."[2] David Cannadine explains that his survey of the landed classes from 1880 to the present "is concerned with wealth, status, power, and class consciousness" which he assumes "were preponderantly masculine assets and attributes" and not much with women, "sex, marriage, and child-rearing," although he at least does acknowledge that books on these subjects are "badly needed."[3] Despite David Spring's admonition that investigation of the family "might well deepen our understanding of aristocratic society," scholarly research on the family, women, and childhood is scattered and fragmentary.[4]

Life below stairs in the country house has likewise been neglected by scholars. Labour historians have shied away from a disappointingly voiceless, servile, conservative, and female group of workers, un-unionized and uninvestigated by contemporaries. Historians studying domestic service have rightly attacked the popular image of high life below stairs in great mansions as atypical, concentrating instead on the vast majority of servants in middle-class households. But the elite sector of one of the largest occupations of all still merits serious analysis, to discover just how its experience differed from that of the typical servant.

This book, then, begins to fill the vast gaps remaining in the history of the landed classes in the period 1815–1914. It demolishes numerous inaccurate stereotypes of sternly authoritarian patriarchs tyrannically ruling over idle, useless wives, repressed but seldom-seen children, and troops of resentful servants. While these popular images were true of some households, they were not typical. Many families and servants led happy, fulfilled lives and coexisted in harmony. The purpose of this book is to reveal how the majority of landed families and their servants actually behaved towards each other.

One difficulty in ascertaining what was typical is that there was inevitably an immense range of behaviour in such a large and diverse population. In each family and staff, all members had their own personalities, with strengths and weaknesses of character which influenced their relationships with each other. Family life was affected by rank and wealth; the duke's peripatetic, opulent, and formal lifestyle was very different from the squire's more modest and confined existence. Many landed families, furthermore, displayed distinctive characteristics from one generation to the next, or belonged to a particular set in Society. Some families were devout Evangelicals or Roman Catholics, or went in for high thinking and plain living; some were preoccupied with politics or addicted to sport; others were domesticated and home-loving, reclusive or even eccentric; while yet others were worldly, frivolous, and impervious to the dictates of Victorian morality. Servants also varied greatly in their background, ambitions, and careers. In every country house community, relations between family and servants were an individual combination of many factors, such as the landowner's rank, wealth, and possessions, the stage of the family's life cycle, its lifestyle and preoccupations, the size and nature of the establishment, the personalities and attitudes of the master, mistress and servants, the provisions made for the staff's comfort and recreation, and the customs, traditions, and atmosphere built up over generations.

Nevertheless, all these households had much in common. They shared the distinctive features of family life and domestic service in the country house. There were widely accepted norms of conduct for both family and servants. To discover typical and normal beliefs and behaviour, I examined hundreds of sources – diaries, collections of letters, autobiographies, biographies, and family histories – for comments on such issues as relationships between husband and wife, parent and child or employer and servant, children's upbringing or servants' attitudes. Typical behaviour is defined as that of the majority of cases in these samples, which, of course, vary considerably in size and sources. No one set of families provided information on all topics.

This book examines, not the family or servants alone, but the entire country house community. Each depended on the other for its very existence. The landed classes were free to run the nation and Society only because other people performed all the domestic chores essential for day-to-day existence. Servants made possible a luxurious leisured lifestyle, taking care of the richly furnished mansion and extensive gardens, preparing elaborate meals, driving the carriages, and raising game for sport. Before guests, servants also acted as symbols embodying the family's power and affluence. The landed family relied on its servants not only for its own comfort, but for its reputation. The omnipresence of servants, moreover, affected all family members. Equally, the family shaped the servants' lives. Serving their master and mistress personally within a private home, servants were uniquely dependent on them, and subject to control over every aspect of their lives. Only by studying both elites together, examining their roles and their relationships within the country house community, can each be fully understood.

Mark Girouard has argued that the country house contained two separate communities, divided by barriers of class, household organization, and architecture; Victorian families, valuing privacy, kept servants out of sight, with elaborate rituals enforcing social distance when contact was necessary.[5] But advice manuals and architectural plans describe the ideal rather than reality. Inhabitants of the country house, along with domestic staff living in outbuildings or estate cottages, still formed one community in other respects.[6] Besides the high degree of functional interdependence, they shared collective goals of maintaining the establishment for the family, its guests, and its descendants. In the country, the two elites were physically isolated not so much from each other as from the wider community, in a closed parish ruled by the landowning family, or at the centre of a vast, largely self-sufficient estate. They held common cultural values, loyal to a traditional hierarchical social order based on authority and deference, and drawn together by the sense of participating in one organic community, with each individual playing a valued part by faithfully performing his or her own duties. Both groups were subordinated to the long-term needs of the dynasty, undertaking roles which maintained and furthered the family's reputation and interests. All were subject to the customs and routines of the country house, and had to conform to established codes of conduct which stressed duty and conformity, not freedom or self-expression. Accumulated family customs and feudal loyalties, and the country house's function as the centre of estate life, brought family and staff together as they jointly celebrated major family events and Christmas. Secluded from public view, and confident of their superior rank, families unbent to invite servants to join them in family concerts, theatricals and cricket matches and at servants' balls. Something of the earlier concept of the great family comprising the whole household persisted. "Our servants and we are all members of a large family, who cannot get on independently of each other," declared Lady Jeune in 1892.[7]

Some historians do recognize the country house community. "Great establishments," asserts John Burnett, still formed "the same kind of total communities they had in the Middle Ages, highly structured, authoritarian and inward-looking, largely self-sufficient and independent of the rest of society."[8] In literature, too, the country house has long symbolized "the qualities and values of community."[9]

The country house community differed significantly from other households containing servants. The country house was far more than a family's home; it was the power base of the nation's political and social elite. For centuries, substantial landowners had formed the nation's ruling class, possessing a disproportionate part of the nation's land and wealth, and heading its social hierarchy. Despite industrialization and the challenge of the middle class, the landed classes reigned supreme until the 1880s. The landed elite consisted of the peerage (dukes, earls, marquesses, viscounts, and barons), landowning baronets and knights, and the untitled gentry. Most peers and baronets were great landowners with over 10,000 acres, but so were the wealthiest gentry. While the term "aristocracy" popularly refers to the nobility, F. M. L. Thompson includes great landowners, and recent historians have used this term to describe the entire landed classes, including the lesser gentry.[10] All were rentiers, obtaining much of their annual income from tenant farmers' rents. Some also derived income from mining or resort towns on their estates, or from urban property. The landed family's primary economic goal was to conserve and augment its land and wealth for future generations, but landowners had to provide for the widowed dowager, sisters and younger brothers, and spent lavishly on conspicuous consumption to keep up their social position.

The country house was the headquarters of this campaign. Most families in Victorian and Edwardian England occupied a rented house for only a few years, at most a generation or two. In contrast, country houses were also family seats, home to succeeding generations of one family, accumulating associations and memories, and holding a central place in the lives of the family's descendants. The country house embodied the lineage's identity and permanence. It was, in Girouard's words, a "power house," designed to inspire awe and respect.[11] Massive and imposing, the exterior asserted the landowner's authority, dignity, wealth, and social status. The house's architecture and interior decoration, its library, fine-art collection, gardens, and park affirmed his cultured taste, education and good breeding. The formal entrance, the large, opulent hall and reception rooms served as a public stage for the rituals of social performance which presented the family to greatest advantage, enhancing its prestige among social equals and exacting deference from inferiors. Open-handed hospitality to both required adequate accommodation, services, and amusements. The house and its surroundings were created for pleasure as well as power, for this leisure class took its recreation seriously.

Finally, the country house was a symbol of community cohesion. As the home of the largest landowner, who ruled the neighbourhood through his public service and control over schools and church, the country house dominated the locality. It was an important source of part-time and temporary employment and charity. Landlords also asserted their authority and benevolence by hosting dinners and balls for tenants and treats for schoolchildren. The country house was, furthermore, the preferred venue for gatherings of friendly societies, volunteers, and other local organizations.

For historians of the landed classes, these various functions define the country house. The Stones regard public display and entertainment as the crucial distinctive function of the country seat, requiring a minimum of 50,000 square feet for family and guest use, including a formal entrance hall and at least four good-sized reception rooms, criteria which exclude many manor houses. F. M. L. Thompson also feels manor houses were barely indistinguishable from large farmhouses, lacking the presence expected of a country house.[12] Architectural historians such as Mark Girouard, however, classify manor houses as country houses, as do other historians of the landed classes such as Heather Clemenson.[13] Girouard, indeed, plays down the importance of display, arguing that the Victorians built their country houses for "family life and entertaining friends rather than for show," placing comfort above luxury and taste.[14] On the other hand, some architectural historians, notably Jill Franklin, are too inclusive: houses built in the country by wealthy businessmen as rural retreats for sport or entertaining on just a few acres were not true country houses; their owners neither relied on a substantial tenanted estate for income nor discharged the squire's traditional obligations.[15]

In this book, I define a country house by its owner rather than by its size or grandeur; it must be owned and occupied by a member of the landed classes, the chief residence on a sizeable estate let to tenant farmers. The house must function as a family seat, theatre of hospitality, and community centre. Even the manor houses of the lesser gentry meet these criteria. In terms of numbers, the lesser gentry were a significant part of the landed classes. In 1873, a survey of landowners with more than 1,000 acres showed that over half of them had less than 3,000 acres. Despite this, the Stones' study of mobility into the landed elite specifically excludes the lesser gentry, whom they label "parish gentry." They argue that less wealthy squires wielded merely local political influence, and pursued a different style of life than the "county gentry," entertaining on a much smaller scale in a consequently less imposing smaller house with different functions.[16]

Other historians readily admit the parish gentry into the fold. M. L. Bush, J. V. Beckett and David Cannadine include them in the "aristocracy," the entire ruling class, whether that rule was at the national, county, or parish level. Like other historians of rural society, they focus on the unifying forces which forged all levels into one class self-consciously distinguishing itself from the rest of rural society. Parish gentry shared with greater landowners a common culture. All ranks were bound together by similar values, ethics, manners, and habits, formed by a widely uniform upbringing and education. They all owned landed estates large enough to be rented to tenantry, enjoying the social and political power and influence conferred by landownership, and recognizing the duties of landownership as well as its privileges. All shared the ideal of the leisured gentleman, shunning employment in farming, trade or commerce, but partaking in government, be it local or national, leading the volunteer military forces, dispensing philanthropy, and enjoying field sports.[17] It was the squire, not the farmer, who dominated his closed parish, as Guardian, patron of the living, supporter and supervisor of the school, and provider of housing and charity. Squires, not farmers, bought coats of arms, squandered land on ornamental parks, kept gamekeepers, and ran the local hunt. Only the gentry were admitted into county Society, forming bonds of marriage and kinship with wealthier landed families. Manor houses had formal reception rooms, pleasure grounds, and park, a setting for entertaining and leisure. They were run by the same routines found in larger country houses. Their staffs, too, considered themselves to be in "gentleman's service."

How was the line between a landed gentleman and a farmer or a country gentleman drawn? Landownership was crucial. Most authorities agree with F. M. L. Thompson that around 1,000 acres and £1,000 in annual rentals were needed to sustain the lifestyle of the landed gentleman.[18] A long pedigree, however, could for a time compensate for diminished landholdings and income. To gain admittance to county Society, a new landowner reduced or abandoned his personal involvement in business, took up field sports and philanthropy, and sought local public office. One important mark of success was appointment as a Justice of the Peace, Deputy Lieutenant or High Sheriff, positions generally reserved for leisured rentiers. The ultimate tests were social acceptance by neighbouring gentry, and deference and respect from social inferiors. Assimilation often took more than a generation, after sons attended public schools and well-dowered daughters succeeded in the marriage market.

Writers on the country house have given a distorted impression by concentrating on the great houses of the peerage and wealthy gentry. In Mark Girouard's *Life in the English Country House*, his chapter on the Victorian country house examines the homes of six immensely wealthy peers, eight *nouveaux riches*, and a baronet whose fortune originated in brewing, but only two county families of longer pedigree.[19] Any balanced picture of life in the country house must include squires and their smaller establishments.

The atypical, too, has dominated our perceptions of family life in the country house: stereotypes still prevail of the tyrannical paterfamilias lording it over the household, the preoccupied father distant both physically and emotionally, the dull, prudish and submissive Victorian wife, or the frivolous, empty-headed social butterfly whose neglected and repressed children cower under bullying nannies and governesses in distant nurseries and schoolrooms. This book demolishes these myths, showing that many marriages remained companionate, characterized by affection and friendship; that wives did have real and valued functions as mothers, chatelaines, hostesses, and philanthropists; and that both parents were involved in child-rearing – typically authoritative, but loving and attentive.

Membership of the landed classes and residence in the country house created a unique family type, with own distinctive demography, child-rearing practices, courtship, and roles for husband and wife. This family type, shaped partly by religious, ideological, and economic developments over the century, derived essentially from the landed classes' own heritage, priorities, customs, and values. The landed family was acutely aware of belonging to a lineage. It was characterized by subordination of individual interests to the family's long-term advancement, a sense of duty to family and class which permeated child-rearing goals, influenced marriage choice, and motivated husband and wife. The nineteenth-century ideology of separate spheres for men and women is not fully applicable to the country house. Gender roles were defined chiefly by the man's position as landowner, and women's relationship to him, but they were surprisingly flexible. The country house family was highly institutionalized and committed to formal public display, yet it valued domesticity and a warm family life.

The family was also influenced by the presence of servants, which limited and altered its behaviour and relationships. The landed family was seldom truly private. Much of its daily life was lived in front of outsiders. Children were bathed, fed, dressed, toilet-trained, chastised, and corrected by nurses and nursery-maids, and educated by governesses or tutors. Women were accompanied everywhere by a servant. Adults were woken by maids, dressed and undressed by a servant, and ate their meals with servants in attendance. Servants washing clothes, making beds, and tidying rooms discovered evidence of their employers' most intimate affairs. The presence of servants often circumscribed spontaneous and intimate behaviour, forcing the family to curb their impulses and feelings and to behave acceptably before them. A rigidly enforced daily timetable for housework and meals denied family members the freedom and flexibility to get out of bed, eat, or even to use a particular room, when they wished.

Landed families maintained social distance from these intruders from another class by a widely uniform code of conduct that formalized and standardized communication with them and mandated their silence and deference. Convention demanded that the upper classes act as if staff attending them did not exist. Servants were depersonalized with uniforms and sometimes by standard names.

Nevertheless, personal relationships between family and servants were stronger and contacts more frequent than all this might suggest. Babies and toddlers loved their nannies, and young children, not yet conscious of class barriers, sought the company and friendship of servants. Teenage boys often became devoted to the gamekeepers, coachmen and grooms who imparted their skills. Their sisters, in contrast, often disliked the governesses who were their constant companions. On acquiring homes of their own, most women and many men took their roles as mistress or master seriously. They hired and fired the staff and formulated the regulations governing servants' behaviour both during and after work. Close relationships often developed with individual servants, and in frail old age, the employers were dependent on the goodwill of their attendants.

The landed classes' behaviour towards their servants was, however, by no means uniform. In some households, the more relaxed, egalitarian attitudes of the eighteenth century survived; liberal employers respected their servants as individual human beings. Early-nineteenth-century Evangelicalism and paternalism revived the patriarchal employer, impelled by a duty to save his servants' souls and protect their virtue. Class consciousness, on the other hand, encouraged formality between family and staff, and allowed the remote employer to reduce the tie to a contractual cash nexus.

A master's treatment of his staff often corresponded with his behaviour towards his own family: while an authoritarian, religious, and paternalist landowner might regard the entire household as his family, ruling them all with an iron hand, a less authoritarian and more companionate husband and father might interfere very little below stairs. Many loving and permissive mothers, however, were strict mistresses, doubtless because they believed a well-organized and morally upright household would be best for their children.

Like their employers, country house servants were a distinctive elite of one of the nation's largest occupations, and the leading one for women. A commentator in 1913 felt sure "no one will deny" that servants who went into large households were a "separate class with all its instincts going out to this sort of work."[20]

To clarify the characteristics that made country house servants an elite, they must be seen in the context of the occupation as a whole. The number of domestic servants increased in the nineteenth century, as population growth and rising incomes increased both supply and demand. The middle classes hired servants to demonstrate their social position in rituals of deference and ceremony, but they had more practical reasons too. Victorian housekeeping was labour-intensive and exhausting. Large families demanded high standards of comfort and cleanliness in houses crammed with mass-produced furniture and dust-catching ornaments, often located in a heavily polluted urban environment. Domestic technology was at a labour-intensive stage too: fireplaces and fuel stoves had to be cleaned and replenished, oil lamps filled, and water carried to washstands and portable baths. Until late in the century, many food ingredients came in an unprocessed state, and numerous foods, beverages or cleaning products were manufactured at home. Many servants assisted in their employer's business, on farms, in shops and craft workshops. Some middle-class householders, it is true, kept no servants, relying instead on female relatives, but there were working-class families who hired help, especially in times of family crisis.[21]

By the early nineteenth century, most domestic servants were female. The tax on menservants and their higher wages were disincentives, but more crucial was the expanding number of households needing just one or two servants to perform the women's work of housework and childcare. Most domestics were life-cycle servants working until marriage. Theresa McBride argues that service in middle-class urban households was a bridging occupation modernizing women from the countryside. Service provided safe lodgings while they acquired urban values, domestic skills, and savings to win husbands.[22] Yet domestic service still retained the traditional culture of deference and dependence.

Domestic service was a survival of pre-industrial patterns of employment, when most workers were "servants" living in their master's household, bound together by reciprocal obligations. By the nineteenth century, industrial workers were leaving home to work in a factory or workshop for fixed hours six days a week, performing a specific, repetitive task to produce commodities sold for profit, which in turn paid wages based on hours worked or piece rates. Notwithstanding some manufacturers' paternalism, typically employer–employee relations were reduced to the cash nexus, with the operative contracting for weekly wages, and employers relinquishing both control over and concern for workers. In many industries, workers eventually organized labour unions, while government investigations produced some protective legislation. In contrast, domestic service remained pre-industrial. Servants were still hired by the year and paid quarterly, half-yearly or even annually out of the master's or mistress's personal income, with board and lodgings a large part of their remuneration. Most servants lived in, their whole time legally at their employer's disposal, and subject to all his lawful demands. Not only did they undertake diverse tasks, but they were obliged to act in a deferential and submissive manner. Domestic servants, however, did not suffer from seasonal or technological unemployment, and might receive medical attention and sick pay. Nevertheless, where alternative occupations existed, service was increasingly shunned. Factory work had many advantages: shorter hours, with evenings and Sundays off, a larger workforce with many social contacts, and personal liberty to dress, court, and relax as one chose. Maids-of-all-work suffered most from the disadvantages of domestic service: isolation and loneliness, an excessive workload and long hours of work, lack of control over their personal lives, and a growing social stigma. Geographically scattered servants could not be unionized, nor was the government interested in investigating and reforming their occupation.

Conditions were far superior in the elite sector of domestic service. "Gentleman's service" in the establishments of the upper classes was characterized by its own patterns of recruitment and labour market, strict divisions of labour, an elaborate internal hierarchy among large staffs, and distinctive values and customs. The experience differed, furthermore, for the four types of servants employed: career servants in service until retirement; life-cycle servants who left it for marriage or another occupation; distressed gentlewomen who reluctantly earned a living as governesses, companions, and lady housekeepers; and the relatively unskilled and low-paid labourers. Each type had its own patterns of social origin, age at entry, promotion, geographical and job mobility, marriage, and retirement. Service in the country house was the pinnacle of the occupation, attracting career servants who rose in social status by their association with the aristocracy, their skills, high pay, and comfortable standard of living within a still deferential rural community. Distressed gentlewomen gained better pay and amenities here than in middle-class households, and the wider social barrier made employment more acceptable. For life-cycle servants, too, country house service offered better rewards and conditions, more company and social life, and specialized training with opportunities for upward mobility. Country houses employed far more men than their middle-class equivalents, mostly as gardeners, stable employees, and gamekeepers, and used more local day and casual labour.

Gentleman's service, nevertheless, remains in the realm of anecdotal popular history. This book is the first to explore the distinctive traits of "gentleman's service," and to apply the same stringent, sophisticated, quantitative, and theoretical analysis given to the occupation as a whole or to urban servants.[23] I examine every aspect of life below stairs in the country house, with the exception of the particular duties of each servant (already well-documented elsewhere).[24]

To reconstruct life above and below stairs, I have made extensive use of primary documents. Quantitative data on the families' and servants' demography, household and community structure, and patterns of employment have been drawn from census samples, family reconstitution, and wages books. Other material on servants has been gathered from numerous letters of reference and job applications, correspondence between family and servants, inventories, rules for servants and other estate papers, a handful of manuscript and published servants' diaries and autobiographies, and oral history interviews. Evidence of the landed classes' family life is more plentiful, including manuscript or published letters and diaries, oral history interviews, autobiographies and memoirs, biographies and family histories.

Although these sources have limitations, it is a mistake to dismiss personal accounts as hopelessly biased and inaccurate. Most diarists intended their diaries to be private, recording not only the events of the day but their own feelings. The upper classes wrote letters much as we use the telephone, to report regularly on domestic details and issues to other family members and friends, in an intimate, confiding, and honest manner. They also produced an abundance of autobiographies, confident of the significance of their lives. A most striking feature of this flood of memoirs and autobiographies is the similarity of their subjects' upbringing, education, interests, and values.[25] Male writers were often public figures self-consciously recording their achievements, skipping over childhood and omitting domestic details. Women's autobiographies give more information about life in the nursery, the schoolroom, and the country house, and about relationships with family members and servants. In contrast to most female middle-class autobiographers, upper-class women who wrote their memoirs were not always unusually intelligent and articulate achievers, rebels or feminists critical of their girlhood.[26] Perhaps they assumed birth alone made them important and interesting. Typically complacent, uncritical of their own privileged position, and convinced of their natural superiority, they wrote approvingly of their upbringing and pursuits. Many recorded their reminiscences for their descendants rather than to make money or to shape their public image, and their recollections are characteristically fragmentary, digressive and formless, less consciously shaped than those of the men towards creating a coherent mythic figure. Thus they tend to be more revealing. An author's judgement of affective relations is often considered unreliable, idealized in retrospect. But artless descriptions of parents' behaviour, their dictates, treats, and customs, are less suspect, and indicate the quality of parent–child relations. The overall impression, moreover, is supported by parental attitudes revealed in letters and diaries. A combination of records written by the upper classes themselves is more reliable than prescriptive literature alone, which sought to change behaviour rather than to reflect actual practices.

Manuscript collections of family papers and household records have proved invaluable in reconstructing the nature and structure of country house communities over the century. Collections spanning much of the century are abundant for the peerage, but rare for the gentry. In three cases it was possible to trace relations between family and servants and household structure over the entire period. The first, the Dukes of Sutherland, were good representatives of the peerage. The Leveson-Gowers were a Staffordshire family with property in Yorkshire and Shropshire. The first Duke inherited the Duke of Bridgewater's canal profits through his mother, Bridgewater's favourite sister. As Earl Gower, his marriage to Elizabeth, Countess of Sutherland, brought him her vast estates in Sutherland in Scotland. Like her two successors, the duchess was a famed Society hostess. One of the wealthiest families in the nation, with total landed properties of 1,358,545 acres in 1873 (worth £141,667 in rentals alone), the Leveson-Gowers owned numerous seats, including Stafford House in London, and Dunrobin Castle in Scotland. Their Staffordshire seat at Trentham was rebuilt at vast expense in the 1830s. Throughout the year, the ducal family made the rounds of its properties, accompanied by a large peripatetic staff. But a considerable permanent staff remained at Trentham keeping the house, gardens, and park in readiness, and the household records in meticulous detail. The mansion was largely demolished in 1910 when the River Trent's pollution became unbearable.[27]

Plate 1 Trentham Hall, remodelled by Sir Charles Barry in 1834–40 for the second Duke of Sutherland

The second case, representative of the lesser gentry, concerns the Dixons of Holton in Lincolnshire, a prosperous farming family transformed into parish gentry at mid-century when Thomas John Dixon decided to become a squire. He acquired more land when he married the heiress to the Searby estate, remodelled and enlarged the house, hired a footman and a bailiff, and took an active role in local affairs, becoming a Deputy Lieutenant and Captain of the Yeomanry. In the 1860s, he bought more land, handed over the rest of his farms to tenants, entailed his estates, bought a coat of arms, hired a gamekeeper and served as High Sheriff. He left 2,275 acres, worth more than £2,300 in 1871. Because his childless son Richard survived him by only three weeks, his unmarried daughter Ann and her widowed sister Amelia inherited the estates in turn, followed by their cousin's son Thomas Gibbons Dixon, a clergyman with a wife and four children, and the property is still in the family. Good estate and household records and many family papers survive. My interviews with Joan and Dora Gibbons also provided much information on the Edwardian period.[28]

The subject of the third collection is an established country gentry family in Wales, the Yorkes of Erddig. Erddig, a moderate-sized mansion built in the late seventeenth century near Wrexham in Denbighshire, was inherited by the Yorke family in 1733, passing in unbroken succession for two hundred years. Simon Yorke II, who inherited in 1804, Simon Yorke III (1834), and Philip Yorke II (1894) all married and had children. The Yorkes preferred a quiet family life at their beloved home, and were unusually interested in their servants, to the extent of commemorating them in portrait and verse. Their refusal to throw any records away has resulted in an outstanding collection on both family and servants. After the reclusive and impoverished Simon

Plate 2 A hunt meeting at Hampton Court

Yorke IV inherited, the staff dwindled, and the neglected house and garden fell into decay. His successor, Philip Yorke III, gave Erddig to the National Trust in 1973.[29]

These three collections draw the wide contours of the landed classes, while more fragmentary family and household papers gleaned from many county record offices fill the gaps. A superb collection of family letters survives for the Arkwrights of Hampton Court in Herefordshire, but their wages books fail to record servants' occupations, and are therefore useless for this study. The barons of Northwick, in contrast, left good wage books, rules for servants, and numerous letters of reference, but the manuscript collection contains few family papers. Using these and other varied sources, I create the most accurate picture yet of daily life in the nineteenth-century county house.

The book covers a hundred years, from 1815 to 1914. By 1815, the end of the Napoleonic Wars, many of the trends that were to alter family life and domestic service in the country house were already evident. The First World War marks a turning point in much of the landed classes' way of life. In the nineteenth century the country house was not immune to changes in the wider world, but in many ways, life above and below stairs showed remarkable continuity.

Early in the nineteenth century, a landed estate was a prerequisite for political and social power. For centuries property had been the basis of participation in government: landowners with a stake in the country were considered independent, responsible, and impartial. The landed classes remained confident that they were the nation's natural rulers, heirs to a long tradition of paternalistic public service. English and Welsh peers inherited a seat in the House of Lords, while the greater gentry controlled the House of Commons. At the county level, the gentry filled the posts of Lord and Deputy Lieutenant, Sheriff, and Justice of the Peace. The landed classes also monopolized the armed forces and the civil service.

Politics and social life were closely linked, with families firmly Whigs or Tories, and partisan party interests dominating many country house parties. Society in the early nineteenth century was small and exclusive, with membership based on rank, pedigree, connections, and patronage. It was an identifiable community of families, sharing a lifestyle and values. This lifestyle focused more on pleasure than duty: the Regency aristocracy and wealthy gentry congregated in London or in spa resorts to amuse themselves with entertainments, fashion, gambling, illicit affairs, and heavy drinking. Socializing was often public, in assembly rooms such as the famous Almacks in London, at masked balls, or in pleasure gardens. Many aristocratic families spent only the winter months in the country. The less wealthy gentry, however, could seldom afford a visit to London, and besides, their political and social activities took place at the county level.

Early in the century the landed classes' monopoly of power was challenged from below. In the decades after the Napoleonic Wars, the dislocations of industrialization and post-war economic distress produced widespread discontent among the working classes, expressed in demonstrations, riots, Luddite machine-breaking, rick-burning, unionization, and popular radicalism culminating in Chartism. The rural poor, suffering the effects of agricultural depression and high wheat prices caused by the corn laws, protested against the decline of paternalist benevolence and the moral economy. At the same time, the middle classes assailed corruption, ineptness, and impotence in government and upper-class arrogance, decadence, and immorality. Over the century, they attacked many bastions of aristocratic power and privilege through the Anti-Corn Law League, the Reform Acts, civil service examinations, the abolition of the purchase system in the armed forces, and the erosion of the Anglican monopoly. In the counties, the powers of the Justices of the Peace were whittled away first by the elective boards created to administer the Poor Law of 1834, highways, schools, and sanitary districts, and then by borough and county councils.

Yet the middle classes sought representation and reform rather than a transfer of power. In the 1830s and 1840s, fear of revolution induced them to turn to the aristocracy to restore firm control, order, and stability. The landed classes tenaciously retained control, showing remarkable resilience and adaptability, with judicious and timely concessions and reforms. Despite competitive civil service examinations and elected county councils, they continued to dominate all levels of government, claiming generations of experience and elite education as suitable qualifications.

The landed classes proved equally skilled in forming a cultural partnership with the middle classes, while simultaneously preserving their social exclusiveness. In response to mounting middle-class criticism of their behaviour, the early-Victorian landed classes reformed themselves, adopting middle-class piety, morality, and seriousness. The middle classes, in turn, eagerly imitated the landed classes' behaviour: they developed a common code of gentility, instilled in the male sex by new or reformed public schools, and attempted to practise the increasingly complex and elusive code of etiquette designed to deny upwardly mobile aspirants entrance to the social elite. Society remained a close-knit, clearly defined community of families linked by intermarriage and kinship. Mid-Victorian social life became more domesticated, intimate, and private. It focused on family events: public entertainments declined in favour of dinners and dances in individual houses and long visits to relatives' country houses. In this period, aristocracy and gentry alike shared the values of piety, morality, and domesticity, the idealization of family life and the home.

Social and political power was buttressed by prosperity. In response to the post-war depression, landowners attracted tenants with estate improvements such as enclosure and drainage, new farm buildings, and repairs, and they borrowed to invest in profitable high farming. Nor were they alienated from the industrial sector: sharing the capitalist ethic of commerce and industry, landowners explored other ways of increasing their incomes, exploiting timber or minerals on their lands, developing urban sites, and investing in stocks and shares. In the prosperous, stable countryside, the landed classes restored their influence. Paternalistic mid-Victorian families took their responsibilities to tenants and dependants seriously, preserving a traditional organic community of authority and deference with philanthropy, hospitality, and discipline.

This golden era ended in the 1870s, when wet seasons, poor harvests, and competition from imported grain, meat and dairy products severely depressed agricultural profits for many years. Landed incomes diminished, owing to falling rents and arrears, and failed tenant farmers proved difficult to replace, even with further investment in the farms. Struggling landowners retrenched, sold off land, let their houses, and encouraged younger sons to take up gainful occupations. Some landowners gave up and put their estates on the market, but few found buyers. With land no longer a profitable investment, landowners bought more stocks and shares. The gentry in arable regions suffered most, and great landowners least, because the latter were buffered by many other sources of income. Though agricultural incomes improved in the Edwardian period, heavier death duties and income taxes worried even the wealthiest landowner. Land sales rose rapidly, mostly to the tenant farmers.

From the 1880s, the urban industrial and commercial interests dominating the economy began to gain commensurate power in politics by winning more seats in the Cabinet, in the House of Commons, and on county councils. Now the wealthy could obtain political power and even titles without first purchasing a landed estate. Society finally admitted unpropertied wealth, vastly expanding in numbers by the end of the century. Wealth, in fact, replaced land and pedigree as the basis of status, as Society once more became pleasure-loving and opulent. Among the fashionable aristocracy, domesticity and duty were displaced by a whirling social life and conspicuous consumption, much to the disgust of the impoverished and alienated lesser gentry. Increasing numbers of aristocrats became peripatetic, flitting from city to Continent to moors and glens. Country houses were now the setting for weekend or shooting parties, or functioned as private retreats for those wishing to remain socially exclusive. The *nouveaux riches* enjoyed the amenities of landownership shorn of its responsibilities by buying or building mansions without estates attached. With new or absentee owners, the traditional bonds between the mansion and the rural community declined. But in the nurseries, nannies still brought up the children, in the drawing room the ladies still entertained, and below stairs the servants still toiled. The essential patterns of the country house community remained.

The book surveys the two parts of this community in turn. First it examines important aspects of the landed family: its demography, patterns of residence, the country house childhood, parent–child relations, courtship and marriage, and the roles of women. Then it focuses on the servants, exploring staff size, demography, the distinctive attractions and rewards of country house service, and relationships between staff members. Finally, the last chapter brings family and servants together to explore the relationship between them.

1

The Demography of the Landed Family

The nineteenth-century landed family had a distinctive demography and structure. Their customs and values influenced rates of marriage, family size and type, and inheritance and occupancy patterns. Primogeniture (the right to succession of the first-born son) was especially important, encouraging heirs to marry, and to eject their widowed mothers and siblings from the family seat. The landowners' primary goal of preserving the estates intact led to lower rates of marriage for younger sons and daughters and, when incomes declined, to smaller families. Changing fortunes, as well as the social calendar, caused surprisingly prolonged absences from the country house.

To obtain a representative picture I took a sample of one hundred inhabited country houses from the 1871 census, when the Victorian country house was at its zenith; the *Return of Owners of Land 1872–3* revealed landed income. Minimum qualifications were around 1,000 acres of land and £1,000 a year, and inclusion in any of the standard social directories: Burke's *Landed Gentry*, Walford's *County Families*, or the "Gentry" or "Principal Seats" sections in county directories. The best available lists of country houses in England and Wales are those published in Walford from the 1880s, and I selected a particularly full list from the 1888 edition. To make it more representative, the sample was structured to reflect both the proportion of peers, baronets, and commoners in the landed classes, and the percentage in each county.[1] Further samples were drawn from the peerage, the baronetage, and Welsh landowners, to discover differences of rank and region.

To examine the impact of landownership on demography, I reconstituted eighty of the one hundred families, with dates of birth, marriage, and death for twenty-five-year cohorts from 1775 to 1899. The other twenty bought their houses after 1820 or sold them by 1905.[2]

22　DEMOGRAPHY OF THE FAMILY

Though impossible to complete, and relatively small, this sample does indicate trends in the demography of the landed classes. Its validity is supported by the similarity of many statistics to T. H. Hollingsworth's demography of the peerage (which includes peers' younger sons and daughters, many of whom merged with the baronetage and gentry by

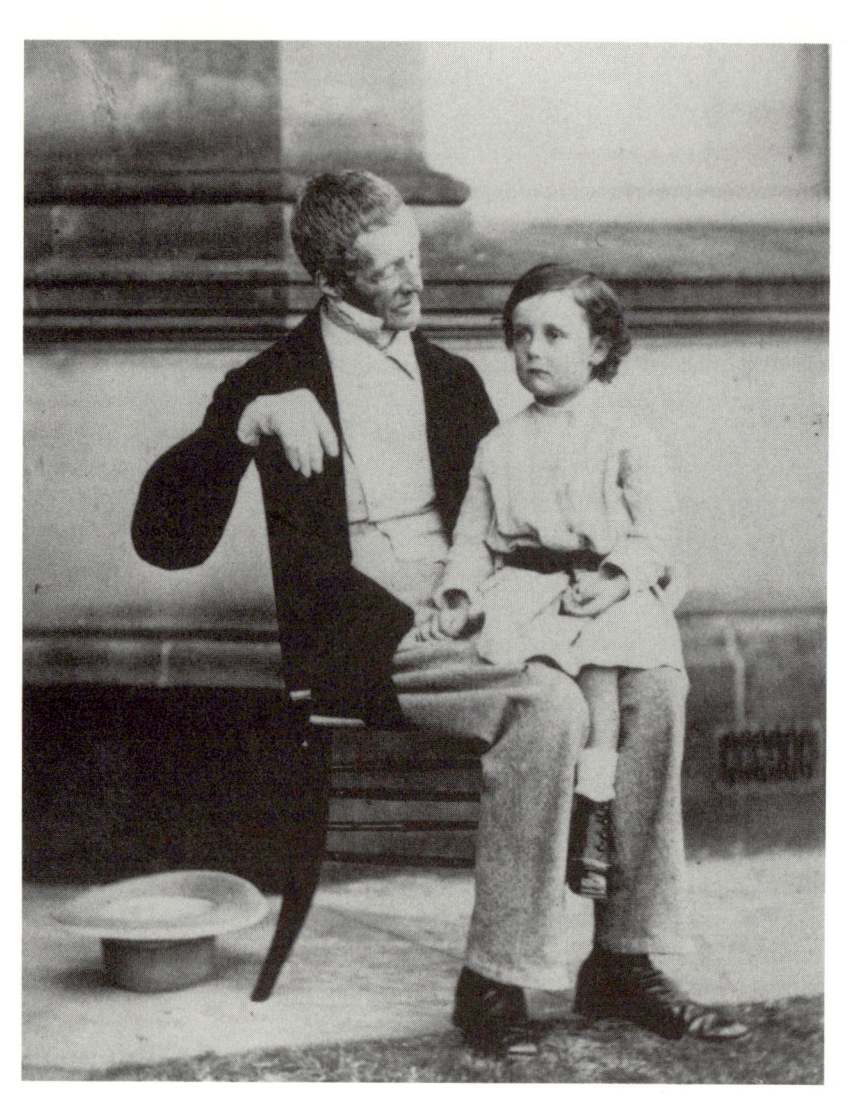

Plate 3　A bachelor and his heir: Ralph Sneyd with his nephew and namesake

marriage and standard of living), and Lawrence and Jeanne Fawtier Stones' statistics from three counties.[3]

In the country house, the individual life cycle – the inescapable events of birth and death and the possibility of marriage and parenthood – and the family life cycle, where family composition was altered over time by the differing life cycles of its members, were both shaped by the landed classes' needs and values.

The family life cycle began with marriage. Nearly 90 per cent of the 238 owners who inherited sample houses between 1815 and 1914 married.[4] Given the imperative of supplying the next heir, the fact that one in ten male owners remained unmarried is surprising. The greater value placed on individualism permitted heirs to make a personal choice, bolstered by primogeniture, which secured the inheritance by entail on a brother or nephew. With the succession to Keele assured by a brother and a nephew, Ralph Sneyd was able to indulge his "thirst for solitude," which gave him "leisure & liberty" to "read & ruminate ... & play with my place."[5]

Table 1.1 Age at marriage of male heirs

Birth cohort	Number	Mean age at first marriage
1775–99	55	29
1800–24	53	29
1825–49	62	31
1850–74	53	32

Table 1.2 Age distribution of male heirs at marriage

Birth cohort	Age 20–4	25–9	30–4	35–9	40–4	45–9	50+
1775–99	12	20	12	7	2	1	1
1800–24	14	22	7	6	2	1	1
1825–49	12	16	19	12	1	2	0
1850–74	10	11	15	9	4	3	1

Heirs to landed estates typically married in their late twenties or early thirties, several years after the rest of the male population (see tables 1.1 and 1.2).[6] Heirs were in no hurry to wed. The landed classes valued maturity, especially in men, and marrying for love took longer than arranged marriages. Lack of income to support a family was not a factor, for most heirs received a larger allowance on marriage.

Heirs' wives, in contrast, tended to marry younger than their sisters. Highly eligible heirs to landed estates enjoyed the first pick of the marriage market's annual offering, and were likely to be accepted with alacrity. The average age at marriage for first wives born after 1800 was around twenty-four, while for all landowners' daughters, it was twenty-seven, falling to twenty-five later in the period.

With the relatively late age at marriage, and untimely deaths, marriages lasted around thirty-one years on average (table 1.3).[7] Few landowners divorced early in the century, but after the Divorce Court, established in 1857, made divorce less expensive and difficult, and social sanctions relaxed, divorces increased.[8] Remarriage after a spouse's death was common early in the century, then fell dramatically in the Victorian era. Later, remarriage rose again with the divorce rate (table 1.3).

Table 1.3 Marriages of heirs and heiresses

Birth cohort	Number	Mean duration of first marriage (years)	Remarried (%)	Divorces
1775–99	50	31	32.2	0
1800–24	57	32	7.0	0
1825–49	64	31	12.7	1
1850–74	56	29	17.8	4

Table 1.4 Distribution of duration of heirs' and heiresses' first marriage

Birth cohort	Years 0–9	0–19	20–9	30–9	40–9	50–9	60+
1775–99	6	8	5	12	15	2	2
1800–24	4	9	11	15	11	5	2
1825–49	4	14	9	19	10	7	1
1850–74	10	5	11	12	12	6	0

Children were fervently desired, not just as a rewarding part of life, but to ensure an heir to the estates. One sample couple, the Pettiwards, produced nine daughters in eleven years in a frantic but futile attempt to secure a son. The landed classes suffered a relatively high rate of infertility. One in seven of the sample's male heirs who married wives of childbearing age remained childless (table 1.5).[9] Desire for an heir undoubtedly motivated second marriages; nearly a third of sample heirs with infertile first marriages remarried, although half of them were doomed to disappointment.

What caused such high infertility rates? Landowners sometimes married very late in life, or to women past their most fertile years. Sought-after heiresses typically came from ominously small families. Some men may have infected their wives with venereal disease. Contemporaries blamed ladies' delicacy and poor health, lack of physical exercise, and tight corsets. Historian Mell Davies argues that tight-lacing was responsible for falling fertility. Tight corsets, he claims, caused uterine displacement and reproductive diseases, malnutrition, and atrophied muscles. Intercourse was painful, therefore less frequent, and undernourishment both reduced fertility and harmed the foetus, resulting in a high rate of miscarriage and stillbirth.[10] It is true that families were largest when corsets were abandoned in the Empire style before the 1830s and infertility rose with severe corseting late in the period. But miscarriage rates remain impossible to quantify, and proving that the wearing of corsets resulted in fewer live births is equally difficult. Davies relies on measurements from fashion plates and formal photographs, but women may have loosened their corsets in private.

Table 1.5 Fertility of married heirs and heiresses[a]

Birth cohort	Number	Infertility (%)	Mean family size	Dead under 20 (%)	Families losing no child (%)
1775–99	56	14	5.9	11	61
1800–24	53	15	6.0	14	60
1825–49	63	12	4.5	9	73
1850–74	55	18	2.8	5	87
1875–99	30	23	3.0	7	78

[a] Excluding marriages where the bride was over 45.

Poor maternal health may thus have been one reason for declining family size. In the early nineteenth century the landed classes deliberately chose to have large families, perhaps, as Judith Schneid Lewis argues, because "an abundant progeny ... helped support one's rank," not only as another form of conspicuous consumption and display but as a means of creating the networks of patronage that provided political and career opportunities in this period.[11] The Church's fulminations against birth control probably discouraged pious Victorian couples from limiting their families.

The cost of educating and providing for younger sons and daughters was high, however, and less easily borne when incomes fell from the

Plate 4 A large mid-Victorian family: George, ninth Earl of Carlisle, his wife Rosalind and their eleven children

1870s onwards. Parents with numerous children might find it difficult to give each child individual attention. Frequent pregnancies, miscarriages, childbirths, and nursing could undermine a wife's health, and ultimately cause her death.[12] These may have been factors in the steady decline of the landed classes' fertility from the 1830s onwards, from an average of six children to around three (table 1.5) – considerably earlier than the rest of the population. (Titled families were apparently slightly larger than those of the gentry.[13])

To achieve this dramatic reduction, these families must have used birth control. The devout, abhorring contraception and abstinence, could reduce family size only by marrying late. Michael and Elizabeth Blount, who were Roman Catholics, had seventeen children. This was apparently a chastening experience for their sons; the first two never married, and the third brother prudently waited until age forty-eight before marrying a woman of forty-three, who did produce a daughter. His heir, a nephew, followed his example, marrying at forty-seven a bride aged thirty-eight. Others did not hesitate to resort to *coitus interruptus*, abstinence during the supposed fertile period, douching, or barrier methods – the rubber condom, the sponge, diaphragm or cervical cap all came into use in the nineteenth century. Lady Constance Lytton told Marie Stopes that birth control had been "practised in our family and by their numerous friends for generations," while in 1886 Mary Drew complained that "the 'American sin'" was "almost universally practised in the upper classes." Refusing to endure a second excruciating childbirth, Lady Sackville insisted she and Lionel take precautions. Abortion might be a last resort. When the Hon. Mrs Stanley became pregnant again after ten children, she soon reassured her husband that a "hot bath, a tremendous walk & a great dose have succeeded."[14]

Deaths reduced family size in the first half of the century, with as many as 14 per cent of the largest cohort, born between 1825 and 1849, dying before age twenty. The eldest son was most vulnerable, accounting for nearly a fifth of all deaths under twenty, perhaps because male newborns are less mature than females, and first births may be most difficult. Over the century, infant and child death rates fell dramatically, much earlier than rates in the general population (table 1.5).[15] In fact, the majority of landowners never lost a child.[16]

Those children who reached adulthood had a good chance of a long life. Among the peerage, for instance, life expectancy rose steadily, and mortality fell relatively rapidly from the 1850s, faster than the general population in the case of women.[17] Firstborn sons remained at higher risk, with twenty-one sample heirs over twenty dying before inheriting. Men who did acquire a country house, and their wives, typically lived to around seventy (table 1.6).

Table 1.6 Mean age at death of landowners and their spouses

Birth cohort	Number	Men (age)	Number	Women (age)
1775–99	59	70	43	67
1800–24	55	68	55	69
1825–49	68	68	58	72
1850–74	54	70	60	69

The family life cycle seldom began or ended in the country house, for it was subordinate to the cycle of inheritance. The paramount goal of the landed classes was to pass on the family inheritance intact to the next generation; to keep together the family's country seat, estates and heirlooms, and to preserve the family name, and, if possible, title. Dividing the estates would leave each new owner with a lower income and consequently reduce the family's power and status.

Most landed families kept their estates intact by primogeniture, passing all these five elements on to just one family member, preferably the eldest son. The strict settlement prevented dispersal. Drawn up on the eldest son's marriage, or his majority, or even with a landowner's will, it entailed the estates on the eldest grandson, often as yet unborn, making the heir merely tenant for life, unable for the most part to sell, alienate, or bequeath the family property he held in trust for his descendants. In practice, the strict settlement was flexible, allowing the owner limited rights to sell outlying properties, mortgage or convey property to trustees, meet obligations to younger sons and daughters, or pay off debts. With this preferential partibility, recently acquired land could also be disposed of at will. These changes took place when father and heir broke and renegotiated the settlement when the heir reached his majority at twenty-one. Otherwise, owners seldom broke the entail, not so much because of legal impediments, as because family and social pressures reinforced their compelling sense of obligation to the lineage. The settlement, always containing elaborate contingency plans should a grandson never eventuate, gave priority to males over females, to downward descent rather than lateral or upward, and failing that, to the most recent branch of the family.

Yet demography often defeated the ideal of continuity in the direct male line. Over a third of sample landowners failed to provide a son.[18] Nearly a fifth of inheritors were only sons. Four inheritors were second or third sons, where the father was free to choose an heir, or the eldest son inherited other property. In eighteen cases, an elder son had died earlier, nine leaving a grandson to inherit. Sample landowners who never married, or had no surviving sons or grandsons, left estates to the next surviving brother, the eldest surviving nephew or great-nephew, a male cousin, or another male relative. Heirs incapacitated by mental illness or retardation might nonetheless inherit, their affairs managed by other family members. Though Richard Roadley Dixon suffered bouts of mental illness, his father still entailed Holton on him.[19]

If no male heir were available, a female could inherit. In the sample, 9.2 per cent of inheritances were by females: eight daughters, two nieces, four sisters, and eight widows.[20] In most cases, family continuity was ensured by requiring the heiress's husband to adopt his wife's name, either by replacing his own or by hyphenation. Widows typically held the property for their lifetime only, with the estates entailed upon the next male heir.

As heirs inherited only on the landowner's death, many of them had already lived half their lives before moving into the country house. The mean age at inheritance rose to the late thirties among heirs born 1800–75 (table 1.7). Wives, siblings, and cousins were the oldest, of course, and grandsons and great-nephews were mostly in their teens and twenties. Around two-thirds of sons and nephews in the 1800–74 cohorts married before inheriting.[21] So did almost all brothers and cousins who inherited. Thus the majority of owners who married did so before moving into the country house, beginning their family life cycle, their housekeeping and child-rearing, in another house. Sometimes the eldest son and his wife resided with his parents. When Harry Toulmin married Emma Wroughton, both sets of parents considered them too young to set up house by themselves, so agreed they should live with the Toulmins at Childwickbury.[22]

Table 1.7 Age at inheritance

Birth cohort	Number inheriting	Mean age at inheritance	Inherited under 21 (%)	Died before inheriting
1775–99	59	32.7	23.7	2
1800–24	60	39.7	8.3	6
1825–49	69	37.3	15.9	14
1850–74	58	38.9	6.8	5
1875–99	30	32.9	26.7	8

Most young couples, however, wanted the privacy and independence of their own home. Great landowners often allowed the heir to occupy a secondary house. In the 1820s, the second Marquis of Stafford rebuilt Lilleshall for his eldest son. Landowners with just one estate had less to offer: in 1820 Sir James Graham's eldest son inhabited a nearby farmhouse "altered and fitted up in a very ... gentlemanlike way." Others wished to avoid proximity to interfering parents. Lady Stanley of Alderley offered her son Edward and his wife a manor house on the Alderley estate, but they preferred Winnington, another family property eighteen miles away.[23]

Heirs lacking spare family houses rented them from other landlords. After eight years at Childwickbury, Harry and Emma Toulmin rented Lord Verulam's dower house nearby.[24] Other heirs lived in London, notably those with an occupation, like the lawyer John Stanhope Arkwright. Among heirs outside the immediate family, married brothers had their own establishment, as did cousins, nephews, and other more distant relatives. Colonel John Picton-Turbervill, heir to his uncle's Ewenny Priory, spent some years abroad in the army, with his children settled in Brighton, before retiring in 1883. The family tried living in Bruges, then rented a country house three miles from the Priory.[25] Likewise, men who bought country houses were often already raising a family in a less prestigious dwelling.

The father's death also changed the lives of the rest of the family. Widows and any unmarried siblings had to move out to make way for the heir and his family. This reluctance to accommodate kin, contrasting with the extended family household of the continental aristocracy, arose in the late seventeenth century when the upper bourgeoisie and squirearchy sought greater privacy and domesticity and reduced ties to kin. The aristocracy followed suit in the following century. By the nineteenth century, vacating the family seat for the heir was the norm, even for bachelors like Ralph Sneyd, who lived alone at Keele Hall, though he had a mother and unmarried sisters living.

While primogeniture gave one individual the bulk of the family's property, the strict settlement provided for the others: a jointure for the widowed mother, portions for the sisters, and capital sums or annuities for the younger sons. Unentailed, recently acquired property was often bequeathed to more needy family members. When the wife was an heiress, her estates might go to a younger son or daughter. Nevertheless, most of the banished discovered that their standard of living fell considerably.

If the eldest son had not yet come of age, or was unmarried with young siblings, the widow did not leave. Generally, a trust was formed, making the mother responsible for the children, household management, and sometimes estate administration. Harriet, Dowager Marchioness of Bath, for instance, ran Longleat during her son's minority for fifteen years, moving out when he came of age.[26] Notwithstanding entail, some owners gave their widows the right to stay in the mansion. John Arkwright, leaving a large family of young children, stipulated his wife could use the mansion until his heir reached age twenty-five. Thomas John Dixon authorized Mary Ann to remain unconditionally at Holton for three years, and thereafter only if their children predeceased her without issue and she did not remarry.[27] Occasionally, widows stayed on permanently after their child inherited the family seat, either by invitation, as at Hesleyside, where William Charlton allowed his mother and aunt to remain, or because they refused to move, as did Mary Ann Dixon, when her daughter Ann bought a dower house for her.[28] A few men lacking surviving sons disregarded primogeniture, and left their estates to their wives. Some, like Lady Shelley, gained everything absolutely, but more typically widows controlled estates for life only, with the property entailed on the next heir, as in the will of George, Lord Northwick.[29]

The vast majority of widows, however, made way for their married sons. In earlier centuries, the rich had either housed a widowed mother in a nearby dower house, or easily accommodated her in their large, well-staffed mansions, and even the lesser gentry had allocated her some rooms. But in the nineteenth century the widow was expected to establish a new home elsewhere. This avoided rivalry between the former mistress and the new wife over household administration, child-rearing and the husband himself, and protected the family's privacy and intimacy.

Consequently, a new home had to be found for the dowager. Some families owned dower houses built for this purpose, or gave her another family house. Cliveden, for instance, was used as the Leveson-Gower dower house. A few widows were bequeathed property of their own: the second Marquess of Westminster, one of the greatest landowners, left his Dorset and Wiltshire estates to his widow for life. She was also residuary legatee to his personal estate, which included land purchased with his private income. Some widows went abroad, or bought their own houses. Though her husband willed her his leased London house, Henrietta Hussey eventually bought a house in Hastings.[30]

Many younger sons had already moved out by the time their father died. Upon graduating from university, or finishing their training, some younger sons lived on unearned income, devoting their lives to sport and other amusements, but most supported themselves with careers in the armed services, the church, the colonial service, politics, or even business. Such occupations normally removed them from the parental home; they set up their own establishments in tied housing such as military quarters or vicarages, rented houses or flats, or resided in a gentleman's club. Primogeniture meant younger sons had relatively small incomes, and, as social norms dictated that they delay marriage until they had accumulated enough capital and income to support a family in the upper-class lifestyle, many married late or not at all.[31]

High rates of bachelorhood deprived landowners' daughters of husbands. Just over 28 per cent of sample daughters born 1800–24 never married, rising to nearly 40 per cent in the next two cohorts, and then falling to just under 29 per cent. In comparison, around 12 per cent of the entire female population never married.[32] The increase in spinsterhood occurred in a generation in which large families with better survival rates came of age in the agricultural depression, when funds for endowing either younger sons or daughters were shrinking. Many younger sons had either departed for the colonies or elected to remain bachelors, while those who did go courting were often discouraged as ineligible by matchmaking mamas. Parents counted on one daughter staying at home to care for them in their old age. Widowers customarily required one daughter to act as mistress of the house, companion, and nurse. Motherless daughters, moreover, lost a key advocate in the marriage market. For her part, the dowager might demand a companion too, or lack the resources to find husbands for her remaining daughters. Finally, not all spinsterhood was involuntary, especially later in the period, when more opportunities in education and social service offered a rewarding life.

Daughters had to remain at home until marriage, and those who failed to marry simply remained there, for income-earning careers were unthinkable until late in the period. At Edwardian Moor Park "the daughters of the house... reached middle age without its having ever apparently occurred to them to start homes of their own."[33] By this time, nevertheless, single career women could live in college halls of residence or settlement houses, or even rent rooms.

When her father died, a single woman normally accompanied her mother to her new home, although she might remain as housekeeper or companion to an unmarried brother, or to assist the new mistress with household management and child-rearing as did Louisa Jebb at the Lyth.[34] Upon her mother's death, a middle-aged daughter faced dim prospects. Sarah, Dowager Lady Lyttleton, worried about providing for her unmarried daughters. If she died in debt, it would have to be repaid out of their fortunes, thereby leaving them "in little better than a dependant situation – after giving them an education, tastes and habits, fit for rich people."[35] Prevented from earning, the elderly spinster lived on her allowance in her own modest establishment, like Charlotte Troubridge, who rented a house in Shepherd's Bush, keeping two servants.[36] Others relied on the family's generosity, "enforced, and often unwelcome, pensioners on the bounty of brothers or more distant relatives."[37] They might live in a house on the estate, or have rooms in the mansion itself. In the 1871 census, Elizabeth Poole, aged forty-one, lived at Marbury Cottage with her former governess as companion and four servants, while the Duke of Northumberland's household included his unmarried sister, Louisa, aged sixty-eight.[38]

Most landowners refused to offer a permanent home to any relative. The nuclear family was clearly the norm. Three-quarters of the census sample were simple family households of only the conjugal family unit: fifty couples with children, thirteen widowers and widows with offspring, and ten couples who were childless or had no children at home.[39] Five country houses contained "no family" households, unmarried heads of household with co-resident mothers, siblings, or stepfamily. There were four solitary households: two widowers with children living elsewhere and two childless widows.

Yet twelve – one in eight of the sample – were extended family households, where relatives joined the conjugal family unit: a widowed mother or mother-in-law, unmarried siblings, a grandson sent from India, a niece, and a cousin. Six were multiple-family households, with two or even three conjugal family units, where a married child and his or her family moved back home. Extended family households were most common among the peerage, doubtless because of their larger mansions and incomes. In a census sample of thirty peers' establishments, nine contained resident kin.

The country house, in fact, acted as an elite welfare institution for the wider kin group. As already noted, an unmarried owner could ask his mother and siblings to stay, and heirs were sometimes encouraged to reside in the family seat. A wife's death left a place to be filled – Lord Devon's daughter kept house for him after her mother died, and after marrying moved her husband and children to Powderham for much of the year. A wife might add her own kin. Archbishop Tait's daughter, for instance, brought her youngest brother to live at Renishaw. Parents sometimes provided a home for a married or widowed child and his or her family. Harry Chaplin married Lady Florence Leveson-Gower, who died after bearing her third child. When he sold Blankney, the Duke and Duchess of Sutherland raised his children with their own. Orphans were taken in by relatives; after the six little Troubridges lost both parents, they went to live with their grandfather Gurney at Runcton. Finally, the physically or mentally handicapped found sanctuary in the country house. In 1871, Charlotte Oglander, an "imbecile from birth," was living with her married brother at Nunwell Park.[40]

As the sample indicates, a country house contained many household types over a century. Inheritance by an unmarried or widowed heir meant a house could be occupied by a lone individual for many years. John, the bachelor Lord Northwick, inherited Northwick in Worcestershire in 1800, his mother dying there in 1818. His nephew, George Rushout, married ten years after inheriting in 1859. Besides a stepdaughter, he had one daughter, who died aged eight. His widow then owned Northwick from 1887 to 1912. At Holton in Lincolnshire, Thomas John Dixon was single when he inherited in 1824, but married less than two years later. After his death in 1871, his widow remained at Holton with the new owner, their daughter Ann, who lived there alone after her mother's death. She was followed by another solitary, her widowed sister Amelia. Only after 1906 did a couple and their children live there again.

The code of inheritance, along with individual and family life cycles, determined how long an owner and his or her family were entitled to live in the country house. Yet demography and legal documents reveal no more than potential patterns of occupancy. Few families, in fact, continuously occupied their country house either during the year or over their tenancy. A fourth cycle, the family's own cycle of migration, altered the actual rate of occupancy from month to month, while changing family fortunes or individual preference caused some owners to be absent for many years.

The aristocracy had an established pattern of migration for social activities: to London in early May for the social Season over the summer, to the country or to Scotland for hunting and shooting in the autumn from August, home to the country house for Christmas, and perhaps an interlude at a seaside resort before the Season, or a trip abroad. Furthermore, the landed classes often made prolonged visits to friends and relatives.

Great magnates with property scattered throughout the British Isles stayed in their own houses wherever they went: a London town house, a castle or lodge in Scotland, country houses on estates in different counties, and even seaside villas. The rest rented London houses and shooting boxes, and took lodgings at resorts. Owners of multiple properties made a round of inspection annually, preferably coinciding with politics or sport.

The Dukes of Sutherland epitomized the migratory habits and multiple dwellings of the very rich. In 1815 the Leveson-Gowers owned Trentham Hall in Staffordshire, Lilleshall in Shropshire, Westhill Park in Essex (until 1847), Richmond (until 1834), Bridgewater House in London, and Dunrobin Castle in Scotland. Two decades later the second Duke of Sutherland took York House in London on long lease from the Crown, renaming it Stafford House. Cliveden, in Buckinghamshire, was acquired in 1847 and sold in the 1890s. The third Duchess, estranged from her husband, built herself a villa in 1873 at Torquay, where she remained until her death in 1888. The Leveson-Gowers leased various houses in Scotland such as shooting boxes at Loch Iver (1840–70s) and at Tarbat (from the 1850s) and a town house in Edinburgh (1850–60s). Trentham Hall was demolished in 1910, and by 1914 the family's principal houses were Lilleshall, Stafford House, and Dunrobin. Successive dukes passed their lives migrating from one house to the next in much the same way. In the 1850s, the family spent the winter at Trentham, returning to London in February or March, then visited Trentham before going to Dunrobin in the autumn. In the 1890s, the fourth Duke and his family usually went to Lilleshall for Easter, returned to London for the rest of the spring and summer, then departed for Dunrobin in August, before dividing the winter between Stafford House and Trentham.[41]

Changing social habits reduced the time many families spent in their country houses by the last decades of the century. Earlier, it was peers who were peripatetic; the gentry tended to remain on their country estates. Railways and later motor transport greatly increased mobility, making the pleasures of fashionable London and the moors of Scotland more accessible. *Nouveaux riches* bought country houses without estates for weekend and shooting parties. Continental resorts also became popular. Increasing numbers of late-nineteenth-century landowners were lured away from country life. Colonel Ralph Sneyd, for instance, inherited Keele Hall in 1888, but, "beset with a certain restlessness, and a penchant for an expensive social life," lived mostly in London, as a member of White's Club, the Royal Yacht Squadron, and the Turf Club. His chief interests in life were shooting and racehorses. By 1900 he was an absentee landlord, renting Keele Hall to the Grand Duke Michael of Russia.[42]

Declining fortunes also caused absences. Families forced to economize often moved into a smaller house, either letting the mansion or simply leaving it empty. This became common when rental incomes fell from the 1870s. John Stanhope Arkwright, for example, could not afford to keep up Hampton Court, so he let the property for several years before selling it and buying a smaller place.[43]

A house could also be let if the family preferred living elsewhere. When Henry Toulmin inherited Childwickbury, his wife refused to return to the house where she had spent early married life under matriarchal rule. Even after her mother-in-law removed herself to St Leonards, she insisted on letting the house. They did eventually move to Childwickbury, but, finding the house too expensive to live in, let it and moved back to the Pre.[44]

The 1871 census provides insights into the normal patterns of occupancy, being taken in early April, when most landed families were still in their country houses. This census was taken before the agricultural depression reduced landed incomes. Suffolk was an average county in its distribution of noble and gentry estates, containing eighty principal seats owned by families with over 1,000 acres and £1,000 a year. On census night, twenty-five families were away, and in one more case the parents were gone. Four of these families had left most of their servants, indicating a temporary absence, but the other houses contained a skeleton domestic staff or caretaker staff. Thus, over a quarter of the principal or only seats were not the current residences of their owners in April 1871. Among parish gentry, occupancy rates were even lower. Of twenty-one borderline gentry families (with landed incomes of between £900 and £1,000), one-third clearly resided elsewhere. Of eighteen families with less land but still listed in Burke's *Landed Gentry*, seven were not resident. Other Suffolk country houses were secondary seats. Such houses were typically acquired by marriage to an heiress or by inheritance, but sometimes by land purchase. Twenty-one families – eight peers, seven baronets or knights, and six squires – owned subsidiary seats in Suffolk. Only one was occupied by a family member, the owner's mother. Seven, all with skeleton staffs, may have been visited by their owners and their retinues at other times, a further six were in the hands of caretaker staff, one had become a farmhouse, and six were let.

The social calendar, rules of inheritance, and other aspects of the upper-class code of values and conduct modified universal life and family cycles to produce a distinct family type. Primogeniture meant heirs were more likely to marry, at an earlier age, than their younger brothers, but individualism meant they wed later and at lower rates than other men.

The upper classes generally had smaller families on average than the rest of the population. Landowners modified the family life cycle by their own codes of inheritance and behaviour. For example, primogeniture kept the house in the family, but evicted the heir's mother and siblings. As head of the clan, however, an owner might offer needy relatives a refuge. As in the rest of the upper classes, fewer daughters and younger sons married than in the whole population, and unmarried daughters often remained at home while younger sons moved out. Finally, landowners spent less time in their homes than did other people, following the rites of their social calendar, and shutting up or letting their country house when they were unable to maintain an acceptable lifestyle.

This chapter has shown which members of the landed family resided in the country house and when they did so. The following four chapters move beyond this to explore their daily lives there, and the relationships between them, beginning with childhood and adolescence, and the relationship between parents and children, then moving on to courtship, marriage, and the lives of women. In all these aspects of life, the country house family had developed its own unique patterns of behaviour.

2

The Country House Childhood

Childhood in the nineteenth-century country house forms a distinct type in the history of childhood. Much of the popular stereotype of Victorian upper- and middle-class child-rearing does apply to the country house childhood; children were cared for by nurses, who imposed firm discipline and rigid routines in segregated nurseries.[1] Yet an upbringing in a country house had many unique advantages and benefits. Landowners' children enjoyed the pleasures of a splendid mansion, extensive gardens, the park and the estate, peopled with interesting and friendly servants and dependants, in a stable, traditional rural community.

The patterns of the country house upbringing were established in the early nineteenth century. Children were raised by the nurse in her nursery until age five or six, when they began lessons with a governess in the schoolroom and, a few years later, boys went away to boarding school. This system was uncritically accepted well into the twentieth century.

The nursery as an institution reached its apogée in the Victorian era. Before the eighteenth century, well-born infants had been sent out to wet-nurses, returning home after a year or two to be reared by nurse-maids in rooms assigned as nurseries. In the later eighteenth century, babies remained at home, as upper-class mothers breastfed their babies or installed the wet-nurse in the nursery. Early-nineteenth-century mothers supervised and instructed the nursery attendant, who acted as the mother's assistant, not her replacement. But soon large families necessitated more under-nurses and nursery-maids to assist the overburdened nurse. Serving an apprenticeship under her, they eventually found places as head nurses themselves, passing their system of childrearing on to the next generation of nursery-maids in turn. The Victorian enthusiasm for subdivision and separation of functions created a clearly defined nursery hierarchy in carefully isolated children's quarters.

A new-born infant spent the first month in its mother's bedroom, attended by the "monthly nurse." Then the baby was handed over to the eagerly waiting nanny. Mothers unwilling or unable to breastfeed engaged a wet-nurse as well. Early in the century, artificial feeding with milk and farinaceous mixtures was unhygienic and lacking in essential nutrients, resulting in a high infant-mortality rate. Wet-nursing was a much safer alternative. Some early-nineteenth-century aristocrats took wet-nursing for granted: all thirteen offspring of Elizabeth Grosvenor were fed by wet-nurses.[2] However, the theory that a baby imbibed personality characteristics, fears of drunkenness, disease and drugs, and maternal-breastfeeding propaganda all made mothers increasingly reluctant to employ a wet-nurse unless their own efforts failed. In 1865, only mounting concern for her ailing new-born son's health persuaded Katherine Russell, Viscountess Amberley, to allow a wet-nurse to replace her. Her mother found a woman "married three months, confined three weeks," whom the doctor examined and approved. As in many other cases, a series of wet-nurses came and went. This first one was removed by her indignant husband, who had not been told about his wife's employment. She was followed by an E. Powell, who left her own baby with another woman. Finally, Lizzy Williams, whose baby had already died, came and remained.[3] Wet-nursing declined in popularity from the 1870s, chiefly because bottle-feeding became safer. Thenceforth, wet-nursing was only chosen for delicate infants.[4]

Wet-nurses only handled the baby during breastfeeding, but this was enough for mutual attachment to grow. The tender-hearted Lizzy Williams loved tiny Frank Russell "nearly like her own."[5] This intimacy was short-lived: most wet-nurses were dismissed after weaning, normally before babies were old enough to miss them. Naomi Bales nursed Lady Greene's infant for just three months, until it was considered developed enough to be hand-fed.[6]

The nurse, or "nanny," undertook the infant's physical care; she dressed it, changed its napkins, washed and bathed it, fed it, even took it into her bed at night early in the century. Most nurses also gave their tiny charges the continuous attentive, responsive, and loving care essential for normal emotional, physical, and mental development. A good nurse cuddled and comforted her babies, smiled and talked to them, and played with them. Beyond babyhood, children remained in the nursery for five or six years. Nurses were not only responsible for physical care, but for training in good personal habits and manners. They gave religious instruction, and sometimes first lessons. Nursery-maids took care of older children, dressing and bathing them, and amusing them.

Unlike mothers of any class, the nurse gave her whole time to her little charges. She slept in their room and ate with them, seldom taking a holiday. Reminiscences stress her omnipresence. As Lady Ann Hill observed,[7]

> There is an immense security in the day-and-night nursery life. When I was in bed, there was always the light under the door, and often the murmur of voices from the other side of it. I don't ever remember her ever being "out", or going away for a holiday, and meals were brought to us in the day nursery by the nursery-maid, so Nanny was never further away than the distance of the bathroom-lavatory, not more than a dozen yards.

Most nurses had deliberately chosen their occupation because they liked children. In autobiographies and other sources, thirty-eight were described as kind and loving, or as loved by their charges, but only eight as cruel, abusive, and unloved. Some families went through several unsatisfactory nurses until a good one was found. The majority, however, possessed qualities and skills ideal for rearing children. The Toulmins' Fanny Rogers, for instance, was kind and patient, sensible and calm. At Renishaw, Nurse Penny played dance tunes on a comb and sang ballads and country songs, and at Stoneleigh Mrs Gailey told wonderful stories and taught the children old-fashioned games.[8]

A nanny complemented typical loving, involved parents, but could also compensate for any parental inadequacies. Some nurses became substitute mothers to motherless children: after Mary Curzon died, Nanny Sibley became "the real prop and backbone" of the Curzon girls' lives. Others made up for parents' neglect or indifference. Only her nanny loved unwanted Edith Sitwell.[9] Nannies acted as buffers, shielding children from marital discord and family crises. In addition, nannies, with their aptitude, training, and experience, understood the nature and needs of small children better than some mothers. Thus, the little Buxtons preferred to confide their "small troubles and embarrassments" to their beloved old nurse.[10]

Not surprisingly, most children loved their nannies, the mainspring of their early years. Lady Sybil Lubbock recognized the small child's total dependence on the nanny, who appeared to provide "everything – warmth, food, clothes, comfort, caresses, support of every kind." To tiny Eleanor Cropper, "Nurse" meant "safe comfortable love," constantly "at the child's beck and call . . . with no other claims upon it."[11] This love continued into adulthood. "I could fall on your neck and kiss you now with as much tenderness as when I was a nasty, dirty, little boy," Lord Wharncliffe wrote to Mrs Ingram.[12] Children even became attached to harsh unresponsive nurses, instinctively seeking affection from the person most available.[13]

Yet the nanny system was not without its drawbacks. Nurses sometimes left when children were young, either dismissed as redundant when the youngest entered the schoolroom, or moving on to advance their own careers. Jealous or uncomprehending parents were insensitive in firing nannies. "Juliet is so silly," complained Lady de Grey. "When I told her she must have a French governess and that her nurse must go, for she was really no use to her now, she just burst into tears and said 'Nanny no *use*! But she *loves* me, Mother.' Of course, I didn't give in, but it was very tiresome."[14]

Abandoned children were grief-stricken, crying for weeks. Children separated from their loved primary care-giver before the age of five or six may suffer deeply, experiencing painful bereavement, bewilderment, and irrational guilt. Losing the mainstay of their world fosters insecurity, and a perception of failing in their first human relationship can hinder their ability to form and maintain later relationships. Jonathan Gathorne-Hardy partly attributes notorious upper-class traits such as inhibitions, coldness, shyness and reserve, to "a system which, at crucial moments, removed the figure from whom they were learning the value of human relationships."[15] Hastings, twelfth Duke of Bedford, believed that the loss of his first nurse "induced a permanent fear-complex" that subsequent care-givers who won his affection might also disappear. Even the departure of an unloving nurse could be traumatic. "Without that familiar, all pervading presence," Lady Cynthia Asquith remembered, "I felt as if my whole known world were dissolving around me – my very sense of Me-ness crumbling back into nothingness."[16]

But the nurse's disappearance did not always cause irredeemable psychological damage. Children are resilient, and much depended on the child's maturity and personality. Many youngsters had already established strong alternative relationships with their parents and siblings. Older children had long passed the most vulnerable age and boys often departed, for school, before the nanny did. Devoted nurses, moreover, kept in touch with their former charges, exchanging letters with them over the years.

The sudden replacement of a beloved nanny with a governess prejudiced grieving and resentful children against the newcomer. The governess was expected to supervise, discipline, and amuse the children, helping to form their characters. Unlike schoolchildren, her charges could never escape from her presence. "Being naughty in lessons always led to reprisals in the rest of your life," complained Viola Bankes, "you could not leave your school self behind at the end of the day."[17] Women usually became governesses out of necessity, regardless of their aptitude for teaching or child care; indeed, some were hired for their piety or gentility alone. The loneliness, bitterness, and unhappiness of the governess's lot was often taken out on the children. Of fifty-five governesses described individually by former pupils, twenty were characterized as harsh or cruel, or disliked.

Many well-meaning governesses found it hard to win their charges' affection. Most children had already grown very attached to their parents, needing no mother-substitute. If the nanny still presided over the nursery, she often vied successfully with the governess for the children's affections. Insular English children might be prejudiced against foreign governesses, with their strange and unappealing habits, foreign accent, or poor English. Teaching methods were seldom enjoyable or interesting, and without examinations or strong parental or societal enthusiasm for female academic achievement, girls had little motivation to learn. Moody, rebellious adolescent girls, or lively little boys, were not easily controlled or very lovable. "Our first governess was Fräulein Alvens, whom Basil continually cheeked," Lady Winifride Elwes recalled. "She chased him round the room with a stick while he dodged between the furniture and Agnes and I stood on the sofa cheering." Many little rascals deliberately baited their hapless governesses, especially baffled foreigners. "We behaved abominably to most of them," admitted Edith Picton-Turbervill, "luring a poor fräulein into a field and then driving the cows at her."[18]

Even so, many governesses were remembered with affection and appreciation; over half of the fifty-five were liked or loved by their charges. These were typically pleasant women with the same warm qualities as a good nanny, some of them gifted teachers. Constance Jones's governess, for instance, was lively, friendly and kind, and made lessons enjoyable.[19] Charlotte Dixon regarded Miss Robertson as her "beloved friend."[20]

The minority of children lacking devoted parents turned instead to their first governess, particularly a nursery governess hired in place of a nanny. John Baker White's parents were divorced, and he was reared by a stern, devout, but kindly governess. When he was sent to school at eight, she left. He was devastated. "Life without her was something I just could not envisage, for she had been so completely part of my being. The future seemed empty, dark and terrible." The orphaned Troubridge children's governess was "all that was left to us of the old life," so they "clung to her and lavished on her deep affection, which she repaid with love and unfailing sympathy." Even abusive governesses were mourned. When their "old Tartar governess" finally departed, the motherless Milne twins felt not just relief, but sadness.[21] Throughout the period, the child-rearing methods of both nannies and governesses were characterized by rigid routine, strictness and discipline, austerity, religious training, and differentiated treatment of girls and boys. Over the century, the daily routine became inflexible, just as it was in the rest of the household. By the 1880s, the typical nursery timetable was: early rising at seven a.m., breakfast at eight a.m., an outing in the morning, dinner at one p.m., another outing in the afternoon, tea at either four or five p.m., children's hour with the parents, then bed at six or seven p.m. As an Edwardian nursery-maid, Sarah Sedgwick discovered that nothing was "allowed to interfere with our time-table, everything happened dead on time."[22]

The schoolroom timetable, though differing between households, was rigidly adhered to once established. Children rose at six or seven, and might do lessons or music practice, or join family prayers, before breakfast. The morning and afternoon were spent in varying combinations of lessons, walks, and rests, with dinner at one or two o'clock, and schoolroom tea at four or five, followed by time with parents or more lessons, then bed by eight. Schoolroom routines were most rigorous early in the century. In the 1820s, the Sitwells began eight hours of lessons at seven a.m., and continued schoolwork after tea as they grew older – "a perfect treadmill of learning" ceasing only on Sundays and Christmas Day. Medical warnings about overtaxing brains and destroying health may have accounted for less demanding schedules late in the period. At Holton, the Gibbons girls had lessons from nine to eleven-thirty a.m., from three to four-thirty p.m., and sometimes after tea in the winter.[23]

The Victorians regarded strict timetables as crucial for inculcating orderly habits and self-discipline. There were practical reasons, too. Timetables reduced decision-making, avoided disputes, and facilitated discipline, especially with the sheer number of children to be controlled in large early-nineteenth-century families. "In a well-run nursery with everything to time outbreaks of naughtiness were rare," affirmed Sarah Sedgwick.[24] Nursery and schoolroom had to synchronize with the rest of the household's routine. Children were, indeed, being conditioned for lifelong subjection to the rigid timetables of large establishments. Nurses' job mobility was another good reason for enforcing a broadly similar routine everywhere. New nurses could easily take over, with little disruption. Perhaps the more diverse schedules encountered by governesses in different households only aggravated their troubles.

A fixed daily schedule ensured an uneventful, even repressed existence. Small children "led such quiet lives, and had so little time to themselves," commented Sarah Sedgwick, "with the two walks, meals regular as clockwork, and the hour downstairs."[25] The routine could be tedious – the Bouveries regarded their obligatory drive as "a terrible chore," and Lady Wellesley recalled "the misery of the daily walk."[26] Yet strict timetables did not necessarily blight young lives. Small children often prefer the security and predictability of routine, and adapt to whatever system is imposed upon them. "I do not remember that the monotony of our existence irked us," wrote Eleanor Acland. "We did not crave for variations and events, but we fully enjoyed them when they occurred."[27]

Strictness and firm discipline were crucial to upper-class child-rearing. Discipline was more severe early in the century, partly due to the Evangelical doctrine of children's innate sinfulness, corrected by breaking the will, and enforcing absolute obedience and subjection to authority. But strictness was also part of the landed classes' effort to reform themselves: parents wanted obedient, correctly behaved children who would undertake their adult duties conscientiously and conform to the upper-class code of conduct.

Nurses, too, were strong advocates of firm discipline. Although some nannies resorted to the slaps and spankings, and the threats of abducting witches, policemen, or sweeps of their own working-class upbringing, many nurses wise in the ways of children used only the mildest punishments, typically denial of treats or time out, or resolved upsets without coercion. Mary Toulmin's nanny, for example, was strict, but patient and kind, with an ability to make children "good when they want to be naughty, by not noticing or by making them laugh." Seeking out the reasons for children's misbehaviour, she never hit them, believing that punishments did more harm than good. Above all, she forbade anyone to call a child "naughty", for that "would break its heart."[28] Corporal punishment was often forbidden in Edwardian nurseries; Sarah Sedgwick's charges were stood in the corner, denied sweets or a story at bedtime. Neither the Norland Nursing School nor the Princess Christian Nursery Training College permitted their trained nurses to slap or spank a child.[29]

It was governesses, rather than nannies, who were notorious for excessive discipline and cruel punishments. They were often imbued with stern religious zeal, or took the traditional view that inflicting fear and pain when mistakes were made most effectively promoted learning and correct manners. Too many governesses seem to have been repressed, neurotic, even sadistic women who ruthlessly exploited their power. The little Toulmins feared the tyrannical Miss Moll, whose frequent punishments of pinches, jabs, and deprivations prompted prayers to get rid of her. Like other terrorized children, they were unable to break "the strictest rule of all children" by telling their parents the truth about her.[30]

Parental demands for obedience and perfect manners, working-class norms, repressive religious beliefs and strict routines coalesced in an elaborate code of rules and restrictions. Insistence on good manners, silent meals and empty plates, and prohibitions on certain toys, activities and foods, were common. Upper-class children had to learn a particularly complex code of values and conduct. Firm discipline can benefit children, who may need consistent rules and a predictable, ordered world to feel secure, and must be socialized to fit into adult society. Yet many nursery and schoolroom regulations were illogical, pointless, or even harmful, causing resistance or undying resentment. Some unfair and irrational rules were accepted without question: as a small child, Lady Diana Cooper thought it only natural that she was forbidden to take a toy in her perambulator, or her doll into the garden.[31] Many children, however, never forgot the experience of being forced to eat cold, congealed and nauseating food refused at an earlier meal. Endless prohibitions and punishments also promoted timidity, inhibitions, conformity, and an obsession with rules.[32] Such an upbringing may have encouraged children to grow up conforming to and supporting the elaborate rules of etiquette which so complicated and confined Society.

Closely allied to discipline and strictness was the austerity of many country house childhoods. Nurseries and schoolrooms were often little islands of plain living in the most luxurious of homes. This was a deliberate policy, designed to promote health and prevent spoiling. Heeding the advice of Rousseau, puritanical Evangelicals, or medical experts, early-nineteenth-century parents ordered plain food, cold baths, hard beds, and unheated bedrooms, to toughen both their children's bodies and their characters, and these practices became standard until late in the period.

Many children were simply dressed, the younger ones in mended and altered "hand-me-downs." Lady Lytton, determined not to bring up her daughters in luxury, allowed them "three dresses – bad, better, best – for winter and summer."[33] Nurseries were sparsely furnished for easy cleaning and for romping, but with unwanted old furniture rather than specifically designed pieces. Nursery menus were an unvarying succession of bland, unappetizing dishes believed suitable for children, such as bread and milk, porridge, boiled mutton, and milk puddings. A simple diet and bare, shabby nurseries contrasted sharply with adult quarters and meals, underlining the gulf between the two worlds.

The austere regime did not extend to playthings. Parents recognized childhood as a distinct stage in life, and play as the young child's proper pursuit, the means of learning many adult roles. Children confined to the nursery for many hours of the day, moreover, needed plenty of playthings and books to keep them busy and happy. Landed parents thus indulged their children with abundant books and toys. A rocking-horse, a doll's house, building blocks, tin soldiers, and numerous dolls complete with cradles, prams and tea-sets were standard. Wealthy parents could easily afford to purchase the growing range of toys mass-produced by a flourishing toy industry. Sometimes the estate carpenter proudly produced custom-made toys like a rocking-horse or doll's house. Plenty of card and board games were provided, too. Children also made their own fun. Leisurely hours confined to the nurseries stimulated complicated imaginative games, numerous hobbies such as stamp-collecting or scrapbook-making, and group enterprises such as a family newspaper, or plays and concerts put on for the servants, guests, or local children.

By the Edwardian period, more worldly and pleasure-loving parents sought children's happiness, not hardiness. Nurseries became more attractive and well-equipped. Edwardian children enjoyed tastier, more varied, and nutritious diets, too.[34]

Austerity often reflected religious earnestness, an integral part of the country house childhood. Nurses taught early prayers and grace at meals, read Bible stories and sang hymns; then governesses, or visiting clergymen, continued religious instruction. Children attended family prayers and church with the rest of the household, and on Sundays found their normal activities forbidden. "In place of our usual toys, our religious sensibilities were cultivated with . . . a Noah's Ark, while a book on the Collects replaced our favourite authors," recalled Frances Greville, Lady Warwick.[35]

Plate 5   The nurse and members of the Lyttleton family in the nursery at Hagley Hall in the 1890s

Evangelicalism, with its emphasis on sin and self-examination, mortality and salvation, coloured early-nineteenth-century religious training. Evangelicals such as Mrs Trimmer and her daughter Selina infiltrated aristocratic nurseries to convert their charges. Mrs Trimmer, Hannah More and others produced a flood of best-selling religious manuals, tracts, and moral tales which reached thousands more nurseries and schoolrooms for several generations. Their graphic depictions of hell and damnation often frightened sensitive children, inducing a morbid sense of guilt and fear. Failure to keep the commandments perfectly haunted Mary Sanderson, who spent sleepless nights reflecting on her sinful nature and fearfully awaiting imminent judgement. The "atmosphere of introspective religion" marred her childhood, "saddened by the Jesuitical system" unknown to her parents.[36]

Later nurses and governesses, realizing the harm of harping on sin and death, taught a more gentle, optimistic Christianity. But religion remained pervasive, stressing the moral values of self-sacrifice and duty. This early training made religion a natural and accepted part of life, its doctrines and values internalized into adulthood. The High Church Miss Harvey instilled in the Chaplin children "a deep love for and a strict observance of religious matters."[37]

Like the rest of Victorian society, and indeed like every culture, the upper classes had differing expectations for boys and girls. Sex differences were less pronounced in infancy and early childhood than today; all babies were dressed in long white robes, and boys wore frocks until the age of four. Then gender was clearly emphasized, when little boys donned trousers, leaving girls hampered by skirts and petticoats. Each sex was encouraged to develop appropriate personality characteristics: boys were expected to be intelligent, courageous, energetic, assertive, resourceful, and independent, while girls were ideally docile, self-effacing, diligent, and sweet-natured. Even in the nursery, a girl was taught to defer to her brothers, and to sacrifice her own interests for theirs. While early-Victorian authorities urged that little girls exercise as vigorously as their brothers, they disapproved of rough sports and boisterous behaviour for older girls. The greater freedom and higher status accorded to boys rapidly became evident to their envious and offended sisters; inevitably, many little girls longed to be boys.[38]

Up to the age of seven or eight, upper-class boys and girls were taught together by a nursery governess. Most girls then remained at home, taught by a succession of governesses. In the early decades of the nineteenth century, many fathers hired tutors for their young sons, or placed them in a clergyman's household. Only from the 1870s did attendance at preparatory school become the norm. While some teenage boys, particularly early in the century, continued to be educated by tutors, most boys typically went on to public school and university.

At boarding school, boys studied Greek and Latin language and literature, the education of a gentleman. More importantly, the public school was supposed to develop manliness, hardiness, and stoicism, counteracting the feminine influences of home. Masculinity was promoted by brutal punishments, grim living conditions, inadequate diets, and bullying and vice among the boys, all of which were tolerated as a form of tribal initiation rite. Reformers sought the same ends through the house system, prefects, and compulsory games. Boys' schools were total institutions, all-masculine communities with their own hierarchies, codes of conduct, customs, and language. They generated intense loyalty and identification, conformity and conventionality, and enormous self-confidence and assurance. School was potentially a rival, alternative institution to the family; indeed, in late-Victorian boarding schools "home – and particularly mothers and sisters – were taboo subjects."[39]

Little boys raised with tender, solicitous care at home found the beatings, bullying, filth, and hunger of preparatory school a great shock. Boys who had endured Spartan nurseries, harsh discipline, and cruel governesses were more prepared: Edward Wood's first school had the same "method and atmosphere" as Miss Hilder's harsh regime. Like most boys, he loathed his preparatory school, and found Eton "very tolerable" in comparison.[40] Many boys greatly missed their families and nurses, feeling very homesick at first, and tearful or depressed when the holidays ended, reluctant to leave their beloved homes, hobbies, and sports. Girls missed their brothers too. At Tolson Hall, life became narrow and dull without the boys; there was no more elementary Latin and algebra, and playtime lost its zest. Home-bound sisters found brothers home for the holidays more self-assured, lordly, and mysterious.[41] Many boys nevertheless became immersed in the world of school. Lawrence Jones admitted that Eton became his life, with holidays becoming "mere interludes in the serious business of living."[42]

The girls left behind in the schoolroom acquired an education not only different in content, but usually inferior in quality. A preparatory governess generally replaced the nursery governess when girls reached the age of eight, and a finishing governess took over in their mid-teens to polish them in accomplishments.[43] Few girls learned any Greek or Latin; instead they were expected to become proficient in French, German, and Italian language and literature, and to acquire accomplishments – music, singing, dancing, and drawing. They studied English literature, history, and geography, and might also dabble in mathematics, art history, or the natural sciences, particularly botany, depending on the governess's interests. Upper-class girls' education was unusually fragmented and haphazard. Instead of attending a school, with a daily series of classes by a set of teachers trained in their subjects, girls were isolated with one governess, who had to range through the various courses of study, deciding for herself what and how she would teach. There was no

Plate 6 Two daughters of the eighth Viscount Cobham and their governess in the schoolroom at Hagley Hall

systematic advancement through any recognized curriculum. A high rate of turnover, as defeated or ineffectual women were dismissed by exasperated employers, often meant that new governesses repeated material or abandoned certain subjects entirely.

Many parents, recognizing the limitations of the English governess, augmented or replaced her with foreign governesses who concentrated on their own language and literature, and hired masters to teach music, drawing, or other subjects. At Runcton, for instance, the village schoolmaster came to teach arithmetic and geography thrice weekly; a music master travelled on Mondays from Lynn, supplemented by the weekly visits of Herr Ludwig from London; a drawing master taught on Tuesday afternoons; and a German master from Lynn spent three months teaching his language, followed by a second governess to impart Italian and literature. Dancing classes were in Lynn.[44] During the London Season, many girls went to dancing classes, or specialist masters; by the Edwardian period, they might also attend exclusive classes in literature, history, and English.

Some girls were "finished" by a year or two at boarding school. Most popular early in the century, these small establishments perfected languages, accomplishments, and etiquette. In the middle decades of the century, when home education was considered safer, attendance slumped, except among the upwardly mobile and the motherless; the Dixons sent Ann to a Miss Matthews in London, and Elizabeth Yandell joined "half a dozen suitable young ladies for music and languages, protocol, painting and polish."[45] By the late nineteenth century, aristocratic daughters, chaperoned by governesses, companions or female relatives went abroad to Germany and France to be "finished" in literature, music, and the arts. Other girls attended more academic middle-class schools such as Cheltenham Ladies' College, or the new female versions of the public school – St Leonard's, founded in 1877, and Roedean, established eight years later.

Recently, M. Jeanne Peterson has attacked the modern condemnation of Victorian home education for girls. She takes a more positive view, arguing that for upper-middle-class girls, home education was largely self-education. Lessons from parents, governesses, and masters were supplemented by much independent reading, and classes and lectures on subjects such as science, art, economics, and anthropology. Girls had access to all the Victorian curriculum, and enjoyed the flexibility and freedom to study in depth any subject that interested them. They acquired the habit of self-education which continued through their lives. As a result, she concludes that upper-middle-class girls were, in fact, highly educated. They, and their parents, took their education seriously.[46]

Some landed families also sought this high standard of education for their girls. W. E. N. Nightingale instructed his daughters for long hours in Greek, Latin, German, French, Italian, history, and philosophy. A local curate taught Elizabeth Yandell Greek and Latin as well as arithmetic, geography, and English.[47] By the end of the century, some parents hired competent masters, trained teachers or female university graduates to give a more serious and thorough education, including classical languages, modern history, philosophy, mathematics, and economics.

The majority of landed parents, however, appear less supportive of girls' education than the upper-middle-class families Peterson examines. Many upper-class parents believed girls needed to learn only enough to attract a husband, by being a pleasing companion, reasonably well-informed, and able to entertain with charming accomplishments.[48] Intellectual prowess was regarded as a handicap in the marriage market, and irrelevant to girls' future roles as wives and mothers. Medical experts, too, advised that overtaxing the adolescent female brain might undermine reproductive health.

Compared to upper-middle-class girls in London, Oxford or Cambridge, landowners' daughters under the control of governesses in country house schoolrooms were less free to pursue their own bent, and had fewer opportunities to attend public lectures and courses. They were possibly also less motivated, preoccupied with hunting or looking forward to being launched into Society. Parents were less supportive too, tolerating inferior governesses who destroyed any love for learning. Lady Granby "had no sympathy with . . . any teaching but history, poetry, the piano and art." Her daughter, Lady Diana Cooper, believed "reading was really all the education I was given."[49] Mary Gladstone, criticized relentlessly by her governess, became convinced of her own stupidity.[50] The quality of upper-class girls' instruction varied enormously, even within the same family, for so much depended on the governess's teaching abilities and personality, on the masters chosen, on the parents' attitude, and on the girl's enthusiasm and dedication. As Peterson points out, however, instruction was only part of education. Many undaunted and intelligent landowners' daughters read a great deal of serious literature for themselves, browsing in well-stocked country house libraries, or taking the advice of relatives and visitors. "Once free of the trammels of the school-room," the Troubridge girls "realised how much... there was to learn." They explored their grandfather's library, and their aunt made suggestions about what to read.[51] Girls also benefited from a cultured environment. They listened to stimulating conversation about literature, current events and issues, and attended concerts, art exhibitions, plays, and lectures when in London. This self-education could continue throughout life.

Despite academic inadequacies, schoolroom education effectively conditioned girls for their future lives as wives and hostesses. Staying at home shaped a girl's personality, expectations, and attitudes so that she accepted her adult roles. Confined to the house and its environs, deprived of wider experience and skills, she often grew up regarding the home as the only possible sphere for her activities. Ruled and regulated by parents and governesses, and waited on by servants, girls found it difficult to develop autonomy and independence. Schoolroom education, lacking competition, examinations, or certificates, stifled ambition. Upper-class girls instead found that inherited status together with the exploitation of personal attractions and talents were the means of advancing their future. They had to groom their personalities and acquire the skills of personal relationships rather than useful income-earning training. Education at home also narrowed their perception of others. Girls were cut off from any female peer group which could bolster resistance to family pressures. In contrast, public schools exposed boys to diverse personalities and social groupings, in a large and influential peer group. They changed status from an inferior junior to an authoritative and powerful senior, gaining experience in directing other people. In school they encountered non-familial authority and norms, and in the classroom dealt with more segmented, impersonal attention. Thus they prepared to become leaders of men in politics, in the professions, and on their estates. Their sisters saw themselves only in relation to the family, relatives and friends, the servants, and the local poor. Most girls envisaged their future roles with such groups, in subservience to their husbands, and in authority over their inferiors.[52]

In the "waiting years" between childhood and adulthood, upper-class adolescent girls' roles were ill-defined and limited. Largely excluded from their parents' social activities, heavily chaperoned on their outings, and denied contact with all but kin and carefully vetted friends and objects of charity, their lives could be aimless, narrow, dull, and boring. The adolescent Margaret Leigh, indeed, viewed Stoneleigh as a prison.[53]

Presentation to the King or Queen at Court drawing rooms, or a local debut at a dance or ball, marked the beginning of adulthood. Early in the century presentation to the monarch was almost exclusively confined to the landed classes, chiefly the aristocracy, but when, by mid-century, this ceremony came to be seen as an entrée into Society, increasing numbers of not only the gentry, but upper-middle-class families or *nouveaux riches* obtained entry for their daughters. By 1891, less than half the women (both debutantes and brides) presented at court were from the landed classes.[54] "Coming out" was the culmination of the upper-class girl's education, her equivalent to the boys' examinations, where her appearance and accomplishments were displayed and compared. For many young women, the change was abrupt, for few of them had much experience in the social graces suddenly expected of them. Yet most debutantes were delighted with the longed-for transformation of their lives. "It was something I looked forward to tremendously," said one, "You thought you were going to be free."[55]

An upbringing by servants, strict timetables, the primacy of religion, and differentiation between boys and girls also characterized childhoods in other classes, but the country house provided further influences which made childhood there unique. The house, with its flourishing social life and many servants, the gardens and park, and the rural community all enriched the lives of country house children. Within the peaceful, safe, stable, and ordered world ruled by their parents, these privileged and cherished youngsters were everywhere courteously welcomed, entertained, and protected. "We enjoyed . . . what children most need," concluded Stephen Tallents, "tranquility, and security and kindness."[56]

They lived in the nation's largest and most beautiful homes, amidst the family's heritage of art and furnishings – a world of spaciousness, grandeur, luxury, and beauty denied most other children. Scampering along lofty corridors, toddling down wide staircases, and ushered into glittering drawing rooms, the child observed and absorbed the beauty of fine architecture, paintings, sculpture, and furniture. Moor Park, wrote Lady Tweedsmuir, fixed her "tastes and standards irrevocably."[57] The house instilled a sense of the past, of family identity and pride, of security and inspiration. Osbert Sitwell "loved the impalpable essence" of Renishaw, "laden with the dying memories of three centuries, pervading the mind like a scent faintly detected."[58] Sitwell, like many landowners' children, was intensely attached to his home. To the Hon. Cynthia Charteris, later Lady Cynthia Asquith, Stanway was "the core of the world." She loved the house "precisely as one loves a human being."[59]

Small children nevertheless often found their homes overwhelming. As a toddler, Cynthia Charteris went downstairs into "seemingly vast, and for a long time uncharted regions."[60] Many young children dreaded venturing into dark, cold, cavernous corridors at night. Edward Cadogan, going upstairs to bed alone, felt "something sinister" about the gloomy staircases, passageways, and recesses.[61] The nursery's few simply furnished, homely rooms were an essential haven for small children, a familiar, safe refuge from the vast, frightening house and the bewildering behaviour of adults. In the drawing-room, Cynthia Milne felt a "shuddering fear" of "the bright lights and intimidating conversation" and "longed for the dim atmosphere and comparative solitude of the nursery floor."[62] As they grew older, however, the spacious mansion became an exciting playground for exploration or lively games. At Stoneleigh, for example, the children raced up and down the galleries and corridors, and played games such as battledore and shuttlecock in the large hall.[63]

Outside lay the gardens, the vistas of smooth green lawns and shady avenues, ornamented with beds of flowers, statues and fountains, and beyond, the park, scattered with majestic trees, edged with woods, wilder and untamed. A private and safe enclosure, the gardens and park were an enchanting playground for children, with space for cricket, croquet, and imaginative games, with trees to climb, lakes and ponds for swimming, boating and skating, and slopes for tobogganing. Often children were allocated small gardens of their own to tend. Both parents and nurses regarded an active outdoor life as healthy and natural for boys and girls alike. The environs of the country house allowed little girls to escape from the confinements and restrictions of a ladylike upbringing – a remarkable number were robust and energetic tomboys. Helen Chaplin, for instance, loved to run and jump, climb trees, and fly an enormous kite.[64] Other girls joined their brothers in cricket or fishing.

Country house children had many pets, both indoors and out: canaries, cats, dogs, and rabbits, and sometimes more exotic creatures too. Most beloved of all were ponies and horses. Babies went out in side baskets on a donkey, then at the age of three or four began riding lessons on a placid pony. In sporting families, horses and hunting became the focus of children's lives. From infancy, the Chaplins were "taught to think, speak and dream of hunting and riding almost like a religion." They began hunting at the age of four, spending as much time as possible on horseback.[65]

On their ponies (normally accompanied by a groom), and on drives or walks with the governess, children explored their father's estates and the surrounding countryside, learning about nature and country life. Visiting the home farm, they fed the animals, collected eggs or tried their hand at milking, making butter or haymaking. Late in the century, many landowners' children roamed the grounds and neighbourhood at will, safe in a quiet, peaceful countryside not yet invaded by the motor vehicle, and protected by the inhabitants' deference, loyalty, dependence, and even affection for their family. Some parents encouraged this independence, but others knew nothing of their offspring's exploits. The Picton-Turbervill boys and girls galloped horses without saddle or bridle while their parents dined, fenced with their father's swords, and filched gunpowder to make fireworks. "Mother, with a large household to run and so many children, knew very little of what we were doing."[66]

Plate 7   The Fitzwilliam children in front of Wentworth Woodhouse, 1908

Freedom within the boundaries of a safe rural community was especially valuable for adolescent girls. Landowners' daughters had more liberty and diversions than girls in wealthy urban families. Even early-Victorian landowners' daughters were allowed to walk, ride, and visit the poor, and later generations enjoyed a wide range of outdoor pursuits. The bicycle liberated teenaged girls such as the Chaplin sisters, enabling them to go unchaperoned "much farther afield than would have been either approved or permitted."[67]

However, within this idyllic environment, some landowners' children were physically and socially isolated. Most country houses were at the end of long drives, miles away from other landed families. Social contact was limited to the distance horses could reasonably travel, about a ten-mile radius. Country house families thus became self-sufficient, turning to each other for friendship, and developing a strong family solidarity and identity, with their own vocabulary, nicknames, jokes, and rituals.

Nevertheless, few children remained isolated for long. Indulgent parents loved arranging magnificent parties both in the country and in London. During the Season, youngsters also met at classes, in the communal square gardens, or in Hyde Park. London meant treats, too: these included prayer meetings and lantern lectures for the offspring of Evangelicals; educational forays to art galleries, the Natural History Museum, and the British Museum; and for the more worldly, pantomimes, plays, concerts, and opera, the Tower of London, the Zoo, and Madame Tussaud's. Many children spent a month at the seaside in late summer, while others travelled with parents to Scottish seats during the shooting season, or abroad. Aristocratic children often followed their parents from one family home to another. The nursery's staff, equipment, and routines accompanied children everywhere.

Close family ties meant many contacts with relatives. Members of the family came to stay for long visits, or returned *en masse* to the family seat to celebrate Christmas or family events. Many children made long and frequent visits to their grandparents or aunts and uncles, befriending their cousins as they played together. Some families, in fact, became almost permanently extended, with large numbers of cousins constantly moving from one nursery to another. Three daughters of the Duke of Abercorn married the Earls of Lichfield, Durham and Mount Edgecumbe, and bore numerous babies. The three families exchanged "hospitality on a wholesale scale" staying weeks at a time with each other.

The cousins "grew up more or less as one gigantic family of thirty-nine with a plurality of residences."[68]

Visitors provided another diversion, and not just at the formal children's hour. At Henham, guests often came to the schoolroom for tea, and they danced with the children in the ballroom before dinner.[69] Many children loved to spy from upstairs on the formal procession into dinner. Mixing with the guests exposed children to interesting people, enlarged their minds, and developed social skills. After the eighth Viscount Midleton inherited Peper Harrow, constant visitors brought a "fresh and illuminating element" into the lives of his children, who, as they grew older, were expected to contribute to the conversation.[70]

Servants also enriched, enlarged, and altered children's lives. Country house children had ready access to them at their work or leisure: at Tolson Hall, the youngsters were "constantly in and out of the kitchen."[71] Children had more knowledge of life downstairs than their parents upstairs, and their role as go-between assisted both employers and staff. "Remarks were often made in front of us which were meant to percolate to our elders," recalled Lady Tweedsmuir, and "household rules were modified" as a result.[72]

Many children, naturally curious, instinctively seeking attachments, and bored with isolated, monotonous nursery life, were attracted to servants, who were often, as one sociologist has concluded, "the simple, hearty kind of folk who enjoy children," and whose duties "were full of interest for the youngsters because they were not part of their own inner family life, and so seemed glamorous and adventurous."[73] Servants were, according to Lady Violet Hardy, more approachable and natural than parents.[74] To young children, the servants' tasks and pleasures were more appealing and comprehensible than their parents' pursuits. The Grosvenor cousins loved going into the servants' quarters, finding the jolly atmosphere there more congenial than the constraints of the drawing-room.[75]

Indeed, servants and children had much in common. Servants were in some ways regarded as children by their employers, and, as such, were denied autonomy over their private lives. Both were subordinate to upper-class adults, isolated with inferior meals and accommodation. Consequently, recalled Sir Osbert Sitwell, "children and servants often found themselves in league against grown-ups and employers."[76] Many servants interceded for youngsters, and acted as conspirators, relaxing regulations, assuaging punishments, and sharing secret pleasures. When the Wood children stood in disgrace behind the door, the housekeeper slipped them cowslip wine and gingernuts.[77] Cooks and housekeepers bestowed other goodies such as chocolate, cakes and bowls to lick, and youngsters waylaid menservants leaving the dining-room to beg leftovers from dinner parties. As soon as the formidable widowed mistress of Kingston Lacy left for a cure abroad, her delighted children rushed to the kitchen to celebrate with the staff. Strict protocol collapsed. Welcome everywhere, the youngsters helped in the stables and kitchen, played with the housemaids, and stayed up late, playing billiards or whist with the menservants.[78] Children gave loyalty in return. The young Charltons knew that the upper servants and laundrymaids were licentious, but never informed their parents.[79]

Servants could even act as substitutes for unloving or inadequate parents or nurses. Motherless Elizabeth Yandell's father neglected her; it was the gardener, Henry, whom she idolized as her closest friend and teacher. At Tolson Hall, when the nurse transferred her limited affections to the new baby, the next youngest would have suffered without her close, compensating friendship with the cook.[80]

The vast majority of autobiographers mentioning servants recall them as friends, who shared in the children's play, or included them in their own amusements. The Stanway footmen were always ready to show the children card tricks, answer riddles, or give them ginger beer or lemonade, while the maids were unfailingly glad to see them, and were also "the best audience for whom to 'dress up'." At Llangoedmor, the boys danced in the servants' hall in the evenings. For many youngsters, tea in the kitchen, the servants' hall, or the housekeeper's room was a highly enjoyable treat. The staff was a ready-made audience for the children's plays. "We put on shows for the whole staff, indoor and out, in the housekeeper's still-room," recalled Viola Bankes, "Such well-trained servants could be relied upon to smile good naturedly as we forgot our lines, giggled or turned our backs."[81] In America, Anne Fremantle regretted the loss of "the multiple extended family" of her country house childhood. Servants were "real friends – or real enemies," she believed, "enormously increasing one's range of understanding and affection."[82]

Because servants would wait on them all their lives, upper-class children seldom learned practical domestic skills. So they were thrilled when the cook invited them to roll out dough and make little loaves or biscuits, or the butler let them polish silver or black boots. Sometimes the lady's maid taught little girls sewing, knitting, and crocheting, and the carpenter allowed the boys to work at his bench.

Outdoor servants were often responsible for inculcating more essential skills: the coachman or groom taught riding, driving, and hunting, and gamekeepers shooting, trapping, and fishing. Many boys formed close friendships with their mentors, who, argues David Roberts, embodied "the world of masculinity" their fathers were "too busy to represent" by their "day to day presence."[83] Sir Tatton Sykes was "a rather distant figure" to his only son, Mark. It was Tom Grayson, a long-serving groom, who helped the boy care for his pack of terriers, taught him to ride, and regaled him with local folklore and legends.[84] Jock Yorke spent many hours with his great friends the coachman, the stern gamekeeper, the huntsman, and the gardener (a keen fisherman), all of them eager to teach him what they knew.[85]

The Yorke boys' relationship with these "frightfully congenial" outdoor men was "very easy, very friendly," with much joking and teasing, and cursing of the boys' errors, yet the menservants were always polite. They were careful not to "exceed," never getting drunk, swearing, or correcting the boys in public. Deferential yet friendly servants helped establish a child's sense of identity and worth. The Cadogans' butler, recalled Lord Cadogan, "treated us all, even when we were very young, with the utmost respect," and the maidservants gave Lady Cynthia Asquith "a specially comfortable sense of one's own Me-ness."[86]

Nannies and parents, in teaching class etiquette, insisted on politeness towards servants. The Yorke boys avoided "anything beastly or rude to any servant, we'd have got absolute stick."[87] Not only was courtesy part of the upper-class code of behaviour, it also prevented servants' resentment and discontent. Intimidating, seemingly omnipotent upper servants inspired and demanded respect. Lady Margaret Barry believed she was really taught her manners by such servants. She and her siblings had to call them by their titles, and were severely reprimanded by their nurses if they mistreated a servant.[88] Some upper servants were even permitted to discipline youngsters. The Bryn Myrddin butler kept a sharp eye on the children's behaviour at table, rapping them on the knuckles for misusing the silverware.[89]

Conflict between servants and children appears to have been rare. However, some harassed and irritable cooks found young visitors a nuisance, and head gardeners resented juvenile theft. A few children were unco-operative by nature; Johnny Stanley's attacks on a housemaid's skirts with a spear were typical of his aggressive and boisterous character.[90]

Servants provided children with a wider experience of life, sometimes disclosing information from which they were carefully shielded. Like all respectable Victorians, parents, nurses and governesses maintained a conspiracy of silence about sexuality and reproduction. Youngsters were forbidden to see the other sex naked, and reading materials were carefully censored. Attempts to satisfy natural curiosity were severely punished. Nevertheless, the persistent eavesdropped, or pumped the less inhibited servants. Lady Emily Lytton pestered maidservants with questions about sex, and overheard the entire story of a housemaid's pregnancy.[91] Children might feel the first awakenings of romance with servants – Stephen Tallents silently adored the housekeeper's maid, helping her wash dishes, and buying her bull's-eyes.[92] Older boys learned much from menservants' talk, and a few had their first sexual experiences with a maid. John Baker White was bathed by the head housemaid, to his "increasing enjoyment," until his father discovered them.[93] In the stables, children encountered other taboo subjects such as racing and gambling. Lady Angela St Clair Erskine placed bets on racehorses through the butler.[94]

Sharing their home with servants meant that country house children were exposed to class distinctions from a young age. As small children, they obeyed their nurses, and viewed the upper servants with awe and respect. They loved their nannies unconditionally and befriended other servants. Soon, however, they saw that their parents had ultimate authority. The children observed the servants' deference and obedience, and the disparity between the speech, dress, and living quarters of parents and staff. Servants addressed the youngsters as "Master" or "Miss", while children used servants' first names.

Gradually, children realized that they themselves had higher status, that their friends could never enter their own social sphere. The open friendship of early childhood was replaced by a certain reserve. "Even children knew their 'place' with servants," one butler explained. "They were friendly without being familiar and though they would play tricks on us . . . they seemed instinctively to know how far they could go. As they grew older they slipped easily into a relationship where although class divisions were not easily defined one felt they were nevertheless there."[95] Most children doubtless assumed this was natural and inevitable.

An upbringing in a household with servants also shaped children's concepts of the working classes. They encountered not the beliefs and behaviour of the urban proletariat or destitute, but those of hand-picked, healthy, submissive, and deferential people who were dependent on their parents. Being waited on by servants convinced landowners' children of their superiority and right to be served by others: "The poor were people who had to work, obviously, for our enjoyment."[96]

A conviction of social superiority was reinforced by contacts with the local community. Normally, landowners' children were forbidden to play with village children, especially by nannies, who often displayed more class prejudice than parents.[97] Even when they were permitted local playmates, class consciousness could intrude. When the Jones boys played with his son, the Cramner bailiff warned the boy, in their presence, "never to forget that he was playing with little gentlemen."[98] Villagers showed ritual deference by curtsying or touching their caps, confirming the children's social superiority. Most upper-class children never questioned deference, inequality, and poverty. "I can't remember wondering why there were rich and poor," admitted Jock Yorke. "I think we accepted it."[99]

Not surprisingly, friendships often developed with outdoor servants and their families. One of Cynthia Charteris's best friends was the coachman's wife, and her playmate was the agent's daughter.[100] Parents and nurses entrusted the children to these families, confident they would encounter nothing untoward. When Lionel Fielden took tea with the head gardener, coachman, bailiff, or lodge-keeper, "the standard of food, comfort and cleanliness seemed no different from that of the Priory."[101] Regardless of inconvenience, estate families had no choice but to welcome their little visitors politely, and their deference and eagerness to please further reinforced self-assurance and class attitudes.

However, the tradition of philanthropy also exposed country house children to less prosperous households. They were taken to visit the elderly, the sick, and the crippled, with gifts of food, clothing, medicines, and tracts; they made and distributed Christmas presents; put on an annual play or treat for the village children; or even shared Sunday School classes or sewing lessons with them. "After lunch we were usually sent out in the pony carriage to take some delicacies to a poor or ill person," recalled Lady Winifride Elwes. "We knew everyone in the village and took the greatest interest in their welfare."[102] Some teenagers ran sports clubs, taught Sunday School, and trained the village choir.

Yet these contacts tended only to reinforce authority and submission, with the gracious patron distributing largesse to a grateful and deferential beneficiary. When Margaret Fletcher accompanied her cousins in their visits to sick or elderly cottagers, she found the governess "did not encourage discussion as to why the poor *were* so poor."[103]

Thus, contacts with servants and the rural poor only confirmed what nannies taught and parents demonstrated: landowners' children became convinced of their superiority as a class, and of their right to dictate to the working class. These unappealing traits were tempered by the sense of obligation instilled in the children, and by their experience of working-class people not as a faceless, threatening mass, but as real individuals.

By the more relaxed Edwardian period, some children mixed more freely with social inferiors. Jock Yorke called in at farms on his rides, and played cricket and football not only with the gardener's children but also the farm boys. Joan Dickson-Poynder and village children had tea at each other's homes, and she loved to play in the farmyards. "I had no feeling about people being superior or inferior at all," she maintained. "It never occurred to me that there was any difference between the children really except that they had less things than I had."[104]

The country house, its guests, its servants, its environs, and its neighbourhood, therefore, enlivened and enriched the lives of most of its children, providing rich, diverse opportunities and experiences while still largely protecting and sheltering them from life's harsher aspects. Admittedly, the country house childhood was often marred by unreasonably oppressive discipline, stultifying routines, the fears and guilt inflicted through religious teachings, and the emotional damage of a beloved nurse's departure. Boys were sent away very young to harsh regimes at school, while girls received an inferior education from governesses they often disliked, enduring a restricted and dull existence until they "came out". The strict code of behaviour tended to repress individuality and enforce conformity. The isolation of the paternalist country house world, with its deferential servants and dependants, also narrowed the children's social outlook and confirmed class prejudices.

Yet country house children enjoyed many unique advantages. Noble or gentle birth in itself gave immediate status and identity, guaranteeing numerous privileges, but also imposing a clearly defined code of conduct, duties, and roles. Nannies were generally loving and capable, and the secure, predictable, and intimate nursery was an appropriate haven for small children in a large and complex household. The nursery's strict routine, firm discipline, and austerity offset the indulgence of wealth and taught stoicism and self-discipline. As children grew older, they enlarged their world, discovering and delighting in their home and the countryside, making friends with the servants and the local people, meeting visitors, visiting kin, moving to London for the Season, or travelling abroad with their parents. Far from being isolated from adults, they found affection and attention among many, developing their sociability and self-esteem. The multiplicity of people available to offer and receive love surely enriched these children's lives immensely. Their parents, nevertheless, were usually the most important people in country house children's lives.

3

Parents and Children

Landownership created distinctive and significant roles for both fathers and mothers in the nineteenth-century country house. While they delegated routine child care to servants, they remained in ultimate command, and most took an active part in raising their children. As part of their reform, landed parents adopted many middle-class objectives and methods, but blended them with their own goals and traditions. Their most crucial task was to inculcate the upper-class code of values and behaviour, as teachers and role models. Most of them did not in fact adopt the authoritarian and repressive mode of child-rearing popularly associated with the Victorian middle classes. A landowner needed no revival of patriarchy to reinforce his rule; his apparently omniscient power already provided him with immense paternal authority. Throughout the century, landed parents typically remained as child-oriented and affectionate as earlier generations, but at the same time became more authoritative, and, for several decades, less permissive. Unlike middle-class fathers, the landowner had nearly as much time and opportunity as his wife did to become involved personally in his children's upbringing and education; and he had also the wealth and inclination to indulge them.

The nineteenth-century landed classes have had a bad press as parents, both from their own contemporaries and from modern historians. Fathers are portrayed as stern, dour and domineering patriarchs, or as virtual strangers to their children, while mothers are neglectful, self-absorbed social butterflies. Lawrence Stone argues that from the mid-seventeenth century to the end of the eighteenth, the gentry, and later the aristocracy, abandoned authoritarian patriarchy to become loving and permissive parents, more domesticated and more personally involved in rearing their children.[1] From the 1790s, however, Stone believes the upper-class family regressed back to an early-seventeenth-century patriarchal, authoritarian, and repressive mode of child-rearing, after the landed classes found permissive child-rearing had produced ill-disciplined, self-indulgent adults, whose dissipated lives tarnished the reputation of their class. Greater autonomy had made them less deferential and obedient, and less dutiful in undertaking traditional obligations. Child-rearing methods therefore became authoritarian and intrusive, again aimed at breaking the child's will and enforcing absolute obedience, with severe punishment if necessary. Piety and conformity were required, while sexuality and individuality were repressed. Only from the 1890s, according to Stone, did parents become more permissive. Paradoxically, early-nineteenth-century upper-class parents "were increasingly turning the whole business of socializing the child over to hired specialists . . . in a physically separate . . . nursery."[2] Other historians endorse the image of neglectful, remote parents. Children reared by nannies, maintains Jonathan Gathorne-Hardy, were alienated from their mothers, and often "hardly knew or actively disliked" their parents. David Roberts finds wealthy early-Victorian fathers "did not bother overmuch with the raising of their children." Many fathers, he claims, "cared little for their children," or found it difficult to become close to them.[3] Numerous modern popular writers perpetuate this stereotype. Anita Leslie is typical. "The parents of Victorian times seem to have been unamused by their offspring. Mothers might see their little ones once a day, the fathers about once a year," she claims.[4]

Modern commentators have drawn their evidence from contemporary critics and from memoirs of unhappy childhoods, especially of the early-nineteenth-century victims of Evangelical zeal, or the neglected offspring of the Edwardian court aristocracy. But these were the exceptions: parents who were remote or domineering because of their own personality problems, rather than any pervasive social norm.

Most memoirs, diaries and letters portray a strikingly different picture: of loving, conscientious and involved parents. Condemned today in the light of late-twentieth-century theories of child-rearing, they were in fact implementing Victorian concepts of the proper roles of fathers and mothers: to form children's characters by instilling religious and class values and by regulating behaviour; to teach them appropriate social skills; and to make their lives happy with love, attention and fun. Most landed parents carried out these duties. Child-oriented and domesticated, they valued their relationship with their children as a significant and fulfilling part of life.[5]

It is true that upper-class parents were frequently separated from their children. Fathers were often absent, involved in estate business, county administration, or politics; or pursuing hunting, shooting, and other sports. Their wives joined them on country house visits or in London, or on trips abroad, leaving young children at home. Many parents found these separations painful. "The parting with one's child is most dreadful," Countess Gower wrote from Paris. "You have no idea of the treasure her little likeness is to us; we have it out and look at it constantly when by ourselves." Children were equally upset. When Lucy Arkwright was in London, her husband reported that baby Jack was perpetually calling out "Mamma tum." Even three years later, she hated leaving him, "on the sofa in an agony of tears." In his father's absence, Jack was inconsolable as early as eleven months of age and as a toddler he exclaimed hopefully "Father is come home" whenever he heard footsteps.[6]

Yet the Victorians, having no theory of maternal deprivation, did not consider such separations harmful. Mothers were not expected to remain constantly with their children, or personally to undertake their day-to-day care. Household, social, and philanthropic duties took priority. Delegating childcare to nurses was a centuries-old, unquestioned custom. Regency mothers trained and supervised their nurses themselves, but when the nursery hierarchy was formed, with the position of nurse more well-defined and specialized, nannies became increasingly the acknowledged experts. As nurses demanded more authority and autonomy, some mothers lost control and access.

Victorian parents were victims of their own passion for regimentation and specialization. Victorian architects segregating specific household functions into distinct territories further isolated children by placing the nursery suite in a separate wing, corridor, or floor, even with its own staircase and outside door. Children recognized the disparate worlds of adult and child. "Mamma, though frequently irradiating the Nursery with her visiting presence, was, however, definitely not *of* it," Lady Cynthia Asquith recalled. "In entering Mamma's own precincts there was definitely a perceptible sense of . . . crossing a frontier."[7] As households adopted strict daily timetables, parents allotted the hour after tea to entertaining their offspring in the drawing-room. Schoolroom children also encountered parents at family prayers and church, or even at lunch. But then boys were sent away to boarding school, seeing their parents only on visits or during the holidays. Throughout childhood and adolescence, therefore, country house children spent much of their daily lives apart from their parents.

Parents nevertheless played a significant part in their children's upbringing and formed loving relationships with them. Their roles as parents evolved from several developments in the late eighteenth and early nineteenth centuries: new child-rearing theories, the religious revival, the "cult of true womanhood," and a reformed code of upper-class values and behaviour.

Eighteenth-century parents had become more concerned than their ancestors with their children's health and education. Inspired by John Locke's *Some Thoughts on Early Education*, and Rousseau's *Emile*, and admonished by physicians in the new field of pediatrics, mothers began breastfeeding and intervened more in the nursery, while fathers sought improved conditions in their sons' schools.[8] Rousseau's insistence on hardening through austerity appealed to early-nineteenth-century parents anxious about both their children's health and the deleterious effects of privilege. Even in the 1850s and 1860s, the Blake Humfreys repeatedly condemned any form of self-indulgence, insisting that their children sit silently on hard chairs around a large table all evening, while the parents took the two easy-chairs.[9]

Spartan conditions were part of the early-nineteenth-century landed classes' prescription for reforming themselves. When they judiciously adopted middle-class values and practices, they gained new parental roles. Like the middle classes, they became more preoccupied with their children's spiritual welfare. Early in the century, Evangelicals converted a number of the aristocracy and gentry, some of whom became Stone's puritanical, authoritarian, and repressive type of parent, banning card-playing, dancing, or theatre-going. Evangelicalism induced many more parents to take their children to church, give them religious instruction, and hear their prayers. Keeping the sabbath, with other pursuits prohibited, left little option but domesticity. The Evangelical movement, indeed, helped to idealize family life and emphasize the father's duty to rule and guide his family, and the mother's to influence and nurture her children.[10]

Evangelicals endorsed the paterfamilias's authority as a God-given responsibility. Among the landed classes, paternalism's revival as a political theory further supported the idea that fathers should rule over their families, commanding respect and obedience. But Victorians did not entirely recreate the seventeenth-century patriarch, for mothers, not fathers, had most responsibility in raising children. Victorian prescriptive literature seldom detailed the functions of fatherhood, nor did it address men; child-rearing was now the mother's province.

Early-nineteenth-century ideals of the nature and roles of women, called by historians the cult of true womanhood, produced a new and important role for middle-class mothers. As the more moral, pious, gentle, and nurturing sex, women were considered more suited to forming a child's character, by example, influence, and active guidance. This function of motherhood was emphasized and idealized, perhaps to justify and compensate for the delegation of physical care and education to servants: "None can supply her place, none can feel her interest," declared Mrs Sandford, the mother "is the best guardian and instructress." Even Edwardian women's magazines assumed that mothers' primary responsibility was to form children's character by setting a moral example.[11]

Advice on child-rearing, directed mainly at the middle classes, did, however, influence the landed classes. The Countess of Airlie bought *Hints to Mothers*, and found her husband reading it. Lady Ridley, given Albertine Necker's *L'Education Progressive*, frequently consulted it for guidance, learning "what a great charge it is to be a mother." She also read a popular manual written by Louisa Hoare, who published her directions to her own children's nurse in 1819 as a guide for mothers. Mrs Hoare quoted Locke approvingly, but her sensible advice also drew on personal observation. Catherine Gladstone's own experience and principles appeared in her preface to Mrs Montgomery's *Early Influences* (1883).[12] Most often, however, young mothers sought advice from their own mothers and married sisters.

The landed classes grafted middle-class ideals of religion, patriarchy, and motherhood onto their own code of conduct, creating a distinct new child-rearing system. Traditions of loyalty and obligations to lineage and kin, the sense of belonging to a dynasty, and the duty to uphold family honour and promote family interests still shaped behaviour and attitudes. Typically, young Lady Emily Lytton took great pride in her ancestry: "I had a tremendous sense of *noblesse oblige* and felt myself to be an aristocrat to my finger-tips." Children soon became conscious of the importance of family honour. Lord Midleton's youngsters tried "to be courteous in public for the honour of the Family, which was sacred."[13]

Boys and girls were taught a well-defined code of behaviour. Both sexes were expected to become well-mannered, courteous, honourable, and charitable, while boys should learn to become dignified, considerate, and chivalrous, and girls had to acquire poise, delicacy, and modesty. Children also needed to master the elaborate system of etiquette devised to maintain social barriers. This code of conduct and values, which both defined and perpetuated the landed classes, could only be learned within the family. "What was owing to rank, . . . to wealth, to age and experience, to good family, to good taste, and to intelligence, all this was taught in the school of the country house."[14] Thus children were raised with a uniform and highly compelling system: learning upper-class values and customs, expected roles and responsibilities, correct social behaviour, and deference and respect to their superiors. "A sense of obligation to things and people to whom you gave way was instinctive," reflected Lady Muriel Beckwith. This duty "to help the future" and "those beneath" remained, providing "a sense of security, a knowledge of which way to turn at the crossroads." The code remained essentially unchanged up to the First World War.[15]

Landed parents' most crucial and distinctive function was to transmit this complex code of values and behaviour by their own example, and by instruction and correction. Parents could form character without being constantly present, for their power and authority, with the bonds of love, made even intermittent encounters effective.

Unlike other fathers, landowners did not go to work for long hours daily to support their families, so they had potentially far more leisure to devote to their children. While many men were often absent from home, the more home-loving landowner could see his children any time of day. Conversely, mothers spent less time with children than ordinary middle- and working-class mothers, for social duties came first. The functional differences between upper-class mothers and fathers were thus reduced.

The landowner's immense authority and power as father was based not on the role of breadwinner, nor on religious dogma, but on his position. His "sovereignty," as Roberts calls it, was "a rule based on customs long held, on a social hierarchy never questioned, and on the enjoyment of a healthy portion of England's wealth."[16] His children soon recognized his power, seeing him administering his estates, distributing largess in the village, sitting on the Bench (as a Justice of the Peace), leading the militia, giving orders to subservient servants, estate workers and villagers, and commanding respect and deference wherever he went. Beyond the nanny-dominated nursery, he seemed to rule their entire world; he was, as Lawrence Jones said, "master of all we surveyed... and his prestige with the tenants and retainers... reinforced his standing with ourselves." Lawrence's father "embodied... all authority and wisdom."[17] To his children, the landowner's sovereignty seemed absolute, ubiquitous, and unchallenged. This immense power meant he could be authoritative rather than authoritarian in ruling his children.

Although the landowner delegated child-rearing to wives, trusted servants and teachers, he "established himself firmly in the children's psyche, employing his exalted position and infallible opinions in the fashioning of their system of values."[18] Wives and servants endorsed his supremacy. "When I was young," one Edwardian peer's child recalled, "he was always held up to me – by both Nanna and my governess, as the ... last judge."[19]

High-minded fathers impressed upon sons and daughters their duties as members of the ruling class. Thus, for example, George Curzon instilled in his daughter Mary "a deep sense of duty to my fellow men, the realisation that life was not all enjoyment and endless gadding."[20] Firmly held principles and high expectations gave fathers immense authority. Edward Wood became increasingly aware of a quality in his father that "seemed to have a claim to our obedience not to be denied." The Wood children developed "a real reluctance to say or do anything that he would not like," and a fear of not meeting his expectations. As they learned his values and standards, they felt obliged to adopt them. Fathers did not have to be explicit. The fourth Baron Lyttleton "never said much to his sons yet somehow they knew that any moral failure on their part would cause him an agony of grief."[21]

The mother's rule over household and servants also gave her authority in her children's eyes. The young Leighs believed their mother "had almost unbounded power over everyone with whom she came in contact." Their "faith not only in her wisdom but in her ability was unlimited."[22] Mothers had their own source of moral authority in the cult of true womanhood. A mother's power, it was argued, lay in the example of her own pious and virtuous character, and in her gentle, loving influence and guidance. In fact, the separation of the upper-class mother from the intimacies and drudgeries of nursery life – from the clothes-changing, bathing, toilet-training and sick-nursing, from childish squabbles, whining and tantrums, and from constant correction and chastisement — meant that she was often idealized. Lady Cynthia Asquith observed: "Our realisation that Mamma, however fond of us and however available, was yet all the while busily engaged with concerns quite outside our own existence and as yet unguessed at, added much to her glamour."[23] For most country house children, Papa and Mama were the centre of their lives. Their primary attachment was not to the nurses and governesses who cared for them all day, but to parents seen intermittently. The strong love between parents and children is a theme expressed over and over again in diaries, letters, and memoirs. The Jones children all adored their mother, for instance, "and wanted nothing better than to be with her," while the little Toulmins regarded their mother as "our safety and our happiness and all the world to us," and Lady Angela Forbes's father was "the great keynote and influence" of her childhood.[24] Despite frequent separations and the nursery system, these close, loving relationships developed because of parents' active role in rearing their offspring: not only in training and socializing them, but also in joining them for play and fun. Mothers were more involved with infants and toddlers, but fathers became more committed as their offspring grew older.

Mothers, of course, had the first, biological ties with their babies, through pregnancy, childbirth, and breastfeeding. Virtually all landowners' wives were eager to bear children, since providing an heir was their paramount duty. Childbearing was a source of pride and achievement, especially when they produced the first son.[25] In most families, subsequent boys and girls were equally welcome, for numerous younger sons were no great asset. As Lady Stanley told her son, "a girl is better than a boy" for "there is less trouble & expence [sic] in setting the former forward in the world, let alone their being often greater comforts to parents."[26] Early in the century, when the landed classes favoured large families, wives typically devoted around eighteen years to childbearing.[27] Pregnancy, childbirth, and childcare often preoccupied them during these years, forming constant topics of discussion with mothers, mothers-in-law, married sisters, and friends. However, later in the century, childbearing took up less of women's lives, as they found other means of fulfilment not only in social life, but in the public duties increasingly expected of upper-class women. In 1885 the Duchess of Sutherland thought her first, difficult birth, which produced a daughter, "an uncalled for shame and hardly worth it," an attitude that would have astonished her predecessors.[28] Possibly, small families among the court aristocracy reflected a declining enthusiasm for babies. However, for most of the landed classes, the economic imperative to have fewer children may have enhanced the value of each child, ensuring that he or she was more than ever wanted and cherished.

Childbirth was a family occasion, with everyone hovering nearby, and the womenfolk encouraging and supporting the labouring mother. Husbands, too, were often present – their absence "was considered somewhat improper." In her study of politicians' wives, Pat Jalland found that their husbands were nearly always present to give comfort and emotional support during labour and to share in the joy of the birth. William Gladstone stayed whenever possible throughout Catherine's labours, Lionel Sackville-West held Victoria while she suffered, and Lord Burlington was "the greatest comfort" to his Blanche.[29] Being present at the birth doubtless helped these fathers bond with their babies.

Early-nineteenth-century handbooks on lying-in assumed that the new-born baby would sleep in the mother's bed, even in her arms.[30] In the 1860s, Emma Toulmin stayed in bed with her babies for three or four weeks.[31] This practice was ideal for mother-child bonding. Even when newborns slept in cradles nearby, mothers soon grew deeply attached. Lady Ridley regretted her son's transfer to the nursery, for she liked "so much having him close to me all day and being able to watch him asleep."[32]

Many mothers also developed close bonds with their infants through breastfeeding. From the eighteenth century, increasing numbers of aristocratic and gentry mothers chose to breastfeed rather than rely on a wet-nurse, persuaded not only by Rousseau, but by physicians worried about infant mortality. Nineteenth-century mothers also nursed because of the growing distaste for working-class wet-nurses discussed earlier, and as a means of spacing births. The nurse either sent for the nursing mother or took the hungry infant to her. Babies seem to have been demand-fed for most of the century, but Edwardian mothers, influenced by new "scientific" methods, nursed at fixed intervals, and less often during the night.

Early in the nineteenth century, concludes Judith Schneid Lewis, the majority of aristocratic mothers still did not nurse their own babies, though breastfeeding may have been more common among the domesticated lesser gentry.[33] Maternal breastfeeding in the landed classes evidently peaked between 1840 and 1880, amid heightened insistence on nursing as a desirable and virtuous duty. Many mothers, anxious about their babies' health and survival, felt obliged to breast-feed, despite difficulties. Lady Ridley thought nursing tedious, but, if "Baby thrives all else is nothing."[34] In 1874 a writer on infant care could claim, "There are few women in the present day willing to allow this dearest privilege of a mother to devolve on a stranger."[35]

Infants naturally grow attached to the person who lovingly feeds them, reassuring young mothers in their new role. Victorian authorities on childcare such as Dr Bull recognized that maternal breastfeeding was "plainly intended to cherish and increase the love of the parent herself, and to establish in the dependent and helpless infant . . . affection and confidence."[36] Thus, Lady Dover found her baby's "shout of delight and decided acknowledgement of me as her nurse, make me think her very adorable."[37] Early- and mid-Victorian mothers, perhaps, saw breastfeeding as their best opportunity to form a close, intimate and rewarding relationship with infants taken over by nurses. Countess Gower dreaded weaning her daughter "as a sort of separation from the darling thing," and later complained when forced through illness to wean a son: "I miss my nursing of the little boy even more as I recover."[38]

By the 1850s more nutritious patent infant foods became available, endorsed by the medical profession and by writers on infant care. When the germ theory induced nurses to sterilize feeding equipment, bottle-feeding also became safer. In the late nineteenth century, many upper-class mothers rapidly shifted to bottle-feeding, just when women's role as mother was being played down, and nurses acquired greater control. In the 1870s, Lucy Arkwright's babies were fed on cow's milk, Swiss milk and the traditional "tops and bottoms" (bread crusts soaked in milk), and in 1903 Louisa Yorke chose Allen and Hanbury's food.[39] By the Edwardian period, most mothers had forfeited this opportunity to build an intimate bond with their infants.[40]

"In the upper and middle classes, mothers, if they nourish, do not tend their infants," declared a women's magazine in 1867. With so many other competing responsibilities, the new mother was not expected to care for her baby herself.[41] But to the Victorians, personally giving physical care was not an esteemed or essential part of mothering. Elizabeth Missing Sewell regarded it as a menial task, fit merely for servants, who could do the job better anyway. After all, "through life they must be more or less dependent for their bodily needs upon their inferiors in station."[42] In any case, changing soiled napkins, attempting to soothe a colicky baby, dressing a writhing, screaming infant or trying to feed a stubborn spitting one, wiping runny noses, or mopping up vomit do not necessarily arouse warm maternal feelings. Perhaps, indeed, it was easier to find babies adorable when they were presented clean and cooing, in a froth of lace and ribbons, and speedily removed when troublesome. Victorian child-care manuals actually opposed full-time mothering. It was an inconvenient distraction for the busy chatelaine and spoiled the baby: "children accustomed to their mother's undivided attention are liable to become self-willed, exacting, helpless."[43]

Mothers were nevertheless expected to supervise and direct the nursery. Ideally, mother and nurse worked together in co-operative partnership; Lady Leconfield and her children's nurse had "a mutual absorption in the children's progress." When separated from them, she insisted on nearly daily reports detailing their health and progress.[44]

Fearful of losing a child, mothers were often preoccupied with their little ones' health. Questions and advice on remedies for childish ailments dominate family letters. Mothers dosed and nursed their sick children themselves. Catherine Gladstone, for instance, frequently administered medicines and purges, and both she and William cared for their daughter Jessy during her long and fatal bout of meningitis.[45]

Young mothers might lack the confidence and expertise to intervene. Lady Ridley struggled valiantly but vainly to control her irascible nurse, Wells, who resented her orders as interference. Distrusting Wells's methods and bad temper, Lady Ridley repeatedly resolved to dismiss her, but her courage failed her. Since mothers could not be constantly in the nursery, unknown abuses could take place. Only on her death-bed was Lady Ridley told of Wells's harshness towards the children. Lady Amberley belatedly discovered that her apparently excellent nurse had been not only starving but actually torturing her adored baby boy.[46] Nevertheless, we can acquit mothers of intentionally neglecting their babies. It was the nursery system, not a lack of maternal care and concern, which allowed cruel nurses to remain undetected.

Even the timid Lady Ridley did her best. Eager to be a good mother, she consulted her doctor, her mother, and child-rearing manuals. She attempted to assert her will, forbidding Wells to order anything for the baby without her permission. Ultimately, she amazed herself by lecturing Wells, telling her "such unpleasant truths." More self-assured or older mothers simply took charge. Catherine Gladstone, "jealous for her authority," was "arbiter in all nursery questions."[47] Such mothers insisted on ready access to their infants. At Erddig, Louisa Yorke visited or took out her babies as she pleased, standing in when Lucy was sick or had to go out. Whenever time permitted, she romped with the boys in the nursery, and wrote her letters there.[48]

Upper-class mothers have been condemned for not caring for their babies themselves. The theories of Sigmund Freud, Erik Erikson, John Bowlby, D. W. Winnicott, and Mary Ainsworth have created the conviction that babies need an intense and exclusive relationship with their ever-present mother to develop a mentally and emotionally healthy personality. None but a mother can fill an infant's needs, they argue, and only in continuously caring for her child will she herself be fulfilled and well-adjusted. Without this maternal nurturing, Gathorne-Hardy claims, upper-class children could not love their mothers but turned to nurses instead.[49] However, recent studies have shown that an exclusive primary bond with the mother is not biologically necessary: babies form multiple attachments to familiar people, with the first and strongest not always being the full-time mother at home.[50] A baby reared in an upper-class nursery, therefore, could become attached not just to its nurses, but to family members, and might well become closer to the mother than to the care-giving nurse. By two and a half, Eleanor Cropper regarded her nurse's love as "not quite so dear as Mother's."[51] Nor does brief contact prevent a mother from loving her baby, as studies of the kibbutz and Bruderhof communities have proved.[52] In numerous letters and diaries, aristocratic and gentry mothers demonstrate devotion to their babies. Anne Frewen was typical. In letters to her husband she chronicled their firstborn's development: his behaviour when brought downstairs, his learning to walk, his outings in the pony cart. His slightest illness made her "feel so fidgety."[53]

Anne Frewen knew her husband wanted news of their baby's progress. While fathers were generally less involved with their children as infants, some delighted in them, especially the first baby. On leaving for Ireland in 1828, Lord Clifton begged his wife, "Let me hear exactly how J.S. and his nurse are getting on, kiss the sweet baby for his old papa." Frequent letters reiterated the same concern and affection: "I must insist upon your sending for Cawdell or Betsey if there is any difficulty about carrying him, as air and exercise are indispensable for the continuance of his health." Months later, again separated, he sent messages: "I hope he will remember me," and "Kiss my sweet da Ta for Tata; the sweet little thing how I long to see him." Similarly, John Hungerford Arkwright adored his first child, Jack. In correspondence with Lucy, he discussed new teeth and a rash, and told of purchasing a bed and a perambulator. He loved visiting little Jack in the nursery, taking him for rides and bringing him down for breakfast and lunch.[54]

Such fathers lost none of their delight in later arrivals. Sir Matthew Ridley, noted his wife, was "so tender and full of feeling and affection" towards their new-born twins. In 1834, Thomas John Dixon wrote

Plate 8 Reginald Windsor Sackville-West, Baron Buckhurst, later the seventh Earl de la Warr, with his son

proudly that nine-month-old Amelia was eager to come to him and almost cried when he gave her back to the nurse and left the nursery.[55]

As babies grew into toddlers, parents became even more involved in their upbringing. Now children were more amusing and independent – weaned, toilet-trained, walking, and talking – and could respond to parental influence and training. Fathers uninterested in infants enjoyed toddlers more. Lord Salisbury, for instance, felt ill at ease with his babies until they grew old enough to hold a conversation with him.[56] Toddlers were old enough to go downstairs for "children's hour." Some parents were fairly decorous, reading stories or playing board games, but others romped without restraint. Edith Cropper played the piano while her children danced, and leaped about the furniture with them.[57] This Victorian version of "quality time" gave fathers greater opportunity to come to know their children than many middle-class fathers who worked long hours. Before the Victorians are condemned for allotting only one hour a day to interacting with their children, it is worth noting that a 1983 study found that on average American housewives spent less than ten minutes a day playing or reading with their pre-school children.[58] These nineteenth-century children enjoyed more of their parents' undivided attention than do many modern children.

While parents accepted the necessity and value of nursery routines, their desire to be with their children often took precedence. Mothers appropriated their offspring whenever they wanted their company: while they attended to business in their sitting-room, ordered dinner and put out stores, received visitors, or went out calling, on walks or drives, or on charitable visits to the poor. Lady Ridley took her toddler out on walks, and eventually kept him with her most of the day. Mothers often put their children to bed, or kissed them goodnight. "I like the evening when Mutterkin comes and cuddles us for a good long time, reading us poetry . . . and telling us about when she was little," Eglantine Jebb wrote in her diary. When her husband was away, a mother might allow a child to sleep in her bed – a treasured treat for Countess Denbigh's large brood, as the cuddle and conversation in the morning helped each one feel special.[59]

Fathers could also encounter their children at any time of the day. In some families, the children went to their father's dressing-room each morning to watch the fascinating ritual of shaving.[60] Thomas John Dixon's letters to his wife in the 1830s revealed a genial Papa who welcomed his children's company: "Little Ann when I arrived home this morning was delighted to see me and did nothing but talk all the time I was at breakfast." She was "very desirous to be with me when I am in the House." On other occasions he wrote, "Little Richard is on my knee and doing all in his power to prevent me from writing to you," and "trots after me and is not willing I shall escape . . . without taking him." Clearly this early Victorian was no stern, remote paterfamilias. Nor was Sir George Sitwell, second Baronet. After lunch together, recalled his daughter, he would sometimes "tie the napkins to our little shoulders and, jumping us off chairs, send us flying across the room with widespread white wings, imagining ourselves to be birds."[61] A Papa such as Sir Lawrence Jones was often "the parent who stood for small indulgences, for slight relaxations from the rules." Lord Halifax interrupted lessons "for a ride or an expedition, or on a wet day for a romp in the stable-loft," while Lord Leigh loved to take his children to entertainments and bought them toys and gifts "on every possible occasion." [62]

His generosity was typical: many landed fathers showered their offspring with playthings and pets. In the 1850s, Robert Blake Humphrey supplied "a swing, a see-saw, a rocking-boat, a yacht, several rowing

Plate 9 George Howard, Viscount Howard, later ninth Earl of Carlisle, playing "race" with his sons

boats, also a billiard-room." Sir Thomas Dyke Acland obtained rabbits, doves, ponies, dogs, lambs, and even a tame bear! He had a miniature Swiss cottage built as a playhouse.[63] David Roberts attributes the "benevolence" of landowners to "their sovereignty, their latitudinarian outlook and their great wealth."[64]

But it was not all fun and frolic. Upper-class parents did not simply regard their offspring as amusing playthings. They took seriously their responsibilities for the children's physical, intellectual, moral, and spiritual development. Some gentry mothers made their children the focus of their lives. In the 1890s, Lady Jones, eschewing more worldly pursuits, devoted her life to making her children happy, healthy, and, above all else, good. Educating them herself, she single-mindedly set out to mould them to her will. Her "watchfulness for faults of character, of behaviour, of manners, of deportment, was close and unremitting. No lapse ever went undetected or unreproved." Lonely widowers might also immerse themselves in child-rearing, like the fourth Duke of Newcastle who lived for his ten children, strictly supervising the spartan regime he imposed, teaching and nursing them in sickness, and carefully limiting their contact with the outside world.[65]

Most landed parents conscientiously undertook their children's spiritual and moral training. Fathers conducted family prayers, and some regularly read the Bible to their youngsters, or gave them scripture lessons, but mothers most often heard the first prayers and Bible verses. Lady Midleton led her brood in prayer early each morning, hearing the psalms, scripture verses, and hymns learned by heart, and even writing out books of inspirational verse for them.[66] Many parents strictly observed the sabbath, taking the family to church and giving Bible readings and lessons. Ever in the less religious Edwardian period, when numerous families abandoned family prayers and relaxed Sunday observance, pious mothers continued religious teachings. Marian Yorke heard her boys' prayers daily, read the Bible, and sang hymns with them on Sundays.[67]

Motivated, perhaps, by a desire to spend more time with their children, many mothers also gave first lessons in reading, before each little one joined the others in the schoolroom. Lady Midleton and Lady Radnor both taught their many children to read. Other concerned mothers closely superintended early education. Countess Gower became obsessed with her children's lessons, vetting all books, and resenting the governess's arrival.[68]

Fathers might also be interested in early education. William Gladstone and Sir Lawrence Jones taught Latin in the schoolroom, and the second Marquess of Westminster gave exercises in Latin verse to his family, also reading Gibbon, Shakespeare, and Scott's poems to them in the evenings.[69] Some fathers literally took over the schoolroom. Sir Thomas Dyke Acland regarded his five motherless children's education as sufficiently important to abandon public life. Though he carefully selected tutors and governesses, "he taught them himself from time to time." He "kept most careful records in notebooks of their progress," constructed "elaborate timetables and plans of work," and purchased "the best educational books then known."[70] Fathers often taught their offspring to ride and hunt, and sons to shoot and fish. Sir Thomas Fowell Buxton took his youngsters hunting, and rode with them every morning while in London. He also taught them to swim and to skate.[71]

Parents also undertook the less pleasant task of disciplining their children, as part of their duty to shape character and behaviour. Lawrence Stone argues that under the influence of Evangelicalism, parents once more saw children as innately sinful, seeking their salvation by breaking their wills with severe punishments, such as locking miscreants for hours, even days, in a dark closet, on bread and water. Linda Pollock agrees that there was a greater incidence of corporal punishment, harsh discipline, and insistence on absolute, unquestioning obedience in the early nineteenth century, but concludes that "the majority of children did not experience such a discipline."[72]

How far did this new severity affect the landed classes? Historians have too readily based their evidence on the sufferings of Lord Shaftesbury (born 1801), Elizabeth Grant (born 1797), or the killjoy Evangelical aristocrats. Yet cruel, repressive parents were unusual: Sir Tatton Sykes, who whipped his children and deprived them of all creature comforts, was a well-known eccentric, and Barbara Charlton (born 1815) called her stern father's child-rearing theories "original." In fact, Pollock finds no "real evidence to suggest that the upper classes were any more strict than the middle" – probably less so. David Roberts suggests that Evangelical, urban, middle-class fathers were more likely to be preoccupied with original sin and punishment than the latitudinarian, easygoing, and very powerful landowners who, often absent, delegated correction to nurses, teachers, and wives.[73]

Mothers, now responsible for nursery discipline, were more reluctant than fathers to inflict pain or cruel deprivations. Some mothers may have been influenced by the growing number of child-rearing manuals which reflected Enlightenment optimism about the child's nature, advocating gentle correction through reasoning and shaming, but they also developed their own ideas by observing their children's characters and stages of maturation. Louisa Hoare did insist on subordinating toddlers who asserted their will, but only because parents could subsequently grant more liberty and indulgence. She advocated "an authority . . . firm but affectionate; decided, yet mild; imposing no unnecessary restraints; but encouraging every innocent freedom and gratification, exercised according to the dictates of judgment, and supported by rewards and punishments." She favoured promoting good behaviour, with as few rules as possible. Punishments should be gentle, immediate, unconditional, and realistic, such as removal from the table, confinement in a well-lit room, or loss of privileges.[74] Typically, mothers decreed that naughty children must be put in corners or sent to bed, endure more lessons or forfeit treats. Corporal punishments were mild last resorts: Lady Lyttleton pinched the offender's hand in a letter-press, while Catherine Gladstone wielded a Japanese fan. The Gladstones disciplined by "love, example and explanation," and felt anguish on the rare occasions when they considered spanking necessary.[75]

Child-rearing manuals support Pollock's conclusion that discipline became less severe in the second half of the century. Whipping was condemned; so was breaking the will.[76] Late-Victorian parents were reluctant to whip their children. The kindly William Cornwallis-West, obliged to chastise his son George, sent him to fetch a stick. Naturally, George chose the thinnest and driest, which snapped at first contact. "Dear! dear!" his father exclaimed, "What a pity! But there it is." And that was the end of the matter.[77]

Throughout the period, most landed parents controlled their children without whippings or sadistic deprivation, relying instead on children's awe and respect for their authoritative power, and desire to seek the beloved parent's approval. "My mother meant everything in my life and my devotion to her influenced all my outlook," recalled Lady Emily Lutyens. "A word from her did more to influence me than all the scoldings in the world, and to give her pain was the only punishment I really minded."[78] Jock Yorke could not recall being smacked or beaten but a "ticking off from either parent was quite something. . . . We didn't do it again." Often a few words or a facial expression sufficed to induce remorse. Lady Lyttleton "checked hot unkind words or squabbles" simply by shaking her head slowly, with an expression of "displeasure and sorrow."[79] Withdrawing love was also effective: when the irrepressible Gerald Tyrwhitt was "sent to Coventry" by his despairing mother and the servants, he felt his offence "against the rules of order and decency . . . far more acutely."[80]

Daniel Blake Smith found the same pattern in the planter elite of the late-eighteenth-century Chesapeake. Noting that recent research has shown that "children are more likely to adopt the behaviour of nurturant" parents, he observes that "many planters appear to have gained the lifelong gratitude and respect of their children more from fond paternal treatment than from assertions of authority or coerced obedience."[81]

Liberal, permissive parenting was rare early in the century, but became common by the end of the period. Evidence supports Lawrence Stone's assertion that more permissive child-rearing methods reached the upper classes in the 1890s.[82] Many late-Victorian and Edwardian parents were less serious and religious than their grandparents, less devoted to duty and discipline than to the pursuit of pleasure and the enjoyment of wealth. The new sciences of psychology and sociology, and the teachings

Plate 10 Louisa Yorke with her sons Phillip and Simon

of educationalists such as Froebel and Montessori, created interest in child development. Parents were now less intent on crushing the child's assertiveness and individuality, and even more eager to enjoy their children. Popular child-rearing theories advocated promoting and ensuring the child's happiness as much as virtue.[83] The Rev. Thomas Gibbons Dixon is a good example of the Edwardian liberal father. He was not at all strict, never spanking his four children. Indeed, when he teased their mother too much, the youngsters pummelled him! When they were small, he romped and played games with them, and later he let them "help" with his architectural plans, and told them stories on walks and at bedtime. Likewise, the seventh Duke of Richmond and Gordon empathized with his children's point of view. "Wise enough to read between the lines" when their "iniquities were brought to his notice," he often took their side. Colonel Picton-Turbervill "was an amazingly indulgent parent," according to his daughter. "Extraordinarily patient," he never exhibited anger or "laid down the law."[84]

In such families, egalitarian relationships continued into adolescence. Edith Picton-Turbervill and her twin sister were "great pals with father," talking over many topics as they strolled round the garden every fine day after breakfast. Some hitherto firm parents became more lenient, confident that their training had been successfully internalized. The first Earl of Cranbrook "relaxed the chains of discipline, and preferred advice and example to coercion."[85]

In most families, however, earlier permissiveness was replaced by stricter control as parents began training their adolescents for adulthood. Boys' preparation began earlier, when they were sent to school. Why did loving parents commit their precious sons to boarding schools notorious for inferior teaching, poor diet, inadequate heating and sanitary facilities, epidemic disease, excessive discipline, bullying, and homosexuality? Long-established tradition, maintenance of status, and making suitable contacts were factors, but the most important was the building of character. Fathers feared that the feminine influence of devoted, tender mothers, nurses, and sisters, and their gentle and permissive child-rearing methods, would result in an effeminate weakling. Mothers wanted to prevent sons' sexual involvement with maidservants. Parents also worried that boys would be corrupted by the "incessant, base, excessive complaisance and flattering" of menservants.[86] Only the boarding-school regimen, parents believed, could harden a boy and inculcate the public-school ethos of independence, stoicism, courage, honour, loyalty, and manliness. The public school thus complemented rather than replaced parents' own training.

Jonathan Gathorne-Hardy argues that boarding school only completed sons' alienation from their parents. "Brought up by nannies, sent away to school at seven, many of them hadn't the faintest idea of what their parents were like. This was especially true of their fathers."[87] On the contrary, most boys had established firm bonds with both parents. Loving parents found parting with their boys very painful. When Willy, her beloved eldest son left, Catherine Gladstone felt as if she had lost part of herself. At the dreaded end of one holiday, she wrote, "I call it a kind of slow poison, one going after another." On taking his eldest son to Eton, it was William, third Baron Lyttleton, who wept unrestrainedly.[88]

Such parents consoled themselves by not relinquishing control entirely. They continued to affirm their love, instil values, and mould behaviour through letters and visits. Many wrote frequently, often weekly, with detailed family news interspersed with questions and advice about the boy's health, morals, and activities. John and Lucy Arkwright's letters to their son Jack at Eton are good examples. In one early letter, his father counselled him, "never tell a lie to get yourself out of a scrape – choose your friends from *gentlemen* whose habits & conversation are manly and chaste – and don't do anything you would be ashamed to let me or your mother know." Lucy Arkwright added, "Always tell us everything, & never keep anything from us. We always treat you with *perfect* trust & confidence & you must try to treat us in the same way." Their son dutifully sent them a copy of his diary and expenses. His parents admonished him about extravagance and a poor report, and discussed his future with him. His father was particularly eager to hear every detail of his son's life: "I am longing to know who is your fagmaster, & how you get on in that way & what boys you are getting to know."[89] This shared masculine experience could forge an additional bond between father and son. When home for the holidays, schoolboys enjoyed more respect and freedom, gaining a new status as companions to their fathers. Arthur Jebb always looked forward to his son's holidays when they could fish, shoot, hunt, study nature, and have long talks.[90]

Teenage daughters, in contrast, remained in their parents' care. Determined to preserve their daughters' purity and innocence, and to cultivate other feminine attributes valued in the marriage market, parents became more repressive. When their daughters entered their teens, mothers became stricter and more intrusive, carefully shielding them from the adult world. Adolescent girls were expected to be submissive, agreeable, cheerful, and dutiful companions to their parents. They came down to meals, played music and sang with them, and went hunting and riding with their fathers. Later in the century, they played tennis and bicycled with their parents, and accompanied them to functions such as flower shows and garden parties. Mothers also took their daughters on philanthropic visits to the local poor. In some households, girls mingled with the guests, encouraged to learn from their conversation, but not to speak unless spoken to.

Apparently conflict seldom disrupted relationships between most adolescent girls and their parents. Instead, the governesses who supervised and disciplined girls from day to day bore the brunt of adolescent irritability. Perhaps, as Carrol Smith Rosenberg found in nineteenth-century American middle-class families, there was less tension when the lives of daughters were to be so similar to those of their mothers.[91] Girls were also thoroughly conditioned to obedience and conformity, after strict nursery discipline and strong identification with their authoritative but loving parents.

When she "came out," a girl became even closer to her mother. Only a mother, or her upper-class stand-in, could introduce a girl into Society. "The most demanding stage of motherhood," argues Leonore Davidoff, "was in the grooming and presenting of . . . daughters when they reached their middle and late teens."[92] The mother taught her daughter correct social behaviour, chose her clothes, presented her at Court, and introduced her into Society at balls, parties and so on, relentlessly acting as a chaperon to protect her reputation and vetting acquaintances, until a suitable suitor successfully proposed. Barbara Charlton, for instance, paid endless visits, "wishing to cultivate friendships" before her daughter came out, then gave many dinners and two dances during the Season, "all on Fanny's behalf."[93] In the marriage market, where an untarnished reputation was essential, these unsophisticated, ignorant and innocent teenagers could easily commit social blunders, or find themselves in compromising situations. Furthermore, mothers feared that their daughter might fall in love with an unacceptable man or worse, lose her virginity. As a result, they might become domineering. Lady Jeune recommended limits on daughters' freedom until age twenty-five. "With the ignorance of youth, the strength of its impulses, the unscrupulousness of men, and the temptations of life, how could we trust any girl to herself?"[94] When her daughter, aged twenty-two, visited friends without informing her, Lady Schreiber was furious. "While she remains under my roof I must be responsible and keep her with me, and prevent independent action."[95] Ideally, the mother was a friend, whose control and advice was thus willingly accepted. "The *strongest* feeling of my heart," Louisa Sneyd told her daughter, "*is* the wish that you may look upon me as your attached friend."[96] At this age, unmarried daughters became their mother's constant companions and concern.

Fathers also found grown-up daughters pleasant and useful companions, and reinforced their wives' teachings. John Grey regarded his daughter Hatty as "a dear companion and confidential friend." Lady Rose Fane's father, overhearing her complaint that trying on a gown was a bore, told her it was her duty to dress well to please him and her mother. This advice was not resented, for she believed that pleasing her parents was her paramount duty.[97]

Parents were often very autocratic in suppressing their daughters' desires to pursue unconventional goals. Florence Nightingale was not unusual in being forbidden to study mathematics, and many daughters were forced to abandon dreams of becoming a nurse, attending university or appearing on the stage.[98] Late in the century, however, many young women demanded and obtained more personal freedom as part of a more egalitarian relationship with their parents. "There is a greater *camaraderie* between mother and daughter," declared Lady Jeune. "The old system of severity and repression is past." As for fathers, "the girl of to-day . . . entertains a fine, manly feeling of friendship for her father."[99]

This close and loving relationship did not diminish when children left home and married. When a daughter married, her own family felt her loss deeply.[100] The Countess of Radnor found having to give up her only daughter and "playmate" a "terrible trial," for they had been "absolutely happy together." John Grey was desolate, with "feelings of regret and loneliness of heart," when each of the daughters he loved and cherished was married.[101] But parents and children kept in touch with frequent letters and visits. "I think of you and Mr Lucy every day," Sir John Williams assured his newly married daughter, "and pray for the happiness of you both day and night."[102] Young wives often sought their mother's advice on domestic affairs, childbearing and childcare. The strength of affective relations between many landed parents and their children is shown in their lifelong devotion to each other.

Most upper-class children grew up conforming to their parents' hopes and plans. David Roberts considers this proof of the effectiveness of parents' efforts to socialize the next generation. None of the sons or daughters of the early-Victorian peers he studied "showed any signs of rebellion, any falling away, indeed any widening at all of the generation gap." As David Spring has suggested, the strength, unity and persisting power of the nineteenth-century landed classes can be traced to their system of child-rearing.[103] Psychoanalysts treating children of very wealthy families in the United States, where parents had been frequently absent from home, mothers were remote, even cold and unloving, and servants cared for the children, found their patients narcissistic and aimless, lacking self-esteem, motivation, and discipline, and so unable to work, or to love.[104] If upper-class parenting had been as poor as the popular stereotypes depict, landed children would surely have exhibited some of these personality problems. Instead the aristocracy and gentry were characterized by enormous self-confidence, a clear code of ethics, a strong sense of duty, and the ability to form deep, lasting relationships. They became mature, responsible, and loving adults because parents fulfilled their task of instilling values, through a close, affectionate relationship with their children.

The landed classes' child-rearing system formed the basis of the upper-class code of conduct, and of their stability, self-confidence, and authority in Victorian and Edwardian England. Nineteenth-century landed parents were as benevolent, affectionate and child-oriented as their eighteenth-century forebears, but not as permissive. While nineteenth-century landowners reasserted their authority, few regressed to Lawrence Stone's stern seventeenth-century patriarchy; they created their own milder nineteenth-century version, based on their powerful position and on a compelling code of conduct and values. The dominant type of landed father provided effective authority, firm guidelines, and acceptable discipline and training, yet was generous, loving, and often fun to be with – even permissive at times. Stone's paterfamilias did appear early in the century, with the revival of paternalism and Evangelical fervour, but even earnest, pious fathers could be warmly affectionate and fun-loving. Mothers, with less authority than fathers, were more intimately involved in rearing babies and small children. Loving and caring, most of them were, by the standards of the day, good mothers. Modern commentators have overemphasized the delegation of physical care and the barriers of the nursery, overlooking women's roles in breastfeeding, supervising the nursery, teaching early lessons, giving religious instruction, forming character, and bringing out daughters. The nineteenth-century aristocracy and gentry were neither physically nor emotionally remote from their children. They chose to spend much time with their youngsters, not only to teach and train them, but to enjoy their company and make them happy. Frequent contact enabled parents to build close, loving relationships which allowed them to moderate discipline as children willingly internalized their values. These parents achieved a balance between permissiveness and control; an effective blend of love and discipline. The success of their goals is shown in adult children's willingness to accept parental advice and guidance in courtship, and to take family interests into account in their choice of spouse.

4

Courtship and Marriage

In marriage, as in child-rearing, the nineteenth-century landed classes showed continuity rather than a reversion to seventeenth-century authoritarian patriarchy. Just as they remained affectionate and child-oriented as parents, so their marriages continued to be companionate. The landowner's courtship and marriage had distinct characteristics, derived from his or her position in the family and in society, and influenced by the aristocratic code of conduct. These factors affected motives for marriage, the role of parents in courtship, relations between husband and wife, and the chances of marital happiness or dissolution.

According to Lawrence Stone, the gentry and then the aristocracy developed the companionate marriage in the seventeenth and eighteenth centuries. Husbands and wives came to regard each other as best friends, preferring each other's company and seeking a romantic, intimate, loving relationship, both emotionally and physically. Traditional patriarchal domination over wives fell into disfavour as individual rights assumed a new importance, so that relationships between husband and wife became more egalitarian. But paternal authority was revived in the early nineteenth century, repressing women and reducing their status in marriage. "The new ideal of womanhood involved total abnegation, making the wife a slave to . . . her husband."[1] More recent research, however, challenges this conventional view of nineteenth-century marriage. Judith Schneid Lewis finds mutual respect typical in aristocratic marriages before 1860, while Pat Jalland's political wives 1860–1914 "enjoyed more contented and less repressed relationships with their husbands than the stereotypes . . . have suggested." Joan Perkin goes so far as to assert that the upper classes contained "the most liberated group of wives in the country," most of whom "did not feel dominated or oppressed."[2] While landowners' wives were, in part, content because they had been socialized to accept subordination to husbands, they were rescued from demeaning helplessness by financial independence, the positive elements of separate spheres, and their valued functions in the family. Both the ideal and the norm remained affectionate companionship.

For the landed classes, nevertheless, marriage was not just a mutual satisfaction of emotional and sexual needs, but a crucial social institution, upheld as a duty to both family and class. When an heir decided to marry, far more was involved than establishing a household and a family. For centuries, marriage had been not only the occasion for arranging the future transfer of the family's property and wealth in the marriage settlement, and the means of acquiring more with the bride's dowry, but an opportunity to advance the family's interests through useful connections with other families of comparable or greater power and status. The heir was thus more subject than other sons to the pressure to marry well. But by the early nineteenth century marrying for love had become the social norm, even for the landed classes, producing potentially conflicting motives.

Upper-class parents routinely directed their children's courtships. Matchmaking was a mother's acknowledged role and duty, but a father was both the ultimate authority for consent or veto, and a loving parent seeking his children's happiness. Men participated in every stage of their children's courtships, even if indirectly through female intermediaries. Fathers and mothers negotiated on their child's behalf with other parents both by letter and interview. Many parents actively promoted or discouraged a candidate, while others merely offered advice. Serious suitors requested permission to court or propose, and most couples wanted their fathers' consent and approval. Finally, the two fathers met to hammer out the marriage settlement.

Landowners' children openly and eagerly sought parental advice and support, demonstrating the depth of love and trust forged in earlier years, and vindicating parents' child-rearing methods. A close, loving relationship meant the younger generation had internalized parents' values and goals in courtship, and thus more willingly accepted guidance. "Without persuasion or compulsion," acknowledged Lady Cowper, "there is so much influence produced on a good heart by seeing the wishes of those you are fond of."[3] Most parents, who deeply loved their children for themselves, rather than as heirs or heiresses, made the child's future happiness the main priority. Having brought their children up in a warm and affectionate relationship, parents hoped they would find the same happiness in marriage. In families where parents were more remote, or closely controlled and dominated their children, both parents and children tended to stress material benefits. Only a small minority of parents autocratically arranged marriages or pressured unwilling sons or daughters into wedlock.

Since the seventeenth or eighteenth centuries, historians agree, love had gained importance as a consideration in choosing a spouse; in the nineteenth century most of the landed classes regarded it as essential.[4] Judith Schneid Lewis sees no dichotomy between "arranged" and "romantic" marriages in the period 1760–1860, arguing that most matches involved both instrumental and affective motives. "Parents were rarely immune to the emotional needs of their children, and children were just as unlikely to ignore their own material welfare." She does see changes over time, nevertheless, with traditional motives more often dominant among eighteenth-century parents, and the emergence of romantic love as a prerequisite in the nineteenth century. The Romantic period in art and literature made sudden, headlong "falling in love," with intense passions and emotions aroused, an approved form of love for marriage.[5]

Plate 11 Croquet was a popular occasion for flirtation: Bowthorpe Hall, Norwich

The landed classes tried to channel such emotions by ensuring that their young people met only potential spouses of suitable background. Before the seventeenth century, parents had arranged their children's marriages. Candidates were few, usually limited to their own rank and county, and negotiations between families often took place by correspondence or through intermediaries. Then, from the seventeenth century, as compatibility, affection and companionship became priorities in marriage, parents began allowing children to conduct their own courtships, retaining the right of parental veto. Freedom of choice could only work if a young person could choose from several potential spouses. At the same time, parents wanted their children to encounter only the socially acceptable. So, in order to widen the pool, yet limit contacts, the landed classes created socially exclusive entertainments where young people could mix freely under supervision. As the upwardly mobile new rich gained access to this marriage market, an elaborate, formal code of etiquette was devised to exclude them. Young unmarried ladies were rigidly chaperoned to prevent seduction or unsuitable attachments.[6] At first, much of this socializing took place at the county level, but the landed classes also gathered in spring and summer in London, then in Bath or other spa towns. In the Victorian period, the London Season became the mecca for matchmaking. Early in the century, the less wealthy gentry brought out daughters at local balls and dinners. When transportation improved and Society became less exclusive, increasing numbers of gentry daughters were presented at Court and participated in the London Season. Back in the country in the autumn for shooting and then hunting, young people attended dinner parties with their neighbours, and county balls. They also embarked on a round of country house visits. Matchmaking hostesses prepared guest lists with an eye to bringing eligible young men and women together. Romance blossomed more easily in the country, where young people could ride, drive, and even walk unchaperoned.[7] Retreating to the private territory of country homes became an important tactic when a vastly enlarged London Society including large numbers of non-landed families no longer met the parental goal of exclusiveness.

Because the dynasty's fate depended on an heir's marriage, parents were more determined to guide and influence him than his younger brothers. Far more concerned about the bride's social status and her dowry, they tried to prevent mesalliances by limiting his circle of acquaintances. Heirs to great estates found their pool of potential brides small. When the seventh Lord Londonderry "contemplated wedlock he had met only six or seven possible girls. Each . . . had been purposely placed next to him at dinner because they were by birth and upbringing qualified to entertain as a great political hostess."[8] Parents might veto unsuitable choices, and promote their own candidates. The thirteenth Duke of Norfolk sent his eldest son on the Grand Tour "in order to forget a Miss Pitt." As Lord Cranborne was "the last of a very noble and ancient house, and the heir of a very large property," his parents wished "to see him settled" and "often proposed to him several persons."[9]

Most heirs and their parents assumed that mutual attraction and attachment were essential before a marriage took place. "The whole is a lottery, unless grounded on strong affection & mutual esteem," Lady Holland told her son. Lord Lincoln objected to his father's direction of his courtship, insisting that such delicate matters "should begin with the parties themselves," and there could be "no parti-making . . . if there is to be happiness."[10] But an heir should only fall in love with someone suitable. "Fall in love with your head as well as with your heart," Lady Selborne advised her son Roundell in 1909. "As the choice of a wife is a very important thing, it ought to be submitted to your judgement before you give free rein to your affections. . . . Affection that is inspired by the judgement is a much higher and more lasting affection than that which depends merely on the passions."[11] Heirs normally internalized a sense of obligation to the family's interests which made their choice prudent. Spencer Stanhope kept a list of "wiveables," gradually crossing out candidates who "would not do."[12] Lord Blandford revealed his priorities when he protested his brother Randolph's whirlwind courtship. "Do you marry for a fortune? No! Do you marry to get children? No! Do you marry because you have loved a woman for years? No!"[13]

Many a young man searching for a wife was assisted by the womenfolk of his family. Mothers dutifully held expensive entertainments during the London Season or invited one eligible young lady after another to visit the family seat, while aunts brought young people together at their own house parties. The third Duchess of Sutherland paraded a succession of Society beauties before her son Cromartie. Finally, when Lady Blanche St Clare Erskine was summoned, he took a fancy to her fourteen-year-old sister, Lady Millicent, invited to keep young Lady Alexandra Leveson-Gower company. Once a young man had expressed his preference, his mother might act as an intermediary, doing some preliminary investigation of his prospects to spare him an embarrassing rejection. One lady had "a regular maternal-matrimonial interview" with Louisa Bowater's mother, to ascertain if Louisa were engaged, and if her son had any chance.[14]

Once attracted to a woman with the right background and interests, an heir sought her company, normally delaying a proposal until he knew her well, and felt sure he loved her. Lord Clifton thought Emma Parnell "a person with whom I am sure I could fall sufficiently in love to make me wish to marry her, but I know not how I can pass time enough in her society to make me judge whether I could safely do so."[15]

Men had greater freedom than women in courtship. They were usually older, more worldly and experienced, and had enjoyed far more independence. Men customarily initiated and controlled the courtship (with Mamas discreetly manipulating them behind the scenes), while women, strictly chaperoned, waited passively for a proposal. Young ladies were subject to greater parental pressure and control, for females were held to have less judgement and reason in affairs of the heart, and to be too easily led astray by ambitious, unscrupulous fortune-hunters. Besides, a daughter had more to lose; she took her husband's social standing, whereas he lost neither his status nor the family estates by marrying beneath him.

Until late in the period, marriage was the only career open to a landowner's daughters: the only alternative was to remain at home under parental authority, and then be forced out on their father's death, to depend on others or survive on a meagre allowance. As Mabell Ogilvy, eighth Countess of Airlie, said, "A woman's only hope of self-expression ... was through marriage. Whether we would ... succeed in getting husbands was our main preoccupation."[16]

An upper-class daughter was well aware that an heir to a landed estate was a far better catch than younger sons, and that her own family might gain from the new connection, especially if she married above her own rank. But primogeniture ensured that there were not enough landowners' heirs to go around, creating competition in the ballrooms. A young woman receiving a proposal from a landed proprietor or his heir was thus more likely to be urged to accept him, to be strongly tempted to do so herself, and to weigh up other considerations besides love and attraction."

A few parents tried to force their daughters into marriage. Early-nineteenth-century patriarchal fathers believed they knew best; Sir John Williams insisted seventeen-year-old Mary Elizabeth accept George

Lucy of Charlcote, despite her tearful protest that she did not and could not love him. She gave in: "I had been brought up to obey my parents in everything and, though I dearly loved Papa, I had always rather feared him. I felt I dared not disobey him." Her mother supported him, assuring Mary Elizabeth that, "Love *will come* when you know all of Mr Lucy's good qualities."[17] Ambitious mothers felt their reputation was enhanced by good matches for their daughters. Lady Saltoun forced Lord Zouche to marry her daughter, though he did not love her, and attempted to break off the engagement. Young and unsophisticated, Lord Zouche was convinced of his duty to marry, while his bride, only eighteen, was no match for "an impecunious father and a scheming mother."[18] Other ambitious mothers simply sabotaged courtships by anyone but a landowner or his heir. The "unashamedly worldly" Lady Stanley was "determined that her daughters should not marry younger sons," while in 1892 Lady Stanhope nipped a younger son's courtship of her daughter Katherine in the bud: "it would not do, and I think we shall steer clear of its complications."[19]

Some young women themselves decided to wed men they did not love, in order to acquire independence and an establishment of their own, to escape an unbearable family situation, or because they despaired of an unrequited love. Lord Ferrers successfully wooed Lady Ina Hedges-White after her brother's marriage ended her happy years as hostess at Bantry House. Georgiana Moncrieff adored Lord Tyrone, but when he failed to propose, she settled for the Earl of Dudley, twenty years her senior.[20]

Other brides simply had an unromantic view of marriage. Upper-middle-class Margaret Potter "found great difficulty in expressing emotion and . . . neither expected nor sought an emotionally compelling relationship in marriage," just one "in which clearly established roles and duties were combined with enough affection to satisfy" her needs. She preferred "prudent and proper marriages – and the young man's income and background always took precedence for her over any endearing personal qualities." When she met Henry Hobhouse, owner of the Hadspen estate, they became engaged after only two weeks' acquaintance.[21]

Indeed, a minority of practically minded females placed material gains above all in their marital ambitions. Sir John Williams's four daughters considered one guest's "<u>greatest</u> charm was that he had ten thousand a year, a fine place, and a splendid collection of pictures."[22] Landowners recognized the attractions of their position. Dearman Birchall distrusted the motives of a neighbour's daughter blatantly pursuing him. After all, she had been openly in love with the previous owner of Bowden Hall. "Is she capable of loving me for my own sake," he asked himself, or "is she playing for the Hall[?]"[23]

Most young women, and their parents, however, considered personal happiness important. Lord Clarendon told Miss Eden that "want of great fortune or rank was all nonsense & ... we had long ago made up our minds that our daughters sh[oul]d marry anyone we thought w[oul]d really make them happy provided the poverty was not extreme."[24] Some parents even allowed daughters to conduct their own courtships, still hovering anxiously near to offer guidance and encouragement. Writing of her daughter Emily's engagement, Lady Stanley was deeply conscious of "all the responsibility we should take upon ourselves in allowing her to follow her inclinations & what she believed her happiness."[25] Young ladies demonstrated their commitment to sexual attraction and love as prerequisites to marriage by turning down proposals from wealthy, titled landowners because they felt no love for them. Despite her family's urgings, Mary Glynne refused to marry Lord Gairlie, for she "could not and would not love" him.[26]

While some young heiresses were pushed into advantageous marriages by determined mamas, a surprising number of heiresses were able to make up their own minds. The orphaned Ethel Fane, heiress to Earl Cowper, could have made a brilliant match, but fell in love with William Grenfell, "by no means a great catch." Lord Cranborne met Mr and Mrs Gascoyne's approval, but the match was still their daughter's own "decided choice."[27] One development which allowed heiresses greater freedom to choose for themselves was the custom of protecting their property from avaricious fortune-hunters by placing the wife's estate in the hands of trustees, or even giving it into her own control.

Many a proposal came from an heir or landowner to whom a young woman was attracted, but did not yet love. Susceptible to her family's encouragement, and aware of the advantages of marriage to an eldest son, she might gamble that he would make her happy. Victoria Sackville-West, having refused Lord Hardinge of Penshurst among others, accepted her cousin Lionel. "For love? I really don't know. ... I am very tired of fighting against life." By marrying the heir to her beloved home, Knole, she could stay there.[28] Parents concerned for their daughter's happiness did not pressure her into accepting an advantageous proposal, but gave her support and advice while she slowly made up her mind. In 1829

Lord Ashley fell deeply in love with Emily, the beautiful, adored daughter of the fifth Earl Cowper. He rapidly proposed, reported her mother,

> when she knew him very little, and she of course refused. He then intreated her to take time to know him . . . but . . . she must soon make up her mind . . . and this we of course leave entirely to herself because if she likes him he is a very suitable match for her, and if not she will find somebody else she likes better. . . . We are now preparing to go to Chatsworth where . . . she will have plenty of oppor[tuni]ty of seeing other people and deciding by comparison whether she prefers him to all the world.

Emily took eight months to decide to accept him.[29]

Maturity of both years and mind facilitated wise decision-making. Teenage girls desperate to escape the confines of the schoolroom were likely to have a very narrow, immature view of life, and little self-confidence. They could be easily dazzled by a glamorous suitor and susceptible to parental pressure. Many of them also had naive and romantic ideas about marriage. Belle of the Season in 1824, sixteen-year-old Jane Digby agreed to marry Edward Law, second Baron Ellenborough. "His handsomeness, mature years and racy reputation would have been enough to attract an unsophisticated girl, who had been taught that the height of happiness in marriage was a house in Mayfair, a country house at Wimbledon, a fine coach, blooded horses, liveried footmen and ample 'pin money'."[30] Both Leonore Davidoff and Pat Jalland assume a debutante had only two or three seasons to display herself before being considered a confirmed spinster.[31] But this pessimism is unwarranted; the mean age at marriage for heirs' wives was twenty-four, seven or eight years after coming out. Many women waited until their early twenties, when, argues Lawrence Stone, "young people know better what they are about, their identity is more firmly established, their experience of the world is larger, and their judgement more mature."[32] Wise parents recognized this. Mr Gascoyne declined to promote the romance between his daughter and Lord Cranborne, judging their acquaintance too brief and Frances too young. He told Lady Salisbury that his daughter's "ideas of the world" and of herself "might alter materially."[33] Despite first class honours in the Cambridge Examination for Women, Emily Jowitt hesitated to accept Dearman Birchall because she felt too young and inexperienced at twenty to become mistress of a country house. "It is an awfully responsible position for me but somehow I... believe I shall have strength for it but oh dear how young I feel."[34]

As in most cases, her parents were closely involved in the decision. Dearman proposed to Emily before obtaining her parents' consent, but then had long talks with them concerning Emily's objections, and his consequent doubts, following their advice to go home and think things over. After he successfully renewed his suit, he met with John Jowitt again to negotiate the marriage settlement.[35]

A young heir and his fiancée were heavily dependent on parental approval, for it was the two fathers who supplied the income they would live on, through the marriage settlement. Once both sets of parents had agreed to the match, lengthy and sometimes acrimonious negotiations ensued over the settlement, which specified the amounts the two families would allot the bride and groom. Both sides set up trusts, in

Plate 12 A suitable match: the wedding in 1909 of Captain Henry Phillips, eldest son of Sir Charles Phillips, first baronet of Picton Castle, Pembrokeshire, and an heiress, Victoria Gwynne-Hughes, only child of John Gwynne-Hughes of Tregyb, Carmarthenshire

which the capital invested yielded a certain annual interest income, ranging from 4 to 10 per cent. The groom's trust provided an annual income until he inherited, while the bride's family gave her an annual allowance called pin money while her husband lived, and a dowry which supplied the jointure, the annual income for widows. The agreement also resettled the estates on the as yet unborn heir, and specified the funds allocated to other potential children.

Few grooms and brides, let alone their families, ignored the material aspects of the match, but many made actual or prospective emotional attachment their primary consideration. Pat Jalland is probably correct in suggesting that most upper-class young couples continued to rely on a more calculated, temperate form of love, "inspired by judgement rather than passion." First ascertaining compatibility not only of personality, but of "social and economic interests," they allowed themselves to grow to love each other.[36]

Still, there were differences between social groups, and changes over the century. The highest aristocracy was more likely to limit the field severely, and to pressure a child to make a good match. Early in the period, some fathers still used traditional patriarchal power to force reluctant offspring into marriage, and older women occasionally retained a cynical, materialistic attitude towards matrimony. "Women are not like men," Mary Glynne's Aunt Neville told her, "they cannot chuse, nor is it creditable or lady-like to be what is called in love." Even when ladies succumbed to this ill-regulated emotion, "in good society, the heart is remarkably prudent, and seldom falls violently in love without a sufficient settlement," observed the first Baron Lytton in 1833.[37] Nevertheless, mercenary marriages did provoke disapproval even in the worldly Regency period. In 1823, Lady Cowper was scathing about the rumour that Lady Elizabeth Cunningham was being forced by her mother and brother to marry the uncouth Lord Burford, evidently attracted by her dowry. "One really feels quite sorry to think of such a nice girl . . . being *persuaded* to do a thing so disgraceful," she wrote. "I think it lowers the Girl terribly in everybody[']s estimation."[38] Married couples were expected to enjoy each other's company: when Lord Ellenborough sought to divorce his unfaithful young wife, newspaper commentaries blamed him for neglecting her and denying her companionship.[39]

Romanticism and domesticity had the greatest impact in the middle decades of the century. Family life was most appreciated in this period, with frequent childbearing and a narrower range of outside activities encouraging wives to focus their lives on the home. Men and women wanted to marry for love and enjoy a companionate marriage. As Society became more exclusive and enclosed, parents could allow their young people to mingle freely and fall in love within the narrower circle.

By the end of the century, Society was no longer just one big family where everyone knew everyone else. It had expanded to include the *nouveaux riches*, the upper-middle classes, foreigners, and even prominent writers, artists and painters. To restore family fortunes and maintain their increasingly elaborate style of living, more heirs pursued daughters of wealthy American or British businessmen. Less hard-headed men found beautiful actresses irresistible.[40] The competition for eldest sons grew fiercer in consequence, with mamas more determined to snare them. Some aristocratic young women, now less attracted to the prospect of babies and household management than to a whirling social life and a wider range of activities outside the home, accepted men who could provide these excitements. Such women often became engaged without a leisurely courtship to establish well-tried affection, evidently considering the gains worth the risk.

Motives for choosing a spouse did influence chances of happiness in marriage. Where courting couples realistically sought compatibility of background as well as personality, tried to discover each other's characters, and cultivated a warmly affectionate love rather than a blinding passion, their marriages were companionate, characterized by friendship and mutuality. Those who fell passionately in love faced the risk of eventual disillusionment. Matches made for money and status were least likely to produce a loving relationship, but worked if neither spouse expected personal happiness from the other.

Successful marriages were more often due to the wife's efforts to adapt herself to her husband's needs and wishes rather than to a mutual sacrifice. Mrs Earle maintained that "in nine cases out of ten, if marriages are unhappy, it is the fault of the woman."[41] Middle-class advice books urged women to mould their lives around their husbands' demands. "The love of woman appears to have been created solely to minister; that of man, to be ministered unto," expounded Sarah Stickney Ellis. A wife should have "a respectful deportment, and a complying disposition, ... with a general willingness to accommodate all household arrangements to a husband's wishes." The burden of the companionate marriage thus rested on the wife. "It is for woman, not for man, to make the sacrifice," insisted Mrs Sandford. The true wife, according to Charlotte M. Yonge, devoted herself to sparing her husband "all vexatious details – giving him her sympathy in all his desirable pursuits, and exerting herself to share whatever he likes her to share in, and adapting herself to his moods with ready tact."[42] The landed classes did read such literature; Julia Leigh lent her fiancé *Woman's Mission*, with passages underlined.[43]

Upper-class girls internalized this doctrine of wifely devotion, aspiring to its ideals when they married. Numerous landowners' wives did their best. Lady Cardigan found her husband only enjoyed walking, driving and riding, so "naturally I put my own hobbies aside and entered into all his favourite pursuits." Lady Halifax "deliberately subordinated" her own considerable abilities to advance her husband's public life and give solace in their private life, practising "an habitual self-effacement." The Countess of Lovelace's "ideal of wifely duty" included listening with apparent interest to everything her husband had to say.[44] In her journal, Lady Boileau wrote questions for daily self-examination which reveal the difficulties wives had in suppressing their own needs.[45]

> Have I been dutiful and affectionate in my manner, as well as in my feelings, towards my dear husband this day?
> Have I listened to him when speaking to me, with attention, with a desire to understand his meaning, with a readiness to enter into his views, to agree with his opinions?
> Have I guarded against my disposition to contradict and to find objections to what he says?
> Have I taken care neither to be sulkily silent, or hasty in answering him, in conversation?
> Have I taken submitted with a cheerful humility when he has thought right to reprove me for or point out any of my faults?
> Have I resisted with all my strength all desire to defend myself even if I should not have seen my fault?
> Have I felt grateful for his advice and admonition, and tried sincerely to believe his motive is to do me good?
> Have I shewn myself ready to arrange my occupations to suit his hours and his convenience, and that without tormenting him with questions?
> Have I tried in everything to consult his wishes?

Most wives turned to their husbands for advice and support. To Molly Bell, the husband was "the person to whom you wanted to refer everything, who was the standard by which you measured things."[46] Men much older than their wives were generally more patriarchal, already accustomed to command, and set in their ways. Timid young wives looked up to these husbands in awe.

Landowners took male dominance over wives for granted, as a result of their upbringing, their powerful position, and prevailing social theories. An eldest son was deferred to by siblings and nurses, becoming convinced of his own right and ability to direct the lives of others and expect submission from them. Once he inherited, his power over his household and estate, and in the rural community, only reinforced his confidence in his right to rule. The Victorian social order was still intensely hierarchical, so organizing the family as a hierarchy of authority and submission seemed natural. Both the popular early-Victorian social doctrine of paternalism and the Evangelical revival stressed men's duty to rule and guide their households. The subordination of wives was justified as much by appeals to nature or common sense as by Scripture. Throughout the period, prescriptive literature aimed at middle- and upper-class women insisted on women's inferiority and dependence on men's superior powers for protection, guidance and support. Early in the nineteenth century, women were considered to be delicate and weak in constitution and temperament, and less intelligent than men. Medical theories reinforced these stereotypes and later the theories of evolution were harnessed to support traditional views of female inferiority. Finally, the law upheld male dominance. Under the common law in the early nineteenth century, a married woman had no separate legal existence: all her property belonged to her husband, she could not dispose of it herself, or make a will without his permission; she could not sue or be sued for contracts; and he had legal custody of the children, even in a legal separation. He even had the right to beat or imprison her. Wives' legal position did slowly improve: limited custody of young children in 1839, and greater custody in 1886; rights to earned and inherited property in acts passed from 1870 onwards; rights to a separation order and maintenance in cases of aggravated assault in 1878, and maintenance after desertion in 1895.

Patriarchal dominance did not necessarily result in an unhappy marriage, as wives were brought up to expect and accept it. Though Sir John Boileau was a domestic tyrant, he and his wife Catherine "remained deeply in love with each other. Her quiet, serene, meek beauty gave him peace. His manliness, . . . consistency, . . . determination, . . . principle and courtesy held her, as once they had won her."[47] Brought up in a rigidly hierarchical society, argues M. Jeanne Peterson, women accepted subordination as "a fact of the social order and a fact of family order" rather than as a mark of personal inferiority or oppression.[48] Very few landed wives expressed any discontent with the norms of male domination and female submission.

Nineteenth-century male dominance was, in fact, not as pervasive as the despotic paternal absolutism of the early-modern patriarch, who had the legal right and responsibility to control and chastise wife, children and servants as his own property. This had long been undermined by the ideal of domesticity, developing among the gentry and aristocracy by the late seventeenth century, and becoming the prevailing norm by the 1820s.[49] Domesticity involved "partial egalitarianism in familial relations."[50] Marriage was idealized as a close and loving companionship between friends. Women's status within the family rose as they became more involved in child-rearing and took over household management.

From the 1790s the Evangelicals developed new definitions of masculinity and femininity, in the ideology of "separate spheres." Gender roles became spatially defined: men went out as breadwinners and family representatives into the corrupting and impure world of commerce, industry and politics, while women ruled the home, idealized as a physical and moral retreat. Isolated and protected from the world, women remained morally uncorrupted, preserving the virtues and emotions destroyed there. The wife was for the first time considered morally superior to her husband, an acknowledged influence and guide. At first, leading promoters of these new gender divisions, William Cowper and Hannah More, envisaged their implementation in landed society. But the next generation of authors wrote for the middle classes, where men went out to work. By the 1830s and 1840s, the doctrine of separate spheres was widely accepted and remained the basis of prescriptive literature on gender throughout the period.[51] As part of their prudent reforms, the early-nineteenth-century landed classes incorporated the concepts of separate spheres into their own redefined gender roles.

Separate spheres theoretically improved the wife's status in marriage by giving her not only power over the home, but a new moral authority which could encourage a husband to respect and value his wife. John Hungerford Arkwright told his fiancée he agreed with Ruskin's view that women were superior to men in their power for good and evil; he looked to her as his guide, and her influence was his "sweet hope."[52]

Upper-class gender relations, however, were not shaped by the ideology of separate spheres alone. Middle-class concepts of the separation of public and private spheres were not completely applicable to the country house, where home and work were intermingled. The house was the headquarters of estate management, the centre of the family's economic enterprise, and the setting for many community events. Family life was not entirely private: births, the heir's coming of age, his marriage, and his funeral were all public celebrations. Male landowners did not leave home to go to work daily. They were involved in household and staff management, in charge of the menservants, stables, and gamekeeping. The husband acted as host at balls, parties, and other social functions, presiding with his wife at dinner parties, or taking guests for drives, rides, and tours of the property. As the next chapter will show, wives, too, had public duties in philanthropy, and could assist their husbands in estate management, and behind-the-scenes political manoeuvrings as hostesses. Fathers and mothers shared the responsibilities and joys of parenthood. The needs and customs of their own class thus created less rigid gender roles and territories.

Where husbands earned all the income, middle-class wives' economic dependence actually reduced their real power. Landowners' wives were better off: pin money meant they were not entirely dependent on a husband's generosity, and could keep day-to-day personal expenditure private. Landed fathers used the law of equity to give their daughters some property of their own, a "separate estate" held through a trust. The daughter's portion was usually a capital sum left untouched, with the annual interest given to her for her "sole and separate use." This was typically part of the daughter's marriage settlement, but further capital could be inherited after her father's death. In marriage settlements, Mary Ann Dixon got £200 a year in 1827, Lady Ridley in 1841 and Lucy Arkwright in 1866 both received £300 a year, Mary Bosanquet was given £400 in 1862, and the aristocrat Lady Elizabeth Belgrave was allotted £600 in 1819.[53] The highest aristocracy and wealthiest *nouveaux riches* contributed dowries of as much as £50,000 with £2,000 annual income, but portions of £10,000 with annual incomes of £400 became more typical. John Arkwright left portions of £10,000, for instance, to each of his five daughters. By the late nineteenth century, capital of £25,000, providing an annual income of £1,000 was typical.[54] Thus, while upper-class women still depended on male generosity for financial support, this was an institutionalized obligation few fathers refused to undertake: class expectations as well as paternal affection ensured it. To protect a married daughter and her children from a profligate husband, some fathers also gave her estates of her own, under the equity system of law, which allowed property to be bequeathed or given as a gift for a married woman's separate use, either with or without a trustee. Separate incomes gave upper-class wives "independence and self-confidence," argues Joan Perkin. Provided for under equity, rather than suffering under the common law, "they were often not aware of the legal disabilities they *did* have, because they were not subjected to them, and consequently saw no problem until something went seriously wrong with the marriage."[55]

Finally, most men continued to cherish their wives as companions and friends, valuing them too highly to bully or neglect them. Circumstances favoured the growth of affection and companionship. The remarkably uniform upper-class upbringing, inculcating similar habits, tastes, attitudes, interests, and behaviour, promoted harmony. Landowners were generally less subject to money worries which caused

Plate 13 A companionate marriage: Mr and Mrs John Sperling of Dynes Hall playing chess

tensions in other marriages. Most heirs received an annual allowance large enough to maintain a high standard of living even before they inherited the estates. Then the couple received a much greater unearned income and an ample home, already splendidly decorated and furnished, in a beautiful, romantic setting of gardens and park. They had far more time to enjoy each other's company than couples in classes below, with the husband free of daily employment, and his wife relieved of childcare and housework. They could enjoy leisure hours together, taking exercise or pursuing hobbies. Household management, entertaining, leisure, and child-rearing were also shared between them. Mutual dedication to family interests, the home, the estates, and the community brought couples together in a companionate partnership approaching that which M. Jeanne Peterson finds in upper-middle-class marriages, where the "central fact of marriage was parity and partnership between husband and wife. The sharing of both affection and work made for marriages that often appear more fully companionate than those in our own time."[56] While frequent separations meant landed couples had less opportunity to do so on a day-to-day basis, they, too, worked together, not just on the political husband's parliamentary career, but to advance the interests of the family. They could act as each other's confidantes, advisers and helpers in a working partnership, running the household and the estate. Absences necessitated reliance on the partner at home. Letters between John and Lucy Arkwright, for instance, contain numerous requests for items from home or town or errands, and consultations over domestic, family, and financial problems.[57]

Husbands and wives, however, were not forced to rely on each other to meet all their emotional needs. They found other sources of support in their families of birth. Country house couples were not so isolated from kin as Stone's model of the companionate marriage suggests. As Judith Schneid Lewis points out, domesticity's more intense affective relations created bonds between parents and children, and between siblings, that were unlikely to diminish when the young people left home. Continued intimacy is clearly evident in frequent visits and voluminous correspondence. The wife, especially, remained emotionally tied to her mother and sisters, who gave the expert advice and encouragement a husband could not provide, as she adjusted to married life and her new role as lady of the manor, then faced pregnancy, childbirth, and child-rearing. Many wives corresponded frequently, even daily, with their parents, sisters, and close women friends. Brides were typically welcomed into their husband's family as a new daughter and sister, receiving the same affection and support, especially from their mothers-in-law.[58] A marriage thus embedded in a wide network of affective ties was under less pressure.

A houseful of servants also influenced the upper-class marriage by moderating behaviour. Irate couples were less inclined to brawl openly within sight or hearing of a servant, and had to conduct arguments in civil tones until they reached the privacy of their own bed. Even devoted couples found spontaneous and intimate behaviour curbed by the omnipresence of servants, the attendance of lady's maids and valets, and the strict timetables of domestic routines.

Some historians have assumed that the nineteenth century was an era of sexual repression and prudery, when husbands were insensitive, even brutal, towards unresponsive wives.[59] Certainly, the Victorians were reticent on the subject, not openly demanding sexual fulfilment as a priority of marriage, but private diaries and letters indicate a mutually satisfying sexual relationship was the norm. Wives such as Lady Lyttleton and Lucy Arkwright made delicate allusions to loneliness in bed and hunger in letters to absent husbands, while Lady Sackville's diaries in the first years of marriage were full of coded references to frequent, rapturous love-making. Molly Trevelyan also recorded nights of "wonderful love" and the Trevelyans' "mutual delight in a passionate sexual relationship shone through their correspondence." After five years of marriage, she believed it "a very perfect state of things that we are not ashamed of our love and our desire."[60]

The companionate marriage remained both the ideal and the norm in the nineteenth century. "Typical of many aristocratic marriages," concludes Lewis, "was a mutual esteem and shared regard that grew throughout a couple's years together." Most of Pat Jalland's political wives "established loving, close and fulfilling relationships with their husbands."[61] Married couples' letters and diaries portray many close relationships. The second Marquess and Marchioness of Westminster felt a mutual devotion which lasted all their married life; Lady Elizabeth considered her husband nearly perfect; her diary and letters show her delight in his company and her misery when they were apart. Letters between Lucy and John Arkwright reveal continuing romantic love and closeness. Fifteen years after their wedding, Lucy wrote, "I have been thinking of you so much my darling, & I miss my old baby so dreadfully."[62]

Nevertheless, some marriages which began happily enough eventually failed. The landed classes' lifestyle could actually undermine the companionate marriage: the different duties and interests of the two sexes could serve to part them. Men were often away from home on estate matters or public service. Their passion for hunting and shooting was not always shared by their wives, who endured long hours of boredom while the men were out shooting. Lady Wortley was not alone in complaining, "I sometimes feel that for part of the year I am married to a gun, not a man."[63] Pregnant or nursing women, or mothers busy with a full nursery, often preferred to remain at home while husbands travelled for business or pleasure. Margaret Hobhouse, eager for her husband to have a career, stoically accepted their separation when his parliamentary duties kept him in London, while she stayed in Somerset with the children.[64] Unless a wife accompanied her husband wherever he went, she had less opportunity to share in his work than the wife of the upper-middle-class professional man, who lived near his workplace in the city and returned home in the evenings.

Many social activities separated the couple. Women normally made calls alone, and dominated the afternoon "at homes" popular from the 1850s. Men organized and participated in shoots with women very much spectators. Even when acting together, spouses paid attention not to each other, but to their guests. Yet many of the wife's social activities occurred when her husband was busy with other commitments, and without outings and guests, her life in the country would have been dull and lonely.

Landowners were also more likely than men in other classes to marry women much younger than themselves. Men who delayed wife-hunting, secure in their perpetual attractions, sometimes snatched up the belle of the Season in her first year out. These marriages by older men set in their ways often deteriorated as their young wives matured, gaining a stronger sense of identity and more self-assurance. "I do not like being interfered with or contradicted," the thirty-year-old Marquess of Stafford told his teenage bride, "I am so much older than you and cannot possibly change." They led very separate lives, with no mutual tastes or interests. The marchioness, yearning for friendship and culture, turned to other livelier men for the companionate relationship she had hoped for in marriage.[65]

Incompatibility of personality or background was a common cause of unhappy marriages, especially when the couple did not love each other initially, or lived with family members opposed to the interloper. Sir George Sitwell married Lord Londesborough's daughter Ida mainly for her pedigree. He was an austere, serious, unemotional man, while his teenage bride was passionate and volatile. Despising her husband, she indulged in reckless extravagance and gambling in her boredom and unhappiness. John Baker White, a quiet, shy, and moody young man, was totally wrapped up in estate management, hunting, and shooting. He chose a well-educated, sociable daughter of a solicitor. She had no interest in country life. After they moved in with his hostile mother, whose attacks on his wife were abetted by his equally antagonistic married sisters nearby, the marriage soon failed.[66]

When couples had married for motives other than love, it required a real effort to create a loving relationship. The strong sense of duty among the gentry, and the aristocracy in the middle decades of the century, gave an incentive, and many achieved a comfortable companionship over the years. Some brides who felt little for their husbands tried hard to learn to love them. Mary Elizabeth Lucy made the best of her forced marriage: "I often communed with my heart and strove to forget how I had loved and been loved, and then at last my whole life became as fondly devoted to my husband as if he had been the object of my earliest affection."[67]

Sometimes the desire for personal happiness overrode this sense of obligation, and disappointed husbands and wives might seek love elsewhere. Wives such as Lady Sykes or Venetia James with impotent or sexually inept husbands sought sexual satisfaction through affairs.[68] Marriages where both parties expected sexual gratification in adultery, common among the highest court aristocracy in 1800, were replicated by their descendants. "Throughout the century," concludes Allen Horstman, "a 'fast' set existed where marital fidelity was not highly valued."[69] While adultery was more frequent and more overt early and late in the century, it was simply better hidden in the middle decades, for fear of public opinion. At all times, affairs were supposed to be "conducted with great discretion. People weren't expected to cause or make a fuss or scandal."[70] Husbands were supposed to keep their hands off unmarried women (who were expected to be virgins at marriage, thus ensuring the legitimacy of the first-born child), and the straying wife first had to produce at least one clearly legitimate heir. Certain sections of the late-Victorian and Edwardian aristocracy indulged in numerous affairs, notably the Marlborough House set – Prince Edward and his courtiers and friends, the hunting set of Melton Mowbray, and the Souls, an exclusive group of friends who valued each other's intellect, wit, aesthetic taste, and conversation. Lady Granby's behaviour was typical. This cultured and artistic Soul married the handsome but stupid heir to a dukedom. When she and her husband lost interest in each other, he began a series of liaisons with actresses, while she took as lovers Montagu Corry, who fathered a daughter, Violet, and then the Soul Harry Cust, to whom she bore Diana in 1892. "Sex was a fact of life" in Lady Diana Cooper's childhood, as she watched Lady Granby, like other fashionable hostesses, allocate bedrooms for guests so that spouses were separated and lovers adjacent to each other. Many of the Souls did not follow the older prescription of marrying on the basis of well-tried affection. In consequence, perhaps, only three of the fifteen couples forming the core of the set, estimates their historian, were really happy.[71] In the more permissive atmosphere of the last decades before World War I, those few aristocratic women who were driven into marriage were particularly vulnerable to seduction. Lady Zouche, for example, committed adultery with the notorious Wilfrid Blunt and several others before finally obtaining a divorce.[72] Adultery does seem to have been rarer among the gentry, who more often married for love, and moved in more conventional circles where respectability mattered immensely.

Discreet adultery sometimes allowed the outward form of loveless marriages to endure. Anything seemed better than undermining the institution of marriage and publicizing the elite's shortcomings. Lady Greville held that "a really nice woman would endure any suffering rather than air her sorrows in the lurid glare of the divorce court."[73] Until late in the century, divorce was anathema to the respectable majority of the landed classes, a scandalous, humiliating last resort for extreme cases. The religious revival promoted Biblical arguments against divorce, and the ideal of companionate marriage made a divorce more psychologically painful, when the estranged couple had to admit the failure of their love.[74] Divorce was also difficult, time-consuming, and very expensive. Initially, only men could seek divorce, first suing the co-respondent, then getting a separation in the Ecclesiastical Court, and finally obtaining a private Act of Parliament, with high fees and embarrassing publicity at each step. Divorced wives were denied custody of their own children until 1839, were ostracized by Society, even by their own families, and were expected to lead the rest of their lives in shamed seclusion. In 1857, the divorce court was established, yet the double standard remained: husbands could sue for adultery alone, but wives had to also claim cruelty, or desertion and non-support.

Thus only a handful went as far as divorce, chiefly among the "fast set" in the court aristocracy. Infidelities and divorces clustered in certain families, such as the Pagets, Pellews and Berkeleys, who attracted spouses and friends from families with similar proclivities.[75] Frequently, it took the wife's flight with her lover to induce the husband to divorce her. Carlotta Polderoy was unhappy with her older, eccentric husband. By the time Henry Polderoy finally realized they were often "strangers to each other," it was too late. He returned home one day to find she had run off with a friend of his. Once divorced, she married her lover.[76]

Other couples obtained a legal separation and lived apart. Neither Charles, Duke of Marlborough, nor Consuelo Vanderbilt had wanted to marry each other, but he needed her fortune, while her ambitious mother bullied and emotionally blackmailed the young Consuelo into accepting him. After eleven years of marriage, irreconcilably incompatible, they agreed on a separation in 1906. They were awarded equal custody of their two sons, and the duchess moved to the London house built for her by her mother.[77] Some wives did not demand separation orders. Lady Orford, for instance, simply took her daughters to live in Italy.[78]

Most estranged couples, unwilling to face the notoriety of divorce, lived separate lives in the same house. This was easy in the country house. Many of the domestic occasions which brought husband and wife together regularly, such as meals, family prayers, and church-going, were formalized and attended by servants and guests. Separate bedrooms were not unusual, and dressing-rooms, boudoirs and smoking-rooms further reduced contact. Downstairs, rooms were divided into male and female zones: billiards room, library and dining-room for men, and the drawing-room for women. George, ninth Earl of Carlisle, and his wife Rosalind had married for love, but the latter's strong will and opinions eventually alienated her husband. By the 1890s, "their territories were kept almost wholly apart." He shunned his wife's sitting-room, and she never entered his sitting-room, smoking-room or studio. Men could also escape without exciting unfavourable comment by attending Parliament or arranging hunting and shooting trips. Lord Carlisle lived in London, returning to Naworth only for shooting and Christmas, while his wife remained at home, only going to London for her committee meetings.[79]

The low divorce rate among the landed classes was as much a matter of class and family pressures as of legal difficulties and expense. An internalized sense of duty or loyalty to family and class kept many unhappy couples together. Lady Battersea blamed the Craven divorce on the pair's lack of a "well-defined sense of duty."[80] Marriage was not simply a matter of personal happiness; it was an institution involving clearly defined roles and obligations for both husband and wife. The newly married Mary Elizabeth Lucy "prayed to God that I might be ever mindful of my duty as a wife, and be diligent in the discharge of such duties as His providence should allot me."[81] Unhappy spouses found consolation in the numerous duties owed to family, class, and community.

The rising divorce rate at the end of the period is related to a declining sense of duty and diminishing religious convictions. By the Edwardian period, divorce had become more common, if not more acceptable, particularly among the highest aristocracy. Submission to the overriding demands of family and class was finally yielding to the desire for personal happiness and fulfilment.

Individuals who did divorce often remarried, as did those whose unhappy marriages were ended by a spouse's death. Remarriage was even more common among the bereaved who had enjoyed a happy marriage. Viscountess Barrington believed an older man's readiness to remarry "may be taken as an appreciation of his happiness under the first regime, and ... his helplessness without a wife."[82] George, Lord Lyttleton, disliked celibacy, suffering an "extreme longing for a companion." This impoverished father of twelve, not surprisingly, wanted a barren wife past childbearing with plenty of money.[83] Supported by annual income from their jointure, upper-class widows had less economic incentive to remarry than other widows. Young widows left in charge of estates, such as Henrietta Bankes, refused suitors to protect their son's inheritance.[84] But some displaced dowagers missed their former position: Lady Cowper found widowhood "a great trial ... after having enjoy'd every comfort and a happy Home." Marrying her former lover, Lord Palmerston, not only improved her "worldly position" but enabled her to receive her children in appropriate style.[85] Other lovers were also finally united in holy matrimony. The third Duke of Sutherland outraged his family by marrying his mistress, widow of an Indian civil servant, just three months after his estranged wife's death.[86] Freed of parental direction, with an heir and an income secured, widows and widowers had more liberty to marry whom they pleased. Lady Lindsey chose a clergyman, and her daughter, Lady Charlotte Guest, fell in love with her own son's tutor.[87] Without family "influence or management" George, Lord Lyttleton, won the wealthy widow Sybella Mildmay, who "told her father she had married the first time to please him and the second . . . to please herself."[88]

The landed classes' eagerness to remarry after widowhood or divorce shows how much they valued companionate marriage. Even within the early-nineteenth-century revival of patriarchy, most upper-class couples expected mutual love and friendship in marriage. While they prudently confined spouse-hunting to suitable social circles, the majority chose a partner on the basis of well-tried affection. An heir's courtship was nevertheless more closely controlled by parents, and more likely to be influenced by pragmatic motives of individual and family interests. While husbands remained dominant, patriarchy was modified by the ideal of companionate marriage, and by the greater autonomy and authority granted to wives not only by separate spheres but by the roles and privileges of their social position. Similarity of background and the advantages of the country house way of life promoted marital happiness, yet paradoxically unhappy marriages were more easily endured when estranged couples dutifully undertook the roles of master and mistress of the country house.

As the duties of a male landowner are well known, the following chapter concentrates on those of country house women, roles underrated and often overlooked by historians but recognized by contemporaries as essential for the family's continuing success.

5

Country House Women

Apart from their roles as companionate wives and involved mothers, landed women had many other recognized, distinctive and demanding functions to perform for their families, class, and community: as housekeepers and hostesses, as participants in Society, and as philanthropists. Some women also made significant contributions in the predominantly male spheres of estate management and politics. Another important role, that of mistress of servants, is dealt with in chapter 10.

Ownership of a landed estate carried with it a prescribed set of duties for both men and women. Historians have exhaustively scrutinized men's roles as landowners, entrepreneurs, politicians, public officials, and philanthropists. Far less is known about women's roles. Indeed, it is widely assumed that they had none. "Condemned to rot in idleness," these "idle drones" supposedly wasted their days on "novel-reading, theatre-going, card-playing and formal visits." According to conventional wisdom, troops of servants deprived upper-class women of any valid role as housewives or mothers. "They had nothing to do except be weak and ineffective, forced by lack of activity into often totally wasted lives."[1]

Most historians of the landed classes have been preoccupied with activities in which women played little or no direct role, since few females inherited estates, nor could they vote, let alone enter Parliament or serve in the armed forces. Except in demography, where women's marriages and childbearing are undeniably important, these historians omit or devalue women's roles. Beckett's *Aristocracy in England*, for instance, covers only men's roles and activities, and discusses philanthropy and London Society without mentioning women's crucial role in both. David Cannadine deliberately excludes women from his equally massive survey of the landed classes after 1880, although he does recognize "an urgent need for more women's history of upper-class women."

But his assumption that "wealth, status, power, and class consciousness" were "preponderantly" male concerns shows a lack of awareness of women's roles and contributions.2 Status and class consciousness were very much female business. No history of the landed classes can be comprehensive and accurate unless it includes the women.

Until recently, women's historians have had scarcely more enthusiasm for upper-class women. Research on nineteenth-century British women concentrated on the working classes, with increasing interest in the middle classes, but the aristocracy and gentry were largely disregarded. Jane Lewis's survey, for example, examines only working- and middle-class women, with no explanation as to why the upper classes have been omitted. Leonore Davidoff's book on Society, published in 1973, was long the sole serious study including upper-class women. But like Pat Jalland, she does not differentiate between the landed classes and the urban upper middle classes. In the last few years, historians of British women have begun to identify the distinct characteristics of landed women, beginning with Judith Schneid Lewis's study of childbearing in the aristocracy. Joan Perkin's book on women and marriage makes some important assertions about upper-class women. Pamela Horn, prolific popular historian of the Victorian countryside, produced the first survey of landed women's roles, but it is anecdotal and descriptive, omitting both the theories of others, and critical analysis by the author herself, so it is by no means the last word on the subject.[3]

Far more important is M. Jeanne Peterson's thesis in her study of upper-middle-class women. She challenges persistent stereotypes of the Victorian woman, arguing that their birth and rank enabled upper-middle-class gentlewomen to expand their sphere beyond prescribed female roles and territory. The Paget women and their friends assisted husbands in their careers, controlled or managed money, pursued further education and energetic physical exercise, worked in philanthropy and education, and developed their own talents in writing and the fine arts. "With the exception of public officeholding, no corner of Victorian life seems to have been closed to the gentlewoman in the sense of action and doing; she did not have the title, but she often had the role."[4] The wide range of opportunities gave gentlewomen meaningful, satisfying, and rewarding lives. This model applies equally to women of the landed classes.

Like upper-middle-class gentlewomen, landed women's gender boundaries were defined more by their birth and social status than by prescriptive literature. Primogeniture, and the landowner's rank, shaped gender in the country house. It was women's relationship to a male landowner as daughter, wife, sister, widow, and mother that defined their roles, delineated their sphere of action, and granted the privileges which made it so wide.

Landed women's liberty increased over their lifetime. Few females were more closely guarded and heavily restricted than young, unmarried daughters. They were kept out of the public eye, although in the country they took exercise and performed good works in the neighbourhood. Marriage to a landowner brought more freedom and independence. A wife enjoyed not only the use of her husband's wealth and property, but her own pin money. Joan Perkin claims equity law, which "gave them legal protection and access to separate income and property," allowed upper-class wives the "independence and self-confidence to behave pretty much as they liked, subject only to the mores of their class."[5] A wife had recognized, demanding, and significant functions both in and beyond the home, as mother, manager of household and servants, hostess, and philanthropist. These roles carried with them power, status, and resources; and they were not confined to wives. Bachelor owners often asked their mother, sister or another female relative to perform the duties of mistress of the household and hostess. Unmarried women remaining with parents or brothers could assume the roles of hostess or philanthropic Lady Bountiful. Single women who inherited estates had the most freedom, followed by widows, whose jointure provided financial support, freeing them from male control for the first time in their life. Widows usually valued their autonomy. Mary Elizabeth Lucy agreed to stay with her son and his wife provided she could have a bedroom and a boudoir where she would "never be in the way, and ... feel thoroughly independent."[6] Widows now had the opportunity to expand their own hobbies and interests; only in widowhood did Lady Stanley of Alderley actively promote higher education for women, helping found Girton College.[7] They were also free to abandon public duties, like Harriet, Dowager Countess Granville, who "entirely gave up the world, and lived in the most absolute retirement."[8] In Society, the dowager lost none of her power; with her accumulated experience and knowledge she maintained control of social placement and matchmaking.

A landowner's wife served the primary goal of advancing the family's interests in her roles of mistress of the household and maidservants, hostess, and philanthropist. But within the landed family, gender roles were not rigidly assigned to women or men. Men of the "leisure class" had the time and opportunity to interest themselves in domestic matters and social arrangements, and as paternalist landowners, they were expected to undertake philanthropy. With their social status assured by birth and marriage, landed women had more freedom to enter the public sphere than middle-class women. In the country, the public domain was always open to upper-class women: they could safely go anywhere with propriety on their families' estates. From the mid-Victorian period, they were also increasingly able to enter the public arena in the city without losing caste.[9] Tolerance of eccentricity as an upper-class trait also permitted unconventional behaviour. Over the century, landed women expanded their sphere into activities normally reserved for men. The companionate marriage discussed earlier was an important factor: couples were eager to share their lives and assist each other in their work. The roles of men and women in the landed classes were characterized by the flexibility M. Jeanne Peterson found among upper-middle-class couples, where "there were tasks that were customarily his. Others were entirely open to negotiation, and others yet were her duty. . . . Couples arranged, according to personal preference, how they would work out the particulars of the distribution of labor. But there was never any doubt that the labor belonged to them both."[10]

Thus, the male spheres of estate management and politics were not entirely closed to landed women. A few women owned or ran estates, many women took an intelligent interest in national politics, and an increasing number of them played a supportive role in their menfolk's political campaigns. By the end of the century, women were entering local government themselves.

Single women and widows who inherited estates discharged many of the landowner's responsibilities themselves. Young widows ran the estate under trustees, until the heir came of age. When her husband died in 1904, Henrietta Bankes dedicated herself to ensuring her little son would inherit a prosperous, thriving estate.[11] Older widows who inherited the estate for life also often supervised estate administration themselves. Mrs Baker White, for example, ran Street End with just a bailiff to assist her.[12]

Many female landowners did a good job. Lady Sitwell restored the Renishaw estate to solvency by the time her young son grew up, and the Countess of Yarborough efficiently ran Brocklesby during her son's

Plate 14 Rosalind Howard, Marchioness Howard, with her estate agent

minority, evidently paying off mortgages of £100,000.[13] Mrs Meynell Ingram "had a great aptitude for managing her properties."[14] Inheriting Waddesdon at the age of fifty-one, Alice de Rothschild personally managed every department of the estate, sending detailed instructions when abroad. When in residence she daily inspected the gardens and home farm. She built schools and recreational clubs and a nursing home for the village. Ann Dixon was a conscientious landowner, too, repairing dilapidated cottages, installing piped water and drains, and rebuilding the school.[15]

Some wives assisted their husbands in estate management, especially women with useful talents. Mary Elizabeth Lucy became her husband's secretary, helping him with his business letters, and even writing some of them herself. Lady Fielding managed her spendthrift husband's finances, supervising all the estate, garden, and stable accounts. Lady Wenlock was trained in architecture, and planned the improvement and building of estate cottages.[16] Wives often managed the estate in their husbands' absence: Lady Stanhope reported to her politician husband in 1878 that the farm stock book was up-to-date, the list of leases was ready, the new brick machine was working well, and the dairy wall had been cemented.[17]

Other women undertook major projects on the estate. Some ladies engaged in building, and others redesigned the gardens. Harriet Leveson-Gower, Duchess of Sutherland, took notes on the houses and gardens she visited abroad, incorporating what she admired most into her own houses. She was responsible for the alterations at Dunrobin and Lilleshall, and for the rebuilding of Trentham, while Cliveden was largely her own creation.[18] Working with a co-operative architect, the widowed Mary Elizabeth Lucy rebuilt the Charlcote parish church to her own design.[19] The second wife of the eleventh Earl of Pembroke designed an entirely new Italian formal garden west of Wilton, which took her many years to complete.[20]

A few wives even ran estates themselves. As she grew up in the 1860s, Maude Hemmings was her father's constant companion on the Bentley estate. When she married Colonel George Cheape of Mull, they lived on her father's Scottish estate, which she ran while her husband was abroad on business trips. Mr Hemmings left both Bentley and Glaschorrie to his daughter, and it was she, not her husband, who managed the property and took up breeding horses, cattle, and sheep. Soon her estate workers were calling her the Squire of Bentley.[21] Until her death in

1825, the Duchess of Rutland managed all her husband's affairs, including his estates, where she took a great interest in planting and farming.[22] Viscount Howard handed over the management of his substantial estates to his wife in 1888. She wanted "a sphere . . . of my own which shall make my life have some definite persistent effort about it – some incentive to learn and to achieve." She found estate management involved learning about farming methods, building, coal mining and forestry, and frequent travelling between the Morpeth, Naworth and Castle Howard estates. Despite her mistakes, the estates' net annual income rose from about £15,000 in 1892–4 to nearly £25,000 by 1911–13.[23] Mr Davidson of Otterburn bought Ridley Hall for his wife Susan. "She was a capital manager of her large estate," observed Augustus Hare, "entered into all business questions herself, and would walk for hours about her woods, marking timber, planning bridges or summer houses, and continuing walks."[24]

Because they were women, female owners could not undertake the full range of a landowner's duties, in Parliament, the militia, or local government. Excluded from participating as voters or representatives, wives played an unseen but still vital supportive role in politics. Women of the landed classes were generally well informed and interested in politics, keeping up with current issues and developments. Often strongly partisan, many politicians' wives were widely read, fervently discussing political questions in correspondence and with men at social gatherings. Politicians' wives also acted as confidantes, listening to and supporting their husbands, but, it seems, rarely trying to influence them directly, except in their ambitions for the husband's career advancement. Some great ladies became renowned political hostesses, entertaining politicians in their London houses or country seats. "A number of political careers were enhanced," concludes Pat Jalland, because "wives were good hostesses capable of making interesting conversation and helping guests to mix easily."[25] Until the late 1840s, the great houses of London "still acted as closed camps for their political party interests."[26] When party politics became fluid in the 1850s and 1860s, political hostesses could bring together diverse interests. With the formation of the Conservative and Liberal Parties, this function declined. But after the 1883 electoral reforms, political wives acquired a more public means of supporting their husbands, in auxiliary organizations which trained party members as unpaid election campaign workers. By far the most successful was the Conservatives' Primrose League. Many of the officers were upper-class women, and the Ladies Grand Council was both active and influential. Gradually, members gained experience and confidence in canvassing; after 1900 they organized campaigns and gave many public speeches. The ladies' high social status meant they could appear in public without losing caste. This political campaigning did not alienate upper-class men, who accepted it as an extension of women's supportive role as wives and mothers. Nevertheless, "by seeking to inform women on political issues as though they were men, and by employing women in the role of instructors and leaders," the Primrose League helped undermine the norms of separate spheres.[27]

By 1914, participation in women's political organizations had convinced many ladies of the need to support women's suffrage. In earlier decades, landed women had been largely indifferent towards this issue, complacently confident that their privileged position gave them "more important indirect political influence" than would a vote, and the few who were either pro- or anti-suffrage hesitated to take an unwomanly public stand.[28]

Landed women first entered politics in local government. From 1875, landed women could serve as Poor Law guardians, from 1894 as district and parish councillors, and from 1907 as county councillors. Their social status ensured their election as councillors or guardians. Being conservative in values, and deferential to the men, they kept a fairly low profile, but often did more committee work and cared more about conditions in workhouses, public health, infant mortality, and poor housing.[29] Edith Cropper's "longing to make the workhouse children's lives a little sweeter" impelled her to join the local Board of Guardians.[30]

Women were often drawn into local politics through their philanthropic work. Many male landowners neglected their personal obligation to assist the rural poor. Both David Roberts and F. M. L. Thompson found that only a minority of landowners built cottages and schools. Discovering only small outlays for charity in estate accounts, Lawrence Stone dismisses philanthropy as just another leisure-time hobby, a "small minority interest," insignificant in terms of either time or money.[31] But these historians, in focusing entirely on what men did, seriously underestimate the extent of the landed classes' efforts. It was women who primarily dispensed charity in the local community.[32]

Since the Middle Ages, the lady of the manor had been expected to tend the poor and the sick. From the early nineteenth century, this role was expanded and undertaken more energetically and universally, motivated not just by Evangelicalism, but also by the landed classes' decision to reform themselves. Paternalist doctrine revived the traditional obligations of *noblesse oblige*. Thus, in the 1840s, the fifth Earl of Macclesfield and his wife Louisa "considered that their wealth, place and power had been given to them as a stewardship." The countess built schools and a domestic training school, started coal and clothing clubs, and relieved sickness and destitution "believing simply that she was fulfilling her duty."[33] The cult of true womanhood gave women additional authority. Women were regarded as morally superior to men, with a more nurturing, empathetic and sensitive nature, and therefore more suited to philanthropy. "Good works," many women's first venture into the public sphere, were justified as an extension of women's domestic roles as wives and mothers.

Though they lacked their husbands' financial resources, landowners' wives were enabled by their housekeeping role to order soup and clothing made for the poor, give away surplus food or worn-out clothing, and employ the needy. As hostesses, they ran balls, bazaars, fancy fairs, and garden parties to raise funds for charity. They were also in great demand as patronesses or officers of charitable committees and philanthropic organizations. "Pre-eminent by birth and position," the landowner's wife was regarded as the leader of the neighbourhood ladies' charitable efforts. "Not a bazaar can be organised without her patronage and aid; not a charitable committee held, not a church restored," declared Lady Greville, unless "graced by her presence and glorified by her support."[34] Above all, the landed woman contributed her time and skills in human relations. It was most often the ladies who made personal contact with the rural poor, helping and attempting to influence them in many different ways.

All female family members were expected to assume the role of Lady Bountiful; young daughters assisted their mothers, and charitable work was considered the ideal occupation for older single women and widows. Female landowners took benevolence more seriously than most of their male counterparts. Mrs Fielden, for example, "felt it her duty to look after the health, education, and well-being of her dependants and their children."[35]

Most country house women accepted their philanthropic duties without question as inevitable and customary obligations. The particularly dedicated often had additional motives. Many ladies, especially ardent Evangelicals or Roman Catholics, were moved by religious impulses.

Mary Ann Dixon, for instance, longed to "live more for the benefit of others and the promoting of Christ's kingdom."[36] Religious writers on charity inspired and encouraged country house women. After reading the works of Charles Kingsley, Charlotte M. Yonge, and Anna Sewell on social questions, the adolescent Lady Rose Fane and her friends, the vicar's daughters, started a night school for boys and men, then a lending library.[37] Less consciously, others may have found in philanthropy an opportunity beyond their domestic roles to use their idealism, intelligence, energy, and initiative, and to exercise power and control over others. The Lady Bountiful, convinced of her right and ability to direct the lives of social inferiors, was sometimes insensitive and arrogant, entering cottages without knocking to pry and scold, and implementing harsh rules. Lady Wenlock, for instance, sought to expel from the estate any girl whose church-going or conduct was deemed unsatisfactory, while Lady Sitwell ordered compulsory haircuts for her schoolgirls.[38] Among single women, philanthropic work both in the country and in London was a worthwhile and rewarding occupation. Early in the century, it was the only role permitted unmarried daughters outside the home; consequently, many threw all their energies into good works. The deeply religious Caroline Boileau spent her time visiting the poor and sick, and teaching the village children. When she took over as mistress of the household on her mother's death, her father was unable to stop Caroline and her two sisters from venturing unchaperoned into hospitals, workhouses, and slums.[39]

The most common activity was visiting the sick, elderly, and destitute in their own cottages, or interviewing them at the mansion, handing out food, medicine, clothing, or bedding. Mary Ann Dixon provided gowns and shawls for the village women, frocks for the Sunday School girls, and four "baby's bags" containing layettes for newborns. Ladies tried to save souls, by distributing Bibles and tracts, reading and explaining the Bible to cottagers, teaching them to pray, and encouraging them to take communion. Women also organized the traditional annual dole. At Christmas, Mary Ann Dixon presented villagers with shirts, petticoats, and sheets (all cut out by her own hand), and coal.[40]

Women frequently founded and ran institutions promoting self-improvement or self-help. The ladies organized and taught estate Sunday Schools. They also might support the village school, paying the poorest children's fees, awarding prizes for attendance and good behaviour, and donating books and equipment. Some even built, financed and managed

Plate 15   Mary Ann Dixon entertaining the Market Rasen volunteers in 1862 at Holton

their own schools, such as "Mrs Arkwright's Free School" at Hope-Under-Dinmore.[41] The mistress of the country house usually arranged and hosted the annual school treat or Christmas party for children attending local schools and Sunday Schools. Mary Ann Dixon, for instance, did the catering for the Holton school feast, either buying or making pastries and cakes.[42] Ladies instigated and ran savings clubs, to help village families buy cloth, blankets, coal, boots, and even medical care, augmenting the small sums paid in weekly, and purchasing and distributing the goods once a year. They also held matrons' or mothers' meetings to give advice on child-rearing and housekeeping. Presiding over these meetings, the lady led prayers, gave lectures, and read aloud improving novels.

To her audience, and on her visits to housewives and schoolchildren, she expounded not only the virtues of cleanliness, order, and frugality, but also obedience to their betters and doing their duty in the station in which God had placed them. Anne Summers believes home visiting was "the attempt to transpose the values and relations of domestic service to a wider class of the poor." Like servants, they should be "economically and socially dependent, obedient, disciplined, clean and broken in" to middle- or upper-class domestic "methods and routines". She believes a desire to increase both the quantity and quality of domestic servants motivated lady visitors.[43] Certainly, country house ladies took a special interest in village girls, insisting they acquire domestic skills such as needlework in preparation for domestic service as much as for married life. Lady Ridley hoped her school's girls would turn out "clean and respectable and make good useful servants afterwards."[44] Some ladies, like Lucy Arkwright, helped school-leavers find their first job in service, or recommended girls who did well in their petty places. Others contributed outfits, and a few, like the second Duchess of Sutherland, established servants' training schools or laundry schools on the estate.[45] This conditioning for domestic service was neither selfish nor reprehensible. Service was, after all, the leading female occupation and often the only option for country girls. Training in housework and sewing, and assistance in securing good places did give them a better chance to do well in service. Landed women were unlikely to have any self-centred desire to train up maidservants for their own households, for few accepted inexperienced local school-leavers.

Ladies' philanthropy was not confined to the estate. They were just as active when in town, where they visited the poor in the slums, in workhouses, missions, homes, and hospitals, and founded or supported an increasing range of charitable societies and institutions. Residing in Scarborough during her widowhood, Lady Sitwell maintained a cottage hospital, a home for "fallen women," and a club-room.[46] In the 1860s, Catherine Gladstone organized a night shelter in London's East End, started an industrial school and soup kitchens in Lancashire during the Cotton Famine, and, during the 1866 cholera epidemic in London, visited patients and organized a convalescent home and an orphanage at Hawarden.[47] Mid-Victorian aristocratic ladies assisted London's children with orphanages, crèches, a nursery for cripples, schemes for free dinners, and social clubs. Landed women were ideally placed to implement the numerous children's country-holiday schemes developed from the 1880s.[48]

Ladies were equally concerned about working girls and women, founding organizations such as the Girls' Club Union and the Young Women's Christian Association, or joining others such as the National Union of Women Workers. A squire's daughter, Jessie Boucherett, founded the Society for Promoting the Employment of Women in 1859, and Lady Knightley was one of the founders of the Working Ladies Guild, both for middle-class women. A number of such organizations became national societies, such as the Girls' Friendly Society, which made upper- and middle-class women mentors of working girls, and the Mothers' Union, which recruited them to address mothers' meetings.[49] Some young upper-class women joined middle-class volunteers in the Charitable Organization Society, founded in 1869, and the East End settlement houses established from the 1880s. Women were also prominent in other causes, such as missionary and emigration societies and the temperance movement. Lady Henry Somerset and the ninth Countess of Carlisle both served as Presidents of the National British Women's Temperance Association.

Ladies' charitable work in London was characterized by an insistence on the same personal face-to-face relationships experienced in the rural community. They believed that personal friendships between rich and poor would not only alleviate the latter's troubles, but reduce class tensions. By the late nineteenth century, "slumming" was a routine part of the London Season, an antidote to its self-indulgent extravagance. Over-protected young women were especially attracted to the spatial freedom of charitable work in the East End, where they could roam alone unaccosted, and abandon restrictive fashionable dress and formal etiquette.[50]

When they returned to the country, late-nineteenth-century landed women formed local branches of national organizations such as the Mothers' Union, the Girls' Friendly Society, the Brazabon Society (for workhouses), the Boys' Brigade, and the Women's Institute. A number of ladies also promoted the district nursing service, providing midwives and in-home nursing care for the rural poor.[51] Although they sat on numerous committees and boards, many Edwardian chatelaines also continued the more informal, face-to-face traditional philanthropy.

Landed women took the Lady Bountiful role for granted, and most of them diligently carried it out. Indeed, many enjoyed the experience. "Went to see some of the poor people in the village – very pleasant," noted Mary Ann Dixon, while Lady Eden "really loved her good works and much of her life was devoted to them."[52] Country house women gained personal rewards and fulfilment from philanthropy; the Lady Bountiful acquired self-confidence and greater self-worth through developing skills in counselling, teaching, and public speaking, and through receiving the apparent gratitude and deference of those she served. Ladies gained access to the public sphere through philanthropy, not only leaving home to visit the poor or take classes in rural villages or urban slums, but in making numerous public appearances to preside over or give speeches at meetings, open bazaars, and hand out prizes. For Lady Jersey, "public appearances became so much part of her life that she came to move from public to private life and back without self-consciousness or self-importance."[53]

The ladies' local philanthropy served the family, justifying its privileges and strengthening its power and control over the rural community by making the informal, personal contacts crucial for maintaining paternalism and enforcing deference. Paternalism, says Howard Newby, "is most effective on the basis of face-to-face contact": those who "directly experience the social influences and judgments of traditional elite members" will be most deferential to their authority.[54] Charity legitimized social subordination, not just in demonstrating the giver's superiority and the recipient's dependence, but in rewarding only the deferential. Deference was strongest where warm personal ties united the family at the "Big House" with their dependants. Petersham villagers eulogized Lady John Russell as "our much-loved friend," and "really like a mother to many of we 'Old Scholars' " of her village school.[55] In the East End, ladies were serving their class, rather than their own families, by attempting to justify their own privileged existence and reduce class conflict. However, East Enders lived in a very different and more independent working-class culture, and many, while willing to take any assistance offered, were alienated by the ladies' conviction of the superiority of their own ideas and methods, their condescension, and their lack of empathy.

At the national level, landed women's participation and leadership in philanthropic causes brought them into the more respectable and uncontroversial stream of feminism – the campaign to expand women's nurturing role into bettering the lot of the nation's women and children, within the boundaries of women's sphere.[56]

Just as the landed family's philanthropy was chiefly in the hands of its womenfolk, so were its social duties. A landowner's wife had to uphold her husband's position, maintain the family's reputation, further his and the children's interests, and demonstrate class solidarity by offering hospitality to her social circle and attending the public events of the annual social calendar. In Society, only the wife was "accepted as representative and official." It was her job to "organise recognised hospitality," dispense invitations, "initiate or reject acquaintanceships", and pay calls.[57] Women were considered especially suited to the role of hostess, supposedly being more sensitive, perceptive, tactful and understanding, unselfish, kindly, and eager to please than men. Ladies were also responsible for instilling social order, and maintaining morality, propriety, civility, and decorum.[58]

Women's social activities were actually the means of social placement, establishing the gradations of rank integral to nineteenth-century Britain. As the Industrial Revolution created newly wealthy groups demanding social recognition, the established elite from the 1820s onwards created a socially exclusive community, with barriers of "strictly structured access rituals" and an elaborate and ever-changing code of etiquette to confound outsiders and confirm insiders. Women maintained the fabric of Society as "arbiters of social acceptance or rejection," through their power to issue or withhold invitations, choose to pay calls or receive callers, or acknowledge or ignore a passer-by.[59] The great lady, explained a commentator, was "the door-keeper of Society, the Supreme Judge of the final court of Social Appeal." It was "her function to repulse with a word or a smile the wily pretender, to close the door . . . in the face of the vulgar and the insolent, to eject the offender against social laws."[60]

The social role developed throughout the stages of a lady's life. As a teenager, she was launched into Society and put on display. Unmarried daughters were merely expected to assist and accompany their mothers, but a married woman had to take her place in county or London Society. A single woman in charge of her father's or brother's house carried out the same social duties. Wives of high-ranking peers might become great Society hostesses, entertaining lavishly in the family's London mansion. As their children grew up, aristocratic and increasing numbers of gentry mothers went to London for the Season to bring out their daughters and help them find husbands. Finally, dowagers enjoyed the greatest social power, controlling entry into Society, and enforcing standards. "The drawing rooms were pre-eminently the preserve of the senior women: their places of business . . . ; their clearing-houses of information . . . ; their tribunals of justice," explains Anna Sproule.[61]

Participation in Society was a serious, valid function performed for a woman's family and social class; it could even become a career, demanding "the same energy, devotion, and work that a man will give to politics."[62] Denied power in men's world of politics and economics, women constructed an alternative world with its own rules, achievements, hierarchy of power, and prestige. Real talents and skills were demanded of an acclaimed hostess, in selecting the right blend of guests and making a party successful. The hostess could exercise power by engineering romances, by providing a venue for politicians to meet and confer in private, and by denying invitations and cutting the unacceptable in public. A good hostess was skilled in the art of conversation. "To watch Mrs Grenfell presiding over a tea-table, . . . introducing her guests to each other and leading the talk, was a lesson in the art of behaviour," recalled Viscountess Milner. "Her gifts were not in statesmanship, only in the perfect management of statesmen."[63] The Duchesses of Sutherland were great Society hostesses. Stafford House was renowned for its lavish and prestigious entertainments and their country houses were seldom without guests. The duchesses boldly invited unconventional celebrities to their parties. The second Duchess of Sutherland had a penchant for Italian republicans, such as Garibaldi, and American abolitionists, such as Harriet Beecher Stowe. The fourth Duchess was especially eclectic in her invitations: at Dunrobin, one could find "a cabinet minister, a poet, a parson and a social reformer sitting down to dinner together."[64]

In the country, the chatelaine's duties included leaving cards, giving and receiving calls, attending local social functions, holding dinner parties, and having guests to stay.[65] The social role was less demanding for gentry wives. Gentry families' social circles were confined to kin and neighbours, and the lesser gentry did not usually mix with great families. Victoria Yorke and her daughters went calling at least once a week, and received callers frequently, but few guests stayed, whereas Mary Ann Dixon went calling less often and invited more people to stay.[66]

Leonore Davidoff argues that most families "gave top priority to the production of social performances" so that "social goals usually took precedence" over privacy, family life, and personal interests, and dictated the system of household management as well as the layout of the Victorian country house.[67] While this may have been true of the aristocracy and the *nouveaux riches*, the gentry strove less for social recognition. The Yorkes, Arkwrights and Dixons enjoyed a relaxed, informal social life, where guests, often relatives, enlivened rather than disrupted family life. For such families, the social role only became crucial when daughters came out.

A wife's duties in Society were inseparable from her role as mistress of the household. Running the household was generally regarded as the wife's province. Before the eighteenth century, the chatelaine had personally supervised a largely self-sufficient household, ensuring that servants performed their tasks and that all the necessary supplies were stocked. She often assisted in the dairy, and in the stillroom made preserves, cordials, and medicines. In the eighteenth century, however, fashionable great ladies, if not gentry wives, delegated these responsibilities to a hired housekeeper.

Early-nineteenth-century landed women took up the role of housekeeper once again, not just because they were indoctrinated in the prevailing gender system of separate spheres, but because housekeeping fitted into the landed classes' efforts to reform themselves and win the approbation of the middle classes. A lady who supervised her own household was not frivolous and idle, but responsibly and industriously performing her duties as a "true woman." Moreover, the lady of the house ultimately determined the family's reputation among the upper classes (and their servants too).

By the early nineteenth century, prescriptive literature idealized and elevated household management and introduced the home-making role. A housekeeper was no substitute, for she could never diffuse an atmosphere of home or set a lady's example to servants. Nor could she grace the house as its chief ornament or act as hostess. Advice books urged the mistress of the house to adopt industrial principles of efficiency, rationalization, and order to household management, with strict schedules, carefully kept accounts, and inventories.[68] Household management was regarded as the special province of women. Characterized as unselfish, sensitive, patient, attentive to detail, and skilled in personal relationships, they were considered more suited than men to deal with its myriad chores and endless small crises. Men, indeed, were not to be bothered with the trivial details of domestic problems. "A gentleman is not always at home and even if he was one cannot run to him with every worry," noted a former head housemaid. "A large house misses a lady, as we cannot get on so well without her." In one establishment lacking a mistress, the servants endured badly cooked dinners and ruined clothes. "We never saw a lady that would let that go on."[69]

Men were expected to supervise the menservants both indoors and out, the stables, the gamekeeping, and the gardens. The wine cellar was under their jurisdiction. Some men, however, became involved in the other departments. The revival of paternalism did increase early-Victorian landowners' authority over their households, and patriarchal, domineering husbands such as Sir John Boileau superintended and criticized their wives' efforts.[70] Companionate marriage encouraged husbands to take an interest in the home and assist their wives: John Hungerford Arkwright, for example, was fully involved in domestic matters. In other cases it was a matter of personality: Lord Stafford really enjoyed supervising "the details of living, looking after the servants and drains and keeping the accounts."[71] Gourmet landowners were preoccupied with menus and closely supervised the cook.

However, men who took over housekeeping were not regarded as normal. Consuelo Balsan felt George Curzon was wrong to refuse to allow his wife "to take on the burdens that should by right have been hers alone."[72] Most men assumed women were perfectly competent to run their large and complex households, and they may have welcomed the opportunity to relieve themselves of the constant anxiety and frequent, irritating demands involved. The typical male landowner therefore felt compelled to find a lady to act as mistress of the country house. An unmarried owner might turn to his mother, sister or even cousin, and a widower commandeered a daughter. Before the third Baron Northwick's marriage, his sister supervised his household. After his wife died, Richard Congreve asked his sister-in-law to run Burton Manor, and on her death, his three unmarried daughters took over.[73]

Few upper-class girls received any systematic training in household management before marriage, though they might witness their mother's housekeeping tasks, or take over a deceased mother's duties, as did Meriel, Lucy and Lavinia Lyttleton successively at Hagley.[74] Wives of heirs gained some practice by running a smaller household, or, if the couple moved in with his parents, the mother-in-law acted as instructor. Brides of landowners had to learn their new responsibilities rapidly. The day after Lady Ridley arrived at Blagdon, she inspected every room with the housekeeper, and the following day saw the gardens and kennels. Initially somewhat overwhelmed, by the third day she felt "nearly settled" and ready to alter the tea-making. Soon she was planning the flower garden, paying bills, prescribing and preparing medicines for a sick maid, and reforming the butter-making. "I have the housebooks all my own way now," she told her mother, "Matt does not even look at them."[75]

The mistress was expected to do the household accounts, inspect the housekeeper's books, pay the bills and order supplies as requested, approve or suggest menus, and deal with unresolved domestic crises. When the family migrated from one property to another, to London for the Season, or to Scotland for shooting, she supervised the move, selecting servants and ensuring that all the plate, china, clothing, nursery equipment, and other luggage was safely packed and transported. Repeatedly, she had to settle her travelling establishment into a different house in a new locality. She still kept in touch by letter and telegram with staff remaining at other family properties, settling their problems, giving orders, and arranging for supplies of fresh food to be sent from country estates. When the family split into several smaller units — children left behind with their nurses and governess in the country, or sent to the seaside; or a husband and his men friends at the hunting lodge in Scotland — her supervision was further complicated. The mistress of the house was also responsible for making the arrangements for her house guests, organizing transportation, accommodation, meals, and entertainment, an increasingly demanding task when the weekend party became so popular late in the century. A housekeeper could not be expected to know the intricacies of precedence, personalities, and love affairs which dictated seating at dinner and the allocation of bedrooms, and she might not realize the importance of little details such as fresh flowers, new pens, and clean blotters in a visitor's room. For the conscientious hostess, planning for numerous guests was burdensome. Having to ensure that the "vast machinery of service" operated smoothly and unobtrusively severely taxed her memory and energies. "She must spare no effort and despise no trouble," complained Lady Greville. "Her head must be a perfect encyclopaedia, with its varied and always ready knowledge. Then she must never forget, never be ruffled, never be 'caught napping'."[76]

Consuelo Spencer-Churchill, wife of the ninth Duke of Marlborough, came to resent the strain weekend parties entailed,[77]

> for my round of the thirty guest-rooms, accompanied by the housekeeper, was apt to reveal some overlooked contingency too late to be repaired; a talk with the chef more often disclosed an underling's minor delinquency; orders to the butler invariably revealed a spiteful desire to undermine the chef . . . that, if realized, . . . would jeopardize the culinary success of my party. Menus had to be approved and rooms allotted to the various guests. I had, moreover, spent hours placing my guests for the three ceremonial meals . . . , for the rules of precedence were then strictly adhered to. . . . There was . . . a considerable amount of purely mechanical work to be done — dealing with correspondence, answering invitations,

writing the dinner cards and other instructions ... which took up a great deal of my time.

Some landowners' wives, preoccupied with a frenetic social life, or with philanthropy or other pursuits, delegated housekeeping to head servants. This was particularly true of the nobility, who could easily afford competent house stewards, housekeepers, and butlers. Many great ladies did no more than confer with department heads about the day's arrangements, although the scale of their entertaining still made this a demanding task.

Less wealthy and fashionable mistresses, home much of the year, became more involved in day-to-day housekeeping. Not all landowners could afford a housekeeper; nearly half of the baronet and gentry households in the census sample had no housekeeper or cook-housekeeper, and a tenth kept only two or three female house servants. Lower incomes necessitated closer supervision and accounting, and more household

Plate 16 Mrs Sperling and her maid swatting flies at Dynes Hall

chores, not only in the mansion, but in the gardens and home farm. Lady Shiffner sold home-farm produce, paid household bills, and hired and paid the female servants. "Not merely a manager, she performed everyday housekeeping tasks; in 1894, for example, she prepared an inventory of the linen and china," Patricia Blackwell discovered. "The notes in her recipe book suggest that she not only planned menus, but also helped execute them." At Hodnet Hall, Gladys Heber-Percy ran the stables and gardens as well as the house, daily giving orders to all heads of departments, obtaining supplies from the estate, and issuing stores once a week.[78]

The mistress was most involved in the smallest households. Mary Ann Dixon did the household accounts and shopping lists, gave out stores, and arranged and supervised her servants' and daily helpers' work. She checked over the plate, bedding and linen, wrote inventories, labelled and put away wine and spirits, tidied her dressing-room, helped shake carpets, and gathered flowers. In the kitchen she processed the home-killed pig, cooked sweets for dinner parties, made pastries for the school feast, preserved fruit, and even cooked breakfast occasionally. Looking over her own and her children's clothing, she cut out garments and linen for seamstresses to sew. She also designed the garden, superintended and helped with sowing and planting, did the annual pruning, and closely supervised the gardener and his helpers.[79]

Some women relished their role, proud of their ability to run the household efficiently. Margaret Hobhouse "enjoyed being in the position of giving orders and superintending the smooth working of a large household."[80] Not all landowners' wives, however, were temperamentally suited to housekeeping. Domestic matters bored and bewildered Lady Sitwell, who was incapable of keeping accurate accounts. Mrs Gibbons found running a household tiring and trying, and disliked ordering dinners. Yet housekeeping was an unavoidable duty. Mrs Jebb "was not domesticated although she tried hard to be." She "worried over expenses, accounts and the servants. Her diaries are full of resolves to look better after her household."[81]

Far from being idle, the chatelaine often felt overworked. The duties of housekeeping, entertaining guests, and caring for the poor caused unceasing demands on her time. Discussing this problem, Catherine Milnes Gaskell created a representative character who exemplified the overburdened chatelaine. "Household duties are ever with you," complained "Lady Cleremont." "Something in a large household has always to be ordered, and counter-ordered. Telegrams arrive at all hours. Fresh guests come, or... write to say that they are detained at the last moment. Nothing is too small, nothing too trivial, for a woman's ears." Comparing herself unfavourably to her husband, who could insist on uninterrupted solitude for his own work, she lamented, "I as a woman have no recognized leisure." Lady Cynthia Asquith characterized the chatelaine's life as a kind of slavery. "What with the cares of family, household and tenants; incessant village duties;... the trickiness of parochial politics and the perpetual coming and going of guests," she "seldom had a disengaged hour in which to read, let alone follow any pursuit." Running a large country house "left its mistress too little privacy, condemned her to too much unceasing thinking ahead, to be compatible with any satisfying life of her own."[82]

Chatelaines' lives were less frenetic earlier in the century, and among the gentry, where responsibilities and opportunities were more local and limited. In the 1850s, Mrs Blake Humphrey's daily routine began with an early breakfast, followed by fifteen minutes reading the Bible or a sermon to her children. Next, she ordered dinner and gave out the stores. "From about 10 to 11 she wrote her letters and did her accounts, then read some deep book till 12, and either painted in water-colour or walked out into the village till 1." After lunch, she revisited the village, paid calls, or went to Norwich.[83] In the late 1880s, Gaskell identified the growing demands placed on the lady of the house, in the complaint of "Lady Cleremont".[84]

> I try and get through some fourteen hours of work.... Everyone comes to me for advice, orders, sympathy, and information.... I speak in public, open bazaars, address political clubs and associations, write for several magazines, have a numerous correspondence with my own family and with friends, literary and political, preside over and superintend several political and charitable organizations, whilst all the time I have my children to educate and see after, my husband to play lady-in-waiting to, my household matters to superintend and regulate, my parish in sickness to provide and care for, and the county neighbours to call on and entertain.

The lives of country house women had expanded over the century. In the 1820s, women's roles in Society and in philanthropy became established. Regency wives had more freedom than had the first generation of Victorian wives, confined to the home as they were by domesticity, respectability, and notions of female delicacy. Abandoning public gatherings, early-Victorian wives retreated to a private world of face-to-face relationships: the landed classes' social gatherings in London became largely private family functions held in the home; the lady's philanthropy, both in London and at home, was mostly through informal, personal visits; and women's publications were often under a penname. By mid-century, however, the aristocracy and gentry were more active in urban philanthropy, becoming patronesses and officers of many charitable organizations, and volunteering in numerous projects in the East End. Their social life was enlarged, as they transformed formerly masculine events such as the Ascot and Goodwood races, the Eton–Harrow cricket match, and the Henley Regatta into fashionable social fixtures, and added garden parties and other female-dominated entertainments to the social agenda. Late in the century, married women gained more freedom to move about and associate in public places such as restaurants and women's clubs. Athletic young women took up hitherto masculine sports such as golf and yachting, and a few even went shooting and stalking.

Influenced by what contemporaries called the Woman Question (the debate over women's expanding demands and activities), late-Victorian wives began to insist on their own self-development. Like "Lady Cleremont", they aimed "at growing a soul in spite of being a wife, a mother, and a hostess."[85] The concept of men and women occupying separate public and private spheres was breaking down, as women sought a greater role in the public arena. Georgiana Hill thought a new ideal of womanhood was being created in the 1890s, which rejected "physical weakness and mental indolence.... Neither the *rôle* of pleasure nor of domesticity suffices. A woman is expected to share in all the social and intellectual activities around her." Women "decline to be kept in a world of their own," she declared. "They would rather be in the larger world of action, where men will meet them on equal terms, and treat them as comrades and fellows." Now the great lady was expected to develop her mind, to "attend committees and conferences, pore over accounts and blue books." She was part of "the work-a-day world of politics, philanthropy, literature, and even trade."[86]

Upper-class ladies championed the cause of various groups of disadvantaged women and children, supported a growing range of charitable institutions, and published numerous books and articles. Some chatelaines shared country life with the underprivileged and unwell, building

Plate 17 Lady Elena Wickham out shooting c.1897

convalescent homes on the estate, or arranging country holidays for city children. Women now participated in local government, both as electors and as councillors or guardians. Politicians' wives attended debates and public dinners, presided over meetings, and delivered speeches during their husbands' campaigns. In political organizations, notably the Primrose League, ladies continued to develop their political activities and skills, further undermining the concept of separate spheres, and reconciling Conservative politicians to a limited female suffrage. Although most female members had been indifferent or even hostile to women's suffrage, many of them were converted by 1914, through the unending debate over this issue within women's organizations.[87] Enterprising landed women even opened fashionable shops in London, to sell the goods made by their protégées, raise funds for their pet charities by offering produce from the estate, or earn income for themselves by exploiting a talent in dress or hat designing.

Millicent Leveson-Gower, fourth Duchess of Sutherland, exemplified this versatile great lady. Blessed with beauty and an exalted status, she was soon lionized as a brilliant Society hostess. But she wanted her talents and energies utilized in more constructive ways. As a patroness of the arts, she held literary gatherings at Stafford House, and befriended novelists, playwrights and poets, inviting them to stay at her country houses. She read widely, not only in English, French and German literature, but also in social policy and politics. The duchess sought a reputation as an author herself, with two novels and a book of short stories, and put on a play in blank verse under a pseudonym. She was acutely conscious of social injustice, and felt a strong sense of responsibility to help others. Coming to believe that the working classes deserved help to gain the education and skills needed to overcome poverty, she implemented practical schemes on the Sutherland estates to promote economic independence there: these included reviving the homespun tweed industry in Scotland, with annual sales at Stafford House, and creating the Golspie Technical School. In Staffordshire, the duchess campaigned successfully against poisonous lead glazes in the pottery industry, built a holiday home for poor children at Trentham, and founded the Potteries and Newcastle Cripples' Guild. This provided medical care and vocational training in crafts for crippled children in their own homes, a residential home, and a clinic. She tirelessly raised funds for her causes, holding a spectacular bazaar and fête at Trentham in 1908. A prominent member of the Primrose League, she supported women's suffrage, too.[88]

Single women shared in women's widening sphere. Their first opportunity to carve out a career away from home was in religion. On her father's death in 1869, Caroline Boileau became a travelling preacher. Lady Edith Fielding went as a missionary to China.[89] In Catholic families, many unmarried daughters became nuns, while Anglicans joined the Sisterhoods, the Church of England's equivalent orders. Olive Banks shows that the few Victorian feminists from the gentry were more likely than other feminists to demand autonomy and independence for unmarried women.[90] By 1906, it was "more usual" for unmarried daughters "to receive their portions and to seek a life of their own instead of lingering on in the ancestral home."[91] They often went into social work and teaching, careers acceptable as extensions of women's nurturing function. Eglantyne Jebb, for instance, read history at Lady Margaret Hall, Oxford, from 1895. With her strong social conscience, she yearned to do something useful for others. She trained as a teacher, but found she disliked teaching. For two years, she lived with her mother and family in Cambridge without paid employment. Heartbroken when the young man she loved married another, she lost any desire for marriage. She then worked for the Charity Organization Society, undertaking a survey of poverty in Cambridge published in 1906. Accompanying her mother abroad, she wrote a novel about social injustice, and in 1913 went on a relief mission to Macedonia to help refugees there.[92]

The stereotype of idle, useless ladies is clearly inaccurate and invalid. Women of the landed classes led active, purposeful lives, performing valid, useful, and important functions as companionate wife, mother, mistress of household and staff, hostess, participant in Society, and philanthropist. These roles were conscientiously undertaken as recognized and valued duties. Most landed women were contented with their lot. They obtained their sense of identity from their gentle birth and the privileges of rank, and their sense of worth and purpose in life from the satisfaction of doing their duty. Landed women knew they made real and important contributions to their marriage, to their children's upbringing, to the household and even the estate, and to the needy; to the family's long-term reputation and power; and to the survival of their class. This is doubtless why so few landed women were liberal feminists demanding equality with men, and why upper-class women took so long to see the merits of women's suffrage.

Once again, this investigation of women's lives has demonstrated that the landed family living in the country house differed from families in other classes and even from other upper-class families. The same was true of the rest of the country house community – the domestic staff. Country house service was a particular type of domestic service, recognized as the elite sector of the occupation, with its own distinctive characteristics. The landowner's social position, customs, traditions, and code of values shaped life below stairs just as much as they did above stairs.

6

Staff Size

As with the family, this survey of country house servants begins by counting heads. Historians of domestic service and of the country house assert that the landed classes felt obliged to hire the largest staffs they could afford, in order to keep up their social position.[1] But census enumerators' schedules and household records reveal that they often managed with less than the full complement of servants appropriate for their rank and income. A family's changing needs and preferences, rather than conventional standards, determined the types and numbers of servants kept.

All landowners kept servants as a matter of course. The country house way of life could not exist without servants. Like anyone else who could afford it, landowners hired servants to relieve themselves of what they saw as the demeaning, defiling, menial tasks of cooking, housework, laundry, childcare, stablework, and gardening.[2] Like the middle classes, they utilized servants as status symbols and actors in ceremonial social rituals. Yet landowners required larger, more specialized and more masculine establishments than the typical middle-class staff of one to three maidservants.

To begin with, landowners' homes were much larger and grander than the typical middle-class home. With its suite of richly furnished reception rooms, numerous guest bedrooms, labyrinthine service quarters, and extensive gardens, the country house required constant, labour-intensive maintenance. The laborious methods of heating, lighting, and bathing made these tasks more arduous in the country house, as servants had to carry coals, water, and slops much further and more often, clean more steel-grated fireplaces, and light and clean more lamps. Even when gas, piped water and, later, electricity, became available, many landowners stubbornly resisted the new technology as untraditional and decadent.

Servants also performed an important function in manufacturing high-quality domestic products which would otherwise have to be bought. Landed estates had their own resources to do this on a far larger scale than the middle-class household. Gamekeepers contributed game, gardeners grew vegetables, fruit, and flowers, and the dairymaid made cheese and butter using milk and cream from the home farm. In the stillroom, the housekeeper or the stillroom maid prepared jams and preserves, and ladies' maids, housemaids and menservants concocted the powders, polishes, and lotions needed for their work. Maids sewed clothing and stuffed pillows and mattresses. Some remote country houses, such as Hampton Court in Herefordshire, still employed women to spin and weave cloth early in the century.[3]

Another factor which expanded staff size in the country house was the Victorian enthusiasm for specialization and subdivision. Ideally, each group of inhabitants was assigned separate quarters and staircase, according to age, sex, and occupation, and each function was allocated a room, all connected by long corridors. Compartmentalization multiplied the number of rooms to be cleaned and the distance loads had to be carried. Three separate meals were served: to the adult family and their guests, to the children, and to the servants. In great houses, different dinners were served in the dining-room, schoolroom, nursery, housekeeper's room, servants' hall, and kitchen. Each servant was trained in one sphere of work, and was not expected to perform the duties of another. Thus individual servants had to be hired for each branch of service, and, in large establishments, for specific positions within the hierarchy.

The servants themselves created a demand for labour: someone had to prepare their food, wash their dishes, and clean their rooms. In great houses, a steward's-room boy, and a housekeeper's girl served upper servants, a kitchen-maid specialized in servants' meals, and the lowest housemaid and a charwoman devoted themselves entirely to the servants' quarters.

Houses of this scale and complexity were necessary for the conspicuous consumption and open-handed hospitality characteristic of the landed lifestyle. The family changed clothes several times a day, and expected numerous dishes or several courses at meals, served in silverware cleaned daily. Great aristocrats insisted upon fresh flower arrangements every day, ironed newspapers and shoelaces, and even washed coins. Visitors meant more housework and laundry, and more elaborate meals and entertainments. Most landlords preserved game and rode to hounds. Hunting dress took hours to clean.

Servants were also required as "deference-givers." Living symbols of the landowner's status and wealth, they confirmed his power and prestige with their exaggerated deference and obedience in front of impressed visitors. Only well-trained "front-stage" servants could perform the complex ceremonies of etiquette and hospitality correctly, and formalize and regulate their employers' encounters with callers, the lower servants, and even the children.[4]

Finally, servants were plentiful and cheap, paid low wages compared to landed incomes. Accommodating and feeding servants cost less in a roomy country house sustained by the gardens and home farm than in an urban mansion. Throughout the century, an ample supply of recruits eagerly sought country house service. The lesser gentry spent proportionately less on servants than did the nobility, who often owned several house (with all the waste and expense of unsupervised housekeeping and board wages), and whose elaborate public lifestyle required more menservants, costlier in both wages and upkeep than maidservants.

To what extent did rank and income determine staff size? Correlating staff numbers in the 1871 census with the only national survey of rental incomes, *The Return of Owners of Land*, of 1872–3, is the most comprehensive and readily available test. But exact staff size cannot be conclusively deduced from the census alone for numerous reasons. Some servants may have been absent on census night, or a servant who had recently departed might not yet have been replaced. Sometimes an absent family member might have been accompanied by a personal servant or a groom. Indoor servants heading nearby households may have worked elsewhere. In parishes containing several large establishments, it is often impossible to tell where gardeners or grooms living out were employed. They were, moreover, seldom labelled "domestic servant" as required, even when living in the "head gardener's cottage" or "rooms over stables." Some may have worked in market gardens, on farms, or in commercial livery stables. Where the landowner kept up the local hunt, or the parish included a horse stud, calculating the number of strictly domestic grooms is especially problematic. Furthermore, outdoor men living in outlying parts of large estates may have been overlooked. For most census-sample households, no 1871 wages lists survive as a means of correcting errors.

Another serious drawback of the census evidence is the fact that great landowners often possessed several estates, with a caretaker domestic staff in each house, and gardeners and gamekeepers outdoors. Locating the family on census night does not reveal a full picture of their expenditure on domestic servants, particularly where owners were residing in one of their lesser houses. At the time of the 1871 census, the Duchess of Sutherland and two of her daughters were at Lilleshall, with a staff of nine indoor menservants, eighteen indoor maidservants, and five stablemen, assisted by five weekly helpers. On the estate were a dairymaid, two gamekeepers, a gardener, and a garden labourer. The absent Duke had at least his valet with him. Still at Trentham, however, were seven women servants looking after the house, three laundresses, a house carpenter, a baker and brewer, a house porter, a poulterer, a dairy-maid, a coachman, stud groom and four grooms, thirteen gardeners, and at least one gamekeeper. In addition, a skeleton domestic staff remained at Stafford House in London, and at Dunrobin, Tarbat House, and Lochinver House in Scotland, along with gamekeepers and other outdoor men.[5]

Just as accurate counts of staff size are impossible from the census alone, so Bateman's list of landed income cannot reveal the actual disposable income of each of the census sample's landowners in 1871. Many landowners had other sources of income, such as investments and shares, urban property, mines, or other commercial or industrial enterprises. The *nouveaux riches* did not always relinquish profitable occupations on becoming landed gentlemen. What portion of every sample family's landed income was actually available for servants is impossible to calculate, for much could be consumed by debts, jointures, portions, and annuities. In 1852, Ralph Sneyd's gross income was £42,686 (£11,246 from farm rentals and £9,093 in mine rentals) from which £2,089 was paid out in annuities, and £6,607 in interest.[6] He spent £950, just 2 per cent of his gross income, on servants' wages that year, nearly half of it on garden labour. When the sixth Baron Monson succeeded in 1841, debts and jointures severely depleted his only income – farm rentals – to between £6,000 and £7,000 a year. He economized with a staff of around ten.[7]

While the census sample enlarged to 187 establishments shows a broad association of income with staff size, with mean sizes of indoor establishments rising steadily with landed income, from just six servants at £1,000–£2,000 to twenty-two for incomes over £20,000, the wide range within each income bracket indicates that although income set the upper limits, the landed classes did not necessarily employ as many servants as they could afford (table 6.1). Lynne Haims, in her dissertation on country house servants, agrees that "the size of income alone cannot predict staff size." Comparing landed incomes and staffs of forty great landowners with over £10,000 in rentals, she found "no very clear correlation," especially with staffs of over twenty.[8]

Table 6.1 Landed income and number of indoor servants

Income	Number of cases	Mean number of servants	Range
£20,000 +	26	22.26	12–31
£10,000 +	28	15.00	5–21
£ 5,000 +	39	10.34	5–18
£ 4,000 +	21	11.15	2–12
£ 3,000 +	28	7.25	3–14
£ 2,000 +	23	7.16	4–10
£ 1,000 +	22	6.05	4–11

Sources: J. Bateman, *The Great Landowners of Great Britain and Ireland* (1883 edition); *Return of Owners of Land*, 1872–3, Parliamentary Papers, 1874, LXXII; 1871 census of England and Wales.

The census sample gives an average indoor staff size of ten. Nearly a fifth had just seven indoor servants, and almost a quarter kept a smaller indoor staff.[9] Given the difficulties in calculating outdoor-staff numbers, the average total domestic staff of seventeen is a tentative estimate. The results show that by 1871, at least, the landed classes were not intent on maintaining their rank by spending as much as they could on servants.

By this time, rank was not a clear determinant of staff size. In earlier centuries, this had certainly been the case, when great magnates' power was embodied in retinues of hundreds. In the eighteenth century, however, wealth challenged status: prosperous merchants and successful manufacturers emulated the landed classes with large establishments. To reassert their social superiority, the aristocracy felt compelled to expand staff size, especially with "front-stage" menservants. Aristocrats vied with each other in lavishing their growing incomes on impressive establishments. They paid higher wages to upper menservants and sought the ultimate status symbol, a French chef. Keeping vast establishments became more punitive during the Napoleonic Wars, when prices and wages both rose, and new taxes were levied on menservants, carriages, and horses. But when prices and wages fell after 1815, great magnates promptly resumed the contest until the 1830s. At this point some found the extra expense brought no benefits, while others may have considered it judicious, in the face of middle-class criticism and working-class discontent, to consume less conspicuously. In addition, moving the household from house to house by the new railways reduced both the occasion for display and the need for stable staff.[10] For the next few decades, staff size indoors remained stable, although the Victorians did keep more gardeners and gamekeepers than their predecessors.[11]

Plate 18 A typical peer's establishment: the Earl of Sandwich's staff at Hinchingbroke, 1906

Peers were expected to have the largest establishments. When William Onslow became the fourth Earl of Onslow, he felt obliged "to keep up a good deal of state" at Clandon with "a large staff of servants."[12] It was usually nobles who owned the great houses which, according to both contemporary observers and historians, contained between thirty and fifty indoor servants.[13] Yet in 1871 the average size of a peer's indoor establishment was just twenty, with around sixteen outdoor men.[14]

Nobles were supposed in theory to retain a full complement of menservants to carry out public rituals of deference and symbolize their masters' wealth and power. Manuals "considered requisite" a house steward, a prestigious man cook, a groom of chambers, a butler and under-butler, a valet for each gentleman, two or three footmen, and a hall boy or two.[15] But many earls and dukes did without a house steward and few peers employed a man cook.[16] Many of these nobles felt no compulsion to maintain impressive numbers of menservants, at least while they resided in their country seats. A third of the 1871 sample of peers kept fewer than four indoor menservants. Within the peerage, staff size was not rigidly graduated according to rank. Though barons generally did have smaller establishments than their superiors, dukes often kept smaller staffs than lesser peers.[17]

Baronets, ranking above commoners but below the peerage, had establishments commensurate with their lower status, typically around fourteen indoor servants and another ten or so outdoors.[18] Yet they differed little from wealthy commoners: when matched with gentry of similar landed incomes, they had on average only one more servant.

Comparing the peer sample with the rest of the sample of 100 shows that by 1871 title alone did not determine establishment size. While the majority of dukes, marquesses and earls had larger indoor staffs than any commoners, others, like most of the barons, had staffs no larger than those of baronets or wealthy commoners.

The gentry contained gradations of status too, from great landowners accepted in aristocratic circles, through county families, to the lesser or "parish" gentry. Social standing, however, played even less of a role in determining staff size among the gentry. At one extreme, newly gentrified plutocrats boasted establishments as large as most peers'. At the other extreme, historians disagree on the minimum staff compatible with gentry status, ranging from F. M. L. Thompson's five or six to Jill Franklin's fifteen indoors.[19] In the census sample, eight families had fewer than eight servants altogether, but only one – the Hales of Somerton Hall, who survived with a cook, a housemaid, a coachman, and a gamekeeper – fell below Thompson's most accurate minimum of five. Every household manual insisted on one indoor manservant, the symbol of gentility, even for incomes of £1,000, but seven gentry families kept no manservant at all on census night.

The lady's maid or valet also symbolized high status. In first-rate establishments, asserted household guides, each adult family member was allowed his or her own personal servant. All upper-class wives were expected to have a lady's maid, although two daughters could share one young lady's maid in less exalted houses. Yet almost one in five of the sample families with females aged over sixteen on census night employed no lady's maid. Nearly half the families with one lady's maid contained more than one adult female. In the peer sample, all the women had lady's maids, but some daughters still shared. Wealthy men, the manuals presumed, would need a valet; in the 1820s those with incomes over £3,000 expected to afford him, as would men with more than £4,500 in the 1840s.[20] In fact, most of the landed classes relied on the versatile butler to double as valet. In the census sample, only ten households – all with landed incomes over £6,000 – had valets, including three peers and two baronets. Nearly a third of the peer sample, moreover, managed without a valet.

Some historians of domestic service assume that Victorian employers followed the principle advanced in *The Servants' Practical Guide* that "establishments graduate downward as . . . incomes . . . also graduate."[21] According to John Burnett, tables of expenditure published in manuals of domestic economy prove that the middle classes' "pattern of servant-building was regulated by a well-understood system, dictated primarily by income" – a "widely accepted practice" of devoting about 12 per cent of income to servants, plus another 10 per cent for stable staff if a carriage were kept.[22] But such works were intended for the upwardly mobile, uncertain of the establishment appropriate for their new social status, and reflected ideal goals rather than reality. In his study of middle-class households in Rochdale in 1851–71, Edward Higgs discovered that many contained no live-in servants at all, or spent far less than 12 per cent of their income on servants. "Even those households which did employ servants could choose to spend more or less of their incomes to meet their own needs, rather than follow the dictates of Mrs Beeton."[23] Manual-writers themselves disagreed on the requisite number of servants for incomes over £1,000. As some excluded gardeners or gamekeepers in their calculations, only house and stable staff are compared here. In the mid-1820s, Samuel and Sarah Adams, both experienced upper servants, assumed families with £1,000 a year needed four maidservants, a footman, a coachman, and a groom-gardener, whereas *A New System of Practical Domestic Economy* recommended just two menservants and three maidservants. Alfred Cox permitted only two female servants and one manservant in his 1852 budget, but J. H. Walsh thought two men and four women permissible in 1857. No greater consistency occurred for incomes over £5,000. The Adamses suggested thirteen menservants and nine maids, but the *New System* only nine men and ten maids. In 1844 Thomas Webster allotted such incomes twelve servants of each sex, but the more prudent Cox allowed five men and six women.[24]

In any event, the landed classes disregarded these recommendations. Alfred Cox advised that landowners with incomes of over £20,000 could budget for twenty-seven indoor servants; two-thirds of qualified sample establishments were smaller. He also limited those with incomes of £5,000 to nine indoor servants; but half of the sample's ten families with landed incomes of £5,000 to £6,000 kept more.[25]

Owners made their own choices: some regarded a certain staff size as indispensable, while others preferred to spend their money elsewhere. The Hon. Frederick Wynn, an elderly retiring bachelor, was served by "a full establishment" of seven indoor men, twenty-one maidservants, eight in the stables, and sixteen in the gardens. His staff "accepted it as the done thing." He "was only keeping the same establishments as his father and grandfather had, it was his birthright."[26] The Packes wanted impressive establishments at Prestwold and Charles Street in the 1880s; in 1889, they spent 17 per cent of their gross income on servants' wages, board wages, liveries and journeys, and charwomen.[27] The second Duke of Sutherland went into debt, even selling assets and land, in order to lavish vast sums on his household – between £30,000 and £40,000 a year in the 1840s.[28] At his principal seat at Northwick, the second Baron Northwick kept up to sixteen house and stable servants, a considerable staff for one man, but modest for a peer. He obviously preferred spending his money on his magnificent art collection. In 1907, Lady Northwick's income (mainly from investments) exceeded £17,000, yet she spent under £500 on servants' wages, compared to £800 on charity and £1,500 distributed as gifts to friends and relatives.[29] The impoverished sixth Baron Monson wished for "a few extra comforts that we ought to have such as carriage horses and coachman," but spent an eventual surplus on farm improvements. "Social pressures were not irresistible," notes F. M. L. Thompson, "the Monsons gave every indication of managing happily with a domestic establishment of about the size that a plain country gentleman might keep."[30]

Staff size may also have been affected by regional traditions. In Northumberland, Lady Ridley found it was customary to keep few servants.[31]

The gentry's staffs were possibly larger in the Home Counties, where the concentration of new wealth intensified social emulation, than among the more isolated, long-established lesser gentry of the far north. A sample of thirty-four Welsh households suggests that there the landed classes kept slightly more indoor servants than usual but fewer outdoor men.

Rank and income, therefore, influenced household size rather than neatly regulating it. Landowners' incomes limited the optimum size of their establishments, and considerations of rank might induce them to hire certain types of servants. But a greater degree of flexibility and personal choice prevailed than has hitherto been supposed. Each family's individual combination of circumstances, characteristics and interests, and changing needs over the life cycle, could modify the norms of social convention. Nevertheless, this refusal to conform was in itself a function of status: families whose social position was secure could defy convention with unexpectedly small staffs. The eccentricity tolerated in the gentry and nobility included a paucity of servants.

The family's changing structure and size also affected the number and type of servants employed. In most cases, servants were added or eliminated according to need, regardless of income, but families keeping the largest establishment they could afford substituted one type of servant for another as their priorities changed over time. Single owners could manage with a small staff; in the sample, one young unmarried baronet and his sister were served by only a butler, a house-boy, a housekeeper, and two housemaids, despite a landed income of £10,000.[32] At marriage, heirs usually set up a basic establishment, but on inheritance enlarged the staff to reflect their new position. When children arrived, nursery servants and later a governess were hired. Great landowners thought in terms of a head nurse served by an under-nurse and nursery-maids, and later hired a schoolroom maid. In less wealthy families with numerous children, more nursery and schoolroom servants forced economies in other departments, especially expensive menservants. The Pettiwards of Finborough Hall, who had nine daughters, employed a nurse, two nursery-maids, and two governesses among their nine maidservants, but only a seventeen-year-old footman as manservant.[33] Surprisingly, ten sample families with children aged from six to sixteen at home employed no resident governess. These children may have been taught by a local daily governess, but in some cases mothers or sisters undoubtedly gave lessons. Three families without governesses had older daughters at home.

Keeping adult daughters at home could augment or reduce staff. A young lady's maid might be hired. Families eager to marry off daughters may have attempted to maintain a suitably impressive household while they were fully involved in Society. On the other hand, adult daughters' help with housekeeping in gentry families with few inhibitions about housework may have reduced indoor staff. The elderly Dawsons of Aldcliffe, with two daughters in their thirties, employed only a cook and two housemaids, despite a landed income of nearly £3,300.[34] Widowers' daughters sometimes acted as housekeepers for their fathers: three sample widowers with adult daughters at home employed no housekeeper.

An extended family also added staff. The Musgraves of Eden Hall, for instance, housed an extra lady's maid and two nurses for their daughter-in-law and grandchild.[35]

Some widows and widowers living a quiet life alone had unusually small establishments. Richard Durant, aged eighty, was attended by only a housekeeper and a kitchen-maid indoors, though he could well afford more with just over £4,500 a year. Elderly or sick people sometimes required nurses; an "imbecile from birth" living with her brother and his wife at Nunwell was cared for by two nurses, while George, Lord Northwick, hired a male nurse in his last years.[36]

Finally, deaths reduced staff. Nursery staff or the governess were dismissed when a remaining child died, and a lady's maid when her mistress died. On his mother's death, a bachelor baronet sacked about half of his servants, as he "was now alone in the house."[37] After the owner died, most servants were normally discharged, as heirs usually had an establishment already, and selected their own additions. Following Thomas Giffard's death in 1823, only the housekeeper, under-butler, coachman, two gamekeepers, and a gardener continued in his son's service; the next heir paid all the servants off on taking over Chillington.[38] Departing family members removed servants too. The fourth Earl of Ashburnham's widow took eight servants with her to Barking Hall, and the two young lady's maids went with their mistresses. Several of the other servants left, leaving only twenty of the thirty-four under the new earl's employ.[39] The Yorkes and the Dixons illustrate the effects of the family life cycle and individual priorities on staff numbers over time. Three generations of Yorkes lived quiet, informal, and domesticated lives, seldom going into Society or travelling from their beloved Erddig. Consequently, they did not expect sophisticated service from their servants. Simon Yorke II kept a butler, but only one footman, and his wife had no lady's maid. There was a cook as well as a housekeeper, with two housemaids, a kitchen-maid, a laundry-maid, and a dairy-maid. Only a head gardener was kept, and just one gamekeeper. Nursery staff was redundant by 1820, and the governess and tutor left a year later. Upon inheriting in 1834, Simon Yorke III hired a second footman and later a lady's maid, but combined the positions of cook and housekeeper. Four children necessitated a nurse, a nursery-maid, a governess, and then a young lady's maid. A scullery-maid was added once the governess went. By the 1880s, however, Simon Yorke III faced financial difficulties. "Keeping down unnecessary Expenses" evidently included dismissing the lady's maids and replacing the second footman with a hall-boy. After Simon Yorke III's death, the household ran down, for Philip Yorke II did not live at Erddig until his estranged first wife died in 1899. Only after he remarried did his establishment expand, with a cook as well as the housekeeper, both second footman and hall-boy, a third housemaid, two more laundry-maids, and soon a nurse and nursery-maid.[40]

The aspiring squire Thomas John Dixon acquired a manservant as well as a cook, a housemaid, a kitchen-maid, a coachman, and a gardener, along with a nurse, a nursery-maid, and a governess when required. By 1861, a gamekeeper was kept, a lady's maid was hired from 1857 until 1864, and a second housemaid was added in the 1860s. After Thomas John Dixon died, his widow dispensed with an indoor manservant, as did her daughters when they in turn inherited, but the gamekeeper remained. Ann, with 2,275 acres and a rental income of £2,308 in 1873, employed a comparable staff, but her eccentric sister managed with a cook, a housemaid, a coachman, and a gamekeeper. Her successor, the Rev. Thomas Gibbons Dixon, was married with four children. He kept a cook, a housemaid, a between-maid (assisting both the housemaid and the cook), a nurse, a governess, a coachman, a gamekeeper, and a parlour-maid – this last because he was opposed to indoor menservants.[41] In these two households, the continuity of an established scale of living meant that basic staff size remained substantially unaltered, but changing family needs and personal preferences added some servants while making others redundant.

Servants listed on census returns are fewer than expected partly because country houses supplemented or replaced them with casual labour. These daily or occasional helpers were neither classified as domestic servants in census returns, nor listed as full-time servants; consequently

Plate 19 Mrs Jameson Dixon with menservants and Minnie Mumby, at Holton

historians have overlooked them in calculating staff size. In fact, the household could not have functioned smoothly without readily available local help. With the events of family life, guests and social activities, seasonal and intermittent household tasks, and staff absences, the numbers and needs of the household constantly expanded or contracted. To hire sufficient live-in staff for peak demand was impractical and uneconomical. Sending existing servants to assist in another department was neither acceptable to them nor did it promote an orderly, closely regulated routine. Great families, moreover, sought highly skilled and specialized staff who could hardly be expected to scrub their domains themselves. Part-time or temporary outside assistance gave the country house enough flexibility to meet its changing needs while minimizing disruption to its formal organizational structure. When the family moved to Scotland, to other residences, and above all to London, temporary servants could be hired to augment travelling staff. Families entertaining on a larger scale than usual hired extra staff for the London Season.

The most common daily helper, the charwoman, did the heavy rough work such as scrubbing floors, cleaning out water-closets, and the annual spring-cleaning. Labourers were called in to do odd jobs: to clean windows, move furniture, lift carpets, or carry luggage. Boys were engaged in smaller households for such tasks as knife-cleaning, boot-cleaning, running errands, and grooming ponies. Local women also helped in the laundry, as washerwomen or cleaners. In large establishments such as Trentham Hall or Petworth, as many as ten were employed virtually full time while the family was in residence, and an odd-job man hauled in the coals and turned the mangle.[42] In ordinary country houses, washerwomen assisted only on the busiest days, and with the annual washing of blankets and household linen. The washerwoman replaced a permanent laundry-maid entirely in the smallest country houses. At Holton local women came in two days a week to wash and iron until 1909, when the family began sending the laundry out to different village women.[43]

Outside assistance was needed less in the gardens and stables. Wealthy landowners kept sufficient full-time garden labourers, and stablemen performed heavy labour as part of their duties. Many estates also had their own craftsmen for maintenance work. Nevertheless, odd jobs still had to be done. Hussey Packe of Prestwold employed nine gardeners, yet additional labourers got in peat, cleaned orchards, shifted trees, cleaned the boiler, and moved beehives; women were hired for weeding, washing pots, mending netting, sewing blinds, and cleaning up after whitewashers.[44] Local women often worked part-time in country house gardens: in the 1870s, two or three at Casewick, and more at Englefield, worked for several weeks each year.[45] Men, women, and boys were engaged for "farm and garden labour" at Erddig, eliminating under-gardeners altogether.[46] Account books show little extra help in stables, where the work-load varied less, especially as visitors often brought their own coachmen or grooms. Women sometimes found employment in the stables, washing, cleaning, and nursing the sick. At Keele Hall in 1856, for instance, one woman did the washing, another cleaned the stablemen's rooms, and a third washed bed and stable linen.[47] Gamekeepers also needed extra help, as at Casewick, where village men and boys did night-watching, rabbiting or ferreting, and collected nests.[48] During the shooting season, many country houses hired local men and boys as beaters.

The self-sufficiency of the country house required further outside assistance with time-consuming seasonal tasks or work beyond servants' capacities. Local labourers or the odd-job man frequently assisted with brewing the servants' beer, or undertook the task themselves. At Petworth in 1816, two men brewed and another ground malt from March until early April, and again from November to early December, while the odd-job man cleaned the brewhouse, the cellar, and the tubs beforehand.[49] Village women assisted with food preparation: the Prestwold charwoman baked twice a week when the family was in residence, and at Holton local women prepared pork pies and sausages after the annual pig-killing.[50] Women repaired or replaced upholstery, draperies, and household linen, and sewed clothing for both family and servants. At Hampton Court in Herefordshire, needlewomen sewed nightwear, sheets, towels, table-cloths, and articles for the nursery, and at Prestwold a woman came in to make bed-hangings, chair-covers, and curtains.[51]

Local people assisted with the catering for shooting-parties, balls, and garden-parties, for estate events such as rent dinners or school treats, for large-scale family celebrations such as an heir's christening or coming-of-age, and for servants' balls. When all the family gathered at Hickleton for Christmas, villagers joined stablemen and gardeners in carrying food from the distant kitchens and helped with the washing-up. At Prestwold in the 1870s, local men even waited at the annual ball.[52] When permanent staff members departed, went on holiday or fell ill, village women were invaluable temporary replacements. At Erddig early in the twentieth century, the gardener's wife stood in for sick servants, and took over the kitchen when cooks left suddenly. Rushmere's two charwomen not only did the sick housemaid's work, but nursed her themselves.[53]

Individuals who had been called in repeatedly over the years became part of the country house community, more familiar and permanent than many transient lower servants. Alice Unwin, charwoman at Matfen in the 1830s, assisted the housemaids, worked in the kitchen, cleaned the nursery, and did washing in the laundry. From 1842 she cleaned the servants' hall weekly, plucked geese, nursed sick servants, and stood in for absent staff. When the family was at home, she worked three or four days a week.[54] In the smallest country houses, such women could become the mainstay of the household. At Holton, Jane Maddison did washing, cleaning, cooking, housework, and sick-nursing for over twenty years, often working with Mrs Dixon herself. In Mrs Jameson Dixon's time, her former personal maid, married to an agricultural labourer, came in during the day with her daughter to do housework. These daily helpers enabled the Dixons to keep a minimum resident staff.[55]

Another influence on staff numbers was the size of the country house itself, both in the labour required to maintain it, and in the accommodation and work space it offered servants. Jill Franklin directly relates the growth of service wings in Victorian country house plans to a rise in staff size over the period, arguing that owners built their houses to accommodate the number of servants they could afford, or enlarged their service wings to fit them in.[56] Mark Girouard disagrees. Instead he ascribes the growth in service wings to the Victorian preoccupation with propriety, comfort (for both family and servants), orderliness, and efficiency. Compared with their predecessors, these owners sought more privacy, further isolation from the servants' activities, stricter segregation of male and female servants, and higher standards of housekeeping and service. Housing larger families and many more visitors and guests meant more bedrooms, and larger kitchens and laundries.[57] Status-conscious upper servants, too, demanded their own bedrooms, workrooms, and sitting-rooms.[58]

Jill Franklin's theory further ignores the fact that the majority of country houses were built before the Victorian era, and many owners evidently found their service quarters adequate. "It is remarkable," Girouard observes, "how many country houses passed through the Victorian period with no alterations or minor and scarcely noticeable ones."[59] This was true of Erddig, where the eighteenth-century offices remained unchanged, except for the addition of three rooms for the housekeeper between the kitchen and the main block. Of the sample's 100 houses, just a fifth were built or rebuilt after 1815, with another quarter remodelled or enlarged.

Only landowners rebuilding or remodelling with the aim of elevating their scale of living, or accommodating a large family, increased their establishments. Richard Benyon rebuilt Englefield following a fire in 1886 without altering his lifestyle or numbers of staff.[60] In contrast, when Ralph Sneyd replaced his Elizabethan house with the mansion of his dreams, his goal included a more luxurious lifestyle. In 1851, before rebuilding, he kept a valet, a footman, a housekeeper, a cook, two housemaids, a stillroom maid, and a kitchen-maid. In 1864, three years after the new house was completed, the indoor staff included his valet (now promoted to house steward), a French cook, a groom of chambers, an under-butler, a footman, an usher of the hall, a housekeeper, a female under-cook, a stillroom maid, three housemaids, two kitchen-maids, a scullery-maid, and two laundry-maids.[61]

The relationship between house size and servant numbers was further complicated by the varying percentage of servants who slept in the country house. This depended on the availability of separate accommodation for married indoor and outdoor servants, on whether the stables, laundry, or dairy were separate buildings, and on the number of outdoor servants who lived in. Female servants generally lived in, though some laundry-maids slept in separate laundry buildings, and some dairy-maids lived at the home farm. Unmarried indoor menservants joined the main household, but so did unmarried or widowed coachmen, grooms, gardeners, and even bailiffs or agents. Many single grooms and gardeners, and all single gamekeepers, lived out, either residing with parents or relatives, or lodging with the department head, other house or estate employees, agricultural labourers, or widows. Single under-gardeners were sometimes housed together in a garden bothy, and grooms slept in rooms over the stables.

Most married outdoor men had their own cottage or a flat in the outbuildings. Head gardeners usually inhabited a house in the gardens, coachmen often had quarters in the stableyard, and gamekeepers an estate cottage. Married stablemen and under-gardeners usually lived in cottages on the estate or in the village. Occasionally, married coachmen or gardeners had rooms in the main house. In contrast, the majority of married indoor servants, both men and women, had to live apart from their spouses. Apart from couples who found employment together, few spouses lived in. In the census sample only seven butlers' wives lived in. A minority of married menservants lived out, in nearby housing. Three butlers spent census night in the mansion although their wives resided nearby. Fifteen married indoor menservants had gone home to self-contained dwellings, and a valet and his wife lodged with a widow. But fifty-three men and women were living apart from their spouses.

Day and casual workers, of course, lived out, in their own households. Some were parents, wives and children of full-time servants, but frequently the head of the household worked elsewhere. The country house community, then, included several small households clustered round the main one, plus those full- or part-time servants who were in lodgings or members of other nearby families.

This community grew smaller on many estates after the 1870s, as the long agricultural depression reduced landed incomes. Later, death duties and rising income taxes also cut the amount available for household expenditure, just as servants' wage rates rose steadily. Many families began combining positions such as cook and housekeeper, or replacing expensive menservants with cheaper parlour-maids. At Cranmer Hall in Norfolk, for instance, low or remitted rents forced the Joneses to close the laundry, dismiss first the footman and then the groom, and not replace the third gardener when he retired.[62]

Commercial developments facilitated staff reductions. A wide range of products – foods and beverages, household linens and cleaning materials – were now mass-produced. Department stores and mail-order services, the railway network, the telegraph, and later motor transport made commercial goods and services increasingly accessible. Landed families could order in bulk from elite London grocers and other firms, and have goods delivered to the country house. Bakeries delivered bread, breweries supplied barrels of ale, and commercial laundries picked up and delivered the washing. Central heating, plumbing, electricity, and domestic equipment such as washing machines and vacuum cleaners all lightened labour. Temporary domestic help became commercialized too, as growing numbers of professional, well-trained servants became available for hire "on the job," summoned by telegraph or telephone, and arriving promptly by rail. By the 1880s, the nobility and gentry were engaging highly skilled temporary cooks and professional waiters for important social events both in London and in the country. A family could create a suitably impressive staff for the Season in London, then retreat to a modestly staffed family seat. Eventually, catering firms managed the entire arrangements for social functions, held in fashionable hotels and restaurants.

The extent of staff reductions in the years 1870 to 1914 must await study of a larger sample and range of wage records, and of the entire run of census returns to 1911. Jill Franklin cites the obvious trend in house plans toward small compact service wings in this period as evidence that the landed classes deliberately reduced staff size late in the century. The supply of servants contracted, the cost of keeping them rose, and the quality of entrants declined, just as commercial and technological developments reduced household labour. Besides, "there was less social cachet to be had . . . from an outsize establishment."[63] But clients' or architects' preference for smaller service wings reveals new, even avant-garde, ideas in planning and work organization rather than a nation-wide decline in the landed classes' establishments. New, architect-designed houses in any decade represented only a small, atypical proportion of all country houses, and there is no evidence of widespread demolition of unwanted service wings in this period.

Jill Franklin further underestimates the conservatism of many landowners who resolutely refused to install bathrooms or washbasins, and insisted on coal fires and oil lamps. Brewing continued at some great houses, such as Lyme Park, Hickelton, Henham, Longleat, and Shirburn.[64] Many families still ran their own laundries. In large establishments, such as Goodwood and Petworth, laundries were still cost-effective and convenient: frequent entertaining produced vast amounts of soiled linens, let alone clothing; the plant was in place, and the wages and keep of a few laundry-maids were a comparatively minor expense. Economies were made by hiring more local women as day labour, as at Shugborough in 1910. Even lesser houses such as Erddig, Woolley Hall, and Hodnet Hall continued to have their own laundry.[65]

Household accounts show that many families did not significantly reduce their establishments before the First World War. In five Sussex country houses, concludes Patricia Blackwell, "household size seemed to change very little." At Goodwood, where agricultural income fell, retrenchment did not affect staff numbers.[66] At Erddig and Holton, staffs were actually larger in the last decade before 1914 than in 1871. Likewise, Lady Northwick employed more indoor servants than her bachelor predecessor in the 1840s.[67] Some landowners preferred to make cuts elsewhere. Impoverished by his gambling debts, Lord Elcho and his wife talked endlessly of retrenchment, but Stanway was "amply staffed." Instead, the family bought inferior, cheap horses, and travelled third class on the railway.[68] Furthermore, the number of "invisible servants," coming in daily or part-time, multiplied as the live-in staff diminished. Many impecunious families began employing daily help on a permanent basis to replace more expensive live-in maidservants.

To the very end of the period, the family's lifestyle, more than anything else, determined staff numbers and type. Secure in their high social status, the landed classes could disregard any social obligation to match their status and income with a certain staff size. Certainly, falling incomes constrained them, but at any level of wealth, the wide range of staff numbers proves that either personal choice or family needs were paramount. Inheritance patterns and the family or individual life cycle caused variations in the numbers and types of servants employed, while the owners' personalities, needs, and wishes could produce in some a desire to assert their position by the full staff appropriate for the family's rank, but in others a preference for a modest, even socially inadequate, staff. Paradoxically, the landed classes demonstrated their status and wealth not by accumulating as many servants as they could afford, but by keeping only the servants they wished to employ.

Motives determining staff size, then, were far more complex than hitherto supposed. So was the demography of country house servants. Four very different types of servants constituted the domestic staff of the nineteenth-century country house.

7

The Demography of Country House Servants

The staff of a nineteenth-century country house was an ever-changing group of people from diverse social and geographic backgrounds, varying in goals and motives in entering gentleman's service, and wide-ranging in age. The sheer range of occupations in country house service promoted this diversity, but servants themselves played a major role. Four distinct types of servants can be identified: the life-cycle servant who eventually abandoned service for another occupation or marriage; the career servant who made service a lifetime occupation; the "distressed gentlewoman," an impoverished single or widowed upper-or middle-class woman forced to earn a living; and the labourer, an unskilled full- or part-time worker. Each type differed in its pattern of social origins, motives, age at entry, promotion, geographical and job mobility, chances of marriage, and retirement. The distinct nature of country house service can only be understood fully when these four types are recognized. While the four types were found in domestic service elsewhere, the country house offered superior conditions to life-cycle servants, better treatment of distressed gentlewomen, greater opportunities for advancement to ambitious career servants, and more permanent positions for labourers.

The majority of female country house servants were life-cycle servants. Labouring men, too low-paid to support their families, and following traditional norms, sent their children out to earn additional income. Their daughters entered the work force by their early teens, typically working for at least ten years before marrying.

Such parents deliberately sent daughters into service, even when other jobs were available. Each departure meant one child less to feed, clothe and accommodate. Parents regarded service as the most suitable employment for girls, preparing them for marriage both practically and psychologically. Living in a family, under the control and protection of a master and mistress, was seen as more natural for the subordinate and dependent sex. Girls expected to gain valuable housekeeping skills, and to become more cultured and refined. Working for a gentleman's family, explained a former maid, was "a finishing education to every working man's daughter."[1] Some considered factory work degrading, or argued that working conditions in service were cleaner and healthier. Real wages, when room and board were included, were actually higher. Provided with accommodation and food, maidservants could save for marriage, or send money home to hard-pressed parents. Many maids from Juniper Hill sent half or more of their wages home.[2] In general, girls from authoritarian families, which stressed hard work, obedience, sexual purity, and duty towards the family, were most likely to accept unquestioningly the restrictions of domestic service.

Theresa McBride believes maidservants used service as a "bridging occupation" providing "the conditions and opportunities which facilitate the movement from one occupation to another" – in their case, marriage. Country girls took posts in cities as a path of transition to urban life, obtaining not merely shelter, supervision, and security while they grew up; but also a means of becoming independent of their families and geographically and socially mobile.[3]

Many girls, then, entered service to support themselves until they were old enough to marry, improving their prospects with savings and domestic skills. They sought tolerable work, good wages, congenial company, and opportunities to meet men. Enterprising life-cycle servants were attracted to the better conditions, lighter work, and higher wages of country house service, and to the companionship of a large staff with numerous menservants.

Not all life-cycle servants were female. Young boys uncertain about what they wanted to do could enter service with no real intention of making it their career. Some men became servants to accumulate capital to buy their own business, or to acquire skills they could utilize in a related career. Men who had worked in livery stables, hotels, and nursery gardens drifted in and out of country house service, some as casual or temporary employees.

Other servants appear to be life-cycle servants because they took up another occupation as they grew older. Housekeepers and cooks bought lodging houses, former chefs started restaurants, and butlers invested in public houses. However, many of them had not left service prematurely but had reached the usual time of retirement for their particular branch of service. Lady's maids, for instance, were expected to be fairly youthful, so an ageing lady's maid who became a milliner was not necessarily exploiting service as a bridging occupation.

Career servants deliberately made a lifetime occupation of domestic service, working their way up to the rewards of being an upper servant, and making their home in the country house community. Only in country houses could they obtain the first-class training and status which were a passport to situations in the best families. The wider contacts of a large staff, and the interest and help of employers and their friends were also advantageous.

Men, as the chief family income-earners, were more likely than women to see service as a lifetime's vocation. Given the range of occupations available to males, service was a deliberate career choice, based on aptitude and preference. Most head gardeners, coachmen, and gamekeepers were career servants. Ambitious boys entered indoor service intent on becoming butlers and valets. "I mean to get to the top," young Eric Horne resolved, "there seems to be nothing else for me but gentleman's service." Edwin Lee became convinced service would provide opportunities for advancement otherwise unavailable to farm labourers like himself.[4] Men who found marriage incompatible with their job eventually left, but others were determined to remain in service. For example, one married valet turned down an excellent chance to go into business in order to remain in service, even though he had to house his family in a nearby town.[5]

Some girls chose a career in service rather than marriage, perhaps deterred by the drudgery and subordination that was normally the lot of working-class wives. Hannah Cullwick, who worked for several years in country houses before becoming a maid-of-all-work in London, preferred being single: "I *like* the life I lead . . . better even I think than a married life."[6] Country house service was, in fact, the best occupation for a working-class woman who rejected marriage and sought economic independence. A place as a housekeeper, cook, head nurse, or lady's maid in a great mansion provided a good income, a comfortable standard of living, and security through savings and a pension.

There is no simple correlation of upper servants with career servants and lower servants with life-cycle servants. Normally, career servants trained as lower servants, and talented, ambitious life-cycle servants might seek good wages as upper servants before leaving service. A few lower servants were career servants, too, contentedly living out their working lives as a dairy-maid, head laundry-maid or head housemaid.[7] The vital difference between a career servant and a life-cycle servant was less a matter of fate – in finding no alternative to service – than of motivation – at some stage choosing to remain in this occupation.

Distressed gentlewomen usually entered service unwillingly, but they had little choice. They were middle-class women – penniless widows or single women whose fathers had died or become impoverished – who were forced to support themselves, and even their families, by earning a living as a governess, a lady's companion or a lady housekeeper. Well-bred ladies did lose social status on taking paid employment, but entering a private household was the least degrading and blatant way of earning a living. They remained respectable, with their virtue protected; ladylike, waited upon by servants; and womanly, dependent and submissive in a patriarchal household. Status-conscious gentlewomen valued good living conditions and respect more than high wages, and refused to undertake manual labour or mix with the other servants. A lady who advertised in 1845 for a place as "a useful companion to an elderly lady or as a nursery governess" was willing "to make herself useful in any way not decidedly menial. As a comfortable home is her chief object, a small salary would suffice." Similarly, in 1875 a lady's companion desired "not a salary but a lady's treatment."[8] Ladies seeking

Plate 20   The gardeners at Beaulieu

a "surrogate home" rather than viewing themselves as paid employees were attempting to deny the reality of employment, argues M. Jeanne Peterson.[9]

From the 1890s Lady Crawshay led attempts to establish unmarried middle-class women as superior "lady-helps," who would indeed perform the work of the housemaid, the cook, or the nurse. Schools such as the Guild of Aids in Bath and the Guild of Household Dames in Cheltenham provided training. The Norland Nursing School and later the Princess Christian Nursery Training College offered "a new career to gentlewomen by birth and education." However, ladies and their employers were too class-conscious to feel at ease with the situation, and lady-servants proved unsuccessful, except in the nursery.[10]

Tutors were scarcely the male equivalent of distressed gentlewomen. Some tutors were young graduates undecided on a career, or failed schoolmasters who did tutoring as a short-term expedient. Many others were ordained clergymen, who were rewarded with a living in their employers' gift. They lived as members of the family, suffering few or none of the social disabilities endured by the governess.[11] As men, they were expected to earn a living, and tutoring was but a stage in their careers.

The fourth type of country house servant, the labourer, was a local person who performed low-paid, unskilled work. Farm workers, and their wives and children, sought part-time or casual labour in the country house to augment inadequate family incomes. Some part-time work was a kind of forced labour, linked to the husband's job or to a tied cottage.[12]

Men worked as garden labourers, stablemen or odd-job men, not as the first step to a higher-status career, but as permanent positions. With the limited aspirations of securing work and feeding their families, they were attracted by the steadier employment and greater rewards of country house service. Sometimes labourers were men lacking the capacity to do better. Odd-job men, according to Frederick Gorst, were "servants who had never thoroughly mastered their tasks, so they had not been able to rise above the most menial positions.... They were rarely entrusted with a job that required much grey matter."[13] Elderly men went into service at the mansion when they could no longer do more strenuous work. For instance, John Wickerstaff, a farm labourer on the Shugborough estate, eventually became the usher.[14]

Incompetent menservants were not the only ones who changed from one category to another over a lifetime: talented young labourers were encouraged and promoted; life-cycle servants observing the benefits of top positions in great houses developed ambitions to rise; maids and distressed gentlewomen who failed to find suitors resigned themselves to a career in service; nurses became so attached to their charges that they turned down proposals of marriage; and career servants became disillusioned or found service incompatible with marriage. Nevertheless, there are clear differences between these four types in their social origins, mobility, and rates of marriage.

Highest in social status were the middle-class distressed gentlewomen. A few of them were even disadvantaged relatives of the landed elite: both Henry Polderoy and Lord Crewe engaged an elderly cousin as housekeeper, and the Maynards' governess was the illegitimate daughter of aristocrats.[15]

Upper servants often came from higher social strata than lower servants. John Gillis found that housekeepers, cooks, lady's maids, and governesses applying to the Foundling Hospital in London were overwhelmingly from the upper working class or lower middle class. These higher ranks "were considered, and considered themselves, to be significantly superior both socially and culturally" to lower servants.[16] Artisans, tradesmen, shopkeepers, small farmers, and clerks could afford to keep their daughters at school longer, and trained them in the "graces and steady habits" employers wanted for upper servants.[17] Gillis's findings certainly apply to the country house. In the mansions near Juniper Hill, upper servants were "daughters of small farmers, innkeepers and farm bailiffs." Elsewhere, one housekeeper's father was an innkeeper and a cook's was a farmer; lady's maids' fathers included a farmer, a cashier, and a city clerk, and five nurses were daughters of a clockmaker, a publican, a hotel-keeper, a cobbler, and a small tradesman. Menservants' fathers included three farmers, a carriage-maker, and a baker and provender. In some cases, family disaster forced children to seek employment: one farmer died when his son was young, and the baker and provender went bankrupt.[18] Service had advantages over other occupations: instead of an apprenticeship, earnings began immediately, and room and board were provided. It was a haven for impoverished widows and deserted wives, too. The lesser gentry even took governesses from this class: John Baker White's governess was the daughter of a mastercraftsman in a powder works, while Constance Jones's daily governess was a local farmer's well-educated daughter.[19]

Servants' children often entered service themselves as a matter of course. Sons of coachmen, gamekeepers, and gardeners commonly followed their father's calling or chose other departments of service. Charles Cooper's grandfather, for example, was a coachman whose ten children all went into service. Edward Dukes "rejected an opportunity to be articled to a lawyer" to train as a gardener under his father at Kingston Lacy.[20]

Most country house life-cycle servants, like the mass of domestic servants, came from the unskilled working classes. Lower-working-class girls from poverty-stricken homes were handicapped by a lack of education and ignorance of relevant domestic skills. Many of them could not afford the required dresses, caps, and aprons.[21] Yet poor girls with aptitude, intelligence, and determination, or training and references from a smaller household, could attain the lowest positions in a country house, especially if recommended by a teacher, the vicar, or his wife. After labourers' daughters from Juniper Hill had had a year's experience, their mothers asked the vicar's daughter to find the girls places in nearby country houses.[22] Some working-class girls with ability and ambition could even become upper servants. Two cooks at Holton were daughters of a carter and a labourer, and a cook at Erddig was a coal-miner's daughter.[23]

Boys from poor families entered country house service more easily. Smart, willing boys were accepted indoors, and labourers' sons readily obtained positions in outdoor service, both as labourers and as trainees. In the census sample, nearly a third of the outdoor menservants living at home were the sons of farm workers.

Labourers' wives were recruited for part-time or casual work. So were widows, and wives of menservants, estate workers, and even rural tradesmen and artisans. At Trentham, for instance, the sewing women included the wives of a police sergeant, a cabinet-maker, and a house-painter.[24] Former maids who had married local men were especially favoured.

Most country house servants were rural-born. In the 1871 census sample, 79 per cent of the English and Welsh servants were born in country parishes or small towns.[25] Domestic servants as a whole overwhelmingly came from the country.[26] Country girls were almost universally expected to go into service. Few districts offered alternative employment, and rural girls lacked access to or knowledge about the urban labour market. Raised in a hierarchical and deferential community, they accepted the subordination of service. Employers themselves often demanded country girls, reputedly stronger, healthier, more docile, and more obedient.[27]

Familiar with the urban labour market's more varied opportunities, and unwilling to tolerate subservience, long hours, and loss of independence, fewer urban youngsters became servants. Those who did enter service were often reluctant to exchange the excitements of city life for the dull countryside. Nevertheless, one in five of census-sample servants were born in cities and towns. More women were urban-born than men, and more upper servants than lower servants. Furthermore, close to half of peers' upper women servants and only slightly fewer of their upper indoor men were urban-born.[28] As working for a great aristocrat was the career servant's ultimate goal, career servants were more often urban-born than life-cycle servants. Given the wider options available to them, these urban-born were deliberately selecting service as a career. Among outdoor servants, 7 per cent of gardeners, and over 8 per cent of gamekeepers were urban-born, perhaps attracted to the fresh air and freedom of the outdoor life glimpsed on visits to the countryside. Boys' interest in horses must have been easily aroused in cities and towns crammed with horse-drawn vehicles; a third of the coachmen were urban-born.

A small percentage of country house servants came from Scotland and Ireland, and from abroad. Scotland was renowned for good gardeners. Continental servants were status symbols: the most highly skilled and sought-after cooks were French chefs, and French or Swiss lady's maids were also fashionable. The landed classes sometimes engaged foreign tutors, masters to teach music and art, and German, Swiss, or French governesses and nursery staff to impart their own language to their charges.

The four types of servant tended to operate in different labour markets within the landed classes' own separate system. Country house service was more difficult to enter than service elsewhere, not only because it demanded higher standards and better qualifications, but also because the landed classes and their servants had their own networks, newspapers, and agencies. External recruitment was common for lower-level positions, but for higher positions the aristocracy and gentry preferred to hire men and women trained in their own gentleman's service, and circulated good servants among themselves. The further a servant advanced, the more likely he or she was to enter the landed classes' own labour market.

Contemporary commentators and modern historians alike have asserted that landed families recruited their servants from their own estates.[29] Certainly, census-sample garden labourers were typically estate-born, as were over a third of the gardeners and stablemen, a fifth of the coachmen and a quarter of the gamekeepers. But only 13 per cent of lower indoor servants and less than 3 per cent of upper indoor servants were born on the estate. Clearly, the landed classes looked further afield for indoor servants. Mrs Kennard of Crawley Court, for instance, had a deliberate policy of recruiting servants from outside Crawley.[30]

Labourers were very much part of the local labour market. The country house offered low-paid employment at weekly wages, or paid by the task, just as local farmers did. The poor, working chiefly on farms, sought casual jobs in the gardens, park or house to supplement their wages, or when little agricultural work was available. On large estates, department heads usually hired labour as needed, but in smaller households such as Holton, mistresses contacted local women themselves.[31] Life-cycle and career servants entered country house service together, filling similar positions as they trained. Many relied on personal networks to obtain their first place in "good service." Parents, the vicar or schoolmaster or their wives were active on their behalf, or the young people asked kin or friends already in service for help. Ernest King's friend, first footman at Hall, secured for him the post of odd-job boy there.[32]

Entry-level positions in outdoor service were filled by local youngsters. Head servants or their masters needed look no further than the village school to find suitable candidates, and local families were often eager to obtain places for their sons. Hearing that Lord Parkes wanted a garden boy, Jack Brookes' mother sent him along to join twelve other applicants.[33] In the census sample, seventeen of the eighteen garden boys and nine of the thirteen stable boys under sixteen were born on the estate. Some estates offered virtual vocational schools for sons of estate employees. "His lordship and his father before him always held it our duty to train and then place our people, and I feel the same," the head gardener at Staunton Harold told a visitor.[34]

Many hall-boys, pantry-boys, or pages were locally born, too. Parish clergymen and schoolmasters consulted about school-leavers often selected delicate boys unfit for agricultural labour.[35] Half the sample's indoor boy servants under sixteen were from the estate. But indoor boys were more widely recruited, too, through personal contacts, or increasingly through agencies and advertisements. Previous employment in other fields was no hindrance: a printer's boy, an office-boy, a farm labourer and navvy, a paper boy and pub counter boy, and a hotel employee all ended up in country houses.[36]

Girls, however, found entering country house service more difficult. While a few establishments deliberately trained estate-born girls, most aspirants had to go to a "petty place" for a year or two to acquire the basic training and experience, and the outfits, required for country house service. In the sample, only five of the eighteen maidservants under sixteen were born on the estate, and nearly two-thirds of the scullery-maids came from more than ten miles away.

Once in the country house, both life-cycle and career servants competed for the same jobs, operating in the same country house labour markets. Many posts were filled through personal connections. The landed classes sought and offered recommendations by speaking or writing to their family, friends, and upper servants. Below stairs, servants likewise exchanged information about impending vacancies and put in a good word for their own kin or friends. This networking helped Rose Raynor obtain posts in country houses. In London, her neighbour, whose sister was second laundry-maid at Horsley Towers, told Rose of a temporary position there for a third laundry-maid. When her three months were up, the mistress recommended her to a relative, the Dowager Countess of Harrowby.[37] Servants and employers also turned to tradesmen and shopkeepers in related occupations, who often operated informal agencies.

Yet personal networks could not fill every vacancy in an occupation characterized by rapid turnover. Newspaper advertising and registry offices provided convenient and efficient alternatives, expanding as more servants became literate and took advantage of rail travel. Advertising reached a wide audience and produced many replies. The landed classes favoured *The Times*, the *Morning Post*, and later the *Daily Telegraph*, all national newspapers circulating among the upper classes and the wealthier middle classes. Over the century, the number of advertisements in the "situations vacant," "situations wanted," and the cheaper "want places" columns expanded steadily from between five and twenty insertions to over eight columns in *The Times* in the mid-1880s (falling thereafter with a change of policy), and up to seventeen columns in the *Morning Post* in the Edwardian period. Servants often specified that they wanted positions in "a nobleman's or gentleman's family." Far more servants advertised than employers, who preferred to reply to advertisements, though the upper classes did advertise for situations for protégés or former servants, and by the 1880s were using the "situations vacant" columns to ask each other's help in finding staff. Thus the upper classes transferred their system of personal networks to a public forum, when Society was becoming larger and more heterogeneous. Landowners also advertised in county or provincial newspapers, and the *Manchester Guardian* became increasingly acceptable. The Packes advertised for laundresses in the *Yorkshire Post*, the *Nottinghamshire Guardian*, the *Stamford Mercury*, and the *Manchester Guardian*.[38] The *Field*, too, carried advertisements, mostly for gamekeepers, gardeners, coachmen, and grooms, and the *Lady* contained a column for distressed gentlewomen and another for recommended servants. Periodicals for servants such as *Hetherington's Universal Register* also included advertisements for country house servants.

Some of these servants' journals were published by registry offices. Early-nineteenth-century agencies were notorious for victimization, prostitution and false characters, but there were many respectable, well-run agencies by the end of the century. In London, Mrs Massey's and Mrs Hunt's, both established by the 1860s, and later the Regina Agency, catered especially for the upper classes. Some landowners also patronized local agencies. Registry offices had many advantages: managers sifted out unsuitable types, assembled a large selection of candidates for interviewing, and came to know the special requirements of regular customers. Employers wrote for servants' particulars or interviewed them, either sending for them or going to the office themselves. Servants wrote to the agency enquiring after situations, examined the lists in person, or waited at the agency to be interviewed. By the end of the century, the landed classes used agencies frequently.

Career servants restricting themselves to gentleman's service were most likely to operate in a distinct upper-class labour market. Deliberately seeking training in country houses, they followed the required pattern of moving on at frequent intervals to get promotion and experience in different households. They tended to use only the most exclusive agencies or newspapers. William Harrison, for instance, wrote only to Mrs Massey, Mrs Hunt and the Regina for his second place.[39]

Different labour markets existed for each branch of service, all with their own patterns of entry, training, and mobility. Some were more isolated from the general middle-class labour market in domestic service

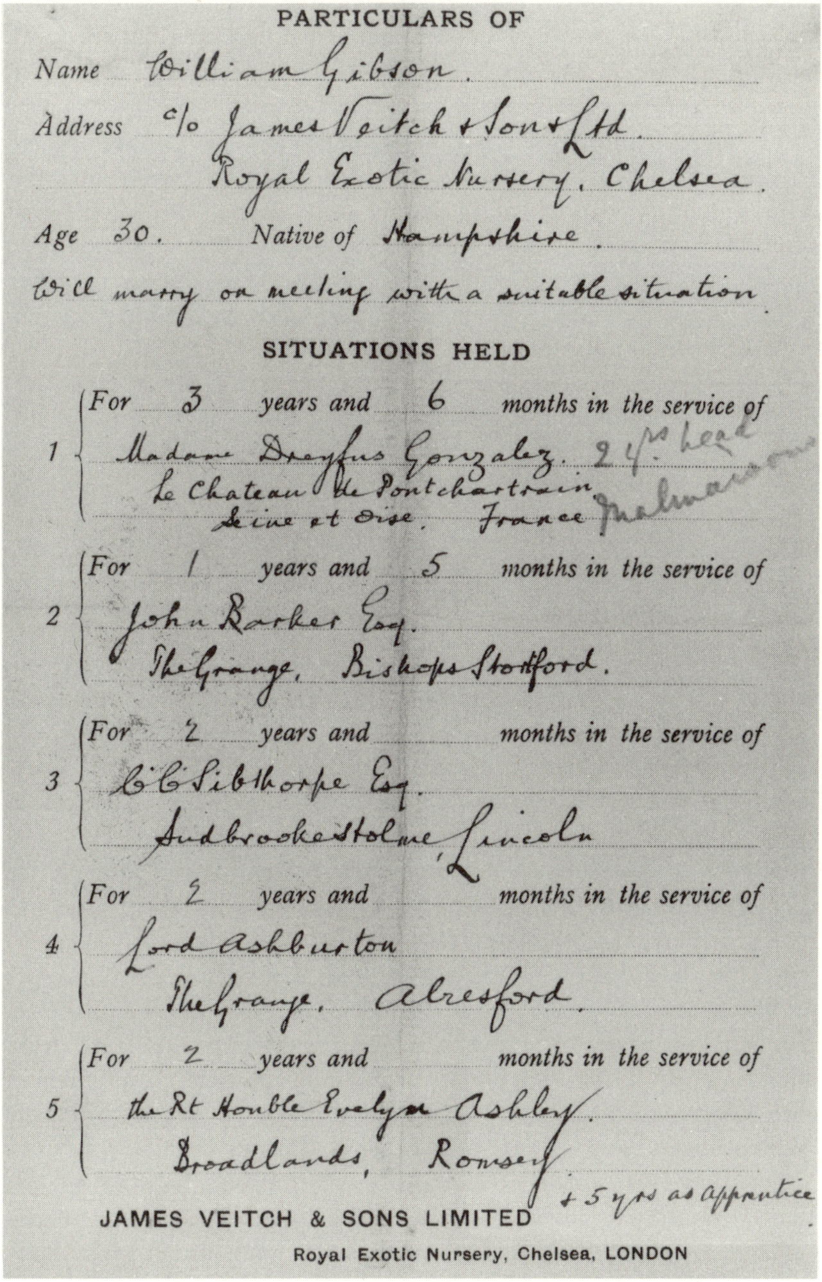

DEMOGRAPHY OF SERVANTS 173

PARTICULARS OF

Name *William Gibson.*

Address *c/o James Veitch & Son & Ltd.*
Royal Exotic Nursery, Chelsea.

Age *30.* Native of *Hampshire.*

Will marry on meeting with a suitable situation.

SITUATIONS HELD

1. For *3* years and *6* months in the service of
Madame Dreyfus Gonzalez. 2 yrs head
Le Chateau de Pontchartrain
Seine et Oise. France *Malmaison*

2. For *1* years and *5* months in the service of
John Barker Esq.
The Grange, Bishops Stortford.

3. For *2* years and months in the service of
C C Sibthorpe Esq.
Sudbrooke Holme, Lincoln

4. For *2* years and months in the service of
Lord Ashburton
The Grange, Alresford.

5. For *2* years and months in the service of
the Rt Honble Evelyn Ashley
Broadlands, Romsey
+ 5 yrs as apprentice

JAMES VEITCH & SONS LIMITED
Royal Exotic Nursery, Chelsea, LONDON

Plate 21 A form sent in application for the position of head gardener at Shugborough, 1907

than others, having their own networks, agencies, and publications. Gardening is an excellent example of a distinct labour market. To become a head gardener, a boy began as an apprentice under a head gardener, became a journeyman, and then a foreman. The best training to be had was in the gardens of the aristocracy, under renowned head gardeners such as Mr Fleming at Trentham, who supervised and taught dozens of beginners at a time, finding them good places for the next stage of their training. The aspiring young gardener sought posts in prestigious gardens which would impress prospective employers. When he had proved himself as a foreman, his head gardener tried to place him as head gardener elsewhere.

Private service was not the only place where a gardener could obtain first-rate training and assistance with job-hunting. He could also go to the Royal Horticultural Society's gardens at Wisley or even the highly regarded Royal Gardens at Windsor and Sandringham. Commercial nurseries both gave training and acted as agencies. From the 1850s, the leading nurseries were James Veitch and Sons in Chelsea, and Dicksons of Chester. These nurserymen offered their services to landowners: they recommended gardeners, supplied printed forms outlining applicants' experience, and sent gardeners to be interviewed. Nurseries also employed out-of-place gardeners until they were found new jobs.

There was a very active grapevine in the gardening world. Trade journals, notably the *Gardener's Chronicle* (founded in 1841), passed on news of impending vacancies, and at meetings of the Royal Horticultural Society gardeners were told of vacancies and urged to apply for them. When the head gardener at Shugborough was about to leave in 1907, the Earl of Lichfield received a flood of letters from gardeners who had either heard through friends or read about it in the *Gardener's Chronicle*. The secretary of the British Gardeners' Association told William Robbins of the impending vacancy, and wrote to William Curtis, advising them both to apply. Six head gardeners wrote to recommend their foremen. Nevertheless, Lord Lichfield contacted Veitch's, who sent particulars of several gardeners, and then applicants for interview.[40]

Other branches of service had similar institutions: in 1885, for instance, gamekeepers advertised for themselves and their sons in the *Field*, or with a keeper's register at a London gunmaker's, while landowners wanting coachmen or grooms could apply to a stable servants' club in London.[41]

Among distressed gentlewomen, lady-housekeepers and companions evidently relied on newspaper advertising like other servants, but in a separate column along with governesses.[42] Eventually, Lady Crawshay organized a registry just for lady servants. Governesses operated in a separate labour market from other servants, partly because of their social class, but also because of the nature and requirements of the occupation. This was an overcrowded occupation, for qualifications could be minimal; good breeding and accomplishments compensated for an inadequate education, and upwardly mobile working-class women only increased competition. Many middle-class governesses offered only their own home education as qualifications, although a number had attended a young ladies' seminary or a charitable institution founded to educate daughters of impoverished gentlemen. From the 1840s, private schools for training governesses were established, and two training colleges, Queen's College and Bedford College. Later in the century, prospective governesses could also attend Charlotte Mason's progressive training college, or even obtain a university education.[43] Governesses did not rise in the ranks like career servants – their education prepared them directly for their first position. Parents could apply to schools training governesses, or reply to advertisements, but both parties preferred to rely on personal networks, asking friends and relatives about vacancies or candidates. When Anne Brontë resolved to become a governess, she found her first place with the Inghams of Blake Hall through a friend, Miss Wooler, and was recommended by Miss Wooler's brother-in-law, the Rev. Edward Carter, who had baptised the Ingham children, and by an old acquaintance, the Rev. James La Trobe.[44] But with the high turnover of unsatisfactory governesses, many families had to resort to advertising or agencies. Agencies, mostly short-lived, often ruthlessly duped and exploited helpless governesses. The Governesses' Benevolent Institution ran an excellent employment agency from 1843, but not until Mr Truman founded his Agency for Governesses in 1901 did governesses and employers have an honest and reliable commercial agency.[45]

A separate labour market apparently existed for governesses to the aristocracy. Once Mary Pinhorn secured a post with the Kay-Shuttleworths, she "never again had to look for a job," as she was circulated around "other leading Liberal families on the strength of Lady Kay-Shuttleworth's recommendation."[46] Kathryn Hughes finds little evidence that governesses to the lower middle class gained access to this market. "The first post that a woman obtained" usually "determined the sort of people for whom she would subsequently work."[47] Most graduates of the Norland or the Princess Christian nursery training colleges were also absorbed by the aristocracy.[48]

There was a national labour market in country house service, facilitated not only by correspondence between landed employers, and by upper-class newspapers and agencies, but by landowners' frequent visits to London. Families moving to the capital for the summer Season took most of their indoor and stable servants with them. London was the centre of personal networks both above and below stairs, and the most important agencies were located there. Many masters and mistresses interviewed prospective servants at their London residence, particularly when patronizing agencies. Lucy Arkwright did her servant-hunting when in London, where she could discuss her needs with numerous friends and relatives, and conduct interviews. In 1883, Emily Birchall went to London specifically to interview cooks, under-housemaids, and laundry-maids.[49] Country house servants sometimes took places in upper-class London homes, but as this was still gentleman's service, they remained eligible to return to the country house community.

Regional and local differences in land use and employment opportunities also affected recruitment: such factors as the density of population, land settlement, local employment, and proximity to urban areas offering other occupations. Rural Wales, for instance, was a region of small tenant farmers employing live-in farm servants and labourers, in peasant communities isolated from Anglicized landlords. Farm girls helped at home, and labourers' daughters became farm servants. In mining areas, however, domestic service was the only employment available for miners' daughters. In a sample of thirty-one Welsh households, over 70 per cent of the lower female servants were Welsh-born, but only a third of the upper female servants. Either most Welsh maids were life-cycle servants, or their employers favoured English servants as upper servants. Just three of the twenty-three lady's maids were Welsh. Welshmen seem to have been far less enthusiastic about domestic service: less than 39 per cent of the lower indoor men and 32 per cent of the upper indoor men were Welsh. Fourteen of the nineteen butlers were English. "Welsh butlers were scarce," affirmed a member of the Welsh gentry, "almost invariably imported from across the border, or from English-speaking parts of South Wales." Again, this may have reflected employers' prejudices against Welsh menservants, but they would probably have been less particular about outdoor menservants, of whom a little more than half were Welsh-born.[50]

The spread of industry into the neighbourhood of a country house offered alternative employment to local people, forcing the landowner to bring in servants from further afield. Nine census-sample households were located near industrial cities or towns, or had a mill nearby. Less than 21 per cent of all their English and Welsh servants were born within five miles, compared to over 30 per cent in the whole sample, and just over 39 per cent were born over fifty miles away, compared to over 31 per cent for all English and Welsh servants. All the indoor servants at Crosby Hall, only six miles from Liverpool, were from over forty miles away, while at Cuerdon, encircled by cotton mills, none of the fifteen indoor servants came from less than twenty miles away. Even the Cuerdon gardener sent all his children into the mills.[51] In contrast, landowners had no trouble finding maids in mining districts. Most of the girls in Bowers Row, a Yorkshire mining village, worked in the seven mansions nearby.[52]

Regional cottage industries, such as glove-making, lace-making, button-making, and straw-plaiting diverted young girls from service. At Southill in Bedfordshire in 1871, many girls and women did straw-plaiting, including a groom's daughters. But gentleman's service still had its attractions: four of the thirteen female servants at Southill came from within six miles. Where farm work was the only alternative, country house service was much sought-after. At Rougham in Norfolk, where most young girls worked in agricultural gangs from the age of eight or nine, three maidservants were born within five miles, and all but the nurse and the governess were natives of Norfolk.[53]

As a class, nineteenth-century domestic servants showed a high degree of mobility, responding to a growing population and declining employment opportunities in the countryside, and the huge demand for servants in rapidly expanding cities and towns. Mobility was accelerated by the improvement in roads, followed by the network of railways, the proliferation of employment agencies, and the spread of literacy. Servants could utilize the penny post, newspaper advertising and the telegraph, and eventually (mostly short-lived) periodicals specializing in advertisements by and for servants. Most employers, furthermore, paid travelling expenses when they hired a servant.

The census returns show differences in geographical mobility between the four types of country house servant.[54] Labourers were the least mobile – 60 per cent of the garden labourers in the sample were born under five miles from the country house. Like agricultural labourers, they seldom looked far for employment, either remaining in their own parish, or moving to a nearby parish on marriage, or because of lack of work at home. Many novice life-cycle and career servants found their first country house places not far from home. But lower servants, changing places frequently, travelled long distances. Nearly a third of the English or Welsh lower indoor servants in the sample were working over fifty miles from their birthplace. The country house's isolated location was in itself a cause of mobility. Moreover, London's function as a labour exchange encouraged movement. Career-oriented servants were especially mobile, because their training and advancement required experience in different kinds of households. George Borell, a gardener born in Suffolk, was apprenticed in that county, became a journeyman in Essex, and a foreman in Cornwall and Ireland, before applying for the head gardener's place at Hampton Court in Herefordshire.[55] Distressed gentlewomen and upper servants were often highly mobile. In the sample, over 53 per cent of English and Welsh upper indoor servants were born over fifty miles away.

Great landowners employed more highly mobile servants than did less prestigious and less wealthy families: nearly 40 per cent of peers' English and Welsh staffs, compared to just over 31 per cent of sample servants as a whole, came from over 100 miles away. The more career-oriented, highly qualified servants were more willing to travel long distances than the less skilled or ambitious staff of the lesser gentry.

Geographical mobility was, of course, closely related to job mobility. Perhaps the most striking feature of the country house establishment was its constantly changing population. This mobility was a major vexation to the servant-employing classes, who in every generation were convinced that in the past servants had faithfully remained in one household for a lifetime. Complaints about high turnover were common in the eighteenth century, and it was certainly a problem by 1815, when advertisements for servants in *The Times* stipulated that a twelve-months' character reference was required, or that "none need apply who are in the habit of changing."[56]

Employers themselves caused some of the turnover in staff, dismissing those they found unsatisfactory, as at Gorhambury, where servants were fired for being, variously, "not much use," "stupid," "not good enough," "a stupid tiresome girl and delicate," and "no good as kitchenmaid."[57]

Servants guilty of moral turpitude (chiefly drunkenness or sexual activity) were promptly fired. Sometimes servants had to quit through ill-health or exhaustion: Charles Cooper was dismissed from a post because he was not strong enough for the work, and was replaced at Fetcham Park when he was laid low with scarlet fever for six weeks. He had to leave Eden Hall when his master went abroad.[58] Lengthy travel was a common reason for reducing staff, along with the need to economize, and when an owner died, many servants were dismissed.

The majority of departing country house servants, however, made the decision to leave themselves. At Bridehead between 1872 and 1908, for instance, just four servants were fired and ten were made redundant, but eighty servants gave notice: ten because of ill-health, seven to marry, four to enter other occupations, and two to emigrate, but most to move on to a better position.[59]

Job mobility was high among lower servants, but generally declined as they moved into senior positions.[60] Labourers were the least mobile, and least affected by changes in ownership. In the census sample nearly 89 per cent of garden labourers' children present were born in the country house's parish. Distressed gentlewomen were dependent on the family life cycle: governesses were only needed for a few years, and companions to elderly ladies faced inevitable redundancy. The turnover in governesses could be high, when irate mothers fired the incompetent, or harried governesses fled their little persecutors. The brief duration of lower servants' service is striking. The lower servant's average stay was just under two years. Around 70 per cent of lower maidservants stayed less than two years, and half of these left within a year.[61] Life-cycle servants moved on frequently, dissatisfied with their treatment, conditions, companions, or wages, or eager to see new places. Many wanted to "better" themselves, to move up to the next rung of the occupation and obtain higher wages. There were few incentives to stay, for places were plentiful and quickly found.

Indeed, mobility was a necessary part of career servants' training and promotion. Lower menservants, for instance, were expected to widen their experience by moving from place to place. Two years was a widely recognized limit. By the 1890s, some footmen had even formed an informal union requiring its members to give notice after two years so others could get a chance to obtain the desired training and references.[62] Charles Cooper is a good example of a typical manservant. After two years as second footman at Brougham Castle, he gave notice, "sorry to give up a good place but one had to get on and gain experience." He spent seven months as first footman to the German Ambassador, then went to Cumberland Lodge for two years. "Seeing no chance of promotion, or an increase in salary, and being ambitious," he explained, "it was only natural . . . that I wished to improve my position and earn a bigger wage." After a similar stint as first footman at Buckhurst, he gave notice. "I was perfectly contented with my place," but "at my age it was time I got out of livery." He obtained the butler's place at Ampthill, where he remained.[63]

Gardeners were also required to move on regularly to gain experience in different kinds of work. James Baynes, born in 1849, started at the age of thirteen under his father at Huntingdon Field, Perthshire. Five years later, he became a journeyman at Courtarchy Castle, and was promoted to general foreman at nineteen. "To gain knowledge and experience," he moved on to Dalkeith Park, "first in the kitchen gardens, thereafter in the [green]houses." The head gardener sent Baynes to his brother, head gardener at Drumlannig Castle, where after eighteen months he became hothouse foreman. In 1875, Lord Belper of Kingston Hall applied for a head gardener, and Baynes was chosen. When Lord Belper reduced his gardens, Baynes left. At Kingston Hall he had been growing for the market, so he decided to try market gardening, and prospered. But by 1892 he wanted to return to private service, applying for situations at Alnwick, Eaton Hall and Trentham, to "try & get to the next rung of the ladder in my profession, as I have all along qualified myself for a first class gardener situation."[64] Once suited, head gardeners remained many years; they had the longest average length of stay in the sample, nearly eleven years.

Only when they reached the peak of their abilities and ambition, or found a congenial household, did upper servants settle down. The landed classes accepted, even encouraged, young career servants' mobility, but naturally wanted excellent upper servants to remain permanently. Servants who had a good relationship with their employers, and found their conditions of work and environment agreeable, stayed longest. While upper servants did stay much longer on average than lower servants, the range of length of service is wide, with some branches more mobile than others. Head coachmen, house stewards, butlers and housekeepers were most likely to remain long periods, but unsatisfactory incumbents were soon got rid of; nearly a third of the wagebook sample's housekeepers departed within twelve months. The Yorkes went through eight housekeepers between 1895 and 1907.[65] Few valets and lady's maids stayed longer than four years, and some less than three months, but others gave many years of devoted service. Ralph Sneyd's valet served him, for example, for over seventeen years.[66] Cooks were the most troublesome; only one in eight lasted more than three years. Upper servants evidently became more mobile over the century. Upper indoor menservants, for instance, stayed an average of nearly eight years in the period 1815–39, but their mean length of service fell steadily, down to five and a half years among upper men hired 1865–89, and under three years in the last quarter of the century.

Promotion and transfer were used as incentives to encourage servants to stay. Promotion was most prevalent among the lower ranks in large establishments, where there were many grades in each department. At Welbeck Abbey, "it was his Grace's custom to promote his own servants," and Goodwood had the sample's highest rate of promotion, but no transfers.[67] In smaller households, there was a surprising amount of movement from one department to another. At Chillington, for instance, three grooms became footmen, two ushers ended up as grooms, a housemaid and a nurse became stillroom maids, and a stillroom maid went into the laundry, as did three housemaids. Another housemaid transferred to the nursery, then became housekeeper.[68]

Promotion, transfer, and length of service varied considerably between one country house and another, influenced by the size, location, and character of each household, and by its owners' personalities and policies. Some country houses were characterized by long service. The Rushouts of Northwick inspired devotion in many of their upper servants: one butler stayed thirty-four years, his footman son succeeded him for nearly twenty-three, and the next butler remained for eleven years. A coachman stayed forty-six years, a housekeeper twenty, and a cook twenty-three.[69] When Sir Richard Frederick died in 1873 aged ninety-three, his butler had served twenty-six years, his footman eighteen, and the laundry-maid fifteen. Perhaps they were hanging on, waiting for legacies! However, an earlier housekeeper had served thirteen years until her death, succeeded by a promoted head housemaid, whose total stay exceeded twenty-eight years.[70] At Erddig the warm relations between family and staff doubtless accounts for the large number of long-staying servants there.

Other households had unusually high turnover rates. Some, like Holton, were subject to the local system of annual hiring from one May-Day to the next, which encouraged servants to move on. Few servants at Holton, on the other hand, gave notice before the year was up, and many stayed longer – one cook remained for over eight years, and a coachman and a gardener remained all their working lives. By the time the Rev. Dixon inherited in 1906, the annual hiring system had disappeared. But Holton's position at the lower end of the landed classes was a disadvantage. His daughter recalls that "the young girls moved away as they grew older & wanted more wages [and] to better themselves." Some left because they did not get on with the parlour-maid. As everywhere, "cooks never stayed very long."[71]

Employers' characters and policies also increased turnover. The third Earl of Verulam had great difficulty in keeping servants at Sopwell and Gorhambury, where the mean length of service was the lowest for any sample household – under sixteen months for upper servants and just over ten months for lower staff. In the 1890s, he rigidly economized in an effort to live within his fallen income, with little entertaining. While his servants were paid the going rate in wages, they evidently could not bear his frugality in running the household. Freeford Hall suffered the second-lowest mean length of service; under twenty-one months for upper servants, and under thirteen for the lower servants. The Dyotts must have been either unusually irascible, or inept in selecting and managing their servants. Between 1816 and 1841 they fired one servant after another, for impertinence, insolence and lack of deference, incompetence, idleness, and drunkenness. Kitchen-maids were "pert" and "giddy," a manservant was a dissembling "tattler," and boys were "worthless . . . & not strictly honest," "good for nothing" and "grievously addicted to lying." Length of service among under-servants was third lowest at Englefield. Richard Benyon's records of his servants' arrivals and departures, with many regulations governing their conduct, give the impression of a strictly run establishment where stern morality ruled. Location may have been a factor too: in Wales, Derwydd had difficulties attracting servants from the 1890s, going through twenty-two cooks, nineteen kitchen-maids, and eighteen under-housemaids by 1912. Sometimes short service for lowest servants may have been encouraged, as at Ashburnham, where youngsters were recruited from the estate, apparently with the intention of training them and sending them on.[72]

Promotion and departure could be influenced by a servant's age: the census sample, newspaper advertisements, and advice manuals show there were recognized patterns for age at entry, speed of promotion, and age limits in each department. The census returns, advertisements, autobiographies, and advice manuals show the patterns prevalent in the second half of the period. Not enough readily accessible evidence survives to ascertain whether these patterns were true of the early nineteenth century. Rising standards of service may have affected employers' willingness to accept very young or elderly servants. Education was another factor. Early in the century, when elementary education was neither free nor universal, many servants entered their first place as mere children — Hannah Cullwick, for instance, left school aged eight in 1841. Schooling was made compulsory until age twelve in 1871, and until fourteen from 1880 (earlier with a labour certificate). Such regulations could not always be enforced. At Juniper Hill in the 1880s, girls left school as early as ten.[73]

By the 1870s, most girls eager to enter country house service had to wait until they reached fifteen or sixteen, not just to accumulate skills and experience, but to gain strength. "Big houses di'n't want little girls of eleven, even as kitchen maids, so the first few years 'ad to be put in somewhere else, afore you even got that amount o' promotion," recalled Kate Mary Edwards. "Big houses expected good service."[74] Only in the nursery and schoolroom, where the work was lighter and applicants were experienced in caring for younger siblings, were there two maids aged thirteen and one aged fourteen in the census sample. Landowners were scarcely more willing to take very young boys as hall-boys, pantry-boys, steward's room boys and pages; only six of the male indoor servants were aged from twelve to fourteen. Head gardeners, gamekeepers and coachmen, however, wanted to train underlings as young as possible, and a boy was immediately useful; indeed, some boys began part-time work even before leaving school. Ten garden boys were aged eleven to fourteen, and nine stable boys were twelve to fourteen. Gamekeepers' sons, "brought up to the business" from childhood, did not become full-time employees until their later teens.

The usual age of entry and advancement and the long-term prospects of each department varied considerably from one position to another. In the decades before 1914, scullery-maids or kitchen-maids usually began at seventeen. Promotion was rapid in this department. Most scullery-maids made the transition to kitchen-maid by the age of twenty, and kitchen-maids soon became cooks. Cooks were assured of employment "up to the extreme limits of working age." But by forty half the sample's cooks had either left or become housekeepers. Advancement to cook-housekeeper or housekeeper was not difficult. Few aspiring housekeepers had the required experience and maturity before their thirties, but they could expect employment until old age – two in the sample were over seventy. Stillroom maids had to gain experience as kitchen-maids before specializing in their early twenties. By thirty, most had left service or become housekeepers.[75] The 1871 sample indicates that housemaids typically entered country house service at nineteen or twenty, but most left by the time they were thirty. Older housemaids were less attractive to employers, but could obtain posts as housemaid-caretakers, or places in smaller households. Laundry work was also a life-cycle occupation, which most women entered in their late teens and deserted by their thirties, even though long-term prospects were good. Laundry-maids who married local men could still work part-time in the laundry, or take in washing.[76]

While girls could enter the nursery at a younger age, some of the sample's nursery-maids and under-nurses were in their twenties. Some labelled "nurse" were under twenty, but over 40 per cent of nurses were

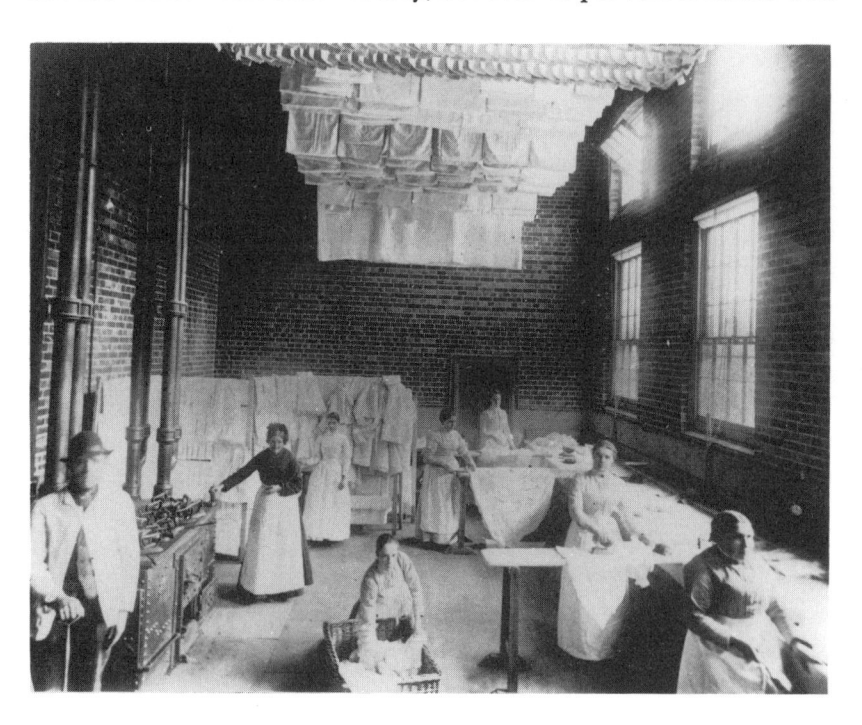

Plate 22 The drying and ironing room of the laundry at Petworth

in their twenties. Many left to marry, rather than face being made redundant as their charges grew up.[77] Yet the landed classes accepted older nurses: good ones were not relinquished until extreme old age. Few lady's maids were under twenty: they needed to be well-educated and thoroughly trained, either as a young lady's maid, or increasingly by an apprenticeship in dressmaking, with lessons from a hairdresser. By 1909 Mrs Massey was recommending they first enter another department to obtain a general training and savings to pay for these lessons.[78] Over half the sample's lady's maids were in their twenties, and under a third in their thirties, but less than 9 per cent were older.

Governesses also entered country house service relatively late, because of their education. The youngest in the sample was nineteen. The optimum age for governesses was between twenty-five and thirty-five.[79] The landed classes favoured younger women: over half were in their twenties. "Few ladies can obtain situations as governesses after they have passed the age of forty," admitted the Secretary of the Governesses' Institution.[80] Some governesses then became ladies' companions. Lady Andover, for instance, retained Miss Steele as her companion after her daughter grew up.[81]

Among indoor menservants, the transition to footman generally occurred at seventeen or eighteen. As an Edwardian hall-boy, George Slingsby heard that any youth who failed to become a footman by twenty "was destined to remain a lower-class servant."[82] Some footmen became valets. Like lady's maids, valets were supposed to be young – most sample valets were in their twenties. But when they grew too old, valets could become butlers. Most men lacked the training, experience, and maturity to become butlers until their thirties. Those who remained in service stayed until their late fifties. The very best butlers reached the pinnacle of house steward, usually at a mature age. Older indoor menservants found it harder to find situations, perhaps because the landed classes considered them inefficient, and unattractive as objects of display.[83] One butler in his seventies dyed his hair to convince his employers he was ten years younger.[84]

Outdoor menservants, in both labourer and career servant categories, were readily employed until old age. Most gardeners began in their teens, serving until their fifties or sixties. Career gardeners spent four or five years as apprentices, several more as improvers or journeymen, and two to eight years as foremen, becoming head gardeners between their late twenties and mid-thirties.[85] With skills which were not easily transferable to other occupations, gamekeeping was definitely a lifetime's career. Richard Jefferies maintained that "once a gamekeeper always a gamekeeper is pretty nearly true."[86] In contrast, the sample indicates that many men who entered country house stables as grooms in their twenties left a few years later, only half of them staying on to their forties. Nearly a quarter of the sample's coachmen were under thirty, and relatively few were elderly. Stable employees were therefore often life-cycle servants, who could work with horses elsewhere.

Prospects for employment in later years was an important consideration, for servants could expect to live a long time. A 1900 census of occupational morbidity and mortality indicates that domestic service was a healthy occupation for men, with a better-than-average life expectancy for all groups. Indoor menservants, however, had a higher-than-average death rate from liver diseases (due to their alcohol consumption, no doubt), diabetes, and suicide. Domestic coachmen and grooms had a lower mortality rate than their commercial counterparts. Strenuous outdoor work ensured that gardeners and gamekeepers had the second and third lowest mortality rates of all occupations.[87] Figures are not available for women, but with better diet and living conditions, less physical labour, and no childbearing, female upper servants probably lived longer than most working-class women.

The staff's age structure and mobility were greatly influenced by servants' marriage patterns. Chances of marriage and its effects on a career in service varied according to gender, type, and department. Nuptiality rates are impossible to calculate for country house maidservants, as their marriages are so difficult to trace. They found potential mates among the male staff and in a countryside otherwise depleted of young women. Over 70 per cent of the sample's female servants were under thirty, so the majority must have left in their twenties, more probably to wed than to descend to less prestigious and less profitable middle-class households. Few married young: their parents' need for remittances and their own desire for savings, restrictions on contacts with men, and high mobility all led to prolonged courtships.[88] Mrs Wrigley was nineteen when she met her future husband. Although her outraged mistress stopped her going out altogether, she remained with her two years, and worked five more years in a country house before marrying her railwayman. Young women who had left a swain behind at Juniper Hill did not leave service for six to eight years.[89] More life-cycle lower maidservants doubtless married, at an earlier age, than career servants, who wanted upward mobility on marriage, and who accumulated savings to attract respectable upper-working-class or lower-middle-class spouses.[90] Annie Cable, who entered service at the age of fourteen, was just twenty-one when she married in 1914. In contrast, when a cook-housekeeper became engaged to the Alnwick Castle butler in 1887, they planned a seven-year engagement.[91]

Few full-time live-in maids were married, reflecting the prevailing norm among both employers and maidservants that married women should become housewives. Employers seldom willingly retained a maidservant who married. Only 3 per cent of the sample's female servants admitted to being married, seventeen of them living apart from their husbands, with only three couples together in indoor service. Children were the main impediment to employment for women. Couples' children were normally boarded out, or forced the wife to abandon her job. When Sarah Cheadle, cook at Freeford, married the butler in 1818, she returned in 1819 until she bore her second child.[92]

If wives were unacceptable in the country house, widows were welcome. Impoverished middle-class widows could exploit their experience as mothers and home-makers to secure positions, mostly as housekeepers, cook-housekeepers or nurses. Their children had to be boarded elsewhere, unless the employer permitted an only child to stay; when the widowed Polly Greenhill became housekeeper for the local squire, her young son went with her. Housekeepers' daughters might become servants themselves, as they did at Trentham and Erddig.[93]

No prejudice existed against hiring married women as part-time or casual charwomen, laundresses, sewing women, and garden labourers. They were middle-aged or even older, seldom with young children still at home.

For one occupation, wet-nursing, maternity was of course essential. Sometimes a local woman obtained lucrative short-term work wet-nursing the landowner's baby. She did not necessarily have to stop breast-feeding her own child: one mother visited the mansion several times a day, and a woodman's wife nursed a peer's son in her home, along with her own baby.[94] More often, however, wet-nurses were recruited from farther afield, to reside in the nursery. As married women were reluctant to leave their families, unwed mothers were increasingly acceptable in the nineteenth century. If the wet-nurse's child had not already died, it was normally placed with a woman who made her living caring for unwanted babies, where it was likely to perish. However, scattered evidence suggests that the landed classes preferred married women or widows. Reresby Sitwell's wet-nurse was from Scotland. Hired with her husband's consent, she left her baby behind. When the cowman's daughter at Blagdon became the wet-nurse, she left her children with her aunt, while her husband went to Liverpool to find work. In 1912, Mrs Astor hired a Mrs Stephal to feed her fourth child.[95]

There was some prejudice against married indoor menservants, as less loyal and dedicated, but sought-after upper servants could marry and remain in service. Just under a quarter of the sample's indoor men over twenty were married. Most indoor men waited until they became better-paid upper servants, marrying in their late twenties or early thirties: nearly half the sample's upper indoor menservants were married.

Marriage was much easier for outdoor menservants, who were assured of permanent employment and usually given a cottage. Employers liked their outdoor men to settle down, and regarded the men's wives and children as a handy source of casual labour. If age at marriage is roughly calculated as about a year before the birth of the first child, over a quarter of the outdoor men were evidently married by twenty-five and nearly another half by thirty, with over a third of the wives older than their husbands. Two-thirds of the coachmen, gardeners, and gamekeepers were married or widowed. Career gardeners delayed marriage until they became head gardeners, while a gamekeeper could not always find a wife willing to endure the loneliness of his cottage and the demands of his job.[96] Labourers had no reason to differ from the other villagers by delaying marriage, but married local women rather than maids from the mansion. Almost all the sample's garden labourers were married, half to wives born in the same parish.

Because they married later, and knew that employers objected to large families, difficult to house and ignore, married indoor servants had fewer children than outdoor men. Butlers advertising for places stressed that they had small families or none at all. In twenty-six Northwick butlers' applications, eight were as yet childless, and only six had more than two offspring.[97]

Altogether, country house staffs had a more complex demographic pattern than did the staff found in the typical small middle-class household. Each of the four different types of country house servant had its own distinct demographic characteristics. Female life-cycle servants, largely from the rural working classes, came originally from surrounding districts in their late teens, but became increasingly mobile, and, like most servants in middle-class homes, left service by their late twenties or early thirties for marriage. Male life-cycle servants were far less predictable, entering and leaving country house service at different ages, and often utilizing their skills in related occupations. Career servants were generally from a higher social class, more often urban-born, and initially highly mobile as part of their training. Once they became upper servants, they were likely to remain in service until retirement, when they sometimes moved into a business of their own. Female career servants were the least likely to marry of all servants. More indoor men married, but unlike outdoor servants they found it difficult to remain in service. Labourers were most similar to the rural working classes in their ambitions, origins, patterns of work, and nuptiality. The country house was also a haven for single and widowed middle-class distressed gentlewomen. Governesses reluctantly entered service in their twenties, and were least likely to marry.

Each of these four types of servant had a different experience of country house service. All of them, nevertheless, enjoyed greater psychological and material rewards than did their counterparts in service elsewhere.

8

Gentleman's Service

Over the nineteenth century, domestic service in middle-class households became increasingly unpopular. Country house service, in contrast, remained sought-after, as a distinct, elite form of domestic service which minimized the occupation's disadvantages while conferring unique benefits. Country house servants received more specialized training, greater job satisfaction, better pay, working and living conditions, and more paternalistic benevolence. The degree to which any individual enjoyed these advantages depended on his or her gender, branch of service, and level of advancement. Life-cycle servants, career servants, distressed gentlewomen, and labourers had differing expectations, and varying degrees of job satisfaction.

"Gentleman's service" was recognized as superior to middle-class service. The majority of domestic servants were employed in middle-class households with a staff of one to three maids. Even the smallest manor house, and the most retiring elderly landowner, employed more, and menservants as well as maidservants. While wealthy middle-class establishments had sizeable staffs, they lacked the country house's traditions, self-sufficient domestic economy, and rural environment. The landed classes' conspicuous consumption and ceremonial ritual required higher standards from their servants. Strict timetables and unvarying routines were most highly developed in the country house, necessitating special training, and endless labour.

While basic skills could be learned in a middle-class home, or in institutions and training schools, only in the country house could servants receive the more systematic and specialized training demanded by first-class establishments.[1] After housemaid Margaret Thomas stepped in as temporary cook in the school where she was employed, she decided to become a cook. Realizing how little she knew, she became a kitchen-maid to "learn to cook properly." The cook told her, " 'You'll never do in a big place, you should have started at the bottom years ago.' "[2] Apprentices to head gardeners on great estates had to perfect their reading, writing, and arithmetic, and study botany, trigonometry, and perspective drawing.[3]

The training given by upper servants was strict, rigorous, and often harsh.[4] Having to combine instruction with operating the department created pressure to teach recruits quickly, and this sometimes degenerated into bullying. Department heads were responsible for the failings of their underlings, and mistakes and insubordination disrupted the smooth running of the household. Cooks, often hot and under pressure, were notoriously irritable. Mistresses who felt department heads were excessively hard on their underlings might be told, " 'I did this when I was young. Why shouldn't she (or he) do it now?' "[5] One head gardener was more positive, believing that if boys "wanted to become good head gardeners they had first to serve; if you can't obey, was his maxim, you'll never command." Yet harshness was not inevitable; this head gardener was also a mentor to his apprentices, helping them sort out personal problems, and generous with praise and encouragement when deserved.[6] Recruits endured their training with stoicism, accustomed as they were to strict discipline from parents and teachers. Ambitious career servants knew they were gaining the sound foundation and recognized qualifications which secured good positions. Training under a talented cook, Margaret Thomas ignored her harsh words because she admired her skill. Charles Cooper met menservants "who had to go through the mill, but never regretted having served under a strict skipper."[7]

Country house servants had more specialized duties than domestics in ordinary middle-class households. The typical maid-of-all-work undertook the full range of household tasks.[8] Even a staff of cook, housemaid, and nurse often performed duties outside their particular calling. Country houses, like other large establishments, offered specialized occupations, to suit different abilities and preferences. On the other hand, they provided more options than urban mansions, with dairy-maids and gamekeepers, and they employed many more men in the gardens and stables. A great aristocrat's establishment might contain even more occupations; in the early 1870s, the Leveson-Gowers travelled with an upholsterer, a piper, a female confectioner, and a plate-maid, and kept a porter, a baker/brewer, and a house carpenter at Trentham.[9]

Young people could even change departments on discovering their own bent. At Staunton Harold, the housekeeper watched her girls carefully, and advised those doing poorly to move to another department when a vacancy occurred. George Slingsby became a garden boy at Rufford Abbey. After seeing the mansion's opulent interior, he resolved to become an indoor servant, and gained the hall-boy's place.[10]

Most servants liked the strict job-demarcation of gentleman's service. The maid-of-all-work could never anticipate demands; she had to be on the alert, willing to undertake new work and meet unforeseen situations. After toiling in dirty, sweaty work, she had to transform herself into a clean, smart "front-stage" maid to answer the door and wait on the family and their guests. Country houses had always been divided into departments, each with its own hierarchy of servants. In earlier centuries, lesser landowners, unable to afford the full spectrum of specialized servants, had combined the duties of different departments. This flexibility continued into the Regency period: Samuel and Sarah Adams, for instance, assumed that housemaids would assist the laundry-maid, and Prince Pückler-Muskau was disconcerted to find coachmen and grooms waiting at dinner, "not always free from the odour of the stable."[11] But soon industrial society's enthusiasm for rationalization, efficiency, and specialization, and the moral urge to separate the sexes, segregated and subdivided each department more rigidly. Averse to exploitation and loss of status, servants firmly enforced job-demarcation, refusing any duties outside their own. Richard Dana and his aristocratic host had to mark the tennis court themselves, because the odd-job man was working far away in the grounds.[12] Strict demarcation, nevertheless, remained impossible for the lesser gentry's few servants: at Holton, the kitchen-maid milked the cow, the indoor manservant worked in the garden and did the mangling, and in the 1890s the coachman cleaned knives, fetched the coal, and helped in the garden.[13]

Country houses not only had more specialized servants, but, according to contemporaries, were more efficiently run than small households supervised by a mistress lacking any "method or system of work." Large establishments were characterized by "greater strictness, greater formality, . . . more order and regularity."[14] The nineteenth-century preoccupation with efficiency and timekeeping resulted in inflexible daily timetables and routines, and tighter work discipline.[15] By the 1850s, Hippolyte Taine described the country house as a perfectly organized machine. Servants were "conscientious, exact, regular, always on time," keeping to their timetable precisely.[16] Gongs and bells announced times for rising, prayers, and meals. Large establishments recorded wages, department accounts or inventory, even numbers at each meal, in specially printed account books.

This formal structure defined each servant's responsibilities and authority, and co-ordinated numerous interdependent activities, so that every item and service was produced when needed, with no one perplexed, offended, or inconvenienced. The routine was fairly standardized in large establishments, which facilitated job mobility and reduced dislocation in a constantly shifting servant population. Servants preferred an uninterrupted, predictable routine with adequate time for meals and leisure. Dearman Birchall, joining the gentry on buying Bowdon Hall, failed to institute the usual strict regime, and so exasperated his butler that he threatened to leave.[17]

> Tothill complains that for years he has never had a comfortable dinner – no time is allowed. Lunch often keeps him till 2.0 or $\frac{1}{2}$2. There is no punctuality. . . . The place is getting harder every year – no consideration for him whatever – it is Tothill here, Tothill there. He can never get to his plate without being rung for. . . .

Plate 23 F. D. Hardy, *After the Party*

The footmen complain they can often scarcely swallow their food before the carriage is wanted, and then they are kept out past their tea time.

Efficient organization did not reduce the heavy workload of many servants. New entrants toiled the hardest. Upper servants protected themselves from defiling, degrading work by making lower servants do it. Youngsters scoured used, soiled objects, fetched and carried heavily laden trays, jugs of hot water, slop pails, and coal buckets. This physical labour sometimes overtaxed adolescents. Martha Foster left Coton Hall "on account of being lowered in health," and left her next place also because the work was too hard.[18] But hard work, the common lot of the working classes, was not necessarily resented. "You didn't seem to take much notice of it in those days," claimed one former kitchen-maid, "'Cos everyone seemed to be working harder."[19] In most country houses, furthermore, an even lower grade of servant, the charwoman and the odd-job man, did the dirtiest and heaviest work.

Later in the century, the workload lightened as landowners installed gas, indoor plumbing, central heating, and, eventually, electricity, and bought household appliances such as vacuum cleaners for their servants' use; and as an increasing range of commercially produced foods, beverages, and household products became available. Anxious employers enticed servants by reducing the workload: by 1913 advertisements for cooks promised "no dairy or baking," and for a housemaid "no fires (radiators)."[20] Yet in many establishments, conservatism, tradition, and a lack of consideration for servants still prevailed. Just before 1914, Margaret Thomas worked in a Yorkshire house lit by candles and lamps, where the plumbing consisted of two cold water taps (in the housemaid's cupboard and outside the kitchen door), and toilets flushed with cans of water filled by housemaids.[21]

Working conditions were influenced by the nature of the duties in different departments, and their location. Hannah Cullwick regretted the change when she became scullery-maid at Woodcote in 1850.[22]

> It was very different work, & a very different place to me after being used to running along the splendid halls & gallery & rooms at Aqualate as a housemaid. And I had learnt to make beds & to do the rooms there for company & all, so that I couldn't help crying

when I came to clean the stew pans & great spits & dripping pan, & live only in a rough outhouse next to the kitchen, & could only get out through the coalhole *unseen*, with no windows to look out for anything.

Indoors, women often worked harder than men. Laundry work, for instance, was notoriously arduous: maids rubbed and lifted wet washing, hung it up, and ironed it with heavy irons, in a hot and steamy atmosphere. In contrast, footmen in large establishments had light duties. They cleaned the silver, waited on table, answered the drawing-room bell, and went out with the carriage. Robust men doing no productive work, they were hired as symbols of the family's wealth and power, so their looks and presence were as important as anything they did. In great houses, they spent much time changing their clothes and fixing their powdered hair, or standing idle in the front hall.

Hard physical labour was compounded by long hours of work. While hours of work steadily fell in factories and other regulated, unionized occupations, domestic service remained characterized by the long hours inevitable when providing for a family's needs from awakening until bedtime. Because employers disliked seeing servants at work, much housework had to be done before the family came down to breakfast. Often the landed classes thoughtlessly increased the burden by ordering many courses for dinner and entertaining late. Under-servants normally arose around six a.m. to prepare for the upper staff as well as for the family, and retired at ten p.m., or later if they were entertaining. This sixteen-hour day did not alter over the century. Some households allowed servants to get up later in winter. But maids still had to awaken early to do their own weekly washing: at three a.m. at Linton Park, and at four a.m. at Northwick.[23] In departments independent of the family's daily routine, hours resembled agricultural labourers' twelve-hour day, with Sundays often free. Stablework began between six and seven a.m. and normally finished about eight p.m., unless carriages came home later. Laundry-maids and dairy-maids generally worked twelve hours. So did gardeners, depending on the hours of daylight. Even governesses had a long day, as they were expected to supervise the children all their waking hours, including meals, and then perhaps sew in the evenings. As Charlotte Brontë discovered, "there is such a thing as seeing all beautiful around you . . . and not having a free moment or a free thought left to enjoy them in."[24]

Long working days were exhausting. One stillroom maid frequently found herself falling asleep on her bed fully clothed, after being "on the go the whole time." Servants aware of improving conditions in other occupations might feel resentful. In May 1872 at Leamington, "a crowded meeting of butlers, coachmen, footmen, gardeners and stablemen demanded shorter hours and more pay."[25]

Despite the hard work and long hours, servants in the country house felt more job satisfaction than the typical servant in a middle-class household. Housework has some innate disadvantages as an occupation. Besides the long hours, it is isolated from the outside world. The work is fragmented, repetitive, and monotonous, and its achievements transitory: clean clothes are worn, meals are eaten, and fires lit. One manservant recognized this when he described footmen's work.[26]

> It is like throwing a stone in a pond, rings are formed in the water, which eventually fades [sic] quite away. So that at the end of his day's work he can show nothing that he has done. He has made nothing, produced nothing, yet he has been constantly on the alert all day, not knowing where his next job will spring from.

Country house servants experienced some of these disadvantages, but their work did become more intrinsically interesting and rewarding with promotion.

Labourers, assigned arduous, dirty, and degrading jobs, probably derived most satisfaction from pay and perquisites, the meals and beer provided, and contact with the exciting world at the Big House. Women called in frequently must have felt needed and valued. Long-serving house labourers often considered themselves indispensable. One old man was infuriated when the squire jokingly told him he needed pensioning off. " 'I've been here all your time, yer father's time, and most of yer grandfether's, and I reckon nobody will have my job so long as old Dick can do it.' "[27]

Many female lower servants' work in large establishments was more monotonous than a maid-of-all-work's diverse activities, for the greater specialization and scale of living meant they mechanically performed the same tasks as part of a rigid routine in the same rooms, day after day. Indoor menservants' work was more varied, but even they followed a set daily routine. This monotony could become boring; indeed, one investigator of modern domestic service found that dislike of doing the same job over and over again led to declining productivity and high turnover.[28] Changing situations at least allowed a life-cycle servant to do her tedious chores in a new environment.

Unambitious life-cycle servants may have considered the wages, food, and company more rewarding than their work. But under-servants did manage to find ways of enjoying their tasks. "Deliberate, narrow identification with the place of work, ... pride in the job no matter how menial, ... or pride in the status and possessions of the employing family allowed servants a certain self-respect," explains Leonore Davidoff.[29] Charles Cooper felt he had "accomplished something" when he saw "a well-laid table covered with beautifully kept silver," and waited on "people who matter." Sometimes, as with a hall-boy who "took a personal pride in a perfectly turned out boot," the desire for perfection became obsessive. Some servants came to regard the objects in their care as their own: one head housemaid in charge of the best dinner service for twenty-five years insisted on carrying the plates and dishes to and from the dining-room, and washing and drying them herself.[30] Finally, the very environment and traditions of a family seat, the "sense of spaciousness, of seasonal rhythm, and old-world beauty about the working routines," could make work more pleasant and satisfying.[31]

Even lower servants could feel gratified in mastering the skills needed for promotion. Unlike ordinary servants, who could at best become a cook or a nurse in a middle-class household, the ambitious country house servant could steadily advance to a more rewarding place as an upper servant in a great mansion, enjoying autonomy, initiative, responsibility, respect, and recognition.

At the top of the hierarchy, the steward or butler and housekeeper supervised the entire staff, ensuring that the complex household ran smoothly and efficiently. They co-ordinated all departments, and made the arrangements required for the family's plans or the arrival of guests. Usually they ran the internal economy, ordering, purchasing, storing, and distributing goods, and keeping careful accounts. They disciplined and protected the staff, sometimes even hiring and dismissing them. The butler or steward dealt with menservants and the housekeeper with the maids, each accountable for subordinates' performance and behaviour. Finally, the steward or butler oversaw security, locking doors and windows at night, and safeguarding the family's valuables.

The heads of departments – the cook, head nurse, first coachman, head gardener, and head gamekeeper – controlled the lower servants in their respective departments, allotting and supervising work and distributing equipment and materials. Fully qualified experts in their chosen sphere, they trained underlings. They might also handle their own accounts, and hire day and casual labour.

Part of the upper servants' role was personnel management: satisfying the family's demands, motivating the staff to perform their tasks efficiently, and promoting harmonious relations among them. Such high-level skills in human relations, power over others, and respect and recognition from subordinates must have been highly satisfying.

Department heads in large establishments enjoyed more autonomy and initiative than servants directed by middle-class masters and mistresses. As Violet Firth pointed out,[32]

> Work, to be interesting, has to be creative; a [middle-class] servant's work is never this, because she is never permitted to have any say in the organization of the house, ... and consequently ... has no intellectual interest in the task; whereas if a person is made responsible for a department ..., he achieves a sense of ownership, and ownership means pride.

Long-serving department heads often demonstrated this proprietary pride. Head gardeners were notoriously possessive. The gardener at Edwardian Knole, recalled Vita Sackville-West, "considered [the gardens] more as his own property than my grandfather's or my father's."[33] Many housekeepers, too, grew to love the house.[34]

Upper servants prided themselves on their skills. A talented cook produced gourmet meals; a butler set the table exquisitely, and served the meal with aplomb. The Buxtons' gamekeeper, Larry Banville, "was totally dedicated, ever anxious to kill the most rabbits, train the best dogs and preserve the most birds for his master."[35] Head gardeners supplied top-quality flowers, and fruit out of season, winning prizes at flower shows and exhibitions. The elite head gardeners of great houses were enormously influential in the development of Victorian horticulture. Acknowledged experts, they raised and tested new species, developed new techniques and landscaping designs, edited and contributed to gardening journals, and served on committees of the Royal Horticultural Society.[36] Skilled servants were rewarded with praise and public recognition. A local newspaper describing a coming-out ball at Port Eliot complimented the housekeeper, cook, and butler: "The whole of the arrangements were carried out in a highly satisfactory manner, under the joint superintendence of Mrs Davis, Mrs Vaughan and Mr Bailey."[37]

Distressed gentlewomen probably enjoyed their work least. Unlike schoolteachers, governesses were isolated from supportive peers, and far more subject to parental interference. Schoolroom teaching was monotonous and confining. Without competitive examinations, estimating pupils' progress was difficult; the governess depended on the family's satisfaction for a sense of a job well done. Her most difficult and disheartening duty was monitoring the children's behaviour. Supervising them at prayers, meals, and play, the governess was expected to influence and discipline her pupils. Too often, parents opposed, undermined, or criticized her efforts. Ladies' companions, too, could find their job a sore trial, forced to sustain a willing, cheerful demeanour in constant attendance on a lady in all her moods.

For most servants, gentleman's service was materially as well as psychologically rewarding. Compared to the typical middle-class maid, country house servants received higher wages, more perquisites, better accommodation and food, and more social welfare.

The landed classes paid higher wages not just because they were wealthier, but because they required more experienced, qualified, and specialized staff. Lady Lyttleton, for example, relinquishing control of Hagley to her daughter-in-law, admitted that some servants were "too well paid" but this ensured "better servants, smiling faces, fewer changes and a right to refuse all perquisites, and to look closely at all pilferers."[38] C.V. Butler reported that the rich seldom complained of inefficiency, as they could "afford to pay high wages and insist on good service in return."[39]

Wage rates in country house service varied enormously, according to the servant's gender, age, experience, skills, and department; the employer's rank, wealth, and policies; and the establishment's size and geographical location. Men were paid more than women, reflecting not only traditional discrimination, but also men's status and ornamental value as front-stage servants, and the greater difficulty of attracting them from other occupations. Even men doing comparable work were better-paid: a parlour-maid assumed a butler's duties but not his wage. For both sexes, however, wages steadily rose as they gained experience and reached a senior position in their chosen department.

Wealthy landowners keeping up their position with first-class establishments offered high wages to the best servants of any rank, whereas

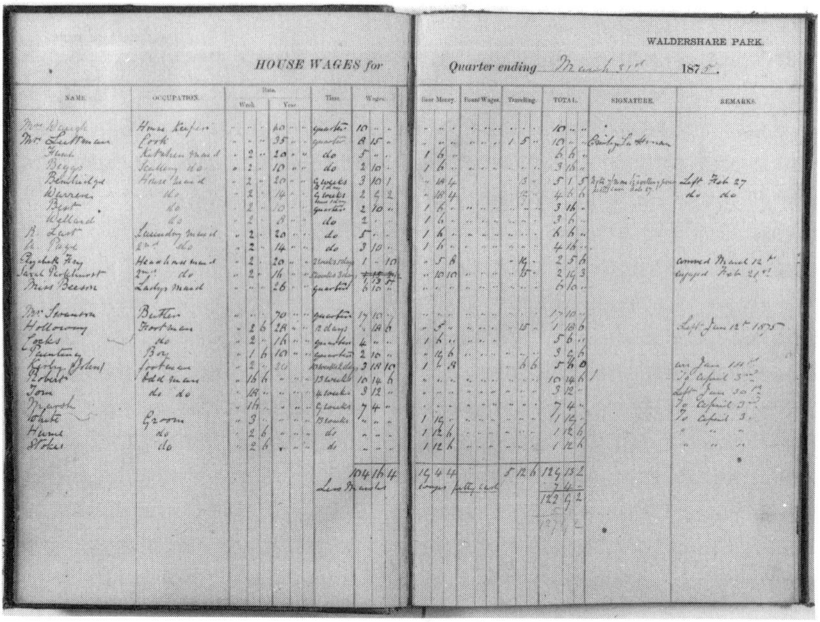

Plate 24 A typical wages book, Waldershare Park

the lesser gentry and families forced to economize, or content with a modest lifestyle, hired less skilled and prestigious servants at lower wages. This meant annual wages for any one category of servant ranged widely, as five establishments show. In 1861, the Earl of Ashburnham paid more to his suitably grand establishment of twenty-six indoor servants, than did retiring bachelor Baron Northwick to his nine. The Giffards of Chillington and the Trollope-Bellews of Casewick kept typical gentry indoor staffs of twelve and thirteen respectively, but the former economized with lower annual wages, which were still higher than those paid by the lesser-gentry Dixons of Holton to their small staff. While Lord Northwick paid his long-serving butler £52 10s per year, the Casewick butler earned £42 and the Chillington man a mere £35. The earl's first footman received £28, the baron's £22, and the Trollope-Bellews' £18. The Giffards could only afford a single footman at £15, while the Dixons kept just one manservant at £21. Lady's maids at Ashburnham and Casewick received £22 each; at Chillington and Holton they had to be content with £11 and £10. Lord Ashburnham's cook earned £60; her counterparts at Casewick, Chillington, and Holton received £30, £20, and £13 10s respectively. The first housemaid (of four) at Ashburnham was well paid at £20 compared to the upper housemaids at Casewick and Northwick (£14) or Chillington (£10), and the Dixons' sole housemaid (£11).[40] Though margins were wide, there was a generally accepted scale of wages for each rank of establishment. "If I choose to offer £25 I can have my choice of any number" of cooks, Henry Polderoy admitted, while Victoria Yorke told her husband, "£8 is the wage boys expect at 14 years."[41]

Wage rates were also affected by geographic location: higher in and near London, and lower in some distant regions. One authority considered Cornwall, Devon, Somerset, and Wales to be low-wage areas, and in Northumberland Lady Ridley found she could pay less than her parents did in Hertfordshire. To determine the usual rate for gardeners in their area of Kent, the Husseys asked their neighbours what they paid.[42]

Most employers negotiated wages with each applicant according to age, skills, and experience, so that wage rates varied for servants hired successively for the same position. Some landowners did offer a standard wage for lower places over many years: at Burwood Park from 1844 to 1871, all under-housemaids, kitchen-maids, and dairy-maids except one earned £10 per annum.[43] Others preferred to offer a high wage initially, hoping to attract and retain good servants. Yet others, such as Lord Northwick, raised a low initial wage if the newcomer did well.[44] Labourers were, predictably, the lowest-paid. Their weekly wages were comparable to the pay of local agricultural workers. At Scotney in 1880, farm and estate wages were identical to wages in the stables and gardens.[45] Without a tied cottage or harvest money, country house labourers' real income was lower, although they had more steady employment.[46] Boys and the elderly received less than a vigorous man. Among the garden labourers at Englefield in 1861, a single lad aged seventeen and a man of seventy-one only earned 9s a week, while men in their early twenties reached the top rate of 11s a week.[47]

Casual workers' wage rates likewise echoed daily rates on farms. Men assisting in the house and laundry at Trentham earned 1s 6d to 2s a day, rising to 3s or more by the 1880s, while part-time garden labourers received 2s a day at Erddig and 2s 6d at Prestwold.[48] For women, the usual rate was 1s a day, but needlewomen and washerwomen often got more. Local rates for women's fieldwork were often lower: at Holton, 6d–8d a day compared to 1s in the house.[49] Regular employment at the mansion could result in significant annual income. Mary Hewitt earned £8 6s at Holton in 1865, and Prestwold's odd-job man accumulated £13 6s in 1871.[50] One form of temporary work, wet-nursing, was exceptionally well paid. Knowing their baby's life depended on the wet-nurse, parents were willing to pay her £1 or more a week, with good food and living conditions, for up to a year.[51]

Casual work also increased full-time outdoor servants' total income. Men earned a little extra after work game-watching, vermin-catching, or waiting at large parties; their wives could obtain full- or part-time employment in the laundry or dairy, taking care of the poultry or a lodge, assisting in the house, or doing laundry at home.

Among life-cycle and career servants, wages were lowest for young, inexperienced beginners in relatively unskilled labour-intensive positions, just as in other occupations. John Mace began as stable-boy at Northwick in 1817 for just 2s a week, and Billy Richardson started in the Norwood gardens at 3s in 1886.[52] Stable-boys and garden boys earned £3–5 early in the century, and £6–8 in later decades. Inexperienced indoor boys commonly received £6–10; scullery-maids, nursery-maids, and even the gentry's youngest housemaids started as low as £4, less than the average maid-of-all-work. Entrants with some experience earned more: for indoor boys, £12–14 prevailed in large establishments from the 1870s; scullery-maids and nursery-maids generally expected around £10; and for lowest housemaids the usual rate was £8–10, rising to £10–12 in the 1860s, and £15 or more after 1890.

Lower outdoor menservants initially did little better than agricultural labourers. "Horticulture has always been tied to agriculture in wage structure," a former Cliveden gardener explained, "a lot of estates would pay agricultural rates," though "the better employers paid a bit more."[53] In the 1860s, the Starkeys' under-gamekeepers got 16s, while under-gardeners began at 13s–15s, with raises to 16s, only 1s more than a farm labourer.[54]

Wages increased with experience and promotion, especially in large establishments, where heads of the lower-servant hierarchy did quite well. First kitchen-maids, for instance, were essentially second cooks, paid as much as £25 or £30. The transition to upper servant meant significant wage increases, and the range of wages for any one position became even wider, because of servants' varying experience and talents, employers' preferences, and the scale and wealth of each establishment. Gender differences in remuneration were greater among upper servants, not merely because menservants were now allowed to marry and support a family, but because the family's reputation depended on their more obvious skills.

Highest paid were men cooks, usually commanding £100 or more a year. The Dukes of Sutherland paid top wages: from £108 in 1818 to £200 in the 1870s. House stewards were well paid too: most earned between £50 and £100, but the Leveson-Gowers paid as much as £210.[55]

As educated gentlewomen, governesses ranked among the highest-paid female servants. Most of the landed classes exceeded the £20–45 typically offered by the middle-class employer. Between £50 and £80 was standard, and well-educated women competent in several languages and many accomplishments expected over £100. The Leveson-Gowers' French governesses commanded annual salaries of £150 and £200 in 1837.[56]

Gender discrimination awarded butlers higher wages than housekeepers, whose responsibilities were not so much less useful as less visible and prestigious. Typically, a butler hired the same year as a housekeeper received around one-half to two-thirds more. In 1876, for instance, the Trollope-Bellews engaged a butler at £76 and a housekeeper at £25.[57] Early in the period, butlers could expect £35–60 in gentry households, and from mid-century £50–80. Aristocrats paid £10–20 more. Housekeepers' wages did not rise significantly over the century: they could expect £30–40. Lesser landowners paid as little as £20, and the wealthiest £50–65.

Although they performed similar services, valets earned about twice as much as lady's maids. Valets could normally expect £40–50 per annum until the 1860s, when £45–65 became common, rising to as much as £70 from the 1870s. Lady's maids started at £16–20 in the first half of the century, but £20–30 in the 1860s, and £25–35 from the 1870s. This unmistakable rise reflects an increasing demand for highly skilled attendants for visiting and travelling.

Inevitably, female cooks were paid far less than men cooks. Female cooks' wages ranged widely, depending on their skills and experience, and on employers' expectations. Some presided over their minions in aristocratic kitchens, or acted as cook-housekeepers. Others were second cooks to a man cook, preparing staff meals, or retained in country seats such as Trentham to cook for permanent servants. The least skilled worked for the lesser gentry, undertaking tasks outside their usual duties, and accepting more intervention in the kitchen. By the end of the century, the subdivisions were clearly defined: "thorough good," or "thorough," "good," "good plain," and "plain." Wage rates for female country house cooks did improve over the century. Regency gentry normally paid cooks less than £20, and the peerage from about £25 to £40. From mid-century £20–35 was common among the gentry, while peers typically paid £40–60.

Nurses were the lowest-paid upper servants, as the least visible and the most "polluted," dealing with bodily wastes, noise, disorder, and grime. Their low ranking was clearly shown when the nurse at Rudding Park became housekeeper as well in 1898; her wages rose from £35 to £45. While the lesser gentry paid as little as £7 a year, most nurses could expect up to £20 until the 1870s, more if employed by peers: the Leveson-Gowers' head nurses received over £30 from the 1840s to the 1870s.[58]

The annual wages of outdoor department heads depended on the scale of the establishment. Highly respected head gardeners of show-piece gardens, training large numbers of men, were well rewarded; at Trentham, head gardeners' wages rose from £100 to £200 over the century.[59] Most head gardeners would be satisfied with £40–65, although grander establishments offered £70–90 from the 1870s. Head gamekeepers' wages ranged between £20 and £80, depending on the importance of game on the estate. Coachmen were the lowest-paid outdoor heads, receiving as little as £16 early in the century; £20–30 remained common until the 1850s, but coachmen's wages did improve to between £30 and 60 thereafter.

Did country house servants' wages rise over the century?[60] F. M. L. Thompson detects a slight fall in the early 1820s, stability until the 1860s, and then rising rates, perhaps due to "intensified competition for good servants." But Jill Franklin believes that "rates for both men and women went up continuously" from 1840, "comparatively slowly until about 1880 then much more steeply."[61] The data in this study indicate that among upper servants, most branches saw their wage rates rise in the 1860s or 1870s.[62] A better measure of change, however, is provided by the lowest servants, whose status and work were most uniform, and who were most likely to be paid at the going rate. Starting wages for scullery-maids, or kitchen-maids in houses without them, lowest housemaids, and lowest laundry-maids, all combined together, show a fall on average in the 1820s from over £9 to below £8, then a long period fluctuating between £9 and £10 until the 1870s, when wages began rising, slowly to the mid-nineties, then rapidly, first to £15, then to £16. To some extent these results correspond to the trend in real wages in the population as a whole, which rose after 1814, stagnated from the 1820s to the 1860s, then climbed until the 1890s, when they fluctuated.[63]

Wages were not a major source of dissatisfaction to either landed employers or their servants. Relatively high wages continued to attract plentiful recruits, who steadily gained more through job mobility. Later in the century, however, rising wage rates were caused not only by heightened competition for good servants, but by pressure from them. In newspaper advertisements and applications, servants increasingly stipulated wages. Lucy Arkwright reported in 1872 that "livery servants are very scarce & will not think of anything lower than £30 or £35," and in 1880 referred to a butler who declined a post "because they only offered him £50."[64]

That wealthy families' employees earned higher wages than the typical maidservant in a middle-class household is hardly surprising. What is less obvious is the fact that real wages were often much higher than money wages. All live-in servants were provided with accommodation, food and drink, and liveries if needed. Many employers also paid for initial travelling expenses, laundry, and medical care. Live-in servants escaped householders' expenses of rates and taxes, too. In 1829, William Kitchener advised that a manservant was "not maintained for less than £20 or £30 per annum." In 1857, J. H. Walsh found a manservant added "at least £50 or £60 a year to the kitchen expenses," whereas a female servant usually cost £20–25 a year or less, an estimate still accepted by Mrs Massey in 1914.[65] Head gardeners, coachmen, and gamekeepers were often provided with free cottages and allowances, as were many married butlers.

The monetary value of accommodation, its furnishings, lighting, heating, maintenance, and cleaning, and the services of other servants, varied greatly from one house to another. The value of servants' food and drink, however, can be calculated from board wages – weekly cash payments given to servants eating in the house for buying their own food when the family was absent, or paid to outdoor single men catering for themselves in their own rooms. This allowance reflected age, status, and gender; men were expected to consume more than women, and boys less, while upper servants received most, for their more expensive food. Typical board wages were 10s a week for lower men, and 9s for lower women.

Upper servants' rates varied more, from 12s to 17s 6d. Rates rose late in the century: lower maids received 11s 6d at Petworth after 1891, and 12s at Taplow Court in 1908.[66] Board wages were lower in the country than the city, and were also influenced by local custom.[67]

Gender differences were also evident in clothing. Lower indoor men-servants, coachmen, and postilions were given livery and working clothes, and gamekeepers, grooms, and stablemen normally received the latter. Some employers even supplied underclothes to footmen, and occasionally a powder allowance. Free clothing meant a considerable saving: a complete outfit for a Prestwold footman cost £16 16s in 1907, and a coachman's £10 8s 9d.[68] Women servants and upper staff usually had to buy their own clothes, cutting deeply into a year's wages. Webster warned maids not to spend more than two-thirds of their wage on dress.[69] But a length of cotton cloth was a common Christmas gift, and a few mistresses supplied uniforms.

Many servants received money allowances: for tea and sugar early in the century, for washing, and eventually for beer. Beer money was determined by sex, status, and age, too: at Erddig in 1905, the butler received 8s per week, the housekeeper, nurse, and footmen 6s, the maids 4s, and the youngest maid and the hall-boy only 2s.[70] With a pint of beer costing $2\frac{1}{2}$–3d servants could imbibe freely. The frugal and abstemious saved their allowances. Annie Cable earned only £1 a month in 1909 as a stillroom maid, but with 5s a week for beer money and washing, she "made a bit." One resourceful footman bought all his underclothes and boots with saved-up beer money.[71] Outdoor staff were often allowed firewood, vegetables, and coal. Even labourers benefited: needy Northwick employees were entitled to dripping from the kitchen, and everyone on the Street End estate got free milk from the dairy.[72]

The greater scale and wealth of the country house meant far better pickings in perquisites than in an ordinary middle-class household. When ordering goods, department heads expected commission or discounts from tradesmen. Butlers were entitled to empty bottles and candle-ends, lady's maids and valets to their employers' cast-off clothing, and head coachmen to worn-out waggon wheels, while stud grooms rented out stallions. Gamekeepers took skins, horns, rabbits, or fawns. Nurses received tips at christenings. Enterprising cooks sold the dripping and kitchen waste, a practice leading to such deliberate spoilage, wastage, and dishonesty that some families forbade it, or allowed a monthly sum instead. When the Duke of Devonshire proposed to raise the chef's wages from £300 to £500, on condition that full accounts be kept and closely monitored, the chef refused, saying he would lose too much.[73] There was enough to spare even for the humblest servants. Daily women often took home gifts of surplus food and cast-off clothing.[74]

Yet another source of income uncommon in a middle-class home was vails, tips from departing guests. Disgruntled employers failed to suppress the practice, and by the end of the century, as a broader social spectrum of guests visited more frequently, demands were made openly. The amount offered depended on the guest's sex and age, the length of the visit, and the host's social position. In the 1830s, Lady Blackett gave housemaids a minimum of 1s 6d. Two decades later, Simon Yorke generally gave menservants and maids 5s each. Edwardian menservants in great houses expected gentlemen to tip a sovereign (£1).[75] Only staff in direct contact with visitors or their servants could count on vails. Profitable vails were an attraction of country house service: some servants, avowed one commentator, actually stipulated on being hired, "for plenty of entertaining."[76] As hall-boy, William Lanceley earned enough in tips from visiting lady's maids to send his entire wage home.[77] Servants in charge of great houses also pocketed lucrative tips from showing visitors around. The whole system of perquisites, vails, and tips was tolerated because it provided additional rewards and incentives, and muted demands for higher wages. Yet when carried on without the family's knowledge or explicit consent, these practices enabled servants to further their own interests at the family's expense.

The feudal traditions and paternal benevolence of the country house also offered greater monetary rewards than were to be found in middle-class service. Indoor servants often resented utilitarian Christmas presents, but outdoor men welcomed food, fuel, clothing, or blankets. Though not legally liable for sick or injured servants, many landowners paid for doctors' visits and nursing care by local women, or for hospital expenses. Early in the century, Lord Hatherton simply made each servant an annual allowance of £1 2s for medicine, but the Packes paid for doctors' visits, a total of £30 10s in 1877, as did the Dukes of Sutherland, with a bill of £121 19s. 6d in 1835. The Blacketts provided a doctor with £50 a year and a rent-free cottage to attend both family and staff.[78] A servant disabled at work might receive compensation. Sir Henry Oglander, for example, left an annuity of £50 to a severely wounded gamekeeper.[79] This care could even extend beyond current employees. The third Duchess of Sutherland arranged for a former lady's maid to convalesce at Trentham, while Sir Thomas Fowell Buxton offered his gamekeeper "anything that his house could afford" for Banville's pregnant and ailing wife.[80]

Upper-class paternalism provided social insurance rarely found elsewhere. Relatively few servants received pensions, which were not the norm in Victorian England. Working people were expected to save providently for their old age, and the well-paid country house servant was in a better position than most to achieve this goal. Pensions were regarded as rewards for long service, and in many households only a few servants stayed for decades. Pensions were also often significantly lower than the former annual wage.[81] Extremely wealthy or liberal landowners were most likely to reward long-serving retirees with pensions, allowances, or rent-free cottages or lodges, and to provide for deceased servants' widows and orphans. Shortly after inheriting, the ninth Duke of Bedford spent around £1,000 on pensions to thirty-two former servants.[82] At Trentham, many retired servants received pensions: a former coachman and a groom each received £30 a year, a poultry-man and a lodge porter £40, and various laundry-maids got between £15 and £25. Two housekeepers retired on £50 and £40 a year. Head gardeners' widows were given handsome annuities of £30 and £50. The Yorkes' retired servants gained a pension and often a cottage. Edward Humphries, a coachman, retired on 7s 8d per week, and after his death, his widow was given 5s weekly.[83] Other estates continued to retain pensioners at a small wage in "the gang," to sweep paths, rake leaves, or do weeding at a leisurely pace.[84]

Legacies and annuities were more widely distributed. A landowner often bequeathed a year's wages to all staff employed at the time of his death, as did John Arkwright in 1858, or left varying amounts according to length of service. Lord Northwick provided annuities of £50 for his butler, under-butler, groom, nurse, and coachman (to be forfeited if invested in a public house), £10 to their widows, and £5 to gardeners and labourers. His head keeper and head gardener received a year's wages if they had served five years when he died, and every other servant two years' wages for ten years' service, three for fifteen or more and four for twenty years and over. A codicil gave everyone who had been in his service a year at his death £100. The second Duke of Sutherland similarly left an annuity of £110 to his valet, legacies to fifteen servants, and a year's wages, up to £100, to all others in service for more than a year. A few left remarkable amounts: the bachelor Ralph Sneyd willed his married manservant and housekeeper £100 a year for life, and £5,000 in trust for their two daughters.[85]

Altogether, country house service offered far greater financial rewards than middle-class service, not only in a higher money wage and opportunities to rise to well-paid positions, but in the savings made by generous board, medical care, clothing, and allowances, and by the gains accumulated through perquisites, vails, and tips, as well as possible legacies and pensions. But the distribution of this largesse varied according to servant type and position.

Labourers benefited least, earning little more than agricultural workers unless employed all year round. Unlike other outdoor men, they had to pay rent. Like farm labourers, casual workers' earnings depended on age, health, and seasonal demand. But as part of the feudal community, they qualified for perquisites or charitable benevolence. Only on great estates such as Trentham, where peers could afford generosity, or on small properties such as Holton, where helpers were known personally, might they expect pensions or legacies. The ninth Duke of Bedford pensioned a porter, a carriage-washer, and a vermin-killer, while Susan Bisset bequeathed £13 to Hannah James, her washerwoman.[86]

Distressed gentlewomen were also relatively badly off. Few earned the £150–200 estimated to be the minimum required to maintain an appropriately genteel standard of living. Although they received board valued at around £30 a year, they paid for laundry, travel, and medical care, and had to buy suitable outfits, so that "under the best of circumstances, a governess's income left her on the very edge of gentility, with no margin for illness or unemployment."[87] Governesses seldom served long enough, or inspired enough affection, to be rewarded with a pension. Furthermore, many of them supported other family members. Thus governesses seldom saved enough for retirement.

Life-cycle servants who changed places frequently and remained lower servants earned fewer fringe benefits, although housemaids, footmen, and grooms could do well from tips. Life-cycle maids earned the lowest wages, had to find their own clothes, and received the smallest board wages and allowances, few perquisites, and the least benevolence. While lower maidservants may not have done better financially than factory workers until later in the century, the benefits of their real wages improved their comparative position.

Career servants, in contrast, could gain relatively high incomes and financial security, particularly if unmarried and settled into one household until a pensioned retirement. Many butlers and housekeepers accumulated substantial savings. Mary Webster, cook at Erddig from 1843 to 1876, left over £1,300 in her will, while James Phillips, head gardener for forty-three years, amassed nearly £4,000.[88] A mere laundry-maid at Shugborough saved £400, which she invested in the estate at 4 per cent per annum.[89] Even married career servants usually did better than the typical rural working-class family. The census returns show

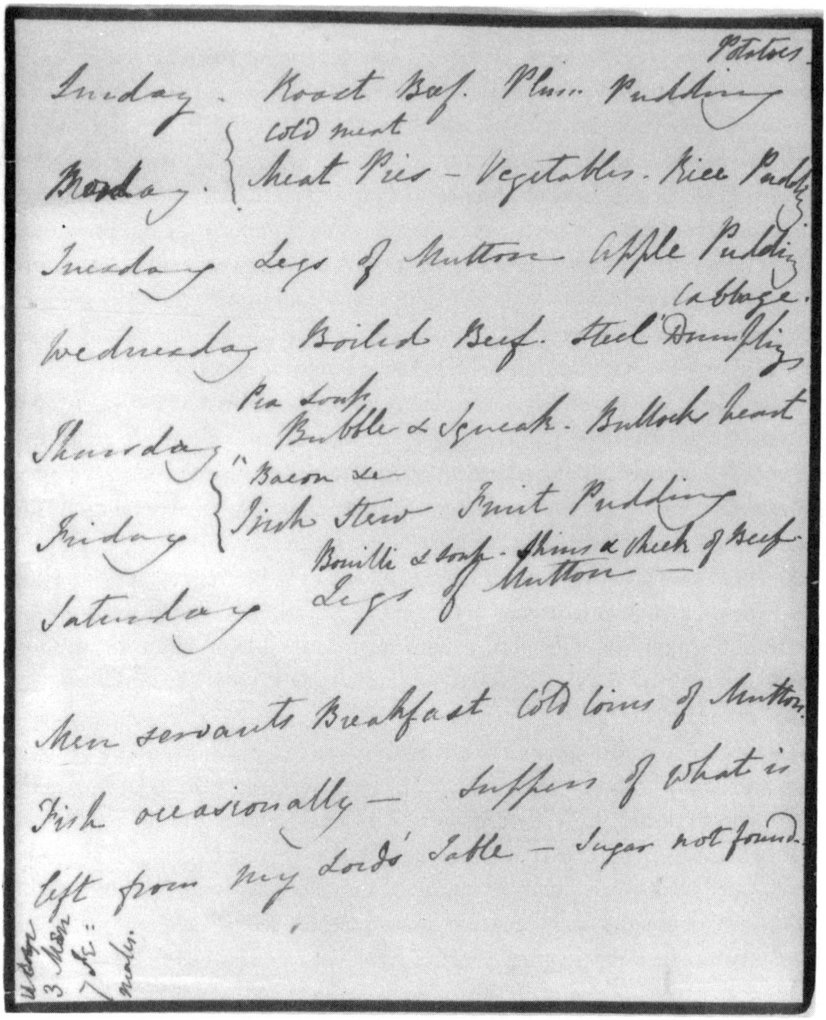
Sunday. Roast Beef. Plum Pudding Potatoes
Monday. Cold meat / Meat Pies – Vegetables. Rice Pudding
Tuesday Legs of Mutton Apple Pudding Cabbage.
Wednesday Boiled Beef. Suet Dumplings
Thursday. Pea Soup / Bubble & Squeak. Bullock heart
Friday Bacon &c / Irish Stew Fruit Pudding
Saturday Bouilli & Soup – Shins & Neck of Beef / Legs of Mutton —

Men servants Breakfast Cold loins of Mutton. Fish occasionally — Suppers of What is left from my Lords' Table — Sugar not found.

Plate 25 A servants' menu from Linton Park

that many could afford to keep children at school until they were thirteen or fourteen, sending them to work later than other working-class children. Some daughters aged thirteen to fifteen were helping at home. Ten upper servants, mostly gardeners and gamekeepers with families or lodgers, actually employed a servant themselves, albeit an inexpensive young girl or older woman.

In an era when many working-class people had deficient diets and lived in poor, overcrowded housing, the superior living conditions of country house service were a significant attraction. The food and sleeping accommodation of middle-class service were, by contrast, notoriously niggardly.

Servants had to be well fed to endure long working hours, and mealtimes loomed large in a monotonous, confined existence. Landowners normally provided ample, nutritious meals, for so much was home-produced at low cost: fresh meat, milk, butter, vegetables and fruit, and often bread and beer. Dishes were plain and wholesome, though sometimes badly prepared by a harassed cook or inexperienced kitchen-maid. Servants' diet became more generous and varied over the century. Early in the period, bread, cheese, and beer dominated the menu, with meat at dinner, and few vegetables, but by the end of the century, cold meat appeared at breakfast, and hot joints, vegetables, and puddings were served at lunch as well as dinner. "Elevenses" or "lunch" of beer (or tea and cocoa for the women), bread, and cheese, were eventually given in the late morning, and afternoon tea with bread and butter and sometimes cake at four p.m. The nutritious meals were a significant benefit, especially for growing adolescents or chronically undernourished villagers.

Diets reflected stratifications within the servant hierarchy. The governess shared the family's every-day fare, joining them for breakfast and lunch when no guests were present, or eating with her charges in the schoolroom. Upper servants enjoyed a richer diet than the lower staff, often taking dining-room leftovers for their supper. At Welbeck Abbey, they also drank wine at luncheon and dinner.[90] Day and casual workers either joined lower servants in the servants' hall or were relegated to the kitchen.

Beer was the usual beverage, either freely on tap or in specified allowances, typically three pints a day for men, and between one and two pints for women. It was refreshing after hard physical work, promoted relaxation and conviviality, and was also nourishing, supplying both carbohydrates and B vitamins.

In the capacious country house, servants' accommodation was, generally, vastly superior to that in most working-class homes, and to the damp, dark basement rooms or cramped, ill-lit, uninsulated, and often dingy and grimy attics serving as servants' bedrooms in most urban dwellings. Landowners could afford to build and keep clean more generous quarters. Conditions in older houses were sometimes still grim: maids slept directly under the roof, and lower menservants in basement dormitories, or even in the servants' hall on let-down beds. One manservant had to guard the silver: at Erddig the footman slept in front of the safe door.[91] Victorian architects improved sleeping quarters, eliminating basements, and sometimes placing servants' bedrooms in wings on the first floor. The servants' bedrooms they designed, concludes Jill Franklin, were "generously sized, perfectly sanitary, usually well ventilated and reasonably warm."[92] Yet while most servants' rooms in Victorian houses had fireplaces, fires were normally banned, for the upper classes believed the lower orders were less sensitive to cold than their betters.

Nor did servants, they assumed, have the same aesthetic sensibilities. One country house architect advocated bedrooms "equal to those of a similar class of persons in their own homes – or perhaps a little better, but not too much so."[93] Thus, lower servants' bedrooms were, in theory, supposed to be minimally furnished with either plain, cheap furniture manufactured for servants, or worn pieces discarded by the family. Lower servants' rooms should enforce anonymity and low status, denying them a pleasant, private retreat.

Inventories, however, show that in practice more comfortable conditions prevailed, with soft feather mattresses over the usual flock ones, half-tester or four-poster beds rather than cheap iron bedsteads, and more furniture. A typical maid's room at Northwick in 1859 contained a half-tester bed with hangings, two oak chests-of-drawers, and a mahogany kneehole chest-of-drawers, besides the usual washstands and carpet strips. Discarded items provided entertainment: one Northwick menservants' bedroom contained an old small billiards table, and sets of chessmen and draughts.[94] Late in the period, some employers, fearing tuberculosis spawned by cold, damp, poorly ventilated, and overcrowded conditions, or the loss of good servants, tried to provide pleasant rooms for lower servants. By the 1880s, at least one servants' bathroom was standard in new houses.[95] A good cottage (the "bothy") for single gardeners was also a great asset, figuring prominently in advertisements for gardeners in the *Gardener's Chronicle*. The bungalow built at late-nineteenth-century Aynhoe had "spacious rooms and separate bedrooms."[96]

While growing up at home, most servants would have slept in unheated, poorly furnished rooms, so austere conditions may not have unduly upset them. Among the girls from Juniper Hill, "sleeping in a large attic . . . was not then looked upon as a hardship, provided they had a bed each and their own chest of drawers and washstands."[97] Indeed, the long hours worked by lower servants meant they seldom used their bedrooms, except to sleep. The spartan conditions were virtually universal, and the means of securing comfort, privacy, and personal territory lay in becoming an upper servant.

As befitted their superior status, most upper servants had their own rooms, often on the first floor, or strategically located where they could guard the lower servants. Nurses slept in or near the night nursery, and governesses and lady's maids were usually on the first floor. Butlers were the least fortunate: many of them had tiny, ill-lit bedrooms in front of the plate room they guarded from burglars. Upper servants' rooms were much better furnished than lower servants' quarters, normally with fireplaces they were free to use. The housekeeper at Northwick had a four-poster bed with dimity hangings, a wool mattress, and four blankets rather than the usual three. Besides the usual fittings, her bedroom contained a Brussels carpet, a large elm chest-of-drawers, two oak tables, seven chairs, and two mahogany chests. Governesses' rooms met middle-class standards: at Hampton Court the governess had mahogany furniture including bookshelves and an easy chair, and a shower bath and foot pan.[98]

Unlike most middle-class employers, the landed classes could afford not only a separate room for the staff's meals and recreation, but offices for the heads of department which also served as comfortable sitting-rooms. Instead of huddling over the kitchen fire, lower servants spent their spare time in the servants' hall, though a few great houses had sitting-rooms or workrooms for each department, and menservants often congregated in the butler's pantry. In older mansions, the servants' hall was in the basement, as at Erddig, but most Victorian architects placed all the offices on the ground floor. Carefully positioned away from family quarters, however, servants' halls were often poorly lit, with a dismal outlook on to the kitchen courtyard. They were normally sparsely furnished, with little more than a large table and benches. The Northwick servants' hall contained an elm table, two benches, a stool, a draft box and writing desk, and a mahogany corner cupboard, and it was ornamented only by a pair of antlers on the wall. By the Edwardian period, some servants' halls were more cheerful: the Holton servants' hall had a polished table and bentwood chairs, a hearthrug on the linoleum, framed *Christmas Graphic* prints, and a whatnot stand. Upper servants, both male and female, gathered in the housekeeper's and steward's rooms, which were comfortably furnished, with personal possessions displayed. The housekeeper's room at Hampton Court contained a mahogany dining-table and chairs, a chintz-covered sofa, a bureau, a carpet, and a hearthrug among its furnishings.[99]

The condition of cottages, lodges, or flats for married servants depended on the landlord's policies. Many dwellings resembled labourers' cottages: badly built and maintained, insanitary, and overcrowded. J. C. Loudon was outraged to find head gardeners on great estates occupying "picturesque but dilapidated cottages with tiny, dark rooms and out-of-door sanitation."[100] Investigations of employees' cottages at Trentham in 1835 and 1842 revealed much sub-standard housing, like a gamekeeper's "very small and uncomfortable" one-bedroom

Plate 26 The head gardener's house at Keele

cottage "in a wretched state of repair." The 1842 report recommended demolishing and rebuilding four of the fifteen outdoor servants' cottages.[101] Early in the century, owners and architects valued pretty exteriors rather than adequate bedrooms or windows, convenience or sanitation. Lodges were notoriously cramped and uncomfortable. Eventually, however, many landlords, motivated by paternalistic benevolence and concern for morality, erected well-constructed three-bedroomed dwellings. Houses for head gardeners and head gamekeepers were often deliberately superior to ordinary labourers' cottages, with three or four bedrooms and a parlour.[102]

One common complaint about middle-class service was the lack of relaxation and recreation. Employers, selfishly demanding all their servants' time, or fearful of their "going wrong," allowed little free time, and disliked letting them go out. Early-nineteenth-century servants seldom had any recognized time off, except for church. Later, legislation reduced hours in factories and other work-places, and the working classes began enjoying leisure after work and on Saturdays. Inquiries repeatedly found lack of leisure time was a leading cause of domestic service's unpopularity.[103] Competing with other occupations offering shorter hours, masters and mistresses increasingly gave an afternoon off a week or every other Sunday, and a fortnight's holiday. Still, unlike other workers, most servants had to remain indoors in the evenings. When work was done, or in any unoccupied moments, many urban servants stayed cooped up in a gloomy basement kitchen, reading novels or popular magazines, sewing or knitting. They were seldom given the time or encouragement to develop other hobbies and talents.

While towns and cities offered more attractions on afternoons off than the countryside, country house service did far more to satisfy needs for relaxation and recreation. With a larger staff, strict demarcation of duties, inflexible routines, and daily help, agreements as to time off were more resolutely adhered to. Servants' meals and hours off were inviolate. Each household regulated leisure time differently. Philip and Louisa Yorke permitted their maids to stay out late up to three times a week, but the Dixons' maids, while free after tea, had to remain in the house.[104]

Landowners acknowledged the need for amusements in isolated rural mansions.[105] In the eighteenth century servants in great houses had freely organized their own entertainments, holding parties called "frolics." Some large establishments continued to have regular dances in the servants' hall, although moralistic Victorian and Edwardian employers

> The Prestwold Hall Servants
> (By invitation of Mr. & Lady Alice Packe),
> on the occasion of the coming-of-age of their son,
> request the pleasure of the company of
>
> _____
>
> at Prestwold Hall, on Tuesday, February 7th,
> at 9.30 o'clock
> ——————— Dancing ———————
> An answer is requested addressed to Mr. Collier,
> Prestwold Hall, stating numbers, when tickets will be sent.

Plate 27 An invitation to a servants' ball at Prestwold Hall, 1889

insisted on greater decorum and supervision. Late in the period, servants' dances were held twice weekly at Longleat, weekly at Rendlesham Hall, and every month at Shirburn.[106] Most landowners gave an annual servants' dance, usually held at Christmas or New Year, but sometimes on the owner's birthday or wedding anniversary, and a wedding or a coming-of-age would also include a servants' dance among its celebrations. Servants from fifteen neighbouring houses were invited to the servants' ball held at Prestwold to celebrate the heir's coming-of-age in 1899.[107] These balls were a great boost to servants' spirits, giving them something to look forward to. Landowners were also munificent at Christmas time, lavish with food, drink, and entertainment. Indeed, many servants at Welbeck "who had very little to go home to anyway actually preferred to stay."[108] Thoughtful employers allowed treats at other times. The Hampton Court servants went to the Leominster Flower Show and the Choral Festival, while the Birchalls gave staff a day's treat to Chepstow and Tintern Abbey in 1883, organized a picnic for them in Cirencester Park in 1896, and sent them to the seaside for the day in 1898.[109]

A few houses provided recreational facilities, the most famed being Worth Park, with its servants' reading room, library, billiard room, and ballroom.[110] Edwardian landowners, anxious to retain increasingly scarce servants, did even more. Some ladies gave maidservants gardens of their own, while one mistress in north Wales not only supplied her maids with books and games, but lent them the car for expeditions.[111]

Many landowners encouraged sport among their menservants: Mr Wingfield provided both equipment and catering for cricket matches at Ampthill, the Buckhurst servants fished and played golf or cricket, and other menservants fished and shot with gamekeeper friends.[112] The Arkwrights took cricket very seriously, asking a prospective butler if he played. Frederick Wynn of Glenliven even hired a professional to coach his menservants.[113]

Servants also used their own initiative. Opportunities for leisure depended on the nature of each occupation, rank, and gender: cooks had afternoons and evenings free; nurses could relax once their charges were in bed; and lady's maids waited up late for their mistresses. Housemaids had leisure time in the afternoons and evenings. Women enjoyed reading magazines and cheap novels, sewing, and entertaining maidservants from nearby houses. Indoor menservants kept themselves occupied while waiting for bells to summon them, and had several hours off every afternoon. They collected crested livery buttons or stationery, did fretwork, silk- and wool work, studied languages, or played musical instruments. Hating idleness, Eric Horne crocheted babies' jackets and shawls for old women while on duty. In his free time he played the concertina, took up the violin and photography, and enjoyed bicycling and reading. As hall-boy, William Harrison sketched and painted in water-colours, with his mistress's encouragement. A footman at Hardwicke Court even got advances on his wages to buy a piano.[114]

Outdoor servants and labourers generally had evenings, and often Sundays, off. Ernest Field, a young gardener at Edwardian Halton, spent his spare time visiting other estates or reading, and joined three or four other young gardeners for Sunday tea at a local inn.[115] In 1889, enterprising gardeners at Prestwold formed a Gardeners' Mutual Improvement Society, with papers and exhibits at their regular meetings, and in 1898 the Lilleshall indoor men and stablemen formed a social club, buying their own billiards table. The club was open from 6 p.m. to 9.30 p.m.;

ale was provided but gambling was forbidden.[116] Head servants had the most leisure and freedom. In the 1820s and 1830s, Ferdinand Ceroti, house steward at Burton Constable, frequently visited friends or invited them to dinner or tea, went coursing and fishing, dined at the Clifford Arms, and took his family on outings. At Wrest Park, seniors read and worked on hobbies "in their private sitting rooms" or studied in the library.[117]

Servants were offered a holiday just once a year, normally when the family was away. William Lanceley found very few servants took up the offer. His first holiday in four years' service "was three days, quite enough at that time," for servants found their "cottage homes and food were no comparison" to living in a country house.[118]

The very environment of the country house enriched servants' lives. They could appreciate the beauty and serenity of the house, gardens, and park. Frances Dade, for instance, "was naturally artistic and thrilled to see priceless tapestries" at Wrest Park.[119] Gordon Grimmett believed service educated him. "It was impossible to live among beauty without it getting under your skin; you learn to distinguish what is good and what is not, you learn taste and appreciation, you look at books lining shelves and eventually you pick one up and begin to read; overheard conversations spark off a desire to know more."[120] Servants were often allowed to explore the park and estate. "The woods, parklands and fields were our pleasure grounds" at Glenliven, recalled Edwin Lee. On their frequent walks, the staff there delighted in identifying wild flowers and observing animals, birds, and fish through the seasons. They even went out at night to spy on families of badgers and foxes.[121]

Servants accompanying the family to London had the best of both worlds. Young William Harrison went sightseeing in the afternoons, and to the theatre if he finished his work in time. On Sundays he visited a museum or the Albert Hall. Frederick Gorst and a footman friend went to restaurants and shows on their evenings off. Gorst enjoyed not only the music hall, but also organ recitals and ballet. Mr Cooper, the art-loving butler at Kingston Lacy, haunted the National Gallery. West End public houses such as "The Running Footman" were gathering places for sociable off-duty footmen and butlers.[122] At the seaside, or shooting-boxes, servants shared a more relaxed and informal holiday atmosphere.[123] So did staff left at the country house for the spring-cleaning. There was an "unaccustomed freedom, an easy gait," at Cramner Hall when the master and mistress went abroad.[124]

Altogether, the rewards of domestic service in the country house were much greater than in the typical middle-class establishment. Work itself was more satisfying: a more rigorous training was the passport to the best jobs; a more specialized and efficiently run household facilitated job demarcation; and promotion through the ranks brought higher and more satisfying job skills into use. The country house establishment offered higher pay, more perquisites and tips, superior food, working conditions, sleeping quarters and facilities for relaxation and recreation, and in many cases a tradition of paternalistic social welfare providing free medical care, legacies and annuities, treats, and outings.

These were not the only advantages of country house service. The maid working alone, or with one or two other women, in a middle-class household led a far lonelier and duller life than the country house servant; the companionship of a large staff of both sexes was a major attraction of gentleman's service.

9

Life Below Stairs

Country house service offered not only material advantages over service in smaller households, but many psychological rewards not found in most middle-class homes. Landowners' servants were able to find an identity and retain more of their self-esteem in the community below stairs. The larger staff provided much greater opportunities for friendship, romance, and marriage. Greater physical isolation in the countryside intensified conflict, but it also promoted solidarity. Servants regulated their relationships with each other with an organizational and status hierarchy copied from their employers. While urban servants became increasingly despised by their own class, the country house staff's relations with the rest of the rural community reinforced a sense of social superiority.

One reason for the growing unpopularity of domestic service in the typical urban middle-class household was its inability to satisfy many human needs: for identity and self-worth as an individual; for a sense of belonging; for friendship and love. Other workers found these outside working hours in family relationships, with friends, and in community roles and duties. Domestic servants, however, endured unusual social isolation. They lived in, with limited hours off and courtship forbidden, and were seldom permitted to invite friends and family to visit. Moreover, domestic service was what sociologists term a "total institution", controlling every aspect of the individual's life – dress, recreation, religious observances, sexuality, and relationships – and imposing a novel, supposedly superior culture. Servants' humanity was virtually denied and their inferiority confirmed when they were treated as if they were not present, or as pollutants degraded by contact with dirt and disorder. They could be depersonalized by uniforms or livery, or by name changes. All this undermined servants' sense of identity and self-esteem.

The nineteenth century was a critical period in the development of a consciousness of these needs. In earlier centuries, most young people had left home in their early teens to live and work in another household, where they were treated very much as family in ordinary households, and as part of an organic community in great houses. In the eighteenth century, the landed classes withdrew from their servants, both physically and psychologically, and greatly reduced the extent of paternalistic interference in their servants' private lives. In a period characterized by "monetary values, casual employment, and impersonal market relationships," says Lawrence Stone, highly mobile and independent servants displayed a "strong sense of self-worth."[1] The combination of employers' class consciousness and religious earnestness made domestic service more of a total institution in the nineteenth century.

At the same time, the working-class family was becoming less fragmented. As a result of the Industrial Revolution, increasing numbers of young workers lived at home until marriage. Mothers became housewives, rearing large families. Thus working-class children developed stronger attachments to their mothers and siblings, which made leaving home to live among strangers harder. Late in the century, the rising school-leaving age meant children lived at home until they were thirteen or fourteen. Education was also cited as a factor in arousing servant discontent: the ability to read and write provided a means of self-expression and of keeping in contact with family members through letters, and cultivated dreams of romance in the popular novels maidservants loved to read.

Thus expectations for psychological and emotional needs were rising just when employers were becoming more reluctant to allow servants to gratify them. Service had always required deference, but relations became more formal in the nineteenth century. While some middle-class employers did treat their young servants as family, especially in the petty-place stage, many others expressed their superior social status by deliberately isolating the maidservant from their own family life, forcing her to eat and relax in the kitchen. Maids-of-all-work were notoriously lonely, while servants working with one or two others had no choice in their companions, who might be utterly incompatible.

Working in the country house was at the same time more damaging and more rewarding. Servants were more depersonalized and humiliated in large establishments where autocratic employers pretended they did not exist. Moreover, these larger staffs adopted the landed classes' own rigid hierarchy and caste distinctions, creating a formal, social structure "below stairs" in their own quarters which inhibited friendships between servants of different ranks and departments. Nevertheless, a larger staff also meant more companionship among those of the same rank or department, and more opportunities for romance. The country house did more to meet servants' social and affective needs, providing not just the friendship, company, and sense of acceptance and belonging that people look for in the work-place, but also the deeper attachments and shared recreations of family life. Outdoor servants could have a family life at home, but indoor servants had to find an equivalent within the servant community. In contrast to the lonely maid-of-all-work, the country house servant was part of the full human drama below stairs. "The servants' hall is a little world by itself," avowed the Adamses, "in which the passions, tempers, vices, and virtues, are brought into play."[2] Life in the country house was simply far more exciting. "There is in the minds of most young servants a great craving to get into large establishments," wrote one commentator. "They are delighted at the idea of seeing so much of life as they must necessarily do among a number of strange men and women."[3] There was more going on above stairs, too. Hannah Cullwick felt lonesome when the family was absent from Woodcote, but when they returned, "company came to stop, & then the winter with all the business as there *is* in a big family, & I forgot I was lonely."[4]

The world below stairs was divided by class and rank, with one or two

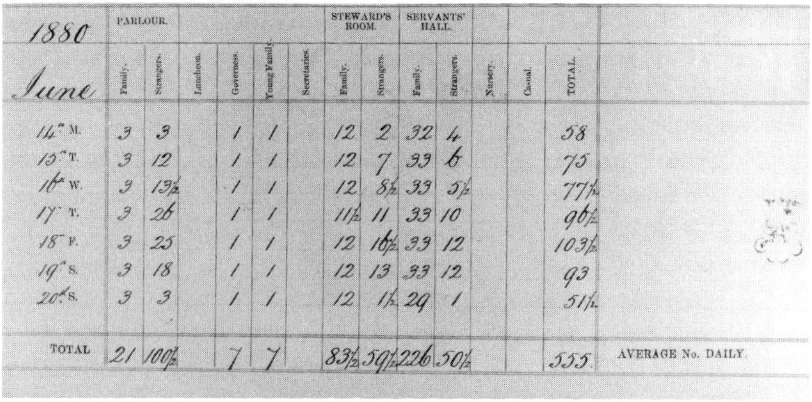

1880	Parlour.						Steward's Room.		Servants' Hall.					
June	Family.	Strangers.	Luncheon.	Governess.	Young Family.	Secretaries.	Family.	Strangers.	Family.	Strangers.	Nursery.	Casual.	TOTAL.	
14th M.	3	3		1	1		12	2	32	4			58	
15th T.	3	12		1	1		12	7	33	6			75	
16th W.	3	13½		1	1		12	8½	33	5½			77½	
17th T.	3	26		1	1		11½	11	33	10			96½	
18th F.	3	25		1	1		12	16½	33	12			103½	
19th S.	3	18		1	1		12	13	33	12			93	
20th S.	3	3		1	1		12	1½	29	1			51½	
TOTAL	21	100½		7	7		83½	59½	226	50½			555	AVERAGE No. DAILY.

Plate 28 A detail from a meals book, from Trentham Hall, showing divisions within the household

gentlewomen keeping aloof from the other servants, who were sharply split between upper and lower staff. While lady-housekeepers had to take their place below stairs, a governess or lady's companion did not work, eat, or socialize with other servants, and expected them to wait on her.[5] Servants found it difficult to treat her as a lady when she lost caste by earning her own living, especially when she was treated coldly by the family. "Some ladies," according to Mary Maurice, "suffer from want of due attention and respect, because the domestics regard them as scarcely their superiors in rank, and others have brought this treatment upon themselves by admitting to undue familiarity and treating them with confidence – and others again from haughtiness and want of consideration."[6] Excluded from the housekeeper's room or servants' hall, governesses and companions were often isolated and lonely. At Roman Catholic Burghwallis, Miss Perkins sought the priest's company, inviting him to supper in her room.[7] Only when the family was in London could governesses socialize, with each other.[8]

In contrast to small middle-class households, in a great house it was upper servants, not the master or mistress, who supervised and directed the under-servants, and controlled their behaviour. Most department heads were strict and severe. Many lower servants were more terrified of the housekeeper or butler than of their master and mistress. Employers wanted department heads to be firm: Mr Holland told Lord Northwick his new footman would require "a *strict stern* butler over him," for only "strong supervision under an autocratic superior servant" who would "work him *hard* and *continuously*" would make Hopkins a reliable servant.[9] "I will not have a steward," insisted Colonel Wyndham, "who is not master of those under him."[10] Not all upper servants were harsh disciplinarians, however. Mr Broughton complained that his butler was too kind and gentle with the "very masterful" lower menservants, and "rather allowed things to slide for the sake of peace."[11] Vantini, the Leveson-Gower house steward in the 1830s, defended his leniency towards the staff, in his imperfect English[12]:

> It has been said that I am to good towards them ... the reason is becose I thing, that a man is more brought to his duty ... by kindness than by rigeur. If I have been kind to them when he has done rong he will listen to your wishes by inclination. In the reverse case he may attend to it for fear and leave the first opportunity.

It may have been easier to accept orders from upper servants than from middle-class mistresses. Lower servants knew their superiors had undergone the same experience, and that they themselves could rise to command others. "The servant in a large establishment is part of a system, and is the *subordinate*, not the *inferior*, of the person in control," explained Violet Firth, "but the servants in a house where the mistress is also the administrator are up against a social system, a viewpoint, a mental attitude."[13] "We lower servants had to walk the chalk-line," recalled Ernest King. "Obey, or else. No-one resented this, all accepted it quite happily."[14]

In a staff of two or three servants, the maids had no choice but to work, eat, and relax in each other's company in a fairly informal and egalitarian way. In contrast, relationships between country house servants were highly regulated and formalized. As in any human group, there was a need to allot roles, define status, and regulate relationships to create harmony, order, and predictability. The staff of a country house, like most work forces, consisted of a group of strangers brought together solely because they worked for the same employer. They were of widely varying ages, personalities, ambitions, and interests, sometimes even of different nationalities. With the high turnover, the servant population was constantly changing. Geographical isolation and restricted contact with the wider world produced an inward-looking community whose members had to endure each other's company day in, day out. Unlike other workers, servants living in could not express their frustrations at home or at the inn. Consequently, divisive and counter-productive tensions could easily build up. Servants dealt with the considerable difficulties of their situation by continuing to adhere to a pre-industrial social order of a hierarchy of ranks, with stratification enforced by rituals and privileges, but with a major division between upper and lower servants. This division had originated with the employment of upper- and middle-class servants in earlier centuries, but was now reinforced by nineteenth-century class consciousness. "Class prejudice among servants themselves is most difficult to combat," complained Lady Willoughby de Broke, "upper servants not caring to associate with the relatives or friends of the under servants." At Welbeck, for instance, the "two groups did not mix socially, the lines were drawn more strictly" than among those they served.[15] While seniors gained their positions by hard work and merit, their sense of superiority was in part derived from their more elevated social origins and education.

The status structure parallelled the organizational structure, each servant being socially ranked according to occupation. Individual establishments had their own systems of ranking: at Welbeck, the under-butler, groom-of-chambers, and head housemaid were considered upper servants.[16] At mealtimes, in church, and at prayers the servants entered and left strictly in order of rank. When there were more than one valet or lady's maid, or when servants accompanied visitors, they joined the procession according to their employer's rank. The distinction between upper and lower servants was expressed in every conceivable way, not only in dress, food, and accommodation, but in the deference lower servants were expected to accord their superiors. Upper servants were addressed as "Sir" or "Madam" by the underlings. To demonstrate their rank and supervisory role, department heads donned formal middle-class dress; even head gardeners wore a dark suit with a stiff collar and a bowler hat to work. Upper servants in earlier centuries had eaten their meals apart, but in most houses they now joined lower servants in the servants' hall as a measure both of economy and discipline. Normally, everyone sat in order of rank, and ate in silence, until the upper servants ceremoniously departed to consume the sweet in their own sitting-room, retaining the custom practised above stairs in the seventeenth and eighteenth centuries.

Servants in great houses took their status system very seriously, with many disputes over precedence. Butlers spent as many anxious moments as their mistresses organizing the procession of visitors into dinner. Servants sometimes even left their places to find a master or mistress of higher rank. After contentedly serving her young gentry mistress for several years, one lady's maid gave notice, saying "I am very happy with you, but it hurts my feelings always to have to walk out last from the 'Hall,' so I want to take a situation with a 'titled lady,' or at least with an 'honourable'."[17] Servants were, in fact, closely imitating the landed classes' status-placement system, demonstrating an identification with their employer's values which enabled them to accept their treatment as inferior menials. Egalitarianism in the servants' hall would have challenged the basic assumptions of domestic service.

The hierarchical system standardized roles, relationships, and behaviour, making them consistent and predictable, and giving stability, order, and security to the individual. Adherence to roles and formal interaction reduced conflicts and personality clashes. Ritual and privilege demonstrated and reinforced upper servants' authority, and enhanced the rewards of upward mobility. "We took the superiority of the Upper Ten seriously," recalled Frederick Gorst, "It was possible to become one of them sometime."[18] As the hierarchical structure was universal in larger households, newcomers were easily slotted in. Regarded as inferiors by their employers, and by the end of the period often despised even by their own class, servants compensated by constructing their own internal status system to satisfy their needs for social advancement and ambition, identity, and a sense of dignity and self-respect.

Yet this system also fostered petty snobbery and harsh treatment of subordinates. Insistence on privilege and demarcation could hinder friendship. Margaret Thomas did not like her first place, for "there was no mateyness in that house, everyone seemed too conscious of their position."[19] Newcomers were intimidated and dismayed by upper servants' haughtiness until they realized it was not personal, but the standard manner thought appropriate. When George Slingsby became a hall-boy, the butler received him "as if he had a nasty smell under his nose. It was an expression that George came to know was generally adopted by all the best butlers."[20] Upper servants' aloofness, pomposity, and arrogance was "part and parcel of the system." As butler, Slingsby found he had to maintain a rigid reserve and act like a stern father towards the under-servants.[21] "Never become familiar with beaters to the extent which gives them an impression of equality," advised a gamekeeper. "Be courteous, . . . but never divest yourself of that something which shows them that you are their superior officer."[22]

Seniors in more modest establishments, who had less to lose, were less overbearing: at Edwardian Erddig, for example, Mrs Brown, the housekeeper, "was not disliked," being "a respected rather than an awesome figure."[23] Smaller staffs were less likely to maintain the elaborate rituals and strict segregation of large establishments, because they necessarily had more contact with each other, and lacked the rooms to maintain separate quarters. In quiet households such as Erddig, where the upper servants were not particularly skilled or ambitious, "there seems to have been far less distinction and fewer barriers between their different ranks than in larger country houses."[24] The smallest country houses contained a few diverse individuals who would have found life very lonely if they kept aloof from each other.

In large establishments, however, a heavy discipline reinforced the segregation of status. At Rufford Abbey, under-servants encountering their superiors were "forbidden to speak, unless spoken to, which wasn't often. Servants of different grades were not allowed to mix freely."[25] Silence at mealtimes inhibited social interaction and relaxation. Segregating departments for greater efficiency and morality also reduced contact. Servants were not permitted to stray into rooms unconnected with their own work. Many kitchen-maids and scullery-maids, for instance, ate all their meals in the kitchen, and never saw the reception rooms and family bedrooms, or the housemaids at work. Nursery staff felt particularly isolated. Sarah Sedgwick and the under-nurse "never mixed with the rest of the staff." Excused from morning prayers and excluded from the servants' hall, they ate supper in the day nursery.[26]

This segregation doubtless intensified the rivalry so common between the upper staff, as they fought over demarcation, and jostled for power and influence with the family. The lady's maid's refinement and pretensions were often resented, and her closeness to the mistress aroused fears that she might carry tales or assume an unwelcome authority. Long-serving nannies sometimes attempted to rule the household, as at Cliveden, where Nanny Gibbons was "a power in the house second only to Mrs Astor . . . and often upset the smooth running of the house and particularly of the kitchen."[27]

Disagreeable upper servants could poison the atmosphere of an entire establishment. Complaining of the nursery cooking, Mrs Newsholm, the Birchalls' cook, gave notice in August, 1876. In October, the footman resigned, saying he could not get on with Sandy, the butler, any longer. When Dearman fired Sandy, the cook agreed to come back, revealing that he had been foul-mouthed and lazy. But her mistress had not "put her in her right place in reference to underlings, and especially the housemaid whom she sometimes took into the storeroom." Other servants spoke up: Mrs Newsholm was "prejudiced and inclined to listen to tales," and "servants had set one another against the place." Even the head gardener "had heard tales enough to induce him to leave ten times."[28]

Promotion within a household could lead to jealousy, duplicity, and insecurity among older servants. In 1903 Charles Booth found that "a 'jumped-up' man" was "eyed with little favour by the other servants."[29] Servants who rose without the usual training were especially resented: when a housemaid was promoted to lady's maid at Knebworth, the upper servants "made her life a misery." Some ambitious servants even attempted to engineer the dismissal of those standing in their way by dropping hints about their work or conduct in their employers' hearing.[30]

Competition and jealousy produced gossip and tale-bearing which undermined group solidarity. "The rivalry between the cook and the housemaid is very disagreeable," grumbled Henry Polderoy. "They come to me with complaints about each other. . . . Often there are sniffs, tears and other signs of coarse emotion.. . . . There are dark and offensive hints of theft, adultery and laziness. I am told of bedclothes which are missing, of bottles mislaid, of stores mysteriously reduced."[31]

Tension was exacerbated by servants' inability to escape from each other's company and the narrowness of their lives. "Jealousy, backbiting," and "slandering" were only natural, argued Eric Horne, when they were all "shut up in a house together, with the same hum-drum duties to do day after day," with "not enough variety of thought to distract" them.[32] Moreover, as most employers discouraged the fulfilment of sexual and affective needs, some unmarried servants became embittered and neurotic, taking their frustrations out on their subordinates. Some individuals quit rather than work with someone they disliked. Among applicants for jobs at Prestwold, James Powell "did not get on with some

Plate 29   Servants in the kitchen at Beaulieu

of the other servants," Lucy Shackleton had a disagreement with the cook, Ann Hayes came into conflict with the upper housemaid, and Ellen Harding was parted with "because she and the Head Laundry-maid did not agree."[33]

Yet it was easier to endure a disagreeable co-worker when there were plenty of others willing to be friendly. The company and friendships of a big staff were an important attraction of service in large houses. "There were eighteen servants kept, so we had plenty of fun," said Charles Cooper of Eden Hall, and Albert Thomas recalled of Holkham, "as it was a large establishment we youngsters had a good time together in the servants' hall."[34]

While friendships between upper and lower servants were discouraged, servants of a similar age and status, working or relaxing together, often became close, especially those in the same department or bedroom. Bessie Gittins, nursery-maid at Erddig, shared a room with the second housemaid, and they became such friends that she asked to become a housemaid. At bedtime, the Erddig maids "would all go to one room and have a good natter." Footmen enjoyed gossiping, joking, and playing pranks on each other. These friendships made all the difference. Hannah Cullwick was sorry to leave Aqualate. "I was got used to the servants & I felt happy for I had a friend or two."[35]

Upper servants also might become close friends. As butler, Eric Horne and a valet became "like brothers" with never a cross word between them. "We had some jolly times together." At another place, the clerk of works, head gamekeeper, head gardener, and head coachman used to join Horne in his office for a friendly chat, telling the latest stories and talking of the day's events.[36] Upper servants were lonely in small households with few other senior staff, for they were not supposed to fraternize with their inferiors. Young George Slingsby felt so isolated as butler at Osberton Hall, where the only other upper servant was the housekeeper, that he returned to being footman. Upper servants left in charge while most of the staff accompanied the family to London or other houses also lacked companionship: Elizabeth Sanders, housekeeper at Goodwood in the 1850s, wrote to her friend, the Duke's secretary, "I miss you as I seem to have no one to speak too [sic]."[37]

The isolation of the country house encouraged friendships between indoor and outdoor staff. At one place, grooms and under-gardeners helped in the pantry in the evenings "more for company than for anything else, for there was nowhere for them to go for miles." In Sussex, a kitchen-maid exploring the estate in her free time befriended and visited the gamekeepers and their families.[38]

Regular part-time and casual workers could become part of the country house community too. Former servants and menservants' wives were on familiar terms with the full-time staff. "In close connection with the Hall, her usefulness is felt by all," wrote Philip Yorke II of the gardener's wife.[39] A wet-nurse might be resented by the other servants, envying her high wages, pampered existence, and power over her employers.[40] Nurses were especially prone to jealousy: the Ridleys' nurse, Wells, made the wet-nurse's life so miserable that she left. The doctor told Lady Ridley to give the baby entirely into the new wet-nurse's care.[41]

Finally, visiting servants provided further opportunities to strike up acquaintances. In great houses, guests brought their own lady's maids, valets, coachmen, and grooms, who worked alongside the family's staff and joined them for meals. After work was over, they would relax in the pantry, housekeeper's room, or servants' hall, sharing news and gossip, and information about job possibilities.

Despite all the quarrels, confinement together in an isolated country house produced a strong *esprit de corps* and sense of community. Group solidarity was often high, with much mutual support. Servants had "a way of clinging together" in "a kind of freemasonry," admitted one butler. Most were "careful not to injure others" and "ever ready to help those . . . not in favour with their employers," finishing off their work "to keep things quiet" and lending clothing or money to an impoverished beginner.[42] Servants concealed each other's crimes and disabilities, too. The Bankes's cook-housekeeper never revealed she knew the nurse had epilepsy, for "no servant at Kingston Lacy would ever tell upon another."[43]

With a staff of both men and women, the country house offered many opportunities for romance and marriage. Courtship was more difficult in domestic service than in other occupations, not only because of the confinement and limited time off, but because employers tried to prohibit it. Unlike maidservants in typical middle-class households, women employed in country houses met a number of male fellow-servants. Although employers discouraged marriage among indoor men, they did not object to married grooms, gardeners, and gamekeepers, who often chose brides from the Big House.

Most employers and their upper servants did their utmost to minimize encounters between the sexes. New houses were designed so that men's work and women's work were in separate places, and their sleeping quarters were carefully segregated, with their own staircases. At Welbeck Abbey, the servants dubbed the maids' corridor the "Virgins' Wing." Strict rules were laid down, too. At Northwick, the housekeeper checked that the maidservants were in their rooms by ten p.m. Women servants were only allowed in the servants' hall for meals, while the menservants were to keep out of the kitchen and laundry as much as possible.[44] Vigilant housekeepers were responsible for protecting the maids' virtue. Some head housemaids were even required to check that menstrual napkins were washed every month.[45] Consequently, some commentators believed country house service was safest for maidservants.[46]

All these precautions failed to suppress human instincts. Footmen, usually chosen for their good looks, had the time and the opportunity to flirt with the maids. Flirtation and courtship added diversion and excitement to dull routine and restricted lives, and could bring a sense of individual identity and worth, as part of the struggle for autonomy and a private life. The two sexes encountered each other in the servants' hall, at prayers, and on the Sunday procession to church, at servants' dances and parties, and in the course of their duties. Once a pair was attracted to each other, clandestine meetings were possible. "Though . . . not allowed in good places, courting is carried on all the same, in a quiet way," admitted a butler. "Sometimes in the housemaid's cupboard, . . . a few words when passing on the stairs; ways and means can always be found to dodge the housekeeper's eagle eye."[47] A footman and a head kitchen-maid left each other notes under the lamp-room mat, and sneaked out at four a.m. for walks in the woods. One housemaid spoke with the man who became her husband when he came in every day to tend the house plants and flowers, and at Longleat, a groom-of-chambers and a nursery-maid had a daily rendezvous over the nursery sink.[48] Under-servants defied the rules: at one house the kitchen-maids met outside men in the potting room after the cook had gone out.[49] Upper servants suffered no restrictions, consulting each other in their work, and eating and relaxing together in the housekeeper's sitting room. Servants also met local individuals on their afternoons off. On Sunday afternoons, the young men of Juniper Hill courted the under-servants of the nearby mansions.[50]

Some love affairs were consummated. Gillis's research shows that most unmarried maidservants' pregnancies were the result of relationships with men of their own class, often anticipating marriage in the traditional manner.[51] Most wages books record occasional dismissals of servants for improper conduct or pregnancy. Caroline Clive noted in her diary "the disgraceful departure of Betsey, the under-nurse, who danced all one Friday night and lay in the next Friday. She so pinched herself in as not to be discovered." (A former footman was the father.) In another house, the head housemaid and the second gardener met at night in a disused wing, helping themselves to their master's drink and cigarettes.[52] Some maids may have been raped by menservants catching them alone in distant bedrooms and staterooms. A third of the raped women petitioning the Foundling Hospital from 1815 to 1845 were victims of fellow-servants.[53] Laundries, separate from the house, were often the Achilles Heel of the morality patrol. The stables and laundry were adjacent to each other at Naworth, and "secret and frequent dances took place in the drying-room." Consequently, pregnant laundry-maids found themselves summarily dismissed. At Hesleyside in the 1820s, the laundry was "nothing but a brothel" with upper servants "among the most licentious."[54] Where the upper servants were themselves lax, promiscuity was rife. The Hesleyside butler, Inkley, slept with several maidservants: one was fired, another left because she was pregnant, a third was dismissed for trying to cut her throat for love of him, and yet another gave notice in the rivalry for his affections. In another northern mansion after 1910, "the male servants used to order their contraceptives in bulk – four gross at a time."[55] Some servants managed to smuggle in a lover from outside. One squire's wife found a villager "descending in stockinged feet from the maid's bedroom, and, after soundly berating him, demanded all particulars. She then produced the bull book, and then and there entered his name, the maid's and the date."[56]

Most maidservants were careful to preserve their virtue, however, knowing a discovered pregnancy meant instant dismissal without a reference. Indeed, the fate of unwed mothers was grim. "Young girls used to be in service in these big houses," recalled a former servant, "and they'd be funny things a-goin' on, and when there was trouble it would be the workhouse. Some went in to have a baby and that was where they'd finish."[57]

Many servants conducted decorous, serious courtships with fellow-servants and outsiders, and by the Edwardian period were permitted supervised meetings within the country house. An estate-office clerk and a kitchen-maid, for instance, went for walks in the fields and woods hand in hand, and in winter attended entertainments in the village hall. He was even allowed to visit her in the kitchen occasionally.[58]

Servants' weddings at the country house were celebrated by both family and staff, who attended the ceremony, put on a wedding feast, and gave gifts to the happy couple. In Wales, Adam Badeau witnessed a wedding between a nurse and a farmer on the estate. The young squire toasted the bride at the wedding breakfast in the servants' hall, and a dance on the lawn followed. The Percys' wedding present to their cook-housekeeper was "a very grand wedding" at fashionable St George's, Hanover Square, and a reception in their town house. Wedding gifts were often generous. Lord Ferrers always gave couples two leather-covered armchairs, and his wife presented them with a breakfast- and a tea-service.[59] Menservants could expect better wages and perquisites on marriage. Sir Lothian Bell's coachman got 15s a week and his clothes while single, but after marriage he was allowed £1 a week, a free cottage, a pint of milk daily, a Christmas goose, a garden, and as much manure for it as he wanted.[60]

The effects of marriage on a career in service depended on the category and gender of the servant. Labourers' marriages seldom even came to the family's attention. Outdoor menservants were encouraged to stay on with higher wages and a place to live. For most female servants, marriage meant an end to their career in gentleman's service. Lower maidservants who married local men, however, often returned as day and casual workers, or took in work. A skilled laundress, for instance, might continue to do the family's fine linen in her own home.[61] Indoor menservants faced a dilemma. Many employers were hostile to married butlers or valets, arguing that they were less loyal and devoted, even tempted to steal from the master for their own families. When Ferdinand Ceroti announced his engagement to a lady's maid, Sir Clifford Constable wrote sourly, "You must be aware that your marrying is inconvenient to me besides being a bad precedent to the rest."[62]

Family life was difficult for an indoor manservant. Many butlers and valets had to live in, housing their families elsewhere. Some employers provided a cottage nearby but long, irregular hours meant the manservant was seldom home. At Woodhouse, a married butler slept at home only on Saturday and Sunday nights. "I cannot say much about my father," one manservant's son commented, "I was very little under his care." Eric Horne's bride, tired of travelling after only one year, insisted on staying in London, and eventually settled in Surrey, where her husband joined her only when he was unemployed.[63] The difficulties of marriage while in service are illustrated in the applications for the butler's post at Northwick Park in 1876. Two butlers had left their previous positions to marry, and another married then left his place because his employer could not provide convenient housing. One wanted to leave his place for lack of suitable accommodation, and four separated from their families wanted the Northwick situation so they could be together in a settled home.[64]

Butlers who had already proved their worth were in the best position. The Estcourts' butler, Stiff, initially gave warning without stating his reason, and only when pressed revealed he intended to marry. In a third letter, however, he had changed his mind. His fiancée, a housekeeper, was not well enough to set up in business with him, so he humbly asked Estcourt if he would object to a married butler, on the same terms as before. His wife would not be an encumbrance, "as she has an Independence & about my own age," and he would rent a cottage himself. Estcourt agreed, confident that Stiff's wife living nearby would not prove an "inconvenience" to him. Other employers were more forthcoming. Lady Alice Packe was upset when her butler wanted to marry, fearing he would want a better place. "Is it not an awful nuisance for me?!" she wrote to her son, "I wonder if I offered him more wages he would stop on." A friend suggested she "do up the rooms over the stables" for him. "Do you think . . . he would like it?"[65]

The sparse evidence suggests that numerous country house maidservants, unlike the vast majority of female servants, were upwardly mobile on marriage. Many working-class life-cycle servants did marry local labourers or artisans. At Trentham, a stillroom maid wed a carpenter, a second dairy-maid a wheelwright, and a second housemaid a railway guard. But at Woolley, the maids often married farmers, and a Hagley housemaid landed a schoolmaster.[66] Women who married under-gardeners or grooms were not upwardly mobile, but working-class maids who wed indoor or upper menservants were. Such men were a better prospect than downwardly mobile urban menservants, "recruited from a slightly lower social station" than urban upper maids.[67] Female upper servants married senior menservants or "men of both lower-middle-class and skilled working-class background," attracted to their nest-egg, as well as their "similarity of background, certified character and steadiness of habit."[68] The elevated status of department heads made them acceptable brides to middle-class men. A nurse at Hampton Court married the estate agent; elsewhere, one housekeeper wed a widowed solicitor, while another married a wool-stapler worth £400 a year.[69] Distressed gentlewomen had the least chance of marriage. As servants, they were considered socially inferior to men of their own class, but would not stoop to wed men of lesser rank. Some did find a husband, nevertheless: at Stoneleigh one governess married a schoolmaster and another a doctor.[70]

For many servants, working in the country house was enough in itself to raise their social status. Country house servants were more respected by rural communities than ordinary servants were by the urban working classes. Many mistresses told C. V. Butler that their servants were the "aristocracy of the village."[71] After the governess, who had few social equals, chiefly in the schoolhouse and vicarage, upper servants ranked highest. Most of them were above the labourers in origin anyway, but all found their jobs gave them prestige locally. They were comparatively well off, dressing and eating well, and freely entertaining their friends in their comfortable sitting-rooms. They had a certain amount of independence, and power over their subordinates, and they could use their influence to help or hinder local people, by purchasing goods, obtaining services, and engaging permanent or temporary staff. As a result, at Juniper Hill, they were "next in importance to 'the gentry.'" A farmworker's son felt that butlers "wouldn't want to know you ... they're superior, ... or think they are." One coachman was "rather circumspect" when he dropped in for a chat at the village forge, "being a man a bit up in the world."[72] Department heads in great houses were accepted as equals by the middle class. Adam Badeau met a doctor proud of his acquaintance with the Bretton Park butler, and a "very respectable" middle-class man who often enjoyed a glass of fine port with a nobleman's butler. When the Shugborough butler retired to Bishton, local directories described him as a "gentleman."[73] "Farmers and small tradesmen," according to Badeau, "look up to the housekeeper and the butler" and "are on a level with the ordinary servants in a great house."[74] Significantly, farmers and tradesmen from nearby towns were guests at servants' balls.[75] Country house labourers, however, remained at the social level of agricultural workers.

One important reason why country house servants found themselves more highly regarded was that the landowner dominated the community. Often virtually everyone in a closed village was employed on the estate, internalizing traditional feudal values. Outdoor servants were a conservative influence on the community. They supported the existing social system, and when enfranchised voted accordingly. On one Edwardian estate, not only did the head gardener vote Conservative but his wife was secretary of the local branch of the Primrose League.[76] Servants were not cut off from the local community, despite segregation in church and rules forbidding or restricting outings to the village. Day and casual labourers came in from the surrounding neighbourhood, and estate carpenters, blacksmiths, masons, and other artisans frequently did work in the house and gardens. Sometimes, as at Erddig, the estate yard and the home farm were close to the service wing. Tradesmen, messengers, and carriers constantly came and went, stopping for refreshments in the servants' hall or kitchen. In 1850, for instance, one or two visitors ate in the Erddig servants' hall every day, including washerwomen, the post-boy, the brewer, carriers, a fly-driver, a rat-killer, and a seamstress.[77] Over meals at the kitchen table or in the servants' hall, these workers and callers must have passed on local news and gossip. Estate employees and their families, even the entire village, attended Christmas treats, dances, and family celebrations, and outdoor menservants might help with haymaking. Individual servants befriended local people. Mr

Plate 30 Cricket outside the gardener's house, King's Bromley Manor

Cooper, butler at Kingston Lacy, frequently visited villagers on his days off.[78]

Servants also entertained friends, with or without permission. Upper servants often invited guests as their privilege, as at Goodwood late in the nineteenth century, where no one questioned the steward's "right to entertain on a liberal scale, whomsoever he chose to invite to his room." Edwardian landowners often readily permitted socializing: one lady's maid gave friends tea in her sitting-room, and a squire allowed his servants to invite their friends for parties until one a.m.[79]

Outdoor servants' social life depended on the location of their homes and the nature of their work. Men living in the stables or gardens became more involved with life at the house than with the village. At Rounton Grange, the coachman's wife befriended the nanny and the lady's maid, her children imitated the gentry in their games, and mealtimes were regulated by the clock tower.[80] In contrast, families scattered about the estate were rather isolated and lonely, especially gamekeepers' families. Gamekeepers were such unpopular suppressers of poaching, "even their wives and children were treated coldly." A maidservant who married a gamekeeper found herself "lonely a good many times" in the lodge where she acted as gatekeeper.[81] Still, families settled permanently in the locality could become involved in village and parish affairs. The garden foreman at Peper Harrow in the 1870s ran a night school for boys, and played the harmonium in the church. George Roberts, gardener at Erddig from the 1890s, served on the parish council and ran the local Sunday School, and John Robson, head gardener at Linton, was treasurer to the Linton parochial church council.[82]

While the insistence on deference, inferiority, and unquestioning obedience in domestic service was inimical to the full expression of individuality, and damaging to self-esteem, servants found compensating sources of worth and identity within the servant hierarchy: in a clearly defined place, with subordinates as well as superiors; in a sense of belonging to a distinct community; and in a gratifying social status within the wider rural community. Servants had more opportunity among the larger staff of a country house to meet their social and affective needs, to make friends, to court, and to marry.

Though relations within the staff dominated the day-to-day lives of many servants, the impact of the family was not negligible. While only a minority of servants developed close personal relationships with individual family members, at least a third of the staff had daily contact with them, and the entire staff felt the impact of their employers' presence and policies. Even if a lower servant seldom saw the master or mistress, ultimately the rules enforced by an upper servant were theirs, or had their sanction. Directly or indirectly, the landed family shaped the lives of its staff.

10

Relations Between Employers and Servants

Servants were attracted to country house service not only by its superior rewards, conditions, and social life, but because the landed classes had a reputation as better employers than the middle classes. Once again, the landowner's social position, traditions, and code of conduct created distinctive patterns of behaviour. The master and mistress were far more involved with their servants than has hitherto been assumed: hiring and firing staff, drawing up rules of conduct, and often taking a personal interest in their domestics. To clarify and codify the complex and varied attitudes and behaviour of family and servants towards each other, I have identified three types of employer here: liberal, authoritarian, and remote; and in this chapter I explore further the different situations of the four categories of servant.

Domestic service was different from other occupations in an industrial economy. Personal residential service to a family resulted in both family and servants conducting their private lives in close proximity. Yet unlike other occupations providing board, servants' whole time was legally at their master's disposal. Because servants lived under their master's roof, he had both the opportunity and the need to control their personal lives. The employer's personality, beliefs, and actions had direct impact on these workers. People employed servants not just to off-load drudgery, but to assert their superior social status by exacting deference and obedience. Thus service demanded a humble demeanour, respectful responses, and a distinctive dress. Deference, according to sociologist Howard Newby, functioned as a stabilizer of the existing relationship of dominance and subordination, maintaining the landed classes' power and privilege. Inherent in this was a tension between the need to maintain social differentiation (regulating social distance both to assert the landed family's superior status and to protect servants' independence), and the need for the staff's "positive, affective identification" with the family.[1]

The landed classes were more effective than the middle classes in exacting deference because of their greater skill and resources in managing this relationship. They enjoyed four major advantages over the middle classes. Firstly, they were not one but two classes above their servants, an established elite wielding great political, social, and economic power. Unlike upwardly mobile new members of the middle class, they did not need constantly to reaffirm their superior status. Thus it was easier for both parties to maintain social distance. An individual's standing in the servant world depended in part on the employer's social status. Like the rest of society, servants revered titles. Working for a duke or an earl held far greater social cachet than serving a mere squire; but even the latter's servants felt superior to those attending a vulgar plutocrat.

With centuries of experience in dealing with servants, the landed classes had developed an effective code of conduct, based on mutual obligations and constraints, and an inimitable style of effortless, confident command in their dealings with subordinates.[2] Gordon Grimmett found the family at Longleat "seemed instinctively to know how to treat servants."[3] These nuances of deportment and address could only be learned in the upper-class home.

Long-established families had built up a mystique of dynasty, a rich accumulation of history and customs transcending any individual owner or servant, which could inspire the staff to preserve and perpetuate the family's heritage and home. The sense of having an " 'organic' partnership in a co-operative enterprise," and a loyalty to the mansion and the estate, in a "common adherence to territory, a solidarity of place," fostered servants' positive identification with the family.[4] At Staunton Harold, for instance, an unbroken "tradition of mutual obligations and service" and "an almost communal enjoyment of the expenditure of wealth" meant employees displayed an even stronger "bond of pride and love of the place" than did Lord Ferrers.[5]

Finally, the landed classes enjoyed "ideological hegemony," a "total social situation" where their views prevailed. Most country houses were isolated from subversive alternatives; they were located on large estates in rural communities where the landowner personally controlled the militia, the bench, schools, the church, farm leases, and many jobs.[6] Landowners' social control included petty rules and regulations for the entire estate.[7]

Even one unappealing feature of the landed classes, their autocratic arrogance, was accepted as a distinction, endured as yet another privilege of rank. Confident of their own superiority and right to command, many members of the aristocracy and gentry were overbearing, condescending, and insensitive in their dealings with the lower orders. In Corbridge, the gentry "were expected to be spirited and to demand much" but not to "understand or have much consideration" for ordinary people.[8] The most bizarre behaviour was due to eccentricity, a celebrated feature of the upper-class personality. Protected by their status, wealth, and privilege, landowners indulged in unconventional behaviour. A mistress who loved dogs assigned one to each servant. The dog accompanied the servant everywhere, even to church. In winter one Duke of Portland sent any housemaid he encountered out to skate on his new rink.[9]

Like their middle-class counterparts, however, landed masters and mistresses were influenced by several nineteenth-century developments. The benevolent concern and intrusiveness of paternalism and religion clashed with the barriers of class consciousness and the detachment of the cash nexus. This tension shaped the employer-servant relationship in the country house.

Conflict between the patriarchal and contractual elements of the master–servant relationship had long existed. In medieval and early modern households, servants were indeed part of the family. The master and mistress were obliged to protect, guide, discipline, educate, and provide for servants as if they were their own children, exacting the same obedience and respect in return. Servants were expected to identify with the family, and to serve its interests with loyalty and devotion. Even the medieval noble's vast establishment was genuinely one community, "a united following of all social ranks, tied to their lord by service and hereditary loyalty, bound together by shared ceremony and ritual, and prepared if needs be to fight for him."[10] The early modern household was still patriarchal, but in the seventeenth century the old concept of the great chain of being was undermined by the scientific revolution, and paternalist theories of government by the Civil War. The family gained greater privacy, banishing domestics to the servants' hall, hiding them with back stairs, and providing sleeping quarters instead of pallets in or near family bedchambers.

In the eighteenth century, the patriarchal model largely collapsed. Religion became latitudinarian, no longer inspiring paternal benevolence and control. Family prayers were abandoned. The Enlightenment's philosophical, political, and economic theories, particularly egalitarianism and individualism, evidently further undermined patriarchy. The Industrial Revolution created alternative occupations with contractual relationships between employer and employee, a more dynamic, fluid society, and a growing middle class whose insatiable demand for servants gave them more bargaining power. Individualistic servants, conscious of their right to liberty, regarded their jobs as contracts, to be exploited for their own benefit. Thus they became insubordinate, left their positions at will, sought independent income through vails, gratuities and perquisites, dressed fashionably, and freely entertained their friends below stairs. Landed families not only tolerated such autonomy but often supplied their own cast-off clothing. The landed classes' behaviour probably resembled their French counterparts, who retained the authority of patriarchy, but not its intrusive concern for servants' well-being.[11] When the cash nexus became the sole tie, relations with servants became more distant in great houses, but also more egalitarian and permissive. In smaller country houses, Merlin Waterson suspects that greater informality in family life may have "encouraged a less formal relationship with staff."[12]

In the nineteenth century, some masters and mistresses retained these more relaxed, liberal attitudes, particularly among the gentry. Mabel Morrison of Fonthill joked and chatted with her grooms and gardeners "on what seemed to be equal terms." Mr Chichester of Hall frequently drank with his butler and footmen after dinner. "My men servants are my friends," he would declare.[13] More than one bachelor master became attached to a servant's children: Ralph Sneyd delighted in playing with his valet's two-year-old daughter, becoming "most twaddlingly fond" of her.[14] The Yorkes of Erddig demonstrated their respect for their staff as individuals with their own life stories and distinct personalities by commemorating them in portraits and verse. This family certainly treated their servants as human beings. Philip Yorke II attended parish meetings at the home of George Roberts, an under-gardener and councillor, who escorted him home afterwards, "and in much converse we engage/ of things pertaining to the age." Louisa Yorke nursed a housemaid with scarlet fever herself, while her visiting father played his cello with a violin-playing housemaid. The Yorke squires regarded family and servants as a single unit. Simon Yorke III complained that one lady's maid "somehow did not quite agree with those of this community." Their historian, Merlin Waterson, concludes that the household at Erddig "was genuinely one community."[15]

These liberal employers were kind and considerate. One housemaid remembered a humane master who carried heavy coal-scuttles upstairs for her, took books to sick menservants, and actually wept when the housemaid's mother suddenly died. His daughters left the drawing-room door open so the servants could hear them play music, even buying special pieces of music for them to hear. John Grey liked to read aloud the novels of Sir Walter Scott while the maids sewed.[16] Because they cared for their servants as individuals, liberal masters were more likely than others to provide for faithful servants in old age with pensions or cottages, and to leave legacies to the entire staff.

At recreation, landed families occasionally treated servants as equals. Adam Badeau encountered young men staying up late who invited the attending footmen to have a cigar and a drink, and to box with them. Elsewhere, housekeepers played cards with their employers, menservants joined the family in cricket matches, and staff members participated in family theatricals and concerts.[17]

Thus, although they still adhered to the established code of conduct in their routine dealings with the staff, liberal masters and mistresses were able to reduce social differentiation at times. Secure in their superiority, they feared no loss of status. "It was the very consciousness of the gulf that made the condescension possible," explained Badeau.[18] Besides, this unconventional behaviour could be excused as just another form of upper-class eccentricity.

In most country houses, however, egalitarianism only occurred at celebrations of major family events such as the heir's birth and christening, coming-of-age, and wedding, and was more a survival of the traditional patriarchal view of the establishment as a great family than Enlightenment liberality. The more relaxed and egalitarian relations of the eighteenth century diminished with the revivals of religion and paternalism and the rise of class.

From the early nineteenth century, a renewed paternalism attempted to restore traditional obligations. Like their ancestors, paternalists believed in an organic community based on authority and deference, in which all performed the duties of their God-given place. With their superior wealth, birth, and education, they were convinced, they knew what was best for their child-like dependants.

Paternalism was reinforced by the Evangelical revival, which portrayed the male head of the household as God's representative and priest, caring for his dependants' souls with family prayers and compulsory church-going, and suppressing immorality. While servants "are members of our family," claimed Mrs Eliot James as late as 1883, "their conduct, their comfort, their general well-being, spiritually and bodily, it is our duty to look after."[19] The religious revival and the cult of true womanhood created a corresponding "maternalism." The mistress was urged to show a motherly concern for her servants' welfare, and to influence her servants by her own character and example.[20]

The landed classes were deeply imbued with the paternalist ethic. The medieval ideal survived on estates great and small, where the term "family" still embraced the entire household. A Northwick memorandum book, for instance, recorded that a laundry-maid "left the famely (sic) the 19th April," while Richard Benyon enjoined his housekeeper to keep "order and quiet in the Family."[21] Early-Victorian families whose sense of duty had lapsed returned to the tradition of *noblesse oblige*, while newcomers enthusiastically adopted paternalism. Sir John Boileau, who bought Ketteringham in 1836, believed his servants were "as much a part of the family as his children, and felt their misbehaviours as breaches in the loyalty of the family more than as breaches of contract."[22] Paternalistic employers were very authoritarian and intrusive, attempting to control the private lives of their staff. John, Lord Northwick, forbade his cook-housekeeper "to go beyond a walk" without his permission, and to report "anything going on" immediately. No maidservant was allowed to wear artificial flowers or "walk out without leave."[23] Paternalism provided the tyrannical with opportunities to persecute and oppress inferiors, yet it could also inspire the benevolent to show a thoughtful concern for servants' well-being and happiness. Lady Macclesfield, for instance, taught illiterate servants to read and write.[24] Paternalists often felt obliged to reward good behaviour with pensions for faithful servants, and legacies to all staff serving any length of time.

Yet while paternalism and Evangelicalism mandated personal involvement, the class system set a distance between family and servants. The nineteenth-century country house contained an upper-class family and mainly working-class servants. Status groups had always used privilege and ritual to assert superiority; now people sought to confirm class membership by maintaining social distinctions, with an elaborate code of etiquette which institutionalized servants' inferiority. Masters and mistresses demanded an exaggerated deference, a display of subservience and humility. Servants, for instance, were expected to stand aside or even face the wall when a family member passed them, and walk several paces behind him or her. For the first time, employers imposed uniforms on lower maidservants. Class consciousness promoted stereotypes about the working classes' inferior morality, intelligence, and personal hygiene. Assigned to clean up human, animal, household, and garden waste, they were defiled by their association with dirt and pollution. The family avoided witnessing these degrading activities and reduced personal contact by receiving small items on a silver salver. Some employers took social distance to extremes. The first Earl of Londesborough, like others, required that all housemaids and gardeners be kept out of sight, and Walter Bankes communicated with his servants only through notes.[25]

Both the need to enforce social distance and this condescending view of working-class inferiority and pollution tempted masters and mistresses to dehumanize their staff. Many rituals asserting social superiority and maintaining the illusion of privacy effectively degraded servants. Well-trained servants preserved an impassive demeanour in front of the family, never expressing their own emotions or reactions. Arrogant and insensitive employers insisted that servants change unsuitable names or allotted successive footmen a standard name like "John". "Servants are looked upon as . . . live furniture, nothing more," Eric Horne bitterly concluded, "moved from one house to another as required, ignoring the live furniture's wish or convenience, it is immaterial whether it be one piece . . . or another."[26]

A second development which created the remote employer was the revival of a contractual relationship between employer and employee. Caroline Stephen labelled this the "commercial" ideal, in which the mistress required "the efficient performance of a certain amount of work in return for board, lodgings and wages," but felt no responsibility beyond "taking care that the food and accommodation are sufficiently good . . ., the wages regularly paid, and the work well done, with due regard to decorum."[27] Remote masters and mistresses were simply uninterested in their servants. Preoccupied by their own political, sporting, or social activities, they left personnel management to trustworthy department heads. Servants working for remote employers were the least likely to receive medical care, pensions or legacies.

Large establishments were most suited to the cash nexus. Great landowners, shielded by the upper servants, the layout of the house, and the organization of work routines, isolated themselves most from those who served them. Kitchen-maid Margaret Thomas saw one mistress on only one occasion — when she summoned Margaret in order to dismiss her.[28] Remote employers' houses thus contained two virtually separate communities, and the lower staff must have regarded the steward and housekeeper as their real employers, and the family much as hotel staff regard guests.

The cash nexus became more common in the last decades of the period, particularly among the fashionable aristocracy, and the *nouveaux riches*, who felt no compulsion to justify their luxurious lifestyle by fussing over menials. But remote employers could be found even among gentry, who perhaps resented servants' intrusion into an intimate family life. The Rev. Thomas Gibbons Dixon tried to ignore the servants at Holton. He referred to them as the 'Theys' and liked them to remain out of sight.[29]

Thus there were three distinct tendencies among employers. But these three tendencies could be intermingled in one household or even in one individual. The master could be one type, and the mistress another. Employers' confidence and power might also wax and wane over a lifetime, from the timid young bride, the confident, busy hostess and mother, the formidable but deposed dowager, to the dependent, sickly old lady. An individual might behave differently towards each of the four types of servant. Over the century, heavily authoritarian types diminished in number. The fashionable aristocracy again became remote, more intent on pleasure than duty. On the other hand, increasing numbers of the gentry grew more liberal. In the 1890s, for instance, Mrs Jebb "had little class-feeling and a genuine interest in people just as human beings." Her family and servants attended a literary society together, where maids openly expressed their opinions, and after a parlour-maid married, the eldest Jebb daughter went to tea with her every Saturday.[30]

Whether motivated by inherited custom, kindness, paternalist theory, piety, or class consciousness, the landed classes were far more involved with their servants than is often supposed. Most employers felt it their inescapable duty to hire and fire staff, and to lay down rules governing behaviour, while many masters and mistresses took a personal interest in individual servants' welfare.

Everyone devoted much time and energy to searching for new servants, firing unsatisfactory ones, and helping individuals leaving without fault find new places. Obviously, only the master or mistress could hire upper servants, and compatibility with personal servants such as valets or nurses was essential. Retaining the duty of hiring and firing gave employers greater control over the membership and quality of their household, reducing the risks of incompetence, exploitation, immorality, and crime. Some employers doubtless relished their power over the lives of others. Servant-hunting was also an absorbing pastime, an endless topic of conversation and correspondence. As Anne Sturges Bourne declared, "getting places & people to fit is one of the chief employments of life."[31] Too often, the hunt was time-consuming, frustrating, and fruitless. Dearman Birchall despairingly recorded his attempts to replace a cook: "We have twice advertised in the Guardian, applied to Mrs Pope, Mrs Massey, Mrs French, and now in Times and Daily Telegraph, so far without success." But success also had its disadvantages; Lord de Vesci had to interview around forty applicants just for one first footman's position. Even when servants were found, the employer's trials did not end. "I am having great trouble with the numerous servants," complained Louisa Yorke. "Some are too noisy, some too grand, some find the work too much. I wonder if I shall ever be quite settled."[32]

Some masters and mistresses had particular prejudices. Early in the century, Lady Hereford shunned literate servants. Fanny Heneage, a Roman Catholic, wanted co-religionists, but Harriet Leveson-Gower, second Duchess of Sutherland, abhorred Roman Catholics. Philanthropic employers attempted to help the underprivileged: Lady Carlisle "took numerous boys and girls from the Workhouse or Outrelief cases," while Archibald Peel gave former convicts jobs in his stables.[33]

Acting on the recommendations of friends, relatives, or servants, or armed with a short-list concocted from newspaper advertisements or supplied by a registry office, employers normally interviewed candidates themselves or wrote for further particulars. An interview was an opportunity to evaluate personality and appearance, and to elicit information on intentions to marry, health, religion, and family background. Richard Benyon, for example, wanted to know if applicants were literate, healthy, and Protestant.[34] Reflecting the Victorian concern for order and efficiency, systematic masters and mistresses such as Benyon prepared not only a checklist of questions and information on duties, wages, allowances, perquisites, time off, household rules, and so on, but also agreements on these points to be signed by the new servant. They often

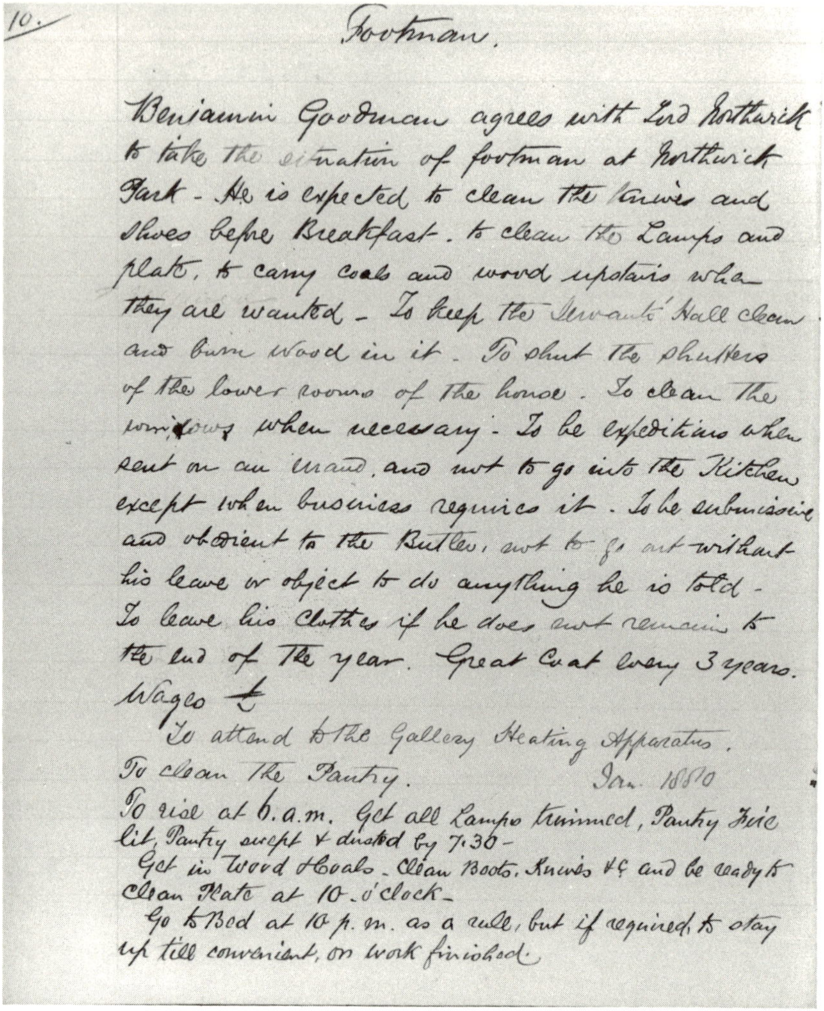

> *10.*
>
> *Footman.*
>
> Benjamin Goodman agrees with Lord Northwick to take the situation of footman at Northwick Park. — He is expected to clean the knives and shoes before Breakfast. to clean the Lamps and plate, to carry coals and wood upstairs when they are wanted. — To keep the Servants' Hall clean and burn wood in it. To shut the shutters of the lower rooms of the house. To clean the windows when necessary. — To be expeditious when sent on an errand, and not to go into the Kitchen except when business requires it. To be submissive and obedient to the Butler, not to go out without his leave or object to do anything he is told. — To leave his clothes if he does not remain to the end of the year. Great Coat every 3 years. Wages £
>
> To attend to the Gallery Heating Apparatus.
> To clean the Pantry.   Jan. 1880
> To rise at 6. a.m. Get all Lamps trimmed, Pantry Fire lit, Pantry swept & dusted by 7.30 —
> Get in Wood & Coals. Clean Boots, Knives &c and be ready to clean Plate at 10. o'clock —
> Go to Bed at 10 p.m. as a rule, but if required to stay up till convenient, or work finished.

Plate 31 An agreement with a footman, Northwick Park, 1880

meticulously kept memorandum books recording the arrival, wage increases, and departure of each servant.[35]

The next step was for the master or mistress to demand the "character," the letter of reference from the previous employer. While some simply followed the standard formula, affirming the basic requirements of honesty, sobriety, steadiness, and respectability, and specifying why the servant left, many characters reveal extensive knowledge and concern, mentioning relevant attributes, commenting on personality, and even evaluating servants' problems and potential.[36]

Writing for a character provided the opportunity to ask questions about particular concerns. Lady Walsingham, for instance, wanted to know if footmen drank, swore, or smoked, or were amorous, dirty, or smelly. Some grew impatient with the virtues demanded: Lady Ruthven answered one letter, "If John Smith could answer to half your demands, I should have married him long ago."[37]

Characters theoretically gave the landed classes great power over their domestics. Denial of a character would end a career in service, and bad references could blight it. In practice, however, the character was not always crucial. Letters revealing faults and unfavourable reasons for leaving did not prevent applicants from obtaining situations, because correspondents were confident that upper servants could correct minor vices. Hussey Packe hired William Davis,[38] though his former employer considered that the footman

> was not up to his work. He wants a strict butler over him and plenty of work to be made efficient. . . . My objection to him was his late hours . . . and slovenliness of habits, these an efficient butler will correct, and I think W. Davis may be made something of as a servant. The servants found him a little "saucy" which can also be corrected.

A bad character, or a refusal to give one, from a family known to be hard on their staff could also be disregarded.[39] Knowing that a character might be forged, falsified, or undeservedly favourable, some servant-seekers also called on the previous employer in order to verify it, to obtain further information and to judge the nature of the household, normally when both families were in London.

Involvement did not end with hiring. The role of master and mistress included promoting desired work attitudes, controlling unwanted behaviour, and solving personal problems and other crises. Their treatment of the staff, and the resultant atmosphere of the household, affected the servants' performance, behaviour, and turnover rate.

Newly hired servants felt the influence of the master and mistress through the rules governing the household. Employers had always sought efficient, deferential, obedient, law-abiding, and honest domestics. The religious revival renewed the obligation to impose religious observances and ensure sexual morality; class consciousness created elaborate rituals of deference and codes of dress; and the family's desire for privacy demanded that servants be as anonymous and invisible as possible. Upper servants diligently enforced their employers' rules.

Pious landowners felt responsible for their servants' spiritual welfare. Lady Darnley read scripture to her maids, while Sir John Boileau heard his footmen's catechism and exhorted his staff to attend Communion.[40] Many more employers contented themselves with instituting family prayers for the entire household either daily or on the Sabbath, while compulsory church attendance on Sundays became virtually universal. At both ceremonies, the staff sat apart from the family. Nevertheless, commentators contended that daily prayers brought family and staff together as one community. Spiritual equality before God supposedly strengthened the sense of common purpose and unity. Church services and family prayers were actually key occasions for social control. The master's spiritual leadership underlined his temporal authority. Like the vicar, he harped on the duty of accepting one's place, using scripture to justify the unequal situations of rich and poor, legitimize his authority, and demand obedience.[41] At Ketteringham, servants "who misbehaved might find themselves held up to public opprobrium in the exhortation after family prayers, and grievous offenders were excluded from prayers."[42]

Both class consciousness and fears of sexual immorality lay behind the imposition of a uniform on lower maidservants: print dresses in the morning and black in the afternoon, with aprons and caps. Employers prohibited current fashions, be they crinolines or bustles, ringlets or fringes, and any ornamentation such as lace, ribbons, artificial flowers, and jewellery. Some employers even insisted on dark, plain dresses and unfashionable black bonnets for church and afternoons off. Richard Benyon instructed his housekeeper to ensure that the maids were "dressed quietly."[43]

Few employers sympathized with maids' natural desire to attract the opposite sex. This was partly because masters and mistresses felt obliged to protect the virtue of young women in their care. Servants' love-lives, moreover, caused trouble: romance within the staff created jealousies, outside attachments introduced illegal guests, even thieves, while both pregnancy and marriage resulted in a tiresome search for a replacement. Denial of servants' sexuality also reflected a reluctance to see them as fully adult beings. Thus masters and mistresses laid down rules segregating the sexes during and after work, restricted outings, and often forbade courtship. Like many other employers, Mary Ann Dixon specified "No Followers." At Rendlesham just before 1914, maids were forbidden to "have anything to do with the men staff."[44] Servants discovered engaging in sexual activity or who became pregnant were normally sent packing. Confronting a pregnant kitchen-maid, Henry Polderoy acted promptly.[45]

> I insisted upon her leaving the house at once. One cannot be too careful or too quick in these matters: a man of my standing must avoid the very shadow of a slur on his reputation or judgement. Although the girl declared that she would be unable to reach her mother's home . . . on the same day, I would not allow her to remain. . . . It would never do to encourage vice by making things comfortable and easy for the sinner.

Some employers were less judgemental and more helpful. "Lord E" asked a vicar to speak to a putative father. "Emma J" had been lady's maid to "Lady X" for twelve years. Lady X willingly wrote a reference for her good character when Emma J applied to place her infant at the Foundling Hospital eighteen months after leaving her service, saying she would take her back but for the bad feeling this would create among the other servants.[46]

Occasionally family members themselves succumbed. In 1835, Francis Seymour, aged twenty-three, longed for a wife, instead of being "obliged . . . to go running after every dirty nurserymaid . . . *pour passer le tems* [sic]," and in 1906, after drinking heavily at lunch, Edward Horner seduced Lady Cunard's beautiful parlour-maid. Another Edwardian, an unscrupulous Oxfordshire squire with an ailing wife, had affairs with maids and then fired them when they became pregnant. In one case, he induced the butler to marry the unfortunate woman.[47] Maids isolated from their own family's protection, enjoined to be obedient and submissive towards their masters, and performing domestic tasks in a man's room out of earshot of others, were unusually vulnerable to rape or seduction. As it was the maid who was blamed and dismissed for losing her virtue, she was unlikely to report the incident. The seducer was able to exploit her ignorance of her own sexuality, romantic fantasies, or unrealistic ambitions. Some female servants may have been willing partners. One governess became mistress of not only her charges' father, but of his two sons. "An impulse from her own nature" most likely led to Elizabeth Ashby's seduction, and she refused to use the money her child's father provided for her and the boy's education. Other gentlemen offered compensation too. Young women from the Fens became housemaids in the houses visited by Prince Edward and his entourage around Newmarket. "Often a girl would come back and soon afterwards her father would be elevated from a humble farm worker to a yeoman farmer, and it would be openly stated that this . . . was due to his daughter having the good looks which brought grace and favour and a little one who was heir to the farm."[48]

Earlier easy-going attitudes towards family bastards sometimes still survived. In 1866, the Earl St Maur, heir to the twelfth Duke of Somerset, made a runaway kitchen-maid called Rosina Swan his mistress. In 1869, he told his parents, and soon after died, asking his mother to take care of Rosina and their children, Ruth and Harold. The duke provided a house and three servants. When their dying mother married a Frenchman, the children moved in with their devoted grandparents. The duke left Stover, and his land at Newton Abbot, to Harold, and £80,000 to Ruth. Ruth was launched into Society and married Frederick Cavendish-Bentinck, whose father himself "had at least one illegitimate family hidden away."[49]

Reports of maidservants' rape or seduction by gentlemen in the Victorian country house are nevertheless rare.[50] Sexual assault may often be less motivated by lust than by a desire to assert power by inflicting humiliation, degradation, and pain. Upper-class men already had such power over servants. Perhaps, too, the eternal vigilance of housekeepers and architects was as effective a deterrent to would-be seducers as piety or a psychological distaste for the lower classes associated with dirt and disorder.[51]

Some virtuous men found themselves falling in love with a maidservant. Divorced and lonely, Henry Polderoy was attracted to his "comely" new housekeeper, Mrs Candybun. He began to "treat her with real confidence," as if he were "talking to a friend," and "to look at her more attentively" when giving orders, admiring her "shapely bosom." One day, Mrs Candybun was so agitated that he finally asked why. Tearfully, she told him another maidservant was making offensive insinuations. She feared his reputation would be harmed. Then she admitted, "You have always been so much more to me than a – a mere master." Pressing his hand, she ran out of the room. "Shaken, hot and uneasy," Polderoy was "deeply touched by her words and action." He consulted the vicar, who advised firing her at once. But next morning Polderoy trembled, fidgeted, and sweated, and asked for hashed mutton instead. Despite gossip among the neighbours, five months passed before he wrote a letter of dismissal.[52]

A few men did face the condemnation of their class by marrying a servant. Sir Harry Fetherstonhaugh, an elderly bachelor, proposed to his dairy-maid. Before the wedding, he sent her to Paris to become educated, but never could persuade local Society to accept her. Servants were equally hostile to working-class mistresses: the footman insulted the new Lady Fetherstonhaugh.[53] Governesses were no more acceptable than maids. John Frewen, heir to Northiam, was disinherited for marrying his sister's governess.[54] In the 1890s, one eccentric and indebted squire actually abandoned his own rank on marrying his housemaid, for she made him sell up and move into a small house near Oxford.[55]

Ladies' liaisons with menservants were even more uncommon and universally condemned. They succumbed chiefly to footmen or grooms, who were chosen for their good looks and whose duties gave them time alone with the ladies. In the 1880s, Adam Badeau was repeatedly told about a deceased duchess who had had an affair with her groom-of-chambers, and a countess "discovered caressing her footman in her own drawing room."[56] In 1855, Mary Gurney was an immature, romantic, and restless wife, bored by her devoted older husband. She and her groom, William Taylor, began an affair while her husband was in London. She became pregnant, and ran away with her lover. An heiress in her own right, she established a household in Sussex. She attempted a "reconciliation" to legitimize a second pregnancy, but her husband, amid rumour that his own two sons were not his, finally divorced her, and she married Taylor.[57]

Concern about the servants' morals was not limited to sex. They might also steal, waste food and materials, get drunk, and disturb the peace by rowdy, quarrelsome behaviour below stairs. Patriarchal employers such as Lord Northwick drew up rules governing servants' behaviour and demanded that head servants keep them informed if "anything goes wrong in the House." Joseph Ablett's rules were displayed in the servants' hall, specifying fines for tardiness, uncleanliness, wasting food, speaking Welsh, blaspheming, cursing, quarrelling, and telling lies.[58] Servants' visitors were also feared as potential thieves, seducers, or consumers of food and drink. Northwick servants required their master's permission to invite friends to meals or stay overnight.[59] Autocratic landowners laid down rules for the whole estate, regulating sexual morality, churchgoing, keeping of animals and gardens, the appearance of cottages, and so on. Lady Courtham, for instance, forbade lace curtains or damask tablecloths in the coachman's cottage.[60]

After establishing rules, employers enforced them, as judges and arbiters. Early in the century, some of them still beat their servants. At the Lambton Races in 1824, Lady Londonderry "in a passion beat her maid till the poor woman fell into hysterics; & Lambton himself fell upon his butler with a stick."[61] While physical punishment soon became unacceptable, masters and mistresses still got away with verbal abuse, although it was certainly not part of the preferred code of conduct. Eric Horne worked for a knight and a baron who were both hot-tempered and constantly swore at their hapless servants.[62] More typically, employers dealt with servants' minor faults with a scolding, more serious ones were readily solved by dismissal, and some crimes by resort to the law. When one dismissed but repentant housemaid pleaded with Anne Frewen to let her stay, her mistress "blew her up roundly" and granted her a reprieve. On returning to "a wasp's nest of domestic troubles," Ralph Sneyd decided it was easiest to "march out the whole female garrison."[63] Often servants caught stealing were simply dismissed, but some infuriated masters called in the police. The Yorkes did both, firing a housekeeper who sold pheasants, and unsuccessfully prosecuting another who finagled over £200 from the household accounts. The Lyttletons were more successful: when the Swiss young lady's maid proved to be a thief, she was prosecuted "as an example to others," and sentenced to fourteen days' imprisonment and hard labour.[64]

Intervention as mediator and peacemaker in staff quarrels was "a recurrent and preoccupying worry."[65] Lucy Arkwright dealt with a "domestic riot." "Housemaid confronting Mrs B in my presence and so on. I have made Jane eat her words about the beer on Sat[urda]y, & given her a piece of my mind."[66] Even the grandest aristocrat might intervene. Anne Leveson-Gower, third Duchess of Sutherland, settled a dispute over precedence at prayers.[67]

A final aspect of managing the staff was to act as a role model, setting a good example and maintaining their respect. Thus the code of conduct also regulated and limited the family's lives, forcing everyone to adhere to the household's routines, attend prayers and church, and to suffer excruciating boredom on Sundays, when Victorian ladies dared not knit, sew, or play cards for fear of shocking the servants.[68] The omnipresence of servants forced family members to conform to the upper-class code of behaviour. As a young lady's maid, Rosina Harrison accompanied her mistress in public, "so that she wouldn't do anything rash or untoward" and "demean herself in front of a servant."[69] Recently, Lady Mander acknowledged, "It is a relief now not to have to try to keep up appearances or to guard one's speech at meals."[70]

Attitudes towards any individual servant depended not just on whether family members were liberal, patriarchal, or remote, but on that servant's occupation, personality, and type, and on the size and nature of the household. The family had to associate with distressed gentlewomen and depended on career servants, but could largely ignore life-cycle servants and labourers. In great houses, aristocrats came to know only their upper and personal servants well, but in the more typical smaller households, the gentry often knew every employee as an individual.

The incongruence in status of her position as both a lady and a servant complicated the family's relationships with the governess. As a gentlewoman, a governess was fit to join the family at meals, or in the drawing room; yet as paid employee, she could not be familiar, and had to exhibit the same obedience, deference, and humility as any other servant. This was particularly awkward in middle-class households, where she was by birth and upbringing her mistress's social equal, and often her superior in education, but had lost her claims to friendship by accepting employment. In the country house, however, the situation was less ambiguous. There the governess was clearly of an inferior social class, not otherwise invited into country house drawing-rooms or dining-rooms. Some commentators believed the aristocracy was consequently more courteous and friendly.[71] A baronet's heir treated Elizabeth Ham "with so much consideration that I cared nothing for my somewhat onerous duties." Mr Elton enjoyed discussing poetry and art with her in the evenings, much to his wife's concern.[72] Yet many employers paid the governess little attention, speaking to her only when necessary. "A private governess has no existence, is not considered as a living and rational being except as connected with the wearisome duties she has to fulfil," concluded Charlotte Brontë. Mrs Sidgwick "does not intend to know me," she complained, "I have never had five minutes' conversation with her since I came – except when she was scolding me." Landowners and their wives often found the governess's company tedious. Lucy Arkwright initially judged Miss Simpson "rather silly, & I find it a little tiresome, having her with me all day, & all evening."[73] Often mothers feared losing authority and influence over their children, or were jealous of their affection for the governess. Both Anne and Charlotte Brontë clashed with their mistress over discipline, and Lady Gower insisted on defining the curriculum herself. Mothers such as Lady Dickson-Poynder who had hated their own governesses were prejudiced against the entire species.[74] On the other hand, a shared devotion to the children could bring mother and governess together. Margaret Hobhouse visited the schoolroom most evenings to discuss the children at length

Plate 32 Emily Mary Osborn. *The Governess*, 1860

with Miss Mandall. Thus some governesses became lifelong family friends. The Dixons' Miss Robertson returned as a lady's companion, and Mary Ann Dixon left £100 to this "friend and companion."[75] Poor relatives who became housekeepers or companions were more acceptable than strangers: Henry Polderoy's elderly cousin, Susan Ardle, who replaced Mrs Candybun as housekeeper, was soon a respected equal and friend.[76]

Employers found it judicious to maintain a good working relationship with upper servants, being dependent on their skills for the family's reputation, on their honesty and integrity, and on their ability to manage under-servants. Compatibility was important. One duchess, inheriting an autocratic housekeeper from her predecessors, "detested her and got rid of her very quickly and had somebody rather humbler and more manageable."[77] Where the family's reputation rested on gourmet cuisine, magnificent gardens, an impressive game bag, or a successful stud, the head servant concerned exercised much power and usually resented interference. Landowners with a passion for these aspects of country house life consulted respectfully with the department head, and deferred to his expertise and advice. Some mistresses were intimidated by a good cook who made it clear she would not tolerate criticism or interference.[78] Unable to afford skilled cooks, many of the lesser gentry endured badly prepared meals rather than offend the cook and undergo another search. The Toulmins, for example, stoically consumed bread and cheese when the mutton was high or the rice pudding undercooked.[79]

Department heads giving long devoted service often gained the respect and affection of their employers. This was particularly true in the nursery. Earlier chapters have shown how deeply many children loved their nannies, and how parents and nurse could share a mutual devotion to the children. A cherished nanny was retained either in another capacity or cared for in her old age. When Mrs Ingram became too old and infirm to serve as nurse, the Duke of Sutherland offered her the post of housekeeper at Trentham, where she could, he assured her, still feel she belonged "to the Family," and he gave her a pension when she finally retired.[80] The majority of nurses who raised an entire family of children stayed on, remaining grown children's confidantes. At Earlham, the old nurse's room was "a gathering-place for all." Young and old alike "came to her perpetually for help," bringing her "their news, their troubles, hopes, [and] interests."[81]

Ladies could also become attached to their lady's maids. A mistress needed her lady's maid to dress and undress her, do her hair and care for her wardrobe, and had to reveal to her the most personal aspects of her life. Over the years, this trusting intimate interaction could create strong ties of affection. Anne Leveson-Gower, Duchess of Sutherland, felt she had "lost the truest, kindest, and best of friends" when her maid, Mrs Penson, died after forty years' service.[82]

Employers had less to do with lower servants. Housemaids' chores were scheduled when family members were out of their rooms, and kitchen servants and laundry-maids worked unseen in their own departments. Footmen and grooms were in attendance, but when not giving orders, the family conventionally acted as if they were not there. In many large establishments, the master and mistress spoke to lower maidservants and lower outdoor menservants only if a problem arose. Remote aristocrats ignored them, but pious, patriarchal employers made it their business to monitor the lives of all their staff, and liberal types were friendly. If maids from Juniper Hill encountered their employers, "her ladyship would ask kindly how they were getting on and how their parents were; or his lordship would smile and make some mild joke."[83]

Plate 33 Mrs Stevens, retired nurse, in her room at Earlham

In the mass of smaller establishments, such as Erddig, Northwick, Hampton Court and Holton, employers were able to get to know each of their servants, but the high rate of turnover among life-cycle servants meant that the family generally became attached only to those lower servants who stayed a number of years.

Day and casual labourers toiled out of the family's sight, yet some paternalist or liberal employers still took an interest in them. The second Duchess of Sutherland, for instance, wrote to the head gardener at Trentham about hiring women to clean the under-gardeners' quarters, and later inspected their work herself.[84] The lesser gentry often came to know their daily servants as individuals. A remarkable relationship developed between the Dixon ladies and some of their daily helpers. Jane Maddison was a former maid married to the Dixons' coachman. For more than twenty years she assisted with cleaning, cooking, washing, housework, and sick-nursing, often working with Mary Ann Dixon herself. A close bond grew up between Mary Ann Dixon and the Maddison family: she paid social rather than philanthropic visits, sent the family doctor

Plate 34 Mrs Jameson Dixon, Mrs Sarah Mumby and her daughter with three maidservants, Holton, *c.*1900

when Mrs Maddison became ill, and even invited her to dinner. Jane Maddison and her husband watched over Mr Dixon on his deathbed, and subsequently, whenever Mary Ann Dixon felt frightened and unwell, Mrs Maddison slept in her room. Mrs Dixon's daughter, Mrs Jameson Dixon, became even more attached to her personal maid, who remained in her service after marrying a farm labourer named Mumby, and the family came to Holton when Mrs Jameson Dixon inherited. Sarah Mumby or her daughter Jenny came daily to do housework and keep Mrs Jameson Dixon company, often late into the night. Their mistress bequeathed £1,000 to Sarah Mumby, and £4,000 and her house in Caistor to another Mumby daughter, Amelia, whom she virtually adopted.[85]

Few servants, however, were treated as true equals. Individuals regarded as family friends still endured condescension and social segregation. Subordination was an inherent and essential aspect of service. Requiring an unrelated social equal to clean up degrading dirt and disorder and to be so subservient and self-effacing was insupportable; therefore servants had to be deprived of their full humanity and regarded as inferiors and overgrown children. Paternalism denied servants personal autonomy, while class consciousness and the cash nexus inflicted a debasing inferiority and anonymity. Deference, suppressed personality and emotions, and the loss of liberty were all inevitable in service, but were intensified by employers' failure to regard their staff as fully responsible, independent adults, their denial of servants' human feelings and needs, and their insensitivity to the servants' point of view. Most masters and mistresses disregarded servants' non-work needs for companionship, love, and sexual fulfilment, and for the privacy and relaxation of home life.

How did country house servants view their employers and their treatment? On the whole, they appear to have been more satisfied with the relationship than were middle-class servants. They tolerated autocrats and eccentrics; appreciated the liberal and benevolent; and, outwardly at least, conformed to paternalist dictates, only resisting when their goals were challenged. Many servants resented the remote employer most. Being treated as an automaton alienated them, claimed Violet Firth, producing a "profound sense of separateness and a consequent indifference to the employer's interests."[86]

The majority of country house servants were from the country, where they had fully internalized deference to upper-class authority, a code instilled by the parson, teachers, and even parents, particularly in communities still isolated by poor transportation and illiteracy, and in closed villages ruled by the landowning family.[87] Among servants raised on great estates, claimed Badeau, "the spirit of servility is innate and ingrained. They firmly believe that the purpose of their creation was to provide proper attendance for the aristocracy." Former servant Alice Butler said, "We all belonged to the same family, and there was a sense of pride in serving in the Big House."[88]

Like many other people, servants looked up to the landed classes as a fascinating, superior species. One butler had acquired "a deeper feeling for 'ladies and gentlemen' as beings apart. It was not snobbishness but something deeper and kinder, ... a faith that those who had ... so much must in some manner beyond understanding deserve it."[89] Some servants were indeed snobs, with their own well-thumbed copies of Burke's and Debrett's genealogies in the housekeeper's room.[90] The landed classes' high social rank and code of conduct facilitated servants' acceptance of their subordination. "The better bred people, the real gentlefolk," a jobbing cook told C.V. Butler, "do treat their employees as flesh and blood, the 'jumped up rich middle classes,' as cattle." The gentry "treated you properly," insisted an Edwardian nurse. "They're brought up to respect you." Among the wealthy, former servants stressed, only the *nouveaux riches* were "penny-pinching and critical."[91] By unquestioningly accepting the class system, servants reconciled themselves to service. "You took it all for gospel truth," recalled Miss Spicer. "You were just contented with your lot."[92]

Social inferiority, moreover, did not necessarily mean a loss of self-respect. Newby found that deferential farm workers perceived their relationship with their social superiors as a partnership of "mutual and harmonious interdependence," in which even the humblest contribution was valuable.[93] This was precisely the ideal promoted by nineteenth-century landowners, and supported by many servants. "No one was servile," insisted Alice Butler, "everyone [else] was in some kind of service – government, civil, military, naval, Church. ... Frankly, I never felt inferior, just a cog in the wheel to help whoever was at the top ... keep the country going."[94]

Country house servants had diverse ways of preserving their self-worth and human dignity in the face of their dehumanization and humiliating treatment as childlike inferiors, either by identifying with the family and its values, and accepting the system, or by resistance. The recognized code of conduct institutionalized the servant-master relationship, distancing and depersonalizing both in a system in which authority and deference were routine rather than deliberate choices in each situation. Submissive behaviour was compulsory for servants; ritualized, habitual, and calculative. Conforming to the code made the relationship predictable and therefore easier for both parties. "I knew exactly where I stood," explained Rosina Harrison, "what I could or could not say and do."[95] Servants learned to handle the tensions of keeping their place "without ever presuming or for a moment 'forgetting themselves,'" noted Charles Booth. Servants "gifted with the tact or experience to tread safely, are not only able to keep with perfect comfort within the line, but even acquire an exceptional dignity of their own . . . very far removed from servility."[96]

Servants' determined adherence to a strict hierarchy among themselves, and upper servants' insistence on the privileges of rank, show their endorsement of the system. When servants behaved just like their betters, the latter's condescending behaviour seemed more natural and acceptable. The hierarchy below stairs also compensated by offering power and prestige within it. Servants regained their self-respect by feeling superior to their deferential subordinates.

To reconcile themselves to their position, many servants relished and exploited the family's very real dependence on them. Judiciously expressed approbation made servants feel indispensable and valued, thus boosting self-respect. "They appreciated you," a former nurse recalled. The gentry were "glad to have you. The majority . . . said they couldn't do without a help."[97]

Career servants often sank their identity entirely into the family, abandoning any independent life of their own. James Macpherson, the bachelor head gardener at Barlborough Hall, had no interests other than his gardens and the children of the family, whom he regarded as his own.[98] When asked why he had not married and retired, an under-butler who had served the Cole family for fifty years replied, "The Cole family is my family; I could not possibly leave them."[99] Women servants demonstrated devotion by rejecting marriage proposals or better jobs. A cook-housekeeper, for instance, refused to marry the head gardener, instead serving the family for forty-five years.[100] Spencer Lucy wanted his bride to take over his mother's lady's maid. He assumed Gates would be eager to regain her status as the mistress's maid. But she refused, remaining with Mary Elizabeth Lucy until her beloved mistress's

Plate 35 The family and their grooms, Shugborough

death.[101] Nurses most often identified with the family. Harriet Ward loved the Locker-Lampson children "with a fierce, maternal love, and lavished all the resources of her heart and strength" upon them alone, despising all other children.[102]

Many other servants gained reassurance of their humanity and worth through their contacts with the children, who were less class-conscious, more friendly, and more interested in the servants' lives than their elders were, and often openly affectionate. They treated servants as intriguing, valuable human beings. Talking or playing with the children provided an enjoyable diversion, and an outlet for servants' own needs for affection and attachment. One old housemaid "preferred the house where there were children running about." She had noticed that walks with the children often cheered homesick young servants. "When you have watched the children grow up," she commented, "they are dear to you all their days." Thus, "Cook often asks after you," Mary Ann Dixon wrote to her daughter Ann at boarding school, "and appears particularly anxious that you should be happy and taken care of."[103] At Kingston

Lacy, the cook expressed her devotion to the girls with expensive Christmas presents of silver hairbrushes and photograph frames, or perfume in cut glass bottles.[104] The presence of children created stronger loyalty to the family. Edwin Lee liked being in a family with children, as they "gave the place a sense of life, purpose and continuity."[105]

Often, servants identified with the landed classes, permanently adopting their attitudes and habits. "You get into their atmosphere," explained Rosa Lewis, "their ways of thinking, . . . living, and . . . feeling, so that you become like them."[106] Gentlemen's servants often acquired their employers' political views: the long-serving Newnham coachman asserted, ' "We was always Whigs, *we* was!" '[107] Retired servants of the "quality" living in the slums of Edwardian Salford were "tidier and sprucer in habit" than their neighbours. "Royalist, ultra-conservative politically, and deeply class-conscious," they were "the apologists and expositors of the whole class system."[108] Former maidservants were frequently more refined and meticulous in their housekeeping than other working-class wives. At Juniper Hill, they held tea-parties, correct in every detail. Arthur Barton's mother retained her "black clothes and her church going, and her reverence for the landed gentry." Likewise, the "idea of the Gentry" haunted Annie Light all her life. " 'Real Gentry wouldn't hear of it," she used to say; "the Gentry always did it like this!' Her tone of voice, when referring to their ways, was reverent, genteel, and longing."[109]

Yet behind a convincing posture of complete devotion and loyalty, servants could also harbour secret opinions of their own. Class divisions preserved a certain distance or detachment between family and servant. In a diary written for publication, Larry Banville showed his affection, respect, and loyalty towards the Buxtons, but still freely criticized their behaviour.[110]

A final way in which servants could fight the dehumanizing and degrading aspects of service was to resort to acts of insubordination, deliberately disobeying household edicts, and acting against the family's interests. Covert resistance depended on the extent to which rules interfered with personal goals. Restrictions on dress, for instance, were resisted, for maids shared their mistresses' love of fashion and desire to attract the opposite sex. Dress was also an expression of individuality and self-worth, and a means of gaining status in their own class.[111] In one house, maids sneaked out in the forbidden smart clothes on Sundays, and the mistress never suspected that it was her strict dress code which caused the unusually high turnover rate among the female staff.[112] Some maidservants risked dismissal in order to meet potential husbands secretly. Illicit affairs may be seen as a form of resistance, but sexual passion had its own impetus.

Likewise, alternative explanations can be found for other behaviours commonly cited as acts of resistance. The high rate of turnover which Leonore Davidoff and Lynne Haims regard as a "device for maintaining self-respect," in the country house was more often motivated by the desire to improve qualifications and wages.[113] Under-servants, indeed, expressed regret about having to move on from a household they liked. Servants who suddenly departed without notice at the most inopportune time were, however, probably vengeful. Margaret Gunston "threw up her place" just when an unanticipated party of guests, without the usual number of attendants, descended upon Wollaton Hall, "thereby adding much to Lady M[iddleton]'s anxieties."[114]

Lynne Haims also considers drunkenness and theft evidence of defiance and insubordination.[115] Certainly, some depressed and alienated servants may have regarded drink as the shortest way out of the servants' hall. But heavy drinking was typical for country house menservants. Until late in the century, servants were served beer with meals. In well-run establishments, menservants obeyed a strict code among themselves to limit drinking, because an inept inebriate only caused them more work and aroused the ire of employers.[116] But when menservants relaxed with more beer in the evenings, upper servants imbibed wine or whisky in the housekeeper's room, or butlers and cooks surreptitiously tippled the wine and spirits in their care, the sheer amount of liquor consumed could result not only in drunkenness, but in alcoholism. Coachmen were also notoriously susceptible, as they were offered alcoholic refreshments at every stop, spent waiting time in the nearest public house, or warmed themselves with flasks of spirits. Once servants became addicted, temptation was difficult to resist. Some alcoholics, such as the butler and a footman at Hall, "died of drink." Consequently, many insurance companies refused to insure butlers.[117] Wages books record numerous dismissals for drunkenness. In many cases, this was due to an obvious inability to perform duties correctly, but the liberating effect of inebriation also prompted many a resentful and hostile servant incautiously to reveal his true opinions.

Theft, more unequivocally an act of disloyalty, may sometimes have been a means of revenge. Again, country houses offered unusually great temptation, with rooms filled with valuable objects, well-stocked pantries and cellars, and opportunities to profit from dealings with tradesmen. Life-cycle servants exploiting service for other long-term goals may have succumbed more readily, but career servants probably regarded small-scale pilfering as their due perquisites. Some butlers pawned the less-used plate to pay their gambling debts, and it was not unknown for disgruntled menservants to abscond with their livery when fired.[118] Stealing could be the result of a sudden overwhelming temptation, but often appears to have been deliberately planned. One butler systematically stole goods from Hesleyside for years, "most cleverly disposing" of them. Nevertheless, former butler William Lanceley concluded that theft of valuables was rare among country house servants. He came across only one case throughout his long career.[119]

Most discontented servants found less drastic and risky ways to restore their self-esteem, in minor acts of insubordination. They "had an unequalled power of taking it out of their master or mistress in subtle ways. Orders could be received with veiled sulks and insinuations of trouble in the background."[120] Some servants asserted their humanity and worth by answering back, notably when departure was imminent. A Starkey butler "gave notice to leave & forthwith commenced to conduct himself most insolently." Other menservants gave notice rather than accept insults to their dignity. In 1875, Sir Lumley Steward's footman quit after being called a "damned rascal."[121] One dismissed and vengeful butler diligently collected moths to put in his master's valuable fur coat.[122] Bad masters aroused most resentment: the irascible Dyotts discharged a number of insolent, disrespectful, or stubborn servants.[123] Novice landowners received little respect either: the Disraelis dismissed an under-butler who failed to obey orders, a coachman who answered his master without "due respect," and another who was "ill behaved" and refused to drive. A housemaid was "incapable and unwilling," and a housekeeper had "a rude manner."[124] But deliberately poor service, such as slowness in answering the bell, banging doors, talking loudly, or giving disrespectful looks, was less tolerated by the landed classes than by the middle classes with their desperate need to retain servants.

The tone of a particular establishment largely determined the level of servants' misbehaviour. Liberal employers, and the more benevolent autocrats, inspired loyalty, honesty, and willing service, but harsh and arrogant employers, or distant and uncaring ones, often provoked a sense of alienation and resentment, expressed in varied acts of insubordination. Landowners who failed to supervise their establishment personally were often ill-served. The bachelor seventh Duke of Devonshire took no interest in household details, and was often absent, providing "plenty of opportunities for below-stairs skulduggery." His valet cheated him for many years; one manservant spent £500 of the housekeeping money on gambling; another, a drunkard, was discovered in a brothel, accompanied by the Duke's own dog; and a housekeeper indulged her friends with flowers and fruit, a visit to Hardwick with Chatsworth servants to wait on them, and a musical party in the Duke's private rooms.[125]

Equally important in maintaining good morale and firm discipline was the role of department heads. Knowing that their own jobs depended on their ability to control their underlings, most of them made every effort to curb illicit activities. The few who were corrupt and dissolute created hotbeds of vice, as did the butler Inkley's rule at Hesleyside.[126] Servants' interdependence at work and at leisure also discouraged anti-social behaviour. Slovenly work was resented by the other servants, who were inconvenienced by it.

Servants shared their own black list of unpopular establishments. When William Lanceley passed on news of vacancies in certain houses, the job-seeker would reply, "Thank you, but I don't think I should care to go there." Lanceley knew of two large establishments "always shunned by servants."[127]

Just how resentful and dissatisfied were country house servants? Upper-class family members confidently believed their childhood homes had been filled with devoted old retainers, while modern historians stress servants' resistance and discontent. My classification into four types helps to clarify this issue.

No one disputes that distressed gentlewomen were highly likely to be unhappy and to experience strained relations with the family. Governesses who were despised and ignored by parents or disliked by their pupils felt rejected and insecure. Determined to retain their status and identity as gentlewomen, they were defensive, readily offended, and easily hurt. Hippolyte Taine observed that governesses "had turned their faces into wooden masks." Even among friends "they remain on the defensive. The habit of keeping a sharp watch and firm control over themselves is too strong."[128] Charlotte Brontë found the "estrangement from one's real character – the adoption of a cold, rigid, apathetic exterior ... painful."[129] Yearning for friendship, however, governesses became attached to affectionate children or kindly employers. At

Hagley, Miss Pearson "clung to Mamma with the whole affection of her earnest mind" and Miss Jourdain was devoted to Lady Elcho.[130]

Life-cycle servants might feel detached, even antagonistic, towards their employers. They were more concerned about working conditions, food, wages, and the social life below stairs than about their employers, and did not identify with a family served for only a year or two. Servants using service instrumentally for their own ends may have lacked a sense of deference and more readily indulged in theft, drunkenness, and other illicit activities. Life-cycle servants more than any other type resented restrictions on personal liberty. Maidservants intent on marriage defied edicts on dress, followers, and visitors, and gave notice when they felt too oppressed. Nevertheless, discontent must not be exaggerated. Many former servants felt respect and loyalty towards the families they served, accepted the system uncomplainingly, and showed their identification with gentlemen's service by their subsequent behaviour. Leah Chegwidden, for instance, "never complained about her years in service," or criticized "the petty restrictions, and she never voted 'Labour.'"[131] Numerous Edwardian servants later recalled country house service with satisfaction and nostalgia.[132]

Labourers and part-time helpers were not likely to feel antagonistic towards their employers. E. W. Martin found that former labourers on Devon estates considered they had been well treated, and "remembered past days with pleasure."[133] In large establishments, where they seldom met the master or mistress, and experienced little more paternalist control or benevolence than other villagers, they might feel pride and loyalty, eagerly following the family's doings. In the smallest houses, a warm personal relationship could develop over the years, as at Holton.

Career servants were most genuinely deferential. To come to terms with the psychological conditions of their career, they supported the system, identified with the family, and internalized its values and rules. Their high mobility as under-servants was simply the approved method of obtaining experience, and most of them were eager to settle down as an upper servant in a compatible household. Many career servants developed a satisfying and successful relationship with the family. Sarah Neal left her job as lady's maid to Miss Bullock with "deep regret. I had," she wrote, "become greatly attached to Miss B."[134] Sometimes, however, intelligent and sensitive individuals forced into service by poverty remained conscious of the humiliating and degrading aspects of service, deeply resenting their treatment.[135]

The psychological impact of service was also affected by gender. Females were brought up to defer to male authority and to accept control by others. As Leonore Davidoff points out, they were "mastered for life," obedient first to their fathers, then to their husbands. Girls who went into service simply substituted employers, or upper servants, for these patriarchs.[136] Women, therefore, adjusted easily to subordination in service. As in other classes, working-class boys were raised as the more privileged sex, granted far more freedom and leisure than their hard-worked sisters. Thus boys developed a stronger sense of their own dignity and rights than girls. While men were, of course, also expected to be deferential to employers in other occupations, the demands for subservience were far greater and far more personal in service, especially for indoor men, who were, after all, engaged in the otherwise female occupation of housework. These men, nicknamed "flunkies", were often despised as servile and therefore unmanly. Eric Horne, a butler, felt the "ordinary working-man looks askance" at the manservant, as "something between a man and a woman, doing women's work, living on sufferance, and not daring to say 'Boo' to a goose."[137] Unlike other working-class men, a servant was a dependant in another's household, without domicile, property, or, in consequence, the vote after the 1884 Reform Act. Gentleman's service, complained Horne, was for "a man who is looking for a sure meal and a bed, and who is willing to forgo his liberty as a citizen."[138]

Menservants dealt with their loss of masculinity by cultivating an extreme haughtiness and dignity in their manner, terrorizing under-servants and visitors alike. Footmen were often very arrogant, and took enormous pride in their looks and dress. Insistent on independence and autonomy, men more often disobeyed orders and more vigorously resisted attempts to control their private lives, taking advantage of their greater scarcity value. In one duke's establishment, two footmen "inclined to resent all authority" sneaked off every night to the local inn. And at Hampton Court, "What is to be done about getting our menservants to church[?]" Sarah Arkwright wondered in 1864.[139] For some men, the psychological damage was too great – male indoor servants had a higher rate of suicide than average. Outdoor occupations were more independent, and clearly reserved for men. Gamekeepers, significantly, had a very low rate of suicide.[140]

Advancing age and length of service might also increase self-confidence and autonomy. Henry Polderoy complained that elderly servants were "insolent and interfering and endeavour to rule our houses and arrange our lives." At Wentworth Woodhouse, where the servants were promoted and never left, "they were all thoroughly spoilt and did just what they liked," once turning away visitors because "it did not suit them to increase the luncheon party." Likewise, at Petworth in 1828, the elderly servants insisted on going to bed early; "they could not stand being put out . . . , and were never interfered with."[141]

Towards the end of the century, a new dissatisfaction became evident in domestic service. With universal education, better communications, more alternative occupations operating on a cash-nexus basis, and the agitation for better conditions in other occupations, servants were more aware of the advantages of other work, particularly independence outside working hours. Other workers had shorter hours and enjoyed unprecedented leisure time, with proliferating facilities to entertain them. Education, rising expectations, and sharper class conflict meant working-class people were more individualistic and more conscious of their own rights and needs, and consequently objected to the humiliations and restrictions of service, particularly as its reputation plummeted among members of their class. Servants increasingly detested paternalistic control of their private lives: they wanted more time off, limited working hours, and freedom to see visitors and suitors. Some younger servants even questioned the inequities of the class system, and the contrast between living standards above and below stairs. While growing numbers of servants preferred a contractual relationship of mutual independence, others disliked the dehumanizing detachment of the remote employer. In 1916, C. V. Butler reported widespread complaints that the employing classes looked down on servants, and treated them as machines.[142]

Yet the Edwardian landed classes experienced no difficulty in attracting all the servants they needed. The abundant evidence of autobiographies and oral-history interviews shows that young people still willingly entered gentleman's service; those raised on the landed classes' estates took service for granted, while others saw it as a worthwhile career. In many ways, country house service was more attractive than ever. The wealthy elite indulged in a glittering social life, and a glamorous lifestyle of lavish spending, even below stairs. Such employers interfered less in servants' personal affairs. The autocratic, pious patriarch or matriarch was becoming rare, and an increasing number of landowners were becoming more liberal in their attitudes. Some of the landed classes responded to the widely reported dislike of service by offering free time and outings, attractive servants' quarters, or new technology to lighten the workload.

Country house servants continued to feel less discontent, and less hostility towards their employers, than did the mass of servants. They were isolated from the highly critical urban working classes, in a more deferential, traditional rural community which still respected them. Their employers were so much higher in rank, and the social distance so great, that servants more readily accorded them deference, awe, and respect. Social differentiation was regulated with an institutionalized code of conduct formalizing and ritualizing daily contacts, making upper-class condescension less personally offensive. The staff, moreover, behaved in much the same way towards each other. Copying the landed classes' hierarchical structure and code of behaviour below stairs helped servants accept their subordination. Servants found the landed classes more skilled and courteous in handling their staff than middle-class employers. Employers in great houses were less personally intrusive than a middle-class mistress supervising two or three servants. Though they usually hired and fired the staff themselves and formulated the strict regulations governing servants' behaviour during and after work, they delegated the day-to-day tasks of supervision and discipline to their intermediaries, the department heads. Landowners' unassailable social superiority meant they could also unbend at times, especially at family celebrations and servants' dances, encouraging servants to feel they belonged to one community. Unlike middle-class servants, country house staff often joined the family in loyally dedicating themselves to the house and the dynasty, and were far more likely to identify positively with the family, and to adopt its values and customs. It took another quarter-century after 1914 before the supply of recruits finally dried up.

Conclusion

The most remarkable feature of the nineteenth-century landed classes was their tenacity in holding on to political and social primacy until the 1880s. Their strength lay both in their refusal to change – in particular their continued insistence on landownership as the legitimate source of power – and in their willingness to compromise, adapt, and reform. Both family life and domestic service in the country house reflect this paradox. Many distinctive features of the two elites remained essentially unaltered over the century. There were, however, perceptible shifts in patterns of behaviour both above and below stairs. Relationships between parents and children, family and servants, and within the servant hierarchy itself, were partly governed by the enduring values of landed society; but the challenges of an industrialized, increasingly democratic society demanded an improved standard of conduct which altered both family life and gentleman's service.

While every country house community was unique to some degree, generalizations can and should be made about the distinctive and characteristic features of the landed family and its servants in nineteenth-century England and Wales. Although the right to follow one's own preferences regardless of conventions was one of the privileges of rank, most families nevertheless did conform to the customary standards of behaviour, which clearly evolved over the nineteenth century. Landownership carried with it compelling obligations and traditions, and many innovations eventually influenced the majority of families and their staffs, or created new customs which became institutionalized. New developments were for the most part gradual and uneven: some individuals and families retained the old ways for a generation or more. Changes reached each sector of the landed classes at different times and with varying impact. Some aspects of life in the country house did not change over the century, however, simply because they were an integral part of landownership. The landowner's values, code of conduct, style of living, and pursuits shaped the lives of the entire country house community. The basic characteristics of the landed family were retained throughout the period, and were a source of its resilience and durability.

In 1815, the landed classes' values were derived from the pre-industrial agrarian society of earlier centuries, in which the main source of wealth, and thus political and social power, was the landed estate. They looked backward to an organic, hierarchical social structure in which birth and rank defined an individual's place in the social order; and in which authority and deference, together with rules of precedence, ruled human relations, and family connections and patronage secured posts and perquisites. At home they preserved an equally organic and hierarchical community, characterized by the authority of men over women, parents over children, and employers over servants and dependants, all bound together in mutual obligation.

The landed classes had their own heritage of values and customs built up over centuries. Central to their beliefs was the priority of the dynasty. The individual's interests and goals were subservient to those of the family – to maintain or raise the family's social position, and to hold, improve, and augment its property for future generations. Key mechanisms for achieving these goals were primogeniture and the marriage settlement. A sense of obligation to the family promoted children's compliance with their parents' wishes and influenced an heir's choice of bride. The traditional functions of marriage in supplying the family with funds and advantageous connections remained factors for many nineteenth-century heirs in their selection of a spouse.

The unique situation of the landed classes shaped gender roles. The nineteenth-century male landowner's authority as a husband and father derived not so much from the ideology of separate spheres, from religious dogma, or even from paternalist theory, as from his real and obvious power as the head of the dynasty, substantial landowner, possessor of great wealth, and member of the ruling class. His power over his children ultimately came from his control of the resources they needed to establish themselves in the world or to marry and set up their own households. Landowners' wives enjoyed greater equality and liberty than wives in the classes below. The marriage settlement guaranteed them separate income, and their rank and wealth gave them greater freedom to follow their own interests. Both the landowner and his wife were subordinate to the primary goal of dynastic continuity; their various roles converged or complemented each other as they worked together to promote and preserve the family. The private sphere of home was not reserved for women, nor the public sphere for men.

Family life in the country house remained unusually public and institutionalized throughout the nineteenth century. To guarantee membership in Society, and to exert authority and exact deference in the rural community, the landed family kept up its position by lavish expenditure on the physical plant and personnel required for hospitality and display. Both husbands and wives had public duties, and were expected to be seen at the social calendar's events. Rites of passage such as the heir's birth, coming-of-age, return from his honeymoon, and funeral were all community events, and christenings, confirmations, and weddings became formal Society occasions. Even at home, the family was on public display before servants and guests, and family members' private lives were circumscribed by the omnipresence of servants.

Several aspects of service in the country house reflected continuity, too. Most landed estates remained traditional pre-industrial rural communities, where inhabitants retained deferential respect for the landowner who controlled so much of their lives. The domestic staff maintained the same hierarchical social order as its betters, with the same insistence on authority and deference, precedence and etiquette. But a servant's rank and privileges were determined less by birth than by achievement. While family connections and upper-class patronage did help individuals obtain places, country house service was fundamentally a meritocracy: better positions were earned by talent, skill, and experience.

Subordination of the individual to the dynasty was found among servants too. Those born on the estate often took it for granted that their role in life was to serve the landowner's family as their parents had before them. Many servants identified with the family, and long-serving upper servants devoted their lives to caring for the mansion and its surroundings. Service on the landed estate had a sense of community and tradition derived from feudal loyalties, family continuity, and a degree of isolation and self-sufficiency. If urban domestic service can be seen as an agent of modernization for rural girls, the reverse was true for servants working in the country house. Gentleman's service preserved and promoted conservative attitudes.

The necessity of keeping servants was never questioned in this period. The landed classes took it for granted that others would do all the domestic chores. A great house, its gardens, stables, game, and park, could not be run without the toil of a large staff, and even the lesser gentry needed several servants. A family's reputation among the upper classes and the local community, and its own personal comfort, depended on the skill and cooperation of servants in maintaining adequate standards in their work and acting in the desired manner. Servants remained symbols of the family's rank and power, actors carrying out the formal rituals which distanced the master and mistress from inferior groups, demonstrated authority, and exacted awe and deference.

The essential nature of domestic service remained unaltered, too. Live-in servants found their whole time was at the family's disposal, and because they were part of the household, their employers attempted to control their personal lives. Servants were hired not just to perform chores considered menial and degrading, but to act in a deferential and submissive manner, acknowledging the employer's superiority. The relationship between master and servant was one of acknowledged inequality. Service was intrinsically demeaning and degrading, damaging to the individual's sense of dignity and worth.

Country houses, nevertheless, attracted an ample supply of servants over the century. The landed family's social status and wealth made country house service the prestigious elite sector of the occupation. Its advantages and distinctive features continued throughout the period. The landowner's social rank inspired respect, awe, and loyalty among his servants, and gave them higher status among their own kind. His lifestyle was glamorous, exciting, and lavish. Blending courtesy and formality, landowners perfected a code of conduct which effectively regulated relations with their servants. Landed families were also more generous than other masters and mistresses in providing good working conditions, decent accommodation, ample food, and more social welfare in the form of medical care, pensions, and legacies. Great houses offered more perquisites and vails, too. Finally, country houses provided opportunities for upward mobility to a higher social status and a comfortable standard of living.

Country houses thus offered benefits to the four distinct types of servant: the life-cycle servant who moved on to marriage or another occupation; the career servant who chose service as his or her lifetime occupation; the distressed gentlewoman forced to earn a living as a governess, companion or housekeeper; and the local unskilled labourer working full- or part-time to earn income for his or her family. These four types were found throughout the century.

All these elements of continuity above and below stairs remained because the landed classes had no intention of relinquishing their way of life. Traditional family values and a large, well-trained, and deferential establishment were sources of strength in perpetuating the aristocratic ideal.

The first development altering the landed family in the period 1815–1914 was the final triumph of domesticity. The shift from patriarchy to domesticity was very gradual and uneven. The new family values were already widespread among the gentry, but Judith Schneid Lewis's close study of aristocratic mothers suggests that it was not until the 1820s that they became the norm among the high aristocracy.[1] For the rest of the landed classes, however, domesticity was an element of continuity rather than an innovation. Like their predecessors, they continued to value and practise companionate marriage. Most courting couples expected to feel love, or at least warm affection, for each other before they married, and then to regard each other as friends and companions as well as lovers. The landowner's privileged position, his leisure, financial security, and luxurious home all facilitated a happy, companionate married life. Most parents were child-oriented and affectionate, personally involved in their children's upbringing, and eager to delight their children with uninhibited play, generous gifts, and enjoyable treats and outings.

Early-nineteenth-century wives were enthusiastic adherents of the expanded concept of motherhood. They willingly bore large families, and often breastfed their infants. A shared preoccupation with childbearing and child-rearing brought them closer to their own mothers, mothers-in-law, and married sisters. Mothers personally controlled childcare and education, dictating policy to subservient nurses and governesses. Child-rearing engendered more responsibilities, but it also gave mothers a respected role within the family.

Many Regency parents, influenced by Rousseau's theories of hardening children, instituted an austerity which became typical of the nursery regime for the rest of the century. Numerous landowners chose to educate sons at home with tutors, rather than to send them to schools notorious for poor teaching and discipline, and no longer socially exclusive. Daughters, however, often attended fashionable boarding schools which emphasized accomplishments, in preparation for the marriage market.

The early-nineteenth-century landed classes generally allowed their children to conduct their own courtships and marry for love because the young people mixed only with eligible social equals. Faced with *nouveaux riches* eager to become socially accepted, upper-class women in the Regency period developed the role of gatekeepers to Society, which they retained until late in the century. Insistent on the importance of rank, pedigree, and connections, they formulated elaborate rituals to identify and forestall unwanted social climbers. This complex system of etiquette formalized and complicated life for both family and servants throughout the nineteenth century.

By the first two decades of the nineteenth century, the fashionable elite was characterized not by a strong sense of *noblesse oblige* or widespread piety, so much as by a desire for personal happiness and pleasure. The decline in patriarchy gave more autonomy to wives, children, and servants. But the pendulum had swung too far. The "abdication on the part of the governors" applied to the nursery too.[2] In the late eighteenth century, according to Lawrence Stone, the shift to affectionate, permissive child-rearing weakened parental authority and discipline. Some fond parents, he argues, spoiled their children. Their undisciplined offspring failed to internalize the norms of good behaviour, and the traditional sense of duty to family, society, and the poor.[3] These children evidently became the dandies, gamblers, idlers, frivolous social butterflies, and adulterous wives whose antics tarnished the reputation of the fashionable aristocracy in the 1820s and 1830s. Most of the gentry had neither the inclination nor the income for the excesses of their social superiors, although a few squires were still uncultured boors obsessed with hunting, gambling, and heavy drinking. Yet even the gentry were more interested in enjoying themselves than in religious or philanthropic duties.

The Regency country house staff reflected the unregenerate ways of its master and mistress. Great magnates sought to maintain their social superiority over aspiring *nouveaux riches* by lavish expenditure on display, including larger establishments, and more "front-stage" menservants dressed in splendid liveries. Conveniently, servants' wages fell for a decade after the Napoleonic Wars. Keeping large establishments for show led to under-employment, inefficiency, and waste below stairs. The household was also far less strictly organized than in later decades, with less job demarcation, but also less free time. Squires' small staffs had to undertake the duties of several different departments.

The decline of patriarchy and piety in the eighteenth century had diminished landowners' sense of responsibility for their servants. Regency masters and mistresses were less concerned than their seventeenth-century forebears with their servants' souls, with regulating their personal lives, or with providing paternalistic social welfare. Servants were consequently more autonomous than later generations of Victorian servants. Many servants themselves were as individualistic, self-interested, materialistic, and pleasure-loving as their masters and mistresses. The early-nineteenth-century landed classes were criticized for being arrogant and rude towards the lower orders, including their own servants. Some masters and mistresses, especially among the aristocracy, had grown remote, retreating to a cash nexus, but in smaller households, more liberal attitudes had led to a greater informality, and more respect for the individuality and rights of servants.

The decline of paternal authority over family and servants generated behaviour which invited middle-class criticism. Permissiveness, extravagance, and worldliness above and below stairs were damaging the landowners' reputation. By the 1830s, the landed classes were facing a rising tide of criticism from below, attacking them as frivolous, dissipated, immoral, selfish, arrogant, incompetent, and altogether unfit to rule. They regained the respect and deference of the rest of society not only by perpetuating the values and social structure of the pre-industrial world as long as possible, but also by meeting censure with reform. The family and its servants played a vital role in this campaign to retain pre-eminence. Child-rearing methods, the roles of women, and the behaviour of servants were all important.

Even in the Regency period, the winds of change were being felt. Evangelicals were infiltrating upper-class nurseries and the universities to convert the rising generation. Evangelicalism encouraged masters and mistresses to intrude into the lives of children and servants, to save their souls and make them virtuous. The role of Lady Bountiful was revived and expanded, with pious ladies visiting cottages and opening Sunday Schools. Compulsory church attendance and family prayers became the norm, as, from the 1830s, the landed classes began judiciously adding middle-class piety, seriousness, and propriety to their own code of conduct. Drunkenness, reckless gambling, fornication, adultery, and other vices diminished, or at least were better concealed from the servants and the public. "Things are vastly improved in the space of two generations," commented Walter Besant in the 1880s. "The general tone, . . . the general manners of society have very much improved."[4] The revival of paternalism in the 1830s and 1840s further validated the landowner's rule, and patriarchal control of dependants, as well as benevolence towards the needy, became mandatory. While this promoted patriarchy in the family too, Stone's assumption that there was a wholesale reversion to the harsh authoritarianism of the seventeenth century fails to recognize the mitigating effect of companionate marriage in the nineteenth century. The middle-class ideals of true womanhood and separate spheres, moreover, both supported and limited patriarchy, by acknowledging women's inferiority and subordination while granting them a sphere of authority and respect within the home. In the early-Victorian years, these theories of gender created an emphasis on women's delicacy and weakness, and confined them more to home and family.

The early- and mid-Victorian landed classes reared children to conform to the rules of propriety and do their duty. Character was developed with austerity, strict routines, religious training, and firm, consistent discipline. Nannies trained in these new priorities and practices passed them on to their underlings, perpetuating a pattern of child-rearing which changed little before 1914. Parents recovered their authority over their children, assuming the crucial role of inculcating the revised code of upper-class values and conduct. Most fathers and mothers did this not by reverting to harsh autocracy and severe physical punishment, but by acting as a role-model of virtuous behaviour themselves, and by exploiting warm ties of affection. Love and respect for their parents motivated children to internalize class values. Girls were now educated at home, within the wholesome and safe family environment, but boys were increasingly entrusted to reformed public schools, which inculcated masculinity as much as the classics, and provided younger sons with qualifications for a career in the new meritocracy. These methods of socializing children were effective in producing a more dutiful, moral, and responsible generation. Moral righteousness, the traditional sense of duty to family and class, and the conviction of superiority engendered by the deference and subservience of servants and the local poor, all combined to create enormous self-confidence and assurance which bolstered the landed classes' claims to continuing dominance over British society.

As a result of all these changes, the mid-Victorian period was characterized by an emphasis on duty toward one's family, class, dependants, nation, and God, and by an even greater focus on family life. Like their parents, couples married for love, and expected affectionate companionship in marriage. They still had large families, and devoted much time and energy to child-rearing. Married couples remained emotionally attached to their parents and siblings, exchanging frequent correspondence and lengthy visits. Society itself became more virtuous and domesticated, abandoning public entertainments during the Season for private events held at family residences. More than ever, Society saw itself as a community of interwoven families. Its exclusiveness, with everyone connected through kinship or friendship, encouraged conformity to the aristocratic code of conduct and values. The ideals of true womanhood and separate spheres still restricted women to running the household, supervising childcare, social activities, and unobtrusive philanthropy. Yet upper-class women were now heading philanthropic organizations and institutions not only in the country, but also in London.

The newly serious landowner and his wife also sought to reform their establishment. Piety and paternalism encouraged greater intervention in servants' personal lives. The early- and mid-Victorian decades were the heyday of the authoritarian master and mistress intent on controlling, disciplining, converting, and improving their servants. Servants had to attend family prayers and church on Sundays. Now the sexes were carefully segregated both during and after work, and feminine fripperies were banned. The need to act as a good example, and to maintain their new image of virtuous propriety, meant that the landed classes felt more constrained by the presence of servants in their home.

Like the middle classes, the landed classes imposed the efficiency, order, and time-orientation of the factory on the household, with strict timetables, work schedules, and job demarcation. Divisions of class promoted stereotypes, formalized relations between family and staff, and encouraged the remote employer to reduce the tie to a contractual cash nexus. Class consciousness was reflected in the uniform for maidservants, depersonalization of servants, and heavier demands for ritualized deference. All these new developments became an accepted part of the country house establishment, taken for granted long after masters and mistresses became more liberal or remote later in the century. The rise of respectability, and the diffusion of notions of separate spheres among the lower-middle and working classes, as much as the stricter discipline imposed upon servants, created a more serious, dutiful, and deferential staff. As Dorothy Marshall noted, "the growth of refinement and propriety hedged in the domestic staff with more restrictions, and though life became less hard it also became less interesting."[5] Thus, in 1854, a butler asserted that gluttons, drunkards, and blasphemers now found it hard to obtain respectable posts. "The morality of religion is . . . fashionable; few persons would acknowledge they profess no regard for religion." Improved "education and moral training" induced young people to "shrink with horror from . . . openly profane persons."[6]

By this time the grandees no longer saw their establishments chiefly as a form of conspicuous consumption. It was not so much income or rank as the family's lifestyle and stage in the life cycle which determined the number and nature of the staff. The majority of landowners had relatively small staffs, and even the very wealthy chose to employ the servants they actually wanted rather than the optimum appropriate for their rank. But this freedom was in itself a reflection of the landowner's secure and assured social status.

In the late nineteenth century, however, the landed classes' position was no longer so secure or assured. The agricultural depression diminished incomes, especially among the gentry, and some families were forced to let or sell their homes. Landowners' control of local and national government was significantly declining, and non-landed wealth was breaking into Society, expanding and fragmenting it. Many *parvenus* bought or rented country houses for weekend entertaining and sport, disdaining traditional local duties. These newcomers were often hedonistic, materialistic, and extravagant. With a new respect for money, the landed classes tolerated, and in some cases adopted, these new attitudes. Decades of fierce controversy over religious doctrines and practices, scientific discoveries, and new schools of thought all undermined religious conviction. The assumptions of separate spheres were also being challenged, as the Woman Question was debated.

High Society responded to the real loss of the landed classes' wealth and power, not by renewed dedication to religion, virtue, and duty, but by a return to an individualistic pursuit of happiness, self-fulfilment, and pleasure, in a welter of extravagance and opulent luxury. The weekend party became the typical country house entertainment, adding to the popular Society hostess's heavy burden. Husbands and wives spent more time away from home enjoying field sports, social visits, or trips abroad. Marital infidelity increased, and unhappily married couples more readily resorted to divorce. Parents, preoccupied with their own pleasures, sometimes became distant and remote, and neglected to act as exemplars and teachers of religion and traditional family values. When young people entered Society, they encountered materialistic, self-indulgent *nouveaux riches* flaunting their wealth and putting on lavish entertainments. The exclusive and intimate marriage market was disintegrating, as aristocratic ladies lost control over admission to Society, and heirs increasingly found brides outside their own class. Ultimately, however, the most fundamental reason for abandoning early-Victorian values was that their basis was fast disappearing: landownership no longer granted the wealth, political, and even social power it had in the 1830s.

Many aristocratic families, and most of the landed gentry, nevertheless clung to the established code of values. Disapproving patrician aristocrats held themselves aloof from Society's junketing, while the beleaguered gentry, unable to afford the growing opulence of the London Season, retired once more to the counties. The majority of Edwardian landed families, in fact, retained the values inculcated by nannies, governesses, parents, and public schools. They remained dutiful, domesticated, and often pious. Their lives still revolved around estate management, local government, philanthropy, field sports, and socializing with neighbouring families and relatives. Their marriages were typically companionate and affectionate. Among the parish gentry, admitted Lady Dorothy Nevill, most households "are models of conjugal peace."[7] Parents enjoyed their children's company and shaped their characters through love, example, and authoritative command. The family attended church regularly, though family prayers were disappearing. Masters and mistresses were still active in running the household and managing the staff. Examining five Sussex country houses from 1880 to 1914, Patricia Blackwell finds more continuity than decline, for "attitudes and habits of life . . . were not changing as rapidly as the objective conditions of landowning."[8]

Nevertheless, there were changes in family life even in these families. Late-nineteenth-century women gained more freedom and independence, as their activities outside the home expanded – in local government, philanthropic organizations and institutions, political organizations, new sports, even their own shops. Girls benefited from university-trained governesses, and academic girls' public schools, though few upper-class women went on to university. Single women gained wider opportunities, with a number of careers now open to the determined. Motherhood became relatively less important in women's lives, as they bore fewer children, abandoned breastfeeding, and devoted more time to their own pursuits. Both parents were often quite liberal, enjoying a more informal and permissive relationship with their children. Children were treated more indulgently than earlier generations, and grew up in more luxurious surroundings.

Many developments of the decades preceding 1914 affected the staff too. Falling incomes prompted attempts to economize by cutting staff, or by replacing expensive indoor menservants with parlour-maids. Another incentive was that wages rates rose, as the rural population supplying the bulk of the nation's servants diminished while the demand from middle-class employers increased. Technological innovations, factory production of goods formerly made at home, and commercial services all reduced labour needs. Landed families increasingly relied on day and casual labour both in the country and in town.

At the same time, however, fashionable Society's frenetic round of entertainment, and its indulgence in new heights of conspicuous consumption, increased the demand for "front-stage" and personal servants. Experienced, efficient lady's maids and valets were in great demand, as were tall, good-looking footmen, skilled butlers, and talented cooks. The number of gamekeepers expanded rapidly, too.

Many socially active aristocrats were growing remote, leaving the day-to-day management of the staff to their upper servants, who perpetuated the strict rules and regulations established by mid-century. Nannies firmly ruled the nursery, often resenting and resisting maternal interference. Less wealthy and less socially active landowners, in contrast, continued to be involved personally with their servants, and often became less authoritarian and more liberal. This was due not only to more egalitarian attitudes, but also to the struggle involved in finding and retaining good servants. Whether as a result of this, or because of the sheer trickle-down effect of extravagance, country house servants saw their standard of diet and accommodation rise, they obtained more liberty, and more effort was taken to keep them happy. Servants themselves demanded better conditions. Compulsory state education from the 1870s made them better informed, more self-aware, and more individualistic. A more domesticated family life created higher expectations of emotional satisfaction and personal happiness. An expanding range of alternative occupations was available, particularly for women. Young people were increasingly rejecting the long hours, lack of liberty, debasing experience of inferiority, and declining status of domestic service.

But growing dissatisfaction elsewhere affected country houses little, for they attracted youngsters who were more deferential in the first place, recognized the advantages of country house service, and found their work congenial and rewarding.

Thus the way of life in the nineteenth-century country house, with its conspicuous consumption and display, its lavish entertaining, hunting and shooting, its nursery and schoolroom, all so dependent on the labour of servants, persisted well into the twentieth century. The symbiotic relationship remained unbroken. "We needed them and they needed us," concluded Edwin Lee, the Astors' butler.[9] Even in the inter-war period, country houses suffered no severe shortage of servants. The patterns set in the Victorian era only disintegrated with the Second World War.

Notes

INTRODUCTION

1. For the nineteenth century, F. M. L. Thompson's *English Landed Society in the Nineteenth Century* (London, 1963; paperback edn, 1971) remains a classic. More recent monographs include M. L. Bush, *The English Aristocracy: a Comparative Synthesis* (Manchester, 1984), and Heather A. Clemenson, *English Country Houses and Landed Estates* (London, 1982).
2. J. R. Wordie, review of J. V. Beckett, *The Aristocracy in England, 1660–1914, Albion*, 19 (1987), pp. 453–4.
3. David Cannadine, *The Decline and Fall of the British Aristocracy* (New Haven, 1990), p. 7.
4. David Spring, "The role of the aristocracy in the late nineteenth century," *Victorian Studies*, 4 (1960), p. 60.
5. Mark Girouard, *Life in the English Country House: a Social and Architectural History* (New Haven and London, 1978), p. 285.
6. Sociologists and geographers have long debated the definition of the term "community." Taking their many viewpoints together, the community may be defined as an interdependent group of stable households within a limited territory. Its members interact as a social group or small social system to meet many of their physiological, psychological and social needs, and share a common cultural bond of community sentiment. Social relationships between all members are not an absolute prerequisite. See Colin Bell and Howard Newby, *Community Studies* (London, 1971), pp. 15–16, 21–53; G. J. Lewis, *Rural Communities* (London, 1979), pp. 29, 31–2, 172–4; Margaret Stacey, "The myth of community studies," *British Journal of Sociology*, 20 (1969), pp. 134–44; Albert J. Reiss Jr., "The sociological study of communities," *Rural Sociology*, 24 (1959), p. 119; William A. Sutton Jr and Jiri Kolaja, "The concept of community," *Rural Sociology*, 25 (1960), pp. 197–8.
7. Lady Mary Jeune, "The servant question," *Fortnightly Review*, 52 (1892), p. 72.

[8] John Burnett (ed.), *Useful Toil: Autobiographies of Working People from the 1820s to the 1920s* (London, 1974; paperback edn, Harmondsworth, 1977), p. 145.

[9] Richard Gill, *Happy Rural Seat: the English Country House and the Literary Imagination* (New Haven, 1972), pp. 5, 14.

[10] Thompson, *English Landed Society*, pp. 14–15; Bush, *English Aristocracy*, pp. 1–4; J. V. Beckett, *The Aristocracy in England, 1660–1914* (Oxford, 1987), pp. 21–2.

[11] Girouard, *English Country House*, pp. 1–2.

[12] Lawrence and Jeanne C. Fawtier Stone, *An Open Elite? England 1540–1880* (Oxford, 1986), pp. 6–7, 11, 51–3, 437–42; F. M. L. Thompson, *The Rise of Respectable Society: a Social History of Victorian Britain, 1830–1900* (Cambridge, Mass., 1988), p. 154.

[13] Girouard, *English Country House*, p. 2; John Harris, "Gone to ground," in Roy Strong, Marcus Binney, and John Harris, *The Destruction of the Country House, 1875–1975* (London, 1974), p. 15; Clemenson, *English Country Houses*, p. 56.

[14] Mark Girouard, *The Victorian Country House* (revised edn, New Haven and London, 1979), p. 16.

[15] Jill Franklin, *The Gentleman's Country House and its Plan, 1835–1914* (London, 1981), p. 4.

[16] Stone and Stone, *Open Elite*, pp. 6–8.

[17] Bush, *English Aristocracy*, pp. 1–4; Beckett, *Aristocracy in England*, pp. 21–2, 39, 41–2, 51; Cannadine, *Decline and Fall*, pp. 8–15. See also Howard Newby, *Country Life: a Social History of Rural England* (Totowa, NJ, 1987), pp. 64–5.

[18] Thompson, *English Landed Society*, pp. 111–13.

[19] Girouard, *English Country House*, ch. 10.

[20] Mrs Dorothy Home McCall, "Another aspect of the Servant Problem," *National Review*, 60 (Sept 1912–Feb 1913), p. 970.

[21] Edward Higgs, "Domestic service and household production," in Angela V. John (ed.), *Unequal Opportunities: Women's Employment in England, 1800–1918* (Oxford, 1986), pp. 133–6.

[22] Theresa McBride, *The Domestic Revolution: the Modernisation of Household Service in England and France, 1820–1920* (London, 1976).

[23] Lynne F. Haims undertook a serious, scholarly study of servants in the great houses of landowners with estates over 10,000 acres, in her dissertation, "In their place: domestic servants in English country houses, 1850–1870" (unpublished Johns Hopkins University PhD dissertation, 1981).

[24] See, for instance, Adeline Hartcup, *Below Stairs in the Great Country Houses* (London, 1980), chs 2 and 3; Pamela Horn, *The Rise and Fall of the Victorian Servant* (Dublin, 1975), chs 4 and 5; Burnett, *Useful Toil*, pp. 146–153;

Samuel and Sarah Adams, *The Complete Servant: Being a Practical Guide to the Peculiar Duties and Business of all Descriptions of Servants . . . with Useful Receipts and Tables* (London, 1825; reprinted as *The Complete Servant* (Lewes, 1989); Mrs Isabella Beeton, *The Book of Household Management: Comprising Information for the Mistress, Housekeeper, Cook, Kitchen-maid, Butler, Footman, Coachman, Valet, Upper and Under House-maids, Lady's-maid, Maid-of-all-work, Laundry-maid, Nurse and Nurse-maid, Monthly, Wet, and Sick Nurses, etc. etc. Also, Sanitary, Medical, & Legal Memoranda; With a History of the Origin, Properties, and Uses of All Things Connected with Home Life and Comfort* (London, 1861; reprinted New York, 1977).

25 Gregory D. Phillips, *The Diehards: Aristocratic Society and Politics in Edwardian England* (Cambridge, Mass., 1979), p. 17.

26 Carol Dyhouse, "Mothers and daughters in the middle-class home," in Jane Lewis (ed.), *Labour and Love: Women's Experience of Home and Family, 1850–1940* (Oxford, 1986), pp. 41–2.

27 Chief published sources for this family are Eric Richards, *The Leviathan of Wealth: the Sutherland Fortune in the Industrial Revolution* (London, 1973); the Duke of Sutherland, *Looking Back* (London, 1957); Denis Stuart, *Dear Duchess: Millicent Duchess of Sutherland, 1867–1955* (London, 1982).

28 Lincolnshire Archives Committee, *Archivists' Report*, 22 (1970–1).

29 The main published source for the Yorkes is Merlin Waterson, *The Servants' Hall: a Domestic History of Erddig* (London, 1980).

CHAPTER 1   THE DEMOGRAPHY OF THE LANDED FAMILY

1 Proportions calculated from Burke's *Peerage* and *Gentry* as roughly 9% peers, 14% baronets and 77% commoners. *Return of Owners of Land, 1872–3*, (3 vols), England and Wales, Vols I and II (*Parliamentary Papers*, 1874, 72, Cmnd 1097); John Bateman, *The Great Landowners of Great Britain and Ireland* (London, 1883); John Burke, *The Peerage and Baronetage of Great Britain* (London, 1871 edn); John Burke, *The Landed Gentry* (London, 1871 edn); Edward Walford, *The County Families of Great Britain* (London, 1871 and 1888 edns).

2 After this time houses were sold during the lifetime of an owner inheriting before 1914, thus not affecting inheritance patterns.

3 T. H. Hollingsworth, "The demography of the British peerage," supplement to *Population Studies*, 18 (1964).

4 The Stones calculated that over 87% of squires and above 1800–49 married. Stone and Stone, *Open Elite*, table 3.2.

5 Sneyd MSS, Ralph Sneyd to Henry Vincent, 15 Feb. 1832, S/HWV/RS, Keele University Library.

6 The sample correlates with the Stones' figures of a median age at marriage in the early nineteenth century of 29 for squires' heirs, and 27 for higher ranks' heirs. Lawrence Stone, *The Family, Sex and Marriage in England, 1500–1800* (Oxford, 1977), p. 46; Stone and Stone, *Open Elite*, p. 96, table 3.2. The male population's mean age at marriage rose steadily from 25 to 27. N. L. Tranter, *Population and Society, 1750–1940: Contrasts in Population Growth* (New York and London, 1985), p. 52; E. A. Wrigley and R. S. Schofield, *The Population History of England, 1541–1871: a Reconstruction* (London, 1981; paperback edn, Cambridge, 1989), p. 437.

7 The Stones found a median of 28 years for heirs' first marriages in all ranks. Stone, *Family, Sex and Marriage*, p. 57; Stone and Stone, *Open Elite*, table 3.3.

8 Hollingsworth, "Demography," pp. 23–5.

9 The Stones' figures are even higher: 23% of first marriages were childless among heirs of the county gentry and above born after 1800. Stone and Stone, *Open Elite*, table 3.3. The average rate of childlessness in the peerage from 1550 to 1950 was 18.6% of married couples, changing little over time. Hollingsworth, "Demography," pp. 45–7.

10 Mell Davies, "Corsets and conception: fashion and demographic trends in the nineteenth century," *Comparative Studies in Society and History*, 24 (1982), pp. 611–41.

11 Judith Schneid Lewis, *In the Family Way: Childbearing in the British Aristocracy, 1760–1860* (New Brunswick, 1986), pp. 218–19.

12 Stone and Stone, *Open Elite*, pp. 97–9; Thompson, *Respectable Society*, p. 58.

13 Tranter, *Population and Society*, p. 60; Hollingsworth, "Demography," pp. 30–1; Sir William Cecil Dampier and Catherine Durning Whetham, *The Family and the Nation: a Study in Natural Inheritance and Social Responsibility* (London, 1909), pp. 138–9.

14 Ruth Hall (ed.), *Dear Dr Stopes: Sex in the 1920s* (London, 1978; paperback edn., Harmondsworth, 1981), p. 51; Pat Jalland and John Hooper (eds), *Women from Birth to Death: The Female Life Cycle in Britain, 1830–1914* (Brighton, 1986), p. 276; Susan Mary Alsop, *Lady Sackville: a Biography* (New York, 1978), p. 143; Nancy Mitford (ed.), *The Ladies of Alderley: Being the Letters Between Maria Josepha, Lady Stanley of Alderley, and her Daughter-in-law Henrietta Maria Stanley During the Years 1841–1850* (London, 1967), p. 142.

15 Hollingsworth, "Demography," pp. 53, 61–3.

16 Actual rates of infant mortality may be higher, for infant deaths may be under-recorded in published sources, and births and subsequent burials may have taken place in London or abroad where they cannot readily be traced.

17 Hollingsworth, "Demography," pp. 61–5.

18 In the sample, 62.6% of inheritances between 1815 and 1914 were by sons,

which correlates well with Stone's calculation that about 37% of squires and above left no son. Stone, *Family, Sex and Marriage*, p. 67.

[19] Dixon MS, will of Thomas John Dixon, 1864, Dixon 2/1/9, Lincolnshire Archives Office.

[20] This correlates with the Stones' findings that 10% of all transfers by inheritance went to women between 1800–29 and 1860–79, with 11% in 1820–39, and a mere 7% from 1840 to 1859 (when the largest birth cohort provided more males). Stone and Stone, *Open Elite*, table 4.2.

[21] This correlates with the Stones' figures: 38% of their heirs 1829–79 first married after their father's death. Ibid, table 3.9.

[22] Mary Carbery, *Happy World: the Story of a Victorian Childhood* (London, 1941), p. 11.

[23] Richards, *Leviathan of Wealth*, p. 15; Hon. Mrs Hugh Wyndham (ed.), *Correspondence of Sarah Spencer, Lady Lyttleton, 1787–1870* (New York, 1912), p. 231; Mitford, *Ladies of Alderley*, pp. 24–5.

[24] Carbery, *Happy World*, p. 21.

[25] Edith Picton-Turbervill, in The Countess of Oxford and Asquith (ed.), *Myself When Young: By Famous Women of To-Day* (London, 1938), pp. 314, 317–19.

[26] David Burnett, *Longleat: the Story of an English Country House* (London, 1978), p. 139.

[27] Arkwright MS, will of John Arkwright, 1858, A63/IV/Box 64, Herefordshire Record Office; Dixon MS, Dixon 2/1/9.

[28] L. E. O. Charlton (ed.), *The Recollections of a Northumbrian Lady, 1815–1866: Being the Memoirs of Barbara Charlton (née Tasburgh); Wife of William Henry Charlton of Hesleyside, Northumberland* (London, 1949), p. 133; personal interview with Miss Joan Gibbons, 14 Jan. 1979.

[29] Will of John Shelley, Bt, 1867, Somerset House; Northwick MS, will of George, Lord Northwick, 1886, 705:66 BA 4221/28, Worcestershire Record Office.

[30] Gervas Huxley, *Lady Elizabeth and the Grosvenors: Life in a Whig Family, 1822–1839* (London, 1965), p. 167; Hussey MS, Benedicta Trotter to Gertrude Hussey, 8 March 1902, F31/1776, Kent Archives Office.

[31] In the three birth cohorts of 1800–74, younger sons' mean age at marriage rose from 31 to 32, around seven years later than the national average, and just over a third never married, compared to around 1 in 10 of the whole male population. Wrigley and Schofield, *Population History*, pp. 255, 437; Tranter, *Population and Society*, pp. 52, 54.

[32] Wrigley and Schofield, *Population History*, p. 437; Martha Vicinus, *Independent Women: Work and Community for Single Women, 1850–1920* (London, 1985), pp. 26–7.

[33] Caroline Grosvenor, "Moor Park," in Susan Tweedsmuir, *The Lilac and the Rose* (London, 1952), p. 120.

[34] Francesca M. Wilson, *Rebel Daughter of a Country House: the Life of Eglantyne Jebb, Founder of the Save the Children Fund* (London, 1967), pp.33–5.

[35] Betty Askwith, *The Lyttletons: A Family Chronicle of the Nineteenth Century* (London, 1975), p. 63.

[36] Hope-Nicholson, Jaqueline (ed.), *Life Amongst the Troubridges: Journals of a Young Victorian, 1873–1884*, by Laura Troubridge (London, 1966), p. 123.

[37] Adam Badeau, *Aristocracy in England* (New York, 1886), p. 47.

[38] 1871 census returns, Marbury Cottage, Cheshire, RG 10 2796 12; Albury Park, Surrey, RG 10 810 1, Public Record Office.

[39] In defining types of households, I have adopted the scheme of classification developed by the historical demographer Peter Laslett, from *Household and Family in Past Time* (Cambridge, 1972), p. 66.

[40] Earl of Halifax, *Fullness of Days* (London, 1957), p. 13; Georgiana Swinton, "The Dew, it Lyes on the Wood: Being the Reminiscences of Georgiana Caroline Sitwell, Afterwards Mrs. Campbell Swinton of Kimmerghame, Book I", in Osbert Sitwell (ed.), *Two Generations* (London, 1940), p. 73; the Marchioness of Londonderry in Oxford, *Myself When Young*, p. 198; Hope-Nicholson, *Life Amongst the Troubridges*, p. 6; 1871 census return, Nunwell House, Isle of Wight, RG 10 1167 20.

[41] Lord Ronald Gower, *My Reminiscences* (London, 1883; new edn, London, 1895), p. 81; Sutherland, *Looking Back*, p. 52; see also Sutherland MS, housekeeping book 1874–5, D593 R/1/9, Staffordshire Record Office, for an example of exact movements.

[42] J. M. Kolbert, *The Sneyds: Squires of Keele* (Keele, 1976), ch. 6, n.p.

[43] Arkwright MSS, letters to John Hungerford Arkwright from family and tenants 1904–11, advertisement to let 1911, A63/IV/Box 216.

[44] Carbery, *Happy World*, pp. 34–5, 150, 215–17.

CHAPTER 2 THE COUNTRY HOUSE CHILDHOOD

[1] See, for instance, Stone, *Family, Sex and Marriage*, pp. 669–72, and Jonathan Gathorne-Hardy, *The Rise and Fall of the British Nanny* (London, 1972).

[2] Huxley, *Lady Elizabeth*, p. 22.

[3] Bertrand and Patricia Russell (eds), *The Amberley Papers: the Letters and Diaries of Lord and Lady Amberley*, 2 vols (London, 1937), I, pp. 403–6, 409, 413–15.

[4] For wet-nursing, see Valerie Fildes, *Wet Nursing: a History from Antiquity to the Present* (Oxford, 1988), pp. 190–204; Ann Roberts, "Mothers and babies:

the wetnurse and her employer in mid-nineteenth-century England," *Women's Studies: an Interdisciplinary Journal,* 3 (1976), pp. 279–93.
5. Russell, *Amberley Papers,* p. 415.
6. John Burnett (ed.), *Destiny Obscure: Autobiographies of Childhood, Education and Family from the 1820s to the 1920s* (London, 1982; paperback edn, Harmondsworth, 1984), p. 289.
7. Gathorne-Hardy, *British Nanny,* p. 247.
8. Carbery, *Happy World,* pp. 39, 47; Swinton in Sitwell, *Two Generations,* p. 16; Margaret, Countess of Jersey, *Fifty-One Years of Victorian Life* (London, 1922), p. 10.
9. Baroness Ravensdale, *In Many Rhythms: an Autobiography* (London, 1953), pp. 24–5; John Pearson, *Façades: Edith, Osbert and Sacheverell Sitwell* (London, 1978), pp. 31–2.
10. Victoria de Bunsen, "A Daughter's Tribute," in George W. E. Russell, *Lady Victoria Buxton: a Memoir* (London, 1919), p. 202.
11. Lady Sybil Lubbock, *The Child in the Crystal* (London, 1939), p. 24; Eleanor Acland, *Good-bye for the Present: The Story of Two Childhoods, Milly: 1878–88 & Ellen: 1913–24* (New York, 1935), p. 25.
12. Sutherland MS, Lord Wharncliffe to Mrs Ingram, 31 Dec. 1875, D593/R/10/7.
13. Diana Cooper, *The Rainbow Comes and Goes* (London, 1958; paperback edn, London, 1984), p. 12.
14. Lubbock, *Child in the Crystal,* p. 133.
15. Gathorne-Hardy, *British Nanny,* pp. 227–9.
16. Hastings, Duke of Bedford, *The Years of Transition* (London, 1949), p. 9; Cynthia Asquith, *Haply I May Remember* (London, 1950), p. 136.
17. Viola Bankes and Pamela Watkin, *A Kingston Lacy Childhood: Reminiscences of Viola Bankes* (Stanbridge, 1986), p. 29.
18. Winifride Elwes, *The Fielding Album* (London, 1950), p. 120; Edith Picton-Turbervill, *Life is Good: an Autobiography* (London, 1939), p. 50.
19. E. E. Constance Jones, *As I Remember: an Autobiographical Ramble* (London, 1922), p. 12.
20. Dixon MS, Charlotte Dixon to Miss Robertson, July 1853, Dixon 10/7.
21. John Baker White, *True Blue: an Autobiography, 1902–1939* (London, 1970), p. 56; Hope-Nicholson, *Life Amongst the Troubridges,* p. 28; Lady Cynthia Colville, *Crowded Life: the Autobiography of Lady Cynthia Colville* (London, 1963), p. 42.
22. Sarah Sedgwick, "Other People's Children," in Noel Streatfield (ed.), *The Day Before Yesterday: Firsthand Stories of Fifty Years Ago* (London, 1956), p. 21.
23. Swinton in Sitwell, *Two Generations,* pp. 27–9; Gibbons interview.
24. Sedgwick in Streatfield, *Day Before Yesterday,* p. 18.

25. Ibid, p. 17.
26. Lady Margaret Barry and Mrs Gertrude Smith, *Lady Margaret Barry & Mrs Gertrude Smith* (Ipswich, 1976), pp. 13–14; Lady Wellesley, "Infancy," in Alan Pryce-Jones (ed.), *Little Innocents: Childhood Reminiscences* (London, 1932), p. 15.
27. Acland, *Goodbye for the Present*, p. 113.
28. Carbery, *Happy World*, pp. 39, 47.
29. Sedgwick in Streatfield, *Day Before Yesterday*, p. 18; Gathorne-Hardy, *British Nanny*, p. 178; Mary Ann Gibbs, *The Years of the Nannies* (London, 1960), p. 185.
30. Carbery, *Happy World*, pp. 192–4.
31. Cooper, *Rainbow*, p. 14.
32. Gathorne-Hardy, *British Nanny*, pp. 260–2.
33. Lady Emily Lutyens, *A Blessed Girl: Memoirs of a Victorian Girlhood Chronicled in an Exchange of Letters, 1887–1896* (London, 1953), p. 9.
34. Bankes and Watkins, *Kingston Lacy Childhood*, pp. 12, 15–16.
35. Frances, Countess of Warwick, *Life's Ebb and Flow* (New York, 1929), p. 18.
36. Elizabeth S. Haldane, *Mary Elizabeth Haldane: a Record of a Hundred Years (1825–1925)* (London, 1926), pp. 45, 62–3.
37. The Marchioness of Londonderry, in Oxford, *Myself When Young*, p. 191.
38. Ibid, p. 175; Carbery, *Happy World*, pp. 52, 135.
39. J. R. De Symons Honey, *Tom Brown's Universe* (New York, 1977), p. 223.
40. Halifax, *Fullness of Days*, pp. 36–8.
41. Acland, *Goodbye for the Present*, p. 212; Asquith, *Haply I May Remember*, p. 160.
42. L. E. Jones, *A Victorian Boyhood* (London, 1955), pp. 175–6.
43. Kathryn Hughes, *The Victorian Governess* (London, 1993), pp. 60–1.
44. Hope-Nicholson, *Life Amongst the Troubridges*, pp. 29–33.
45. Dixon MSS, Mary Ann Dixon to Ann, 5 Feb. 1844, 20 May 1845, Dixon 10/3/6–7; Elizabeth Yandell, *Henry* (London, 1974), p. 118.
46. M. Jeanne Peterson, *Family, Love, and Work in the Lives of Victorian Gentlewomen* (Bloomington, 1989), pp. 34–57.
47. Cecil Woodham-Smith, *Florence Nightingale, 1820–1910* (London, 1950; reprinted 1952), p. 8; Yandell, *Henry*, p. 105.
48. Charlotte M. Yonge lists the minimum requirements for a lady in *Womankind* (London, 1876), p. 39.
49. Cooper, *Rainbow*, pp. 49–50, 53.
50. Pat Jalland, *Women, Marriage, and Politics, 1860–1914* (Oxford, 1986), pp. 11–12.
51. Hope-Nicholson, *Life Amongst the Troubridges*, p. 33.
52. Leonore Davidoff, *The Best Circles: Society, Etiquette and the Season* (London, 1973; paperback edn, 1986), pp. 51, 93; Carol Dyhouse, *Girls Growing Up in Late Victorian and Edwardian England* (London, 1981), pp. 43–5.

[53] Violet Powell, *Margaret, Countess of Jersey: a Biography* (London, 1978), p. 24.
[54] Davidoff, *Best Circles*, pp. 24–5, 52; Cannadine, *Decline and Fall*, p. 346.
[55] "Lady Violet Brandon," in Paul Thompson, *The Edwardians: the Remaking of British Society* (London, 1975; paperback edn, St Albans, 1977), p. 100.
[56] Sir Stephen Tallents, *Man and Boy* (London, 1943), p. 74.
[57] Tweedsmuir, *Lilac and the Rose*, p. 118.
[58] Osbert Sitwell, *Left Hand, Right Hand: an Autobiography* (London, 1944; reprinted 1946), p. 117.
[59] Ibid, p. 109; Asquith, *Haply I May Remember*, pp. 1, 6.
[60] Asquith, *Haply I May Remember*, p. 127.
[61] The Hon. Sir Edward Cadogan, *Before the Deluge: Memories and Reflections, 1880–1914* (London, 1961), p. 30.
[62] Colville, *Crowded Life*, p. 9.
[63] Jersey, *Fifty-One Years*, p. 17.
[64] Helen, Dowager Countess of Radnor, *From a Great-Grandmother's Armchair* (London, 1927), p. 36.
[65] Londonderry in Oxford, *Myself When Young*, pp. 177–8.
[66] Picton-Turbervill in Oxford, *Myself When Young*, pp. 319–21.
[67] Londonderry in Oxford, *Myself When Young*, pp. 208–9.
[68] Lord Ernest Hamilton, *Forty Years On* (London, 1922), pp. 75–9.
[69] Lady Augusta Fane, *Chit-Chat* (London, 1926), p. 53.
[70] The Hon. Mrs Gell, *Under Three Reigns, 1860–1920* (London, 1927), p. 28.
[71] Acland, *Goodbye for the Present*, p. 100.
[72] Tweedsmuir, *Lilac and the Rose*, p. 94.
[73] James Bossard, discussing "Functions of the Domestic Servant in Child Development," in the *Sociology of Child Development* (New York, 1948), p. 270. Although his subject is American households, his analysis is applicable here.
[74] Lady Violet Hardy, *As It Was* (London, 1958), p. 56.
[75] Susan, Lady Tweedsmuir, *The Edwardian Lady* (London, 1966), p. 66.
[76] Sitwell, *Left Hand, Right Hand*, p. 97.
[77] Halifax, *Fullness of Days*, p. 41.
[78] Bankes and Watkins, *Kingston Lacy Childhood*, pp. 58–9, 64, 69.
[79] Charlton, *Northumbrian Lady*, p. 195.
[80] Yandell, *Henry*, pp. 8–9, 27, 56; Acland, *Goodbye for the Present*, p. 195.
[81] Asquith, *Haply I May Remember*, p. 131; Herbert M. Vaughan, *The South Wales Squires* (London, 1926), p. 13; Bankes and Watkins, *Kingston Lacy Childhood*, p. 49.
[82] Anne Fremantle, *Three-Cornered Heart* (London, 1948; US edn, New York, 1971), p. 110.
[83] David Roberts, "The paterfamilias of the Victorian governing classes," in

Anthony S. Wohl (ed.), *The Victorian Family: Structure and Stresses* (London, 1978), pp. 72–3; Lord Willoughby de Broke, *The Passing Years* (London, 1924), p. 49.
84 Christopher Simon Sykes, *The Visitors' Book: a Family Album* (New York, 1978), p. 159.
85 Jock Yorke in *Edwardian Childhoods*, Thea Thompson (ed.) (London, 1981), p. 195.
86 Cadogan, *Before the Deluge*, p. 26; Asquith, *Haply I May Remember*, p. 131.
87 Yorke in Thompson, *Edwardian Childhoods*, p. 194.
88 *Lady Margaret Barry*, p. 20.
89 Vaughan, *South Wales Squires*, p. 28.
90 Alice Buchan, *A Scrap Screen* (London, 1979), p. 3; Vita Sackville-West, *Country Notes* (London, 1939), p. 97; Mitford, *Ladies of Alderley*, p. 164.
91 Lutyens, *Blessed Girl*, pp. 10, 163.
92 Tallents, *Man and Boy*, p. 65.
93 Baker White, *True Blue*, p. 7.
94 Lady Angela Forbes, *Memories and Base Details* (London, 1921), p. 56.
95 Edwin Lee in Rosina Harrison, *Gentlemen's Gentlemen: my Friends in Service* (London, 1976; paperback edn, London, 1978), p. 133.
96 Hardy, *As It Was*, p. 11.
97 Essex oral history archives, interview 2032, p. 33, University of Essex.
98 Jones, *Victorian Boyhood*, p. 51.
99 Yorke in Thompson, *Edwardian Childhoods*, p. 202.
100 Asquith, *Haply I May Remember*, pp. 23, 34.
101 Lionel Fielden, *The Natural Bent* (London, 1960), p. 31.
102 Elwes, *Fielding Album*, p. 116.
103 Margaret Fletcher, *O, Call Back Yesterday* (Oxford, 1939), p. 63.
104 Yorke and Joan Poynder in Thompson, *Edwardian Childhoods*, pp. 196, 226.

CHAPTER 3   PARENTS AND CHILDREN

1 Randolph Trumbach's research on the eighteenth-century aristocracy supports Stone's thesis, but places the transition much earlier, from the 1690s. Randolph Trumbach, *The Rise of the Egalitarian Family: Aristocratic Kinship and Domestic Relations in Eighteenth-Century England* (New York, 1978).
2 Stone, *Family, Sex and Marriage*, pp. 666–84.
3 Gathorne-Hardy, *British Nanny*, pp. 126, 229, 234–5, 239; Roberts, "Paterfamilias," pp. 59–62, 78.
4 Anita Leslie, *Edwardians in Love* (London, 1972), p. 22. See also Barbara

Kaye Greenleaf, *Children Through the Ages: a History of Childhood* (New York, 1978; paperback edn, New York, 1979), pp. 78–9.
5   These conclusions are based on information on 88 fathers and 86 mothers, gathered from autobiographies, biographies, published and manuscript diaries and letters, and oral history interviews.
6   Maud, Lady Leconfield (ed.), *Three Howard Sisters: Selections from the Writings of Lady Caroline Lascelles, Lady Dover and Countess Gower, 1825 to 1833*, revised and completed by John Gore (London, 1955), p. 41; Arkwright MSS, John Hungerford Arkwright to Lucy Arkwright, 26 Feb. 1874, A63/IV/Box 218; Lucy Arkwright to John Hungerford Arkwright, 25 June 1873, 9 March 1875, 27 Nov. 1877, A63/IV/Box 176.
7   Asquith, *Haply I May Remember*, pp. 124–5.
8   Trumbach, *Egalitarian Family*, pp. 190–235, 252–85.
9   Samuel Gurney, *Isabel, Mrs Gurney, Afterwards the Lady Talbot de Malahide, 1851–1932* (Norwich, 1935), p. 18.
10 Ian Bradley, *The Call to Seriousness: the Evangelical Impact on the Victorians* (London, 1976), pp. 36–41, 54–6, 150–4, 179–81; Catherine Hall, "The early formation of Victorian domestic ideology," in Sandra Burman (ed.), *Fit Work for Women* (London, 1979), pp. 15–31.
11 Mrs John Sandford, *Woman in her Social and Domestic Character* (London, 1831), p. 167; Marilyn Helterline, "The emergence of modern motherhood: motherhood in England 1899 to 1959," *International Journal of Women's Studies*, 3 (1980), pp. 596–8.
12 Nancy Mitford (ed.), *The Stanleys of Alderley: Their Letters Between the Years 1851–1865* (London, 1937), p. 23; Viscountess Ridley, *Cecilia: The Life and Letters of Cecilia Ridley, 1819–1845* (London, 1958), p. 132; Blagdon MS, Cecilia Ridley to Lady Parke, 19 Nov. 1843, ZR1/30/27/3, Northumberland Record Office; Louisa Hoare, *Hints for the Improvement of Early Education and Nursery Discipline* (London, 1819; US edn, Portsmouth, 1823), pp. 3–4; Georgiana Battiscombe, *Mrs Gladstone: the Portrait of a Marriage* (London, 1956), pp. 78–9.
13 Lutyens, *Blessed Girl*, p. 11; Gell, *Under Three Reigns*, pp. 8–9.
14 Thompson, *English Landed Society*, p. 96.
15 Lady Muriel Beckwith, *When I Remember* (London, 1936), p. 35; Essex archives, interview 2034, p. 16, and interview 2012, p. 21.
16 Roberts, "Paterfamilias," p. 62.
17 Jones, *Victorian Boyhood*, pp. 76–7, 115.
18 Roberts, "Paterfamilias," p. 71.
19 Essex archives, interview 2018, p. 20.
20 Ravensdale, *In Many Rhythms*, p. 32.
21 Halifax, *Fullness of Days*, p. 7; Askwith, *The Lyttletons*, p. 48.
22 Jersey, *Fifty-One Years*, p. 8.

23 Asquith, *Haply May I Remember*, p. 125.
24 Jones, *As I Remember*, p. 3; Carbery, *Happy World*, p. 38; Forbes, *Memories*, pp. 13, 43, 52.
25 Edith, Marchioness of Londonderry (ed.), *Frances Anne: the Life and Times of Frances Anne, Marchioness of Londonderry and her Husband Charles, Third Marquess of Londonderry* (London, 1958), p. 61.
26 Mitford, *Ladies of Alderley*, pp. 28–9.
27 Lewis, *In the Family Way*, pp. 122–3.
28 Stuart, *Dear Duchess*, p. 41.
29 Violet Powell, *Within the Family Circle: an Autobiography* (London, 1976), p. 11; Jalland, *Marriage and Politics*, pp. 144–6; Joyce Marlow, *Mr and Mrs Gladstone: an Intimate Biography* (London, 1977), pp. 30, 40; Alsop, *Lady Sackville*, p. 118; Leconfield, *Three Howard Sisters*, p. 225.
30 *The Good Nurse; or, Hints on the Management of the Sick and Lying-in Chamber and Nursery* (London, 1825), pp. 177–9; Pye Henry Chavasse, *Advice to a Mother on the Management of Her Children, and on the Treatment on the Moment of Some of Their More Pressing Illnesses and Accidents* (London, 1839, 13th edn, London, 1878), pp. 56, 59–60.
31 Carbery, *Happy World*, p. 25.
32 Ridley, *Cecilia*, p. 131.
33 Lewis, *In the Family Way*, pp. 209–12.
34 Blagdon MS, Cecilia Ridley to Lady Parke, n.d. [1842], ZRI/30/27/3.
35 P. M. Braidwell, *Domestic Management of Children* (London, 1874), pp. 15–16.
36 Thomas Bull, *Hints to Mothers for the Management of Health During the Period of Pregnancy and in the Lying-in Room* (London, 1864), p. 254.
37 Leconfield, *Three Howard Sisters*, p. 244.
38 Ibid, pp. 99, 256.
39 Arkwright MS, Lucy Arkwright to John Hungerford Arkwright, 20 May, 14 Dec. 1883, A63/IV/Box 176; Erddig MS, Diary of Louisa Yorke, 30 June 1903, D/E/2816.
40 Lady Clodagh Anson, *Book. Discreet Memoirs* (London, 1931), p. 363; Powell, *Margaret, Countess of Jersey*, p. 52.
41 *Englishwoman's Domestic Magazine*, 3 (1867), p. 31; Hoare, *Hints*, p. 4.
42 Elizabeth Missing Sewell, *Principles of Education Drawn From Nature and Revelation and Applied to Female Education in the Upper Classes* (London, 1866; US edn, New York, 1866), pp. 72–5.
43 Mrs Pedley, *Infant Nursing and Management of Young Children* (London, 1866), p. 93.
44 Patricia Blackwell, "The English landed elite in decline. A case study of five Sussex country houses" (unpublished University of Sussex MA thesis, 1978), pp. 27–8.

NOTES, PAGES 75–80   297

45 Battiscombe, *Mrs Gladstone*, pp. 49, 82–3.
46 Ridley, *Cecilia*, pp. 118, 123, 150–3, 157–9, 190, 199–200; Russell, *Amberley Papers*, I, pp. 414–15.
47 Ridley, *Cecilia*, pp. 114, 118, 134, 136, 150, 181; Blagdon MS, Cecilia Ridley to Lady Parke, 21 Nov. 1843, n.d. [April, 1844], ZRI/30/27/4; Battiscombe, *Mrs Gladstone*, p. 49.
48 Erddig MSS, Louisa Yorke's diaries, 24 and 30 July, 14, 19 and 21 Aug., 17 Nov., 10 Dec. 1903, 1 and 7 Jan., 7 Feb., 9 July, 9 and 18 Aug., 15 Nov., 10 Dec. 1904, 5 and 22 Jan., 25 March, 3 Apr., 3 and 7 Sept., 5 and 29 Dec. 1905, passim, D/E/2816.
49 Gathorne-Hardy, *British Nanny*, p. 235.
50 Sandra Scarr, *Mother Care/Other Care* (New York, 1984; paperback edn, New York, 1985), pp. 102–4.
51 Acland, *Goodbye for the Present*, p. 25.
52 Scarr, *Mother Care*, pp. 212–22.
53 Blackwell, "Landed elite in decline," p. 3.
54 Lady Elizabeth Cust and Evelyn Georgiana Pelham, *Edward, Fifth Earl of Darnley and Emma Parnell his Wife: the Story of a Short and Happy Married Life Told in their Own Letters and Other Family Papers* (Leeds, 1913), pp. 247–53, 291–4, 296, 299, 302, 306; Arkwright MSS, John Hungerford Arkwright to Lucy Arkwright, 20 and 22 May 1873, 25 and 26 Feb., 3 June 1874, 15 May 1876, A63/IV/Box 218.
55 Ridley, *Cecilia*, p. 170; Dixon MS, Thomas John Dixon to Mary Ann Dixon, 26 May 1834, Dixon 10/1/39.
56 David Cecil, *The Cecils of Hatfield House* (London, 1973), p. 255.
57 Acland, *Goodbye for the Present*, pp. 68–9.
58 Scarr, *Mother Care*, pp. 26–7.
59 Ridley, *Cecilia*, pp. 134, 141, 156, 177; Wilson, *Rebel Daughter*, p. 25; Elwes, *Fielding Album*, p. 117.
60 Cust and Pelham, *Earl of Darnley*, p. 435; Elwes, *Fielding Album*, p. 115; Barry, *Lady Margaret Barry*, p. 8.
61 Dixon MSS, Thomas John Dixon to Mary Ann Dixon, 13 Oct. 1831, 19 June, 26 June 1832, Dixon 10/1/13; Swinton in Sitwell, *Two Generations*, pp. 21–2.
62 Jones, *Victorian Boyhood*, p. 77; Halifax, *Fullness of Days*, p. 18; Jersey, *Fifty-One Years*, p. 17.
63 Gurney, *Isabel, Lady Gurney*, p. 19; Arthur D. Acland (ed.), *Memoirs and Letters of the Right Hon. Sir Thomas Dyke Acland* (London, 1902), pp. 150–1.
64 Roberts, "Paterfamilias," p. 65.
65 Jones, *Victorian Boyhood*, pp. 37–8; John Martineau, *The Life of Henry Pelham, Fifth Duke of Newcastle, 1811–64* (London, 1908), pp. 5, 10.
66 Gell, *Under Three Reigns*, pp. 30–1.

67 Yorke in Thompson, *Edwardian Childhoods*, pp. 200–1.
68 Gell, *Under Three Reigns*, p. 13; Barry, *Lady Margaret Barry*, p. 9; Leconfield, *Three Howard Sisters*, pp. 204, 235, 243, 249–50.
69 Marlow, *Mr and Mrs Gladstone*, p. 45; Jones, *Victorian Boyhood*, pp. 14–15; Huxley, *Lady Elizabeth*, p. 56.
70 Acland, *Sir Thomas Dyke Acland*, p. 147.
71 Russell, *Lady Victoria Buxton*, p. 70.
72 Stone, *Family, Sex and Marriage*, pp. 669–71; Linda A. Pollock, *Forgotten Children: Parent–Child Relations from 1500 to 1900* (Cambridge, 1983), pp. 182, 184–5, 187.
73 Christopher Sykes, *Four Studies in Loyalty* (London, 1946), pp. 13–14; Charlton, *Northumbrian Lady*, pp. 29–30, 36–7; Pollock, *Forgotten Children*, pp. 184–5; Roberts, "Paterfamilias," pp. 62–5.
74 Hoare, *Hints*, pp. 19–32.
75 Askwith, *Lyttletons*, p. 100; Battiscombe, *Mrs Gladstone*, p. 123; Marlow, *Mr and Mrs Gladstone*, pp. 45–6.
76 Pollock, *Forgotten Children*, p. 105; Christina Hardyment, *Dream Babies* (Oxford, 1984), pp. 148, 151.
77 George Cornwallis-West, *Edwardian Hey-Days: or, a Little About a Lot of Things* (London, 1930), pp. 2–3.
78 Lutyens, *Blessed Girl*, pp. ix, 3.
79 Yorke in Thompson, *Edwardian Childhoods*, p. 200; Askwith, *Lyttletons*, p. 100.
80 Lord Berners, *First Childhood* and *Far From the Madding War* (London, 1934 and 1941; combined paperback edn, Oxford, 1983), p. 36.
81 Daniel Blake Smith, *Inside the Great House: Planter Family Life in Eighteenth-Century Chesapeake Society* (Ithaca, 1980), p. 53.
82 Stone, *Family, Sex and Marriage*, p. 680.
83 Helterline, "Emergence of modern motherhood," p. 597.
84 Gibbons interview, 14 Jan. 1979; Battiscombe, *Mrs Gladstone*, p. 124; Beckwith, *When I Remember*, p. 88; Picton-Turbervill, *Life is Good*, pp. 48–9.
85 Ibid., p. 69; Gurney, *Isabel, Lady Gurney*, p. 39; Alfred E. Gathorne-Hardy (ed.), *Gathorne-Hardy, First Earl of Cranbrook: a Memoir, with Extracts from His Diary and Correspondence*, 2 vols (London, 1910), I, p. 5.
86 Frances Ann Kemble, *Records of Later Life*, 2 vols (London, 1882), II, p. 147.
87 Jonathan Gathorne-Hardy, *The Public School Phenomenon, 1597–1977* (London, 1977), p. 224.
88 Battiscombe, *Mrs Gladstone*, p. 123; Askwith, *Lyttletons*, pp. 41–2.
89 Arkwright MSS, John Hungerford Arkwright to John Stanhope Arkwright, 20 and 25 Jan. 1886, Lucy Arkwright to John Stanhope Arkwright, 4 Jan. 1886, A63/IV/221.
90 Wilson, *Rebel Daughter*, pp. 27–8.

[91] Alice Renton, *Tyrant or Victim? A History of the British Governess* (London, 1991), p. 167; Carrol Smith-Rosenberg, "The female world of love and ritual: relations between women in nineteenth-century America," *Signs* 1 (1975), pp. 1–29.
[92] Davidoff, *Best Circles*, p. 54.
[93] Charlton, *Northumbrian Lady*, pp. 258, 266–8.
[94] Lady Jeune, *Lesser Questions* (London, 1894), p. 96.
[95] Earl of Bessborough (ed.), *Lady Charlotte Schreiber: Extracts from her Journal 1833–1852* (London, 1952), p. 107.
[96] Sneyd MS, Hon. Louisa Sneyd to Charlotte Augusta Sneyd, n.d. [1818], S2856.
[97] Josephine Butler, *Memoir of John Grey of Dilston* (London, 1874), p. 285; Rachel Weigall, *Lady Rose Weigall: a Memoir Based on Her Correspondence and the Recollections of Friends* (New York, 1923), p. 59.
[98] Woodham-Smith, *Florence Nightingale*, pp. 30–1; Marlow, *Mr and Mrs Gladstone*, pp. 117, 141–2.
[99] Jeune, *Lesser Questions*, p. 91; Mrs Humphry, *Manners for Women* (London, 1897; Exeter, 1979), pp. 4–5.
[100] Jalland, *Marriage and Politics*, pp. 32–4.
[101] Radnor, *Great-Grandmother's Armchair*, p. 136; Butler, *Memoir of John Grey*, pp. 189, 285.
[102] Alice Fairfax-Lucy (ed.), *Mistress of Charlcote: the Memoirs of Mary Elizabeth Lucy* (London, 1983; paperback edn, London, 1985), p. 36.
[103] Roberts, "Paterfamilias," p. 77; Spring, "Role of the aristocracy," p. 60.
[104] Michael H. Stone and Clarice J. Kestenbaum, "Maternal deprivation in children of the wealthy: a paradox in socioeconomic vs. psychological class," *History of Childhood Quarterly*, 2 (1974), pp. 79–106.

CHAPTER 4 COURTSHIP AND MARRIAGE

[1] Stone, *Family, Sex and Marriage*, pp. 221–69, 325–35, 390–404, 668.
[2] Lewis, *In the Family Way*, p. 35; Jalland, *Marriage and Politics*, p. 288; Joan Perkin, *Women and Marriage in Nineteenth-Century England* (London and Chicago, 1989), pp. 50, 53.
[3] Tresham Lever (ed.), *The Letters of Lady Palmerston* (London, 1957), p. 124.
[4] Trumbach, *Egalitarian Family*, pp. 71, 105, 109, 111; Stone, *Family, Sex and Marriage*, pp. 390–2.
[5] Lewis, *In the Family Way*, pp. 17–20, 30–1.
[6] For the rise of the Season see Stone, *Family, Sex and Marriage*, pp. 316–17; and Davidoff, *Best Circles*, pp. 20–5.
[7] Jalland, *Marriage and Politics*, p. 24.
[8] Anita Leslie, *The Marlborough House Set* (New York, 1972; paperback edn, New York, 1975), p. 30.

[9] John Martin Robinson, *The Dukes of Norfolk: a Quincentennial History* (Oxford, 1982), p. 204; Carola Oman, *The Gascoyne Heiress: the Life and Diaries of Frances Mary Gascoyne-Cecil, 1802–39* (London, 1968), p. 44.

[10] Earl of Ilchester, *Elizabeth, Lady Holland to her Son, 1821–1845* (London, 1946), p. 139; F. Darrell Munsell, *The Unfortunate Duke: Henry Pelham, Fifth Duke of Newcastle, 1811–1864* (Columbia, 1985), p. 16.

[11] Jalland, *Marriage and Politics*, p. 75.

[12] Spencer Pickering (ed.), *Memoirs of Anna Maria Wilhemina Pickering* (London, 1904), p. 11.

[13] Ralph G. Martin, *Jennie. The Life of Lady Randolph Churchill: the Romantic Years, 1854–1895* (New York, 1969; paperback edn, 1970), pp. 76–7.

[14] Stuart, *Dear Duchess*, pp. 29, 35–6; Julia Cartwright (ed.), *The Journals of Lady Knightley of Fawsley, 1856–1884* (London, 1915), p. 63.

[15] Cust and Pelham, *Earl of Darnley*, p. 60.

[16] Jennifer Ellis (ed.), *Thatched with Gold: The Memoirs of Mabell, Countess of Airlie* (London, 1962), p. 40.

[17] Fairfax-Lucy, *Mistress of Charlcote*, p. 28.

[18] Elizabeth Longford, *Pilgrimage of Passion: the Life of Wilfrid Scawen Blunt* (London, 1979), pp. 108–9, 112.

[19] Bertrand Russell, "Lady Carlisle's Ancestors," in Dorothy Henley, *Rosalind Howard, Countess of Carlisle* (London, 1959), p. 21; Jalland, *Marriage and Politics*, p. 48.

[20] Katherine Everett, *Bricks and Flowers: Memoirs of Katherine Everett* (London, 1949; reprint, Bungay, 1951), pp. 43–4; Leslie, *Marlborough House Set*, p. 91.

[21] Barbara Caine, *Destined to be Wives: the Sisters of Beatrice Webb* (Oxford, 1986; paperback edn, 1988), p. 93.

[22] Fairfax-Lucy, *Mistress of Charlcote*, p. 23.

[23] David Verey (ed.), *The Diary of a Victorian Squire: Extracts from the Diaries and Letters of Dearman and Emily Birchall* (Gloucester, 1983), p. 12.

[24] A. L. Kennedy (ed.), *"My Dear Duchess": Social and Political Letters to the Duchess of Manchester, 1858–1869* (London, 1956), p. 113.

[25] Mitford, *Ladies of Alderley*, p. 76.

[26] Battiscombe, *Mrs Gladstone*, p. 16.

[27] Angela Lambert, *Unquiet Souls: the Indian Summer of the British Aristocracy* (London, 1984), pp. 74–5; Oman, *Gascoyne Heiress*, p. 48.

[28] Alsop, *Lady Sackville*, pp. 90, 101.

[29] Lever, *Lady Palmerston*, pp. 182–5.

[30] Margaret Fox Schmidt, *Passion's Child: the Extraordinary Life of Jane Digby* (London, 1976; paperback edn, 1978), p. 32.

[31] Jalland, *Marriage and Politics*, pp. 22, 118; Davidoff, *Best Circles*, p. 52.

[32] Stone, *Family, Sex and Marriage*, p. 318.

[33] Oman, *Gascoyne Heiress*, p. 44.
[34] Verey, *Victorian Squire*, p. 49.
[35] Ibid, pp. 46–50.
[36] Jalland, *Marriage and Politics*, pp. 75–6.
[37] Battiscombe, *Mrs Gladstone*, p. 16; Edward Bulwer-Lytton, *England and the English*, 2 vols (London, 1833), I, p. 137.
[38] Lever, *Lady Palmerston*, pp. 124–9.
[39] Schmidt, *Passion's Child*, pp. 76–7.
[40] Thompson, *English Landed Society*, pp. 301–3; on trans-Atlantic marriages see Maureen E. Montgomery, *"Gilded Prostitution": Status, Money, and Transatlantic Marriages, 1870–1914* (London and New York, 1989).
[41] Mrs C. W. Earle, *Memoirs and Memories* (London, 1911), pp. 245–6.
[42] Sarah Stickney Ellis, *The Wives of England* (London, 1843), pp. 76, 119; Sandford, *Woman*, pp. 3, 13; Yonge, *Womankind*, p. 188.
[43] William S. Childe-Pemberton, *Life of Lord Norton* (London, 1909), pp. 43–4.
[44] Adeline, Countess of Cardigan and Lancastre, *My Recollections* (London, 1909), p. 108; The Earl of Birkenhead, *Halifax: the Life of Lord Halifax* (London, 1965; Boston, 1966), p. 83; Tweedsmuir, *Lilac and the Rose*, p. 34.
[45] Owen Chadwick, *Victorian Miniature* (London, 1960; paperback edn, 1983), pp. 68–9.
[46] Jalland, *Marriage and Politics*, p. 119.
[47] Chadwick, *Victorian Miniature*, p. 70.
[48] Peterson, *Family, Love and Work*, p. 190.
[49] For the rise of domesticity see Stone, *Family, Sex and Marriage*, and Trumbach, *Egalitarian Family*.
[50] Trumbach, *Egalitarian Family*, p. 122.
[51] For the origins of separate spheres see Leonore Davidoff and Catharine Hall, *Family Fortunes: Men and Women of the English Middle Class, 1780–1850* (London, 1987), especially ch. 3.
[52] Arkwright MS, John Hungerford Arkwright to Lucy Davenport, 21 May 1866, A63/IV/218.
[53] Dixon MS, pin money notebook 1861–71, Dixon 10/12/19; Ridley, *Cecilia*, p. 75; Huxley, *Lady Elizabeth*, p. 2; Arkwright MSS, marriage settlement of Mary Bosanquet, 1862, indenture of Lucy Davenport's marriage settlement 1866, A63/IV/Box 64.
[54] Arkwright MSS, John Arkwright's will, 1858, indenture of Lucy Davenport's marriage settlement, 1866, A63/IV/Box 64; Thompson, *English Landed Society*, pp. 100–1; Jalland, *Marriage and Politics*, pp. 58–72.
[55] Perkin, *Women and Marriage*, pp. 5, 50–1, 53.
[56] Peterson, *Family, Love, and Work*, p. 188.
[57] Arkwright MSS, letters between John Hungerford Arkwright and Lucy Arkwright, 1866–1900, A63/IV/63, A63/IV/218, A63/IV/176.

[58] Lewis, *In the Family Way*, pp. 48, 52–5; Jalland, *Marriage and Politics*, pp. 30–1.
[59] Stone, *Family, Sex and Marriage*, pp. 666, 671; Walter E. Houghton, *The Victorian Frame of Mind, 1830–1870* (New Haven, 1957), p. 353; Eric Trudgill, *Madonnas and Magdalens: the Origins and Development of Victorian Sexual Attitudes* (London, 1976), pp. 59–62.
[60] Askwith, *Lyttletons*, p. 91; Arkwright MSS, Lucy Arkwright to John Hungerford Arkwright, 19 Oct., 23 Oct., 24 Oct., 25 Oct., 1866, A63/IV/176; Alsop, *Lady Sackville*, pp. 104–6, 116; Jalland, *Marriage and Politics*, p. 121.
[61] Lewis, *In the Family Way*, p. 35; Jalland, *Marriage and Politics*, p. 130.
[62] Huxley, *Lady Elizabeth*, pp. 13–15; Arkwright MSS, letters between John Hungerford Arkwright and Lucy Arkwright, 1866–1900, A63/IV/63, A63/IV/218, A63/IV/176.
[63] Tweedsmuir, *Lilac and the Rose*, p. 67.
[64] Caine, *Destined to Be Wives*, pp. 133–5.
[65] Stuart, *Dear Duchess*, pp. 39, 63–5, 70–1.
[66] Pearson, *Façades*, pp. 25–6, 28–9, 40, 42–3, 49, 50; Baker White, *True Blue*, pp. 4, 6–7, 14–17.
[67] Fairfax-Lucy, *Mistress of Charlcote*, p. 37.
[68] Sykes, *Visitors' Book*, pp. 49, 57–8, 115.
[69] Stone, *Family, Sex and Marriage*, pp. 391–2; Allen Horstman, *Victorian Divorce* (New York, 1985), p. 117.
[70] Edwin Lee in Harrison, *Gentlemen's Gentlemen*, pp. 127–8.
[71] Forbes, *Memories*, pp. 106–7; Lambert, *Unquiet Souls*, pp. 78–9, 85–6; Philip Ziegler, *Diana Cooper* (London, 1981), pp. 3–4, 14.
[72] Longford, *Pilgrimage of Passion*, pp. 108–9, 112–13, 118.
[73] Lady Violet Greville, *Vignettes of Memory* (London, 1927), p. 258.
[74] Lewis, *In the Family Way*, p. 46.
[75] Horstman, *Victorian Divorce*, pp. 117–33.
[76] C. E. Vulliamy (ed.), *The Polderoy Papers* (London, 1943), pp. 80–2.
[77] Consuelo Vanderbilt Balsan, *The Glitter and the Gold* (London, 1953), p. 148.
[78] Constance Battersea, *Reminiscences* (London, 1923), p. 351.
[79] Henley, *Rosalind Howard*, pp. 45, 114–17; see also Charlton, *Northumbrian Lady*, pp. 75–6, 84–5.
[80] Battersea, *Reminiscences*, p. 157.
[81] Fairfax-Lucy, *Mistress of Charlcote*, p. 33.
[82] Charlotte, Viscountess Barrington, *Through Eighty Years* (London, 1936), p. 133.
[83] Askwith, *Lyttletons*, pp. 148, 151.
[84] Bankes and Watkins, *Kingston Lacy Childhood*, pp. 114–16.
[85] Lever, *Lady Palmerston*, p. 218.

[86] Stuart, *Dear Duchess*, pp. 43–5.
[87] Bessborough, *Lady Charlotte Schreiber*, pp. xi, 45.
[88] Askwith, *Lyttletons*, pp. 169–70.

CHAPTER 5 COUNTRY HOUSE WOMEN

[1] Ronald Pearsall, *The Worm in the Bud: the World of Victorian Sexuality* (London, 1969; paperback edn, Harmondsworth, 1983), p. 64; Stone, *Family, Sex and Marriage*, p. 396; Gathorne-Hardy, *Public School Phenomenon*, p. 233.
[2] Cannadine, *Decline and Fall*, p. 7.
[3] Jane Lewis, *Women in England, 1780–1950* (Brighton and Bloomington, 1984); Davidoff, *Best Circles*; Jalland, *Marriage and Politics*; Lewis, *In the Family Way*; Perkin, *Women and Marriage*; Pamela Horn, *Ladies of the Manor: Wives and Daughters in Country-house Society, 1830–1918* (Stroud, 1991).
[4] Peterson, *Family, Love and Work*, pp. 40–57, 120–30, 133–86, 226.
[5] Perkin, *Women and Marriage*, p. 5.
[6] Fairfax-Lucy, *Mistress of Charlcote*, p. 137.
[7] Russell in Henley, *Rosalind Howard*, p. 21.
[8] Susan H. Oldfield, *Some Records of the Later Life of Harriet, Countess Granville* (London, 1901), p. 1.
[9] In London, upper-class women were not permitted to walk in the streets, ride, or travel, without a male relative or servant accompanying them, and they were banned from hansom cabs, public houses, and music halls. These restrictions were intended to protect the supposedly weak, vulnerable, naive, and innocent sex from criminals, to isolate them from socially unacceptable acquaintances and suitors, and, above all, to segregate them from high-class prostitutes, so that ladies would neither be accosted as such, nor encounter their menfolk's mistresses. But taking a servant along demonstrated rank as much as a need for protection.
[10] Peterson, *Family, Love, and Work*, p. 189.
[11] Bankes and Watkin, *Kingston Lacy Childhood*, p. 35.
[12] Baker White, *True Blue*, p. 6.
[13] Stella Margetson, *Victorian High Society* (London, 1980), pp. 130–1; Meriel Buxton, *Ladies of the Chase* (London, 1987), pp. 65–6.
[14] Birkenhead, *Halifax*, p. 29.
[15] Mrs James de Rothschild, *The Rothschilds at Waddesdon Manor* (London, 1979), pp. 75, 78; Dixon MS, historical notes by T. G. Dixon, Dixon 10/6/3.
[16] Fairfax-Lucy, *Mistress of Charlcote*, p. 33; Elwes, *Fielding Album*, pp. 89–90; Tweedsmuir, *Lilac and the Rose*, pp. 28–9.
[17] Jalland, *Marriage and Politics*, p. 235.

18 Sutherland, *Looking Back*, pp. 35–6.
19 Fairfax-Lucy, *Mistress of Charlcote*, pp. 81–2, 84.
20 Tresham Lever, *The Herberts of Wilton* (London, 1967), p. 208.
21 Buxton, *Ladies of the Chase*, pp. 96–100.
22 Perkin, *Women and Marriage*, p. 78.
23 Charles Roberts, *The Radical Countess* (London, 1962), pp. 136–50; Henley, *Rosalind Howard*, pp. 137–8.
24 Augustus Hare, *The Story of My Life*, 6 vols (London, 1896 and 1900), II, pp. 173, 176.
25 Jalland, *Marriage and Politics*, p. 194. Chapter 7 discusses wives' changing political roles.
26 Davidoff, *Best Circles*, p. 26.
27 Martin Pugh, *The Tories and the People* (Oxford, 1985), pp. 2–3, 43, 46–56.
28 Jalland, *Marriage and Politics*, pp. 210–19.
29 Patricia Hollis, *Ladies Elect: Women in English Local Government, 1865–1914* (Oxford, 1987), pp. 7–10, 365, 371–5, 377, 381, 385–91.
30 Acland, *Good-Bye for the Present*, p. 180.
31 David Roberts, *Paternalism in Early Victorian England* (London, 1979), pp. 120, 122; F. M. L. Thompson, "Landowners and the rural community," in G. E. Mingay (ed.), *The Victorian Countryside*, 2 vols (London, 1981), II, 457–73; Stone and Stone, *Open Elite*, p. 317.
32 For a fuller discussion, see Jessica Gerard, "Lady Bountiful: women of the landed classes and rural philanthropy," *Victorian Studies*, 30 (1987), pp. 183–209.
33 Ethel, Lady Thomson, *Clifton Lodge* (London, 1955), pp. 162–4.
34 Greville, *Gentlewoman in Society*, p. 171.
35 Fielden, *Natural Bent*, p. 31.
36 Dixon MS, notes in Mary Ann Dixon's diary, 1866, Dixon 10/12/1.
37 Weigall, *Lady Rose Weigall*, pp. 69, 71.
38 Lubbock, *Child in the Crystal*, p. 126; Swinton in Sitwell, *Two Generations*, p. 68.
39 Chadwick, *Victorian Miniature*, pp. 170, 177.
40 Dixon MSS, Mary Ann Dixon's diaries, 1838–80, Dixon 10/12/1–10; "Christmas Books" 1834–59, 1861–81, Dixon 10/12/20–1.
41 Arkwright MS, E. D. Paul, "The descriptive list of papers from the Arkwright Collection relating to John Hungerford Arkwright 1840–1905" (unpublished [1964], Hereford Archives Office).
42 Dixon MSS, Mary Ann Dixon's diaries, for example 8 Aug., 9 Aug. 1864, Dixon 10/12/3; 13 Aug., 17 Aug. 1867; 24 July, 30 July 1868, Dixon 10/12/4; 22 June, 9 Aug., 10 Aug. 1869, Dixon 10/12/5.
43 Anne Summers, "A home from home – women's philanthropic work in the nineteenth century," in Burman, *Fit Work for Women*, p. 39.

[44] Ridley, *Cecilia*, p. 133.
[45] Arkwright MSS, schoolchildren's letters of thanks, A63/IV/537, A63/IV/591; Horn, *Victorian Servant*, pp. 36–7.
[46] Sitwell, *Left Hand, Right Hand*, p. 154.
[47] Battiscombe, *Mrs Gladstone*, pp. 129–34.
[48] Baroness Burdett-Coutts (ed.), *Woman's Mission* (London, 1893), pp. 8, 18, 20, 22, 25, 31–2, 39, 77, 85.
[49] Burdett-Coutts, *Woman's Mission*, pp. 39–45, 69; Horn, *Ladies of the Manor*, pp. 119, 126, 128–31.
[50] Vicinus, *Independent Women*, pp. 211–12, 220.
[51] Horn, *Ladies of the Manor*, pp. 131–6; idem, *Victorian Countrywomen* (Oxford, 1991), pp. 211–22.
[52] Dixon MS, Mary Ann Dixon's diary, 29 June 1869, Dixon 10/12/4; Anthony Eden, *Another World, 1897–1917* (London, 1976), p. 44.
[53] Powell, *Margaret, Countess of Jersey*, p. 5.
[54] Howard Newby, "The deferential dialectic," *Comparative Studies in Society and History* 17 (1975), 155–8, 161–3; idem, *The Deferential Worker: a Study of Farm Workers in East Anglia* (Madison, 1979), p. 44.
[55] Desmond Macarthy and Agatha Russell (eds), *Lady John Russell: a Memoir* (London, 1910), p. 257.
[56] Jalland, *Marriage and Politics*, p. 211.
[57] Mrs Waldemar-Leverton, *Servants and their Duties: a Helpful Manual for Mistress and Servant* (London, 1912), p. 269.
[58] Michael Curtin, "Etiquette and society in Victorian England" (unpublished University of California at Berkeley PhD, 1974), pp. 231–3, 265.
[59] Davidoff, *Best Circles*, pp. 15–16.
[60] "One who is in it," "Society as it is," *Lady*, (28 May 1885), pp. 425–6.
[61] Anna Sproule, *The Social Calendar* (Poole, 1978), p. 40.
[62] "One who is in it," "Society as it is," p. 425.
[63] The Viscountess Milner, *My Picture Gallery, 1886–1901* (London, 1951), p. 218.
[64] Richards, *Leviathan of Wealth*, p. 17; George W. E. Russell, *Portraits of the Seventies* (London, 1916), p. 249; Sutherland, *Looking Back*, pp. 36, 43; Forbes, *Memories*, p. 64; Stuart, *Dear Duchess*, pp. 57–9, 61.
[65] Leaving cards and calling were formal preliminaries to making friends in Society. Once two ladies had been introduced to each other, they left cards engraved with their own and their husband's names at the other's house, as an initial overture of friendship. Next they paid each other a call, a formal fifteen-minute visit. Only then could invitations ensue for tea, dinner, and so on. An unwillingness to form a friendship was demonstrated by continuing to send cards instead of calling, or calling but refusing to issue invitations.

[66] Erddig MS, Simon Yorke's diary, 1845–83, D/E 803; Dixon MSS, Mary Ann Dixon's diaries 1838–74, Dixon 10/12/1–9.
[67] Davidoff, *Best Circles*, pp. 89–90.
[68] McBride, *Domestic Revolution*, pp. 27–30.
[69] "An Old Servant," *Domestic Service* (Boston, 1917), pp. 35–6.
[70] Chadwick, *Victorian Miniature*, p. 69.
[71] Stuart, *Dear Duchess*, p. 39. See also Balsan, *Glitter and the Gold*, pp. 174–5; John, Duke of Bedford, *A Silver-plated Spoon* (London, 1959; paperback edn, 1962), p. 24.
[72] Balsan, *Glitter and the Gold*, p. 138.
[73] Northwick MSS, agreements with servants 1859–68, 705:66 BA 4221/23; P. H. W. Booth, *Burton Manor: the biography of a House* (Burton Manor, 1978), p. 34.
[74] Askwith, *The Lyttletons*, pp. 144, 160, 165.
[75] Ridley, *Cecilia*, pp. 69–71, 73, 81, 83–4, 86.
[76] Greville, *Gentlewoman in Society*, pp. 172–3.
[77] Balsan, *Glitter and the Gold*, p. 81.
[78] Blackwell, "Landed elite in decline," pp. 39–40; Cyril Heber Percy, *Us Four* (London, 1963), pp. 29, 31–2.
[79] Dixon MSS, Mary Ann Dixon's diaries, 1838–62, 1864–79, Dixon 10/12/1–9.
[80] Stephen Hobhouse, *Margaret Hobhouse and her Family* (Rochester, 1934), p. 67.
[81] Margetson, *Victorian High Society*, p. 133; Gibbons interview; Wilson, *Rebel Daughter*, pp. 25–6.
[82] Catherine Milnes Gaskell, "Women of to-day," *Nineteenth Century*, 26 (1889), p. 782; Asquith in Streatfield, *Day Before Yesterday*, p. 119.
[83] Gurney, *Isabel, Lady Gurney*, pp. 17–18.
[84] Gaskell, "Women of to-day," p. 782.
[85] Ibid.
[86] Georgiana Hill, *Women in English Life from Medieval to Modern Times*, 2 vols (London, 1896), II, pp. 90–1, 109, 113.
[87] Pugh, *Tories and the People*, pp. 56–7, 66.
[88] Stuart, *Dear Duchess*, pp. 76–85, 91–111; Pugh, *Tories and the People*, pp. 46, 57.
[89] Chadwick, *Victorian Miniature*, pp. 179–80; Elwes, *Fielding Album*, p. 217.
[90] Olive Banks, *Becoming a Feminist: the Social Origins of "First Wave" Feminism* (Athens, Georgia, 1986), p. 86.
[91] Helen Bosanquet, *The Family* (London, 1906), p. 188.
[92] Wilson, *Rebel Daughter*, pp. 56, 59, 65–7, 80–1, 85, 88, 90–1, 97, 102–3, 107, 112, 127–9, 141–2.

CHAPTER 6 STAFF SIZE

[1] Thompson, *English Landed Society*, p. 187; Franklin, *Gentleman's Country House*, p. 87; Horn, *Victorian Servant*, p. 18.

2 For the association of polluting dirt and human waste with servants, see Leonore Davidoff, "Class and gender in Victorian England: the diaries of Arthur J. Munby and Hannah Cullwick," *Feminist Studies*, 5 (1979), pp. 88–9, 95–7.
3 Arkwright MSS, housekeeper's account books 1819–43, A63 uncatalogued.
4 Leonore Davidoff, "Mastered for life: servant and wife in Victorian and Edwardian England," *Journal of Social History*, 7 (1974), pp. 411–13.
5 Census enumerators' returns, 1871: Trentham, Staffordshire, RG 10 2864; Lilleshall, Staffordshire, RG 10 2747; Sutherland MS, wages for all houses 1869–70, D593/R/4/6–7.
6 Sneyd MS, cash book 1852, S2093.
7 Thompson, *English Landed Society*, p. 191.
8 Haims, "In their place," p. 192.
9 The median falls between 8 and 9 indoor servants, with a mode of 7.
10 J. Jean Hecht, *The Domestic Servant in Eighteenth Century England* (London, 1956; reprinted 1980), pp. 2–3; Thompson, *English Landed Society*, pp. 188–91.
11 Girouard, *English Country House*, p. 276.
12 The Earl of Onslow, *Sixty-Three Years: Diplomacy, the Great War and Politics, with Notes on Travel, Sport and Other Things* (London, 1944), p. 17.
13 Thompson, *English Landed Society*, p. 187; Girouard, *Victorian Country House*, p. 28; Thompson, *The Edwardians*, p. 35; Frank E. Huggett, *Life Below Stairs: Domestic Servants in England from Victorian Times* (London, 1977; paperback edn, Stevenage, 1978), p. 19; Christopher Simon Sykes, *The Golden Age of the Country House* (London and New York, 1980), p. 44; David Cannadine, "The theory and practice of the English leisure classes," *Historical Journal*, 21 (1978), pp. 449–50; Badeau, *Aristocracy in England*, pp. 174–5; "A Member of the Aristocracy," *The Servants' Practical Guide: A Handbook of Duties and Rules* (London, 1880), p. 4.
14 In a sample of 33 peers' establishments drawn from the 1871 census, the median for indoor staff was 20 and the mean 20.4, with 27% having 15 or fewer. Only three had as many as 30 indoors. Adding likely outdoor servants brings the total staff on these estates to between 21 and 64 (this last included 18 hunt servants) with a mean of 36.1. A third apparently employed fewer than 30 altogether.
15 *Servants' Practical Guide*, pp. 4–5.
16 In the peer sample, twelve employed house stewards; three of the six dukes, one of two marquesses, and four of eleven earls did without one. Only one marquess and three earls employed a man cook.
17 The order of precedence is: duke, marquess, earl, viscount and baron. When the sample peers were ranked by the size of their indoor staffs, two of the six dukes came first (31 servants) and second equal (30), and another two sixth

and seventh, but the Duke of Devonshire came twelfth equal, and the Duke of Leeds, with a mere 13, trailed at twenty-eighth equal. Earls ranged between second equal and last.

[18] A sample of 30 baronets' staffs gave an average of 13.7 indoor servants and an estimated 9.5 outdoors, with a mean of 23.2.

[19] Thompson, *English Landed Society*, p. 193; Franklin, *Gentleman's Country House*, p. 87. Other figures for indoor staffs include eight (Girouard, *Victorian Country House*, p. 28), ten (Sykes, *Golden Age*, p. 44) and twelve (Cannadine, "Theory and practice," p. 450).

[20] *A New System of Practical Domestic Economy, Founded on Modern Discovery and the Private Communications of Persons of Experience* (London, 1824; revised edn, 1827), p. 437; Thomas Webster and Mrs Parkes, *An Encyclopaedia of Domestic Economy, Comprising Such Subjects as are Most Immediately Connected with Housekeeping* (London, 1844), p. 330.

[21] *Servants' Practical Guide*, p. 5.

[22] Burnett, *Useful Toil*, p. 154.

[23] Edward Higgs, "Domestic service and households in Victorian England," *Social History*, 8 (1983), pp. 207–8. Factors influencing the decision to employ servants, and how many to hire, were remarkably similar to factors affecting staff size in the landed classes. In Rochdale, these included "family size, the number of potential household workers in the family, crises such as widowhood or childbirth, the amount of entertainment undertaken, the relative efficiency of the household plant, the availability of manufactured commodities such as polishes, starch, pickles, jams and so on."

[24] Adams and Adams, *Complete Servant*, p. 16; *New System*, pp. 438–49; Webster, *Encyclopaedia of Domestic Economy*, p. 330; Alfred Cox, *The Landlord's and Tenant's Guide* (London, 1852), pp. 108–10; J.H. Walsh, *A Manual of Domestic Economy, Suited to Families Spending from £100 to £1000 a year* (London, 2nd edn, 1857), p. 221.

[25] Cox, *Landlord's and Tenant's Guide*, pp. 109, 111.

[26] Lee in Harrison, *Gentlemen's Gentlemen*, p. 117.

[27] Packe MSS, Hussey Packe's income and expenditure 1875–89, DE 1749/103; summary note of house bills, 1889, DE 1749/107/3.

[28] Beckett, *Aristocracy*, pp. 303–4.

[29] Northwick MSS, memorandum book 1819–44, 705:66 BA 4221/35, memorandum book 1837–58, 705:66 BA 4221/25; household accounts 1907–12, 705:66 BA 4221/14.

[30] Thompson, *English Landed Society*, pp. 191–2.

[31] Ridley, *Cecilia*, p. 163.

[32] Census enumerator's return, 1871, Hillington, Norfolk, RG 10 1859:6.

[33] Census enumerator's return, 1871, Finborough Hall, Great Finborough, Suffolk, RG 10 1733:1.

[34] Census enumerator's return, 1871, Aldcliffe Hall, Aldcliffe, Lancashire, RG 10 4232:19.
[35] Census enumerators' returns, 1871, Eden Hall, Edenhall, Cumberland, RG 10 5202:11.
[36] Census enumerator's return, 1871, Sharpham House, Ashprington, Devon, RG 10 2094:1; Nunwell Park, Brading, Isle of Wight, RG 10 1167:20; Northwick MS, wages book 1854–87, 705:66 BA 4221/17.
[37] Eric Horne, *What the Butler Winked At: Being the Life and Adventures of Eric Horne (Butler) for Fifty-Seven Years in Service with the Nobility and Gentry* (London, 1923), p. 58.
[38] Chillington MS, servants' wages book 1833–79, D590/650/1–2, Staffordshire Record Office.
[39] Ashburnham MS, servants' wages book 1879–1900, ASH 2611, East Sussex Record Office.
[40] Erddig MSS, household and personal accounts 1792–1821, D/E 428; household and personal accounts 1835–54, D/E 443; personal and estate accounts 1855–92, D/E 2363; servants' wages book 1904–18, D/E 467; lists of servants 1907–18, D/E 1134; vouchers 1865–1913, D/E/ 509; Simon Yorke to Philip Yorke 11 April 1881, D/E/1022; Waterson, *Servants' Hall*, p. 90.
[41] *Archivists' Report* 22, p. 20; Dixon MSS, ledger 1824–37, Dixon 4/10, cash books 1831–72, Dixon 4/14/1–7; servants' account book 1865–72, Dixon 4/18/10; ledger 1872–93, Dixon 22/4/9; cash book 1893–9, Dixon 22/4/13; Gibbons interviews.
[42] Sutherland MSS, household vouchers 1838–90, D593/R/2/18–95; Petworth MSS, weekly wages books, 1816–37, Petworth 2110–32, weekly wages book 1843–52, Petworth 2314, West Sussex Record Office.
[43] Dixon MSS, Dixon 4/14/1–7; household and personal accounts 1833–9, 1854–5, 1858–62, 1865–7, Dixon 10/12/11–14; Dixon 10/12/1–9; household accounts 1891–3, Dixon 4/18/8; Gibbons interviews.
[44] Packe MSS, garden cash books 1875–1921, DE 1346/46/1–2.
[45] Trollope-Bellew MS, garden labour book 1876–89, being catalogued, Lincolnshire Archives Office; Englefield MS, garden accounts 1858–96, D/E By A128, Berkshire Record Office.
[46] Erddig MS, estate vouchers 1865–1913, D/E 509.
[47] Sneyd MS, cash book 1855–6, S2103.
[48] Trollope-Bellew MS, gamekeeper's labour book 1876–99, TB list, p. 68 (being catalogued).
[49] Petworth MSS, weekly wages book 1816, 2110.
[50] Packe MS, house payments book 1869–74, DE 1346/366; Dixon MSS, diary entries of Mary Ann Dixon, 1 Dec. 1867, 11 Jan. 1870, Dixon 10/12/4–5.
[51] Arkwright MSS, housekeeper's account books 1819–43, being catalogued; Packe MS, DE 1346/366.

310   NOTES, PAGES 156–63

52 Halifax, *Fullness of Days*, p. 29; Packe MS, 1346/366.
53 Verse by Philip Yorke II at Erddig; Pitt-Rivers MSS, household and estate accounts 1885–1901, D396 F79–80, Dorset Record Office.
54 Blackett MSS, housekeeping cash books 1831–44, ZBL 288/8.
55 Dixon MSS, Dixon 4/14/1–7; Dixon 10/12/11–14, household and personal accounts 1872–83, 10/12/16; Dixon 10/12/1–9; household accounts 1881–1900, Dixon 4/18/7–9; diaries of Mrs Jameson Dixon 1895, 1902, 1903, Dixon 10/14/2–4; letter from Miss Joan Gibbons to the author, 11 Sept. 1978.
56 Jill Franklin, "Troops of servants: labour and planning in the country house 1840–1914," *Victorian Studies*, 19 (1975), pp. 211–13.
57 Girouard, *English Country House*, p. 276; idem, "Living with the past: Victorian alterations to country houses," in Jane Fawcett (ed.), *The Future of the Past* (London, 1976), pp. 117–18.
58 Huggett, *Life Below Stairs*, p. 18.
59 Girouard, "Living with the past," p. 131.
60 Englefield MS, servants' wages book 1854–94, D/E By A130.
61 Sneyd MSS, cash books 1848–65, S2080–2110.
62 Jones, *Victorian Boyhood*, p. 72.
63 Franklin, "Troops of servants," pp. 220–4, 226–33, 239.
64 Willoughby de Broke, *Passing Years*, p. 5; Halifax, *Fullness of Days*, p. 38; Gordon Grimmett in Harrison, *Gentlemen's Gentlemen*, p. 36; Horne, *Butler Winked*, p. 96; Fane, *Chit-Chat*, p. 52.
65 *A Laundrymaid's Week*, Staffordshire County Museum Services Information Sheet n.d.; Goodwood MS, servants' wages book 1904–18, Goodwood 1097, West Sussex Record Office; Petworth MS, servants' wages book, 1891–1912, Petworth 5111; Heber Percy, *Us Four*, p. 30; Geoffrey Markham, *Woolley Hall: the Historical Development of a Country House* (Wakefield, 1979), p. 54; Erddig MSS, lists of servants 1907–18, D/E 1134.
66 Blackwell, "Landed elite in decline," p. 15.
67 Census enumerators' returns, Erddig, Wrexham, Denbighshire, RG 10 5656, Holton-le-Moor, Lincolnshire, RG 10 3421; Erddig MSS, servants' wages book 1904–18, D/E 467; letter from Miss Joan Gibbons to the author, 11 Sept. 1978; Northwick MSS, memorandum book 1819–44, 705:66 BA 4221/35; 705:66 BA 4221/14.
68 Asquith, *Haply I May Remember*, p. 29.

CHAPTER 7   DEMOGRAPHY OF SERVANTS

1 Michael Winstanley, *Life in Kent at the Turn of the Century* (Folkestone, 1978), p. 167.

[2] Flora Thompson, *Lark Rise to Candleford* (Oxford, 1945; paperback edn, Harmondsworth, 1973), p. 165.
[3] McBride, *Domestic Revolution*, pp. 83–98.
[4] Horne, *Butler Winked*, p. 46; Edwin Lee, in Harrison, *Gentlemen's Gentlemen*, p. 116.
[5] David Vincent (ed.), *Testaments of Radicalism* (London, 1977), p. 119.
[6] Liz Stanley (ed.), *The Diaries of Hannah Cullwick: Victorian Maidservant* (New Brunswick, 1984), p. 170.
[7] "An Old Servant," author of *Domestic Service*, for instance, was a lifelong head housemaid who completely identified with the world of gentleman's service.
[8] *The Times*, 28 Jan., 4 Feb. 1815, 23 April 1845, 14 July 1875.
[9] M. Jeanne Peterson, "The Victorian governess: status incongruence in family and society," in Martha Vicinus (ed.), *Suffer and Be Still: Women in the Victorian Age* (Bloomington, 1972; paperback edn, 1973), p. 14.
[10] Gathorne-Hardy, *British Nanny*, p. 178; Rose Mary Crawshay, *Domestic Service for Gentlewomen* (London, 1877); L.M.H. (ed.), *The Hand-Book of Women's Work* (London, 1876), pp. 41–5; *Lady Servants – For and Against* (London, 1906); Mrs Eliot James, *Our Servants: Their Duties to Us and Ours to Them* (London, 1883), pp. 6–8; *Domestic Servants' Advertiser*, 20 May 1913.
[11] Henley, *Rosalind Howard*, p. 74; Thompson, *English Landed Society*, pp. 82–4; Hartcup, *Children of the Great Country Houses*, pp. 36, 38.
[12] Christopher Holdenby, *Folk of the Furrow* (London, 1913), p. 347; see also the *Field*'s advertisements for gamekeepers and gardeners.
[13] Frederick John Gorst with Beth Andrews, *Of Carriages and Kings* (London, 1956), p. 93.
[14] Pamela Sambrook, *A Servants' Place: an Account of the Servants at Shugborough* (Stoke-on-Trent, 1989), p. 54.
[15] E. S. Turner, *What the Butler Saw* (London, 1962), p. 263; Vulliamy, *Polderoy Papers*, pp. 135–6; Leslie, *Marlborough House Set*, p. 145.
[16] John Gillis, "Servants, sexual relations, and the risks of illegitimacy in London, 1801–1990," *Feminist Studies*, 5 (1979) pp. 145–7.
[17] Ibid, p. 147; *Cassell's Household Guide Being a Complete Enyclopaedia of Domestic and Social Economy, and Forming a Guide to Every Department of Practical Life*, 3 vols (London, 1870), II, p. 182; Yonge, *Womankind*, p. 192.
[18] Thompson, *Lark Rise*, pp. 207–8; Lee in Harrison, *Gentlemen's Gentlemen*, p. 111; Northwick MSS, applications for butler's place 1876, 705: 66 BA 4221/35; Burnett, *Useful Toil*, p. 185; Ernest King, *The Green Baize Door* (London, 1963), p. 8; Gorst, *Of Carriages and Kings*, p. 10; H.G. Wells, *An Experiment in Autobiography* (London, 1934), p. 45; Horne, *Butler Winked*, pp. 19–20; Horn, *Victorian Servant*, p. 57; Carbery, *Happy World*, p. 38; verse by Simon Yorke about Sarah Davies at Erddig; Swinton in Sitwell,

Two Generations, p. 16; Sitwell, *Left Hand, Right Hand*, p. 127; Jersey, *Fifty-One Years*, p. 9.

[19] Baker White, *True Blue*, p. 9; Jones, *As I Remember*, p. 6.

[20] Charles Cooper, *Town and Country: or, Forty Years in Service with the Aristocracy* (London, 1937), pp. 3, 5, 21; Bankes and Watkin, *Kingston Lacy Childhood*, p. 62.

[21] M. Mostyn Bird, *Woman at Work: a Study of the Different Ways of Earning a Living Open to Women* (London, 1911), pp. 111–12.

[22] Thompson, *Lark Rise*, p. 162.

[23] Holton-le-Moor marriage register 1837, 1845, Holton church; verse by Philip Yorke at Erddig.

[24] Census enumerator's returns, 1871, Trentham, Staffordshire, RG 9 1914; Sutherland MS, household vouchers, 1861, D593/12/2/61/1–4.

[25] This figure includes a number of cases in which the place of birth was unreadable, unidentifiable, in the wrong county, or not given. Presumably, many of these were obscure country parishes. Irish and Scottish servants were excluded because many of their birthplaces were recorded simply as "Ireland" or "Scotland" so that rural or urban origins, and distances from birthplace, could not be calculated. Foreigners were excluded for the same reason.

[26] Mark Ebery and Brian Preston, *Domestic Service in Late Victorian and Edwardian England, 1871–1914*, Geographical papers no. 42 (Reading, 1976), p. 77.

[27] Richard Jeffries, *Hodge and His Masters*, 2 vols (London, 1880; republished 1979), II, p. 240.

[28] 20.8% of the sample's English and Welsh servants were born in cities and towns with populations over 2,500. These urban-born comprised nearly 28% of upper indoor servants, but only 21.8% of lower indoor servants. Among the indoor staff, more women than men were urban-born; 32% compared to 23.9% among upper servants, and 24% versus 17.7% among lower servants. Governesses were almost all urban-born, 10 of the 13 British-born coming from London. In a sample of 30 peers' staffs, 47.9% of the upper women servants and 44.8% of the upper indoor men were urban-born.

[29] Elizabeth Alicia M. Lewis, "A reformation of domestic service," *Nineteenth Century*, 33 (1893), p. 128; Sheila J. Richardson, "The Servant Question: a study of the domestic labour market, 1851–1911" (unpublished University of London MPhil thesis, 1967), pp. 109–10; Frank Dawes, *Not in Front of the Servants: Domestic Service in England, 1850–1939* (Readers Union edn, Newton Abbot, 1975), p. 102.

[30] Norman Scott Brien and Ethel Culbert Gras, *The Economic and Social History of an English Village* (Cambridge, Mass., 1930), p. 157.

[31] Dixon MS, Mary Ann Dixon's diary, 22 March 1866, Dixon 10/12/3.

32 King, *Green Baize Door*, p. 9.
33 Mollie Harris, *Another Kind of Magic* (London, 1971; paperback edn, Oxford, 1985), pp. 118–19.
34 Everett, *Bricks and Flowers*, p. 47.
35 Horne, *Butler Winked*, p. 50.
36 Ibid, p. 38; John James, *The Memoirs of a House Steward* (London, 1949), p. 12; Gorst, *Carriages and Kings*, p. 11; King, Green Baize Door, p. 8.
37 Rose Gibbs, *In Service: Rose Gibbs Remembers* (Cambridge, 1981), pp. 11–13.
38 Packe MSS, house payments books, 1869–95, DE/1346/366–8.
39 "The First World War Memoirs of William Harrison," DS/MISC/64, Imperial War Museum, p. 27.
40 Shugborough MSS, correspondence regarding gardener's place 1907, D615/E(A) B4, Staffordshire Record Office.
41 *Field*, 4 April 1885; *Morning Post*, 7 April 1885.
42 See, for instance, *The Times*, 17 July 1882, p. 3.
43 Renton, *Tyrant or Victim*, pp. 92, 150–3.
44 Winifred Gérin, *Anne Brontë* (London, 1959), p. 120.
45 Renton, *Tyrant or Victim*, pp. 109–11, 116–17.
46 Hughes, *Victorian Governess*, p. 43.
47 Ibid, p. 50.
48 *Domestic Servants' Advertiser*, 20 May 1913.
49 Arkwright MSS, Lucy Arkwright to John Hungerford Arkwright, 20 Feb. and 22 June 1871, 22 Feb. and 5 Aug. 1872, 14 Feb. 1873, 23 March 1881, 19 Oct. 1893, A63/IV/176; Verey, *Victorian Squire*, p. 161.
50 Vaughan, *South Wales Squires*, p. 27.
51 Census enumerators' returns, 1871, Little Crosby, Lancashire, RG 10 3837:5; Cuerdon, Lancashire, RG 10 4195:15.
52 Jim Bullock, *Bowers Row: Recollections of a Mining Village* (Wakefield, 1976), p. 47.
53 Census enumerators' returns, 1871, Southill, Bedfordshire, RG 10 1552:17; Rougham, RG 10 1848:6.
54 These statistics concern only those servants whose birthplaces were identified and located, born in England and Wales. Some returns omitted birthplaces, noting only the county, some servants did not know where they were born, some birthplaces were indecipherable, and some were located in the wrong county and were thus inconclusive.
55 Arkwright MS, application for gardener's position 1899, A63/IV/Box 227.
56 Hecht, *Domestic Servant*, pp. 81–2; *The Times*, 7, 12, 23 Jan., 21 Feb., 28 March, 6 April, 8 June 1815.
57 Verulam MS, wages book 1895–1911, D/EV/F 271, Hertfordshire Record Office.
58 Cooper, *Town and Country*, p. 26, 28, 47.

[59] Bridehead MS, wages book 1869–1908, D 289, Dorset Record Office.

[60] Statistics on mean length of service were calculated from the wages records of 10 peers, 2 baronets and 19 gentry families, with additional material from reminiscences, job applications and letters of reference.

[61] Statistics gathered from the wage-book collection do not show any clear trend of declining length of service. But there are too few cases early and late in the period, and the variables are too great, with houses of different size, policies, and geographical location entering and leaving the sample at different times.

[62] King, *Green Baize Door*, p. 19; "Memoirs of William Harrison," p. 27; Lady Clodagh Anson, *Another Book* (London, 1937), p. 107; Lady Willoughby de Broke, "An employer's conclusion," in C. V. Butler, *Domestic Service: An Enquiry by the Women's Industrial Council* (London, 1916; reprinted New York and London, 1980), pp. 105–6.

[63] Cooper, *Town and Country*, pp. 52, 78, 99–100.

[64] Sutherland MS, application for head gardener's position 1892, D593/L/3/65.

[65] Waterson, *Servants' Hall*, p. 91.

[66] Sneyd MS, S2080–S2110.

[67] Gorst, *Carriages and Kings*, p. 133; Goodwood MSS, servants' wages books 1869–1900, Goodwood 1096–7, West Sussex Record Office.

[68] Chillington MSS, wages books 1833–79, D590/650/1–2, Staffordshire Record Office.

[69] Northwick MSS, bundle of servants' wages 1817–18, memorandum book 1819–44, BA 4221/35; memorandum book 1837–58, BA 4221/25; memorandum book 1854–87, BA 4221/17; servants' wages book 1859–1880, BA 4221/23; BA 4221/14.

[70] Frederick MS, wages and board wages book 1844–73, 183/36/6/9, Surrey Record Office.

[71] Gibbons interviews.

[72] Thompson, *English Landed Society*, p. 305; Verulam MS, D/EV/F 271; Dyott MSS, notebooks on servants 1816–41, D661/12/9, Staffordshire Record Office; Englefield MS, D/E By A130; Derwydd MS, servants' wages book 1890–1913, CA 13, Dyfed County Record Office, Carmarthen; Blackwell, "Landed elite in decline," p. 54.

[73] Stanley, *Hannah Cullwick*, p. 35; Thompson, *Lark Rise*, p. 156.

[74] Sybil Marshall (ed.), *Fenland Chronicle: Recollections of William Henry and Kate Mary Edwards, Collected and Edited by their Daughter* (Cambridge, 1967), p. 231.

[75] Mrs E.M. Massey, *Girls Entering Service* (Derby, 1914), pp. 6–7, 10.

[76] Ibid, pp. 8–9.

[77] Ibid, p. 10.

[78] Ibid, p. 11.
[79] Hughes, *Victorian Governess*, p. 31.
[80] G. S., *The Governess*, Houlston's Industrial Library no. 18 (London, n.d.), p. 356.
[81] Schmidt, *Passion's Child*, pp. 22, 179.
[82] Nina Slingsby Smith, *George: Memoirs of a Gentleman's Gentleman* (London, 1984), p. 35.
[83] G. Oram, *Master and Servants; Their Relative Duties* (London, 1858), p. 46; Butler, *Domestic Service*, p. 68.
[84] Godfrey Locker-Lampson, *Life in the Country* (London, 1948), p. 129.
[85] Shugborough MS, D615/E(A)34.
[86] Richard Jefferies, *The Gamekeeper at Home* (London, 1881), p. 37.
[87] *Supplement to the Sixty-fifth Annual Report of the Registrar-General of Births, Deaths, and Marriages in England and Wales*, Part II, *Parliamentary Papers* 18 (1905).
[88] Michael Anderson suggests that maidservants had lower nuptiality rates than other women, in "Marriage patterns in Victorian Britain. An analysis based on registration district data for England and Wales 1861," *Journal of Family History*, I (1976), pp 67–70, 72; Penelope Wilcox confirmed that this was true in Cambridge in the period 1847–70, but found servants wed around a year earlier from 1871 to 1901. "Marriage, mobility and domestic service in Victorian Cambridge," *Local Population Studies*, 29 (1982), pp. 24–8.
[89] Mrs Wrigley, "A plate-layer's wife," in *Life as We Have Known It: by Co-operative Working Women*, Margaret Llewelyn Davies (ed.) (London, 1931; reprinted 1977), pp. 59–60; Thompson, *Lark Rise*, pp. 166–7.
[90] Gillis, "Illegitimacy in London," p. 153.
[91] George Ewart Evans, *From Mouths of Men* (London, 1976), pp. 63, 70; Audrey Le Lièvre, *Miss Wilmott of Warley Place: her Life and her Gardens* (London, 1980), p. 61.
[92] Dyott MS, D661/12/9.
[93] Jean Robin, *Elmdon: Continuity and Change in a Northwest Essex Village, 1861–1964* (Cambridge, 1980), pp. 116–17; census enumerator's return 1871, Trentham, RG 10 2864:3; verse by Simon Yorke at Erddig.
[94] Kate Taylor in Burnett, *Destiny Obscure*, p. 289; Essex oral history archives no. 2012, p. 9.
[95] Lucy Wake (ed.), *The Reminiscences of Charlotte, Lady Wake* (London, 1909), p. 88; Blagdon MS, Lady Ridley to Lady Parke, Dec. 1844, ZRI/30/27/6; Lee in Harrison, *Gentlemen's Gentlemen*, p. 130.
[96] Ian Niall, *The Gamekeeper*, (London, 1965; reprinted Woodbridge, 1985), pp. 123–4, 126.
[97] Northwick MS, applications for butler's place, 1876, 705:66 BA 4221/35; see also Thompson, *Rise of Respectable Society*, p. 74.

CHAPTER 8 GENTLEMAN'S SERVICE

1. Willoughby de Broke in Butler, *Domestic Service*, p. 102; Horne, *Butler Winked*, pp. 114–15.
2. Margaret Thomas, "Behind the Green Baize Door," in Streatfield, *Day Before Yesterday*, pp. 82–3.
3. Joan Morgan and Alison Richards, *A Paradise out of a Common Field: the Pleasures and Plenty of the Victorian Garden* (London and New York, 1990), p. 202.
4. Thompson, *Lark Rise*, p. 164; see also Butler, *Domestic Service*, p. 81.
5. Tweedsmuir, *Lilac and the Rose*, p. 95.
6. Yandell, *Henry*, pp. 21–2.
7. Thomas in Streatfield, *Day Before Yesterday*, p. 85; Cooper, *Town and Country*, p. 188.
8. See Stanley, *Hannah Cullwick*, pp. 5–6, for a good description of duties.
9. Census enumerators' return, 1871, Trentham RG 10 2864:3; Sutherland MS, London wages 1869–70, D593/R/4/6.
10. Everett, *Bricks and Flowers*, pp. 49–50; Slingsby Smith, *George*, pp. 12–14, 23–4.
11. Adams and Adams, *Complete Servant*, p. 106; E. M. Butler (ed.), *A Regency Visitor: the English Tour of Prince Pückler-Muskau, Described in his Letters, 1826–1828* (London, 1957), p. 155.
12. Richard Henry Dana, *Hospitable England in the Seventies: The Diary of a Young American, 1875–1876* (Boston, 1921), p. 75.
13. Dixon MSS, memos on servants' duties, Dixon 22/5/33, Dixon 5/22/36.
14. Willoughby de Broke in Butler, *Domestic Service*, p. 102; "Domestic service – Nelly Armstrong," *North British Review* (Nov. 1853–Feb. 1854), p. 205.
15. Butler, *Regency Visitor*, p. 78.
16. Taine, *Notes on England*, pp. 87–8.
17. Verey, *Victorian Squire*, p. 129.
18. Horn, *Victorian Servant*, p. 203.
19. Essex archives, interview 372, p. 43.
20. *Domestic Servants' Advertiser*, 20 May 1913.
21. Thomas in Streatfield, *Day Before Yesterday*, pp. 91–3.
22. Stanley, *Hannah Cullwick*, pp. 38–9.
23. Cornwallis MS, rules for servants, U24 F25, Kent Archives Office; Northwick MS, agreements with maidservants, 705:66 BA 4221/23.
24. Muriel Spark (ed.), *The Letters of the Brontës: a Selection* (Norman, Oklahoma, 1954), pp. 76–7.
25. Annie Cable in Evans, *From Mouths of Men*, p. 67; M. A. Bienefeld, *Working Hours in British Industry: An Economic History* (London, 1972), p. 106.
26. Horne, *Butler Winked*, p. 78.

[27] William Lanceley, *From Hall-Boy to House-Steward* (London, 1925), p. 14.
[28] Judith Rollins, *Between Women: Domestics and Their Employers* (Philadelphia, 1985), pp. 83–4.
[29] Davidoff, "Mastered for Life," p. 414.
[30] Cooper, *Town and Country*, p. 195; Lanceley, *Hall-Boy*, p. 16; King, *Green Baize Door*, p. 18.
[31] Pat Barr (ed.), *I Remember: an Arrangement for Many Voices* (London, 1970), p. 70.
[32] Violet M. Firth, *The Psychology of the Servant Problem* (London, 1925), p. 33.
[33] Vita Sackville-West, *Country Notes* (London, 1939), pp. 97, 99–100.
[34] Merlin Waterson (ed.), *The Country House Remembered: Recollections of Life Between the Wars* (London, 1985), p. 192; "Housekeeping at Shugborough," Information Sheet FL5, Staffordshire County Museum Service.
[35] Norma Virgoe and Susan Yaxley (eds), *The Banville Diaries: Journals of a Norfolk Gamekeeper, 1822–1844* (London, 1986), p. 67.
[36] Morgan and Richards, *Paradise*, especially ch. 10, "Men of influence."
[37] Baroness Raglan, *Memories of Three Reigns* (London, 1928), p. 104.
[38] Askwith, *Lyttletons*, p. 95.
[39] Butler, *Domestic Service*, p. 84.
[40] Ashburnham MS, wages book 1851–62, ASH 2609; Northwick MS, wages book 1854–87, 705:66 BA 4221/17; Trollope-Bellow MS, wages book 1848–76, not catalogued, Lincolnshire Archives Office; Giffard MS, wages book 1832–79, 590/650/1–2, Staffordshire Record Office; Dixon MS, cash book 1855–72, Dixon 22/4/4.
[41] Vulliamy, *Polderoy Papers*, p. 94; Erddig MS, Victoria Yorke to Philip Yorke [n.d.], N/E 1013.
[42] James, *Our Servants*, p. 126; Ridley, *Cecilia*, p. 163; Hussey MS, memorandum, "Wages of gardeners etc. sundry places 1875," U1776 E108.
[43] Frederick MS, wages book 1844–73, 183/36/6/9, Surrey Record Office.
[44] Northwick MS, agreement with servant, 705:66 BA 4221/35.
[45] Hussey MS, list of workmen, 1880, U1776 E108 253.
[46] At Petworth, house labourers got around 14s a week, "same as the labourers," though their pay fell to 9 or 10s a week at mid-century for a while. Stablemen earned 11–12s a week early in the century, rising to 14s from the 1830s, and between 13s and 18s in the 1870s. Washerwomen received only 8s a week in 1816, rising to 14s by the 1840s. (Petworth MS, weekly wage books 1816–37, Petworth 2110–32, weekly wages books 1845–52, Petworth 2314.) Odd-job men got between 16s and 18s a week at Waldershare in the 1870s. (North MS, wages book 1872–82, U471 A184, Kent Archives Office.)
[47] Census enumerator's return, Englefield, 1871, RG 10 1277:100; Englefield MS, D/E By A128.

48 Sutherland MSS, household vouchers 1816–90, D593/R/2/3–95; Erddig MS, D/E 509; Packe MSS, DE 1346/46/1–2.
49 Dixon MSS, farm servants' wages book 1859–63, Dixon 5/4/5; household and personal accounts 1858–67, Dixon 10/12/13–14.
50 Dixon MS, household and personal accounts, 1862–7, Dixon 10/12/14; Packe MS, DE 1346/366.
51 Fildes, *Wet Nursing*, p. 196; Roberts, "Mothers and babies," p. 286.
52 Northwick MS, bundle of servants' wages 1817–18, 705: 66 BA 6221/35; Starkey MS, menservants' wages book 1858–82, DDSN X/4, Nottinghamshire Record-Office.
53 Geoffrey Tyack, "Service on the Cliveden estate between the wars," *Oral History*, 5 (1977), p. 76.
54 Starkey MS, DDSN X/4.
55 Sutherland MSS, undated wages list 1817–18, D593 R/4/9, London servants 1834, D593 R/1/26/4, wages of London establishment 1840–7, D593 R/4/3, Stafford House wages 1875–7, D593 R/4/8.
56 Sutherland MS, statement of receipts and payments 1837–9, D593 R/1/26/20.
57 Trollope-Bellew wages book.
58 Radcliffe MS, servants' wages book 1897–1908, Rad I 414, West Yorkshire Archive Service; Sutherland MSS, D593 R/4/3; D593 R/4/8.
59 Sutherland MS, garden accounts 1815–55, D593 F/4/1/1–54; garden accounts 1856–1913, D593 F/5/2/1–60.
60 Historians disagree on general wage trends in domestic service. Mark Ebery and Brian Preston argue that wages stagnated, even declined, until the 1870s (Ebery and Preston, *Domestic Service*, p. 92), whereas John Burnett suggests "wages showed a continuous upward improvement over the Victorian period and . . . rose particularly during the closing decades of the century" (Burnett, *Useful Toil*, p. 161). Theresa McBride concludes that wages rose until around 1880, then stabilized and lost their advantage over other occupations (McBride, *Domestic Revolution*, pp. 64, 67).
61 Thompson, *English Landed Society*, p. 195; Franklin, "Troops of servants," p. 222.
62 The sample of wages records collected is inadequate as a conclusive measure of wage trends. Not only is this sample small and incomplete, with few households' records covering more than a decade or two, but the proportion of peer and gentry disbursements in each decade varied greatly, resulting in higher averages in decades with more peers' servants included.
63 Five-year means are used here. Data from M. W. Flinn, "Trends in real wages, 1750–1850," *Economic History Review*, 27 (1974), p. 409; B. R. Mitchell and Phyllis Deane, *Abstract of British Historical Statistics* (Cambridge, 1971), pp. 343–4.

[64] Arkwright MS, Lucy Arkwright to John H. Arkwright, 2 May 1872, 12 Nov. 1880, A63/IV/176.
[65] William Kitchener, *The Housekeeper's Oracle* (London, 1829), p. 133; Walsh, *Manual of Domestic Economy*, pp. 224, 226; Massey, *Girls Entering Service*, p. 6.
[66] Petworth MS, 5111; Taplow Court MS, maidservants' wages book 1908–33, being catalogued, Buckinghamshire Record Office.
[67] James, *Our Servants*, p. 127.
[68] Packe MS, Anthony S. Packe, *Index of Family Papers at Prestwold* (Prestwold, 1974), p. 11, DE 1749/121.
[69] Webster, *Encyclopaedia*, p. 328.
[70] Erddig MS, D/E 467.
[71] Evans, *From Mouths of Men*, p. 64; Lanceley, *Hall-Boy*, p. 163.
[72] Northwick MS, rules for servants, 705:66 BA 4221/23; Baker White, *True Blue*, p. 50.
[73] Sir George Leveson-Gower, *Years of Content, 1858–1886* (London, 1940), p. 7.
[74] Beckwith, *When I Remember*, p. 81.
[75] Blackett MS, Lady Blackett's personal accounts 1832–8, ZBL 288/8; Erddig MSS, personal and estate accounts 1855–92, D/E 2363; "A Lady in Society," *The New Book of Etiquette* (London, 1907), pp. 79–81.
[76] Badeau, *Aristocracy in England*, p. 176.
[77] Lanceley, *Hall-Boy*, p. 13.
[78] Hatherton MS, account book 1841–4, D260/M/E/50, Staffordshire Record Office; Packe MS, house payment book 1873–84, DE/1346/367; Sutherland MS, bill in vouchers 1835, D593/R/21/14/3; Blackett MS, agreement between Sir Edward Blackett and Dr James Andrew Baird Thompson, 26 Dec. 1877, ZBL 35/2.
[79] Will of Sir Henry Oglander, 1874, Somerset House.
[80] Sutherland MS, Anne Leveson-Gower, Duchess of Sutherland to Mrs Ingram (n.d.), D593/R/10/2; Virgoe and Yaxley, *Banville Diaries*, p. 79.
[81] Haims, "In their place," pp. 302–4.
[82] Hartcup, *Below Stairs*, p. 169.
[83] Sutherland MSS, vouchers 1840–55, D593/F/1/47–55; estate accounts 1857–1911 D593/F/5/2/2–58; Erddig MSS, D/E 509.
[84] Ralph Nevill, *English Country House Life* (London, 1925), p. 215; the Duke of Richmond and Gordon, in Waterson, *Country House Remembered*, p. 177; Zoë Ward, *Curtsey to the Lady: a Horringer Childhood* (Lavenham, 1985), p. 13.
[85] Arkwright MS, John Arkwright's will, 1858, A63/IV/Box 64; Northwick MS, Lord Northwick's will, 1879/86, 705: 66 BA 4221/28; Haims, "In their place," pp. 308–9; Sneyd MS, Ralph Sneyd's will (n.d.), S3460.

86 Hartcup, *Below Stairs*, pp. 165, 169; Susan Bisset's will, 1903, Somerset House.
87 Peterson, "Victorian governess," pp. 7–8.
88 Waterson, *Servants' Hall*, pp. 82, 158.
89 Sambrook, *Servants' Place*, p. 15.
90 Gorst, *Carriages and Kings*, p. 132.
91 Waterson, *Servants' Hall*, p. 176.
92 Franklin, *Gentleman's Country House*, p. 103.
93 Robert Kerr, *The Gentleman's House: or, How to Plan English Residences from the Parsonage to the Palace* (London, 1864), p. 222.
94 Northwick MS, inventory 1859, 705:66 BA 4221/13.
95 J. E. Panton, *Leaves from a Housekeeper's Book* (London, 1914), p. 204; Franklin, *Gentleman's Country House*, p. 114.
96 Ted Humphis, *Garden Glory* (London, 1969), pp. 40–1.
97 Thompson, *Lark Rise*, p. 164.
98 Northwick MS, 705:66 BA 4221/13; Arkwright MS, inventory 1858, not catalogued.
99 Northwick MS, 705:66 BA 4221/13; Arkwright inventory; Gibbons interviews.
100 Bea Howe, *Lady with Green Fingers: the Life of Jane Loudon* (London, 1961), p. 84.
101 Sutherland MSS, reports on cottages, 1835, 1842, D593/N/2/2/3/1–2.
102 Anne Tibble, *Greenhorn: a Twentieth-Century Childhood* (London, 1973), pp. 14–15.
103 Edward Salmon, "Domestic service and democracy," *Fortnightly Review*, 49 (1888), p. 41; Nellie Lockhart Anderson, "A servant's view of the servant problem," *National Review*, 61 (1913), p. 126; Butler, *Domestic Service*, pp. 50–5; Firth, *Servant Problem*, p. 35.
104 Waterson, *Servants' Hall*, p.113; Miss Joan Gibbons to the author, 4 Oct. 1978.
105 Beckwith, *When I Remember*, p. 76; Badeau, *Aristocracy in England*, p. 181.
106 Dorothy Marshall, *The English Domestic Servant in History*, General Series no. 13, Historical Association (London, 1949), p. 25; Evans, *From Mouths of Men*, p. 69; D. W. L. Thynne, *Before the Sunset Fades* (Warminster, 1951), p. 17; Horne, *Butler Winked*, pp. 98–9.
107 Packe MS, bundle of returned reply cards, Feb. 1899, DE 1346/436.
108 Slingsby Smith, *George*, p. 78.
109 Arkwright MSS, Lucy Arkwright to John Hungerford Arkwright, 25 June 1873, 2 June 1874, A63/IV/176; Verey, *Victorian Squire*, pp. 164, 166, 227, 234.
110 Cooper, *Town and Country*, p. 114.
111 Butler, *Domestic Service*, pp. 20, 31.

[112] Cooper, *Town and Country*, pp. 87–8, 89, 92; Horne, *Butler Winked*, pp. 57, 152, 119–20.
[113] Arkwright MS, form filled out by William Udall, applicant for butler's position, A63/IV/218; Harrison, *Gentlemen's Gentlemen*, p. 121.
[114] Horne, *Butler Winked*, pp. 54–5, 66, 103, 112, 221; "Memoirs of William Harrison," p. 8; Cooper, *Town and Country*, pp. 180–1; Hardwicke Court MS, servants' wages book 1887–1928, D49/1/17, Gloucestershire Record Office.
[115] Ernest Field, "Gardening memories at Halton," *Country Life*, 154 (11 Oct. 1973), pp. 1062, 1064.
[116] Packe MSS, records of the Gardeners' Mutual Improvement Society 1889, DE 1346/582; Sutherland MSS, records of the Lilleshall Menservants' Club, D593/L/4/38.
[117] Burton Constable MS, diaries of Ferdinand Ceroti 1827–1828, 1830, 1832, DD CC (2) 36B, East Riding Record Office; Violet E. Armstrong, "In service at Wrest Park," *Bedfordshire Magazine*, 19 (Summer, 1984), pp. 182–4.
[118] Lanceley, *Hall-Boy*, p. 23.
[119] Armstrong, "Wrest Park," p. 182.
[120] Grimmett in Harrison, *Gentlemen's Gentlemen*, p. 107.
[121] Lee in Harrison, *Gentlemen's Gentlemen*, pp. 120–1.
[122] "Memoirs of William Harrison," pp. 12–15; Gorst, *Carriages and Kings*, pp. 89, 112, 115; Bankes and Watkin, *Kingston Lacy Childhood*, p. 68.
[123] Gorst, *Carriages and Kings*, p. 98; Cooper, *Town and Country*, p. 109.
[124] Jones, *Victorian Boyhood*, p. 79.

CHAPTER 9 LIFE BELOW STAIRS

[1] Lawrence Stone, *Road to Divorce: England, 1530–1987* (Oxford, 1990), pp. 217–18, 230.
[2] Adams and Adams, *Complete Servant*, p. 174.
[3] Anon., *A Mistress's Council: or, a Few Words to Servants* (London, 1871), p. 21.
[4] Stanley, *Hannah Cullwick*, p. 39.
[5] G. S., *The Governess*, p. 360.
[6] Mary Maurice, *Governess Life: its Trials, Duties and Encouragements* (London, 1849), p. 52.
[7] Charlton, *Northumbrian Lady*, p. 31.
[8] Cardigan, *My Recollections*, p. 22.
[9] Northwick MS, Mr Holland to Lord Northwick, 3 March 1870, 705:66 BA 4221/35.
[10] Petworth MS, Colonel Wyndham to Rev. T. Lockett, 17 Sept. 1839, Petworth 729.

11. Arkwright MS, A. R. Broughton to John Hungerford Arkwright, 5 March 1904, A63/IV/216.
12. Sutherland MS, Vantini to Locke, 22 April 1836, D593/R/1/26/15.
13. Firth, *Servant Problem*, p. 50.
14. King, *Green Baize Door*, p. 11.
15. Willoughby de Broke in Butler, *Domestic Service*, p. 107; Gorst, *Carriages and Kings*, p. 132.
16. Gorst, *Carriages and Kings*, p. 132.
17. Fane, *Chit-Chat*, p. 51.
18. Gorst, *Carriages and Kings*, p. 133.
19. Thomas in Streatfield, *Day Before Yesterday*, pp. 90–1.
20. Slingsby Smith, *George*, pp. 23–4.
21. Gorst, *Carriages and Kings*, p. 202; Slingsby Smith, *George*, pp. 68–9.
22. Owen Jones, *Ten Years of Game-keeping* (London, 1910), p. 229.
23. Waterson, *Servants' Hall*, p. 92.
24. Ibid, p. 13.
25. Slingsby Smith, *George*, p. 28.
26. Sedgwick in Streatfield, *Day Before Yesterday*, pp. 15–16.
27. Lee in *Gentlemen's Gentlemen*, pp. 134–5.
28. Verey, *Victorian Squire*, pp. 84–6.
29. Charles Booth, "Domestic Service," in *Life and Labour of the People in London*, Series 2, Industry 4 (London, 1903), p. 227.
30. Lutyens, *Blessed Girl*, p. 8; Lanceley, *Hall-Boy*, pp. 152–3.
31. Vulliamy, *Polderoy Papers*, p. 92.
32. Horne, *Butler Winked*, p. 275.
33. Packe MSS, letters of reference, 1873–87, DE 1346/437.
34. Cooper, *Town and Country*, p. 26; Albert Thomas, *Wait & See* (London, 1944), p. 29.
35. Waterson, *Servants' Hall*, pp. 111, 116; Stanley, *Hannah Cullwick*, p. 38.
36. Horne, *Butler Winked*, pp. 194, 201.
37. Slingsby Smith, *George*, pp. 64, 68; Dorothy Howell-Thomas (ed.), *Goodwood: Letters From Below Stairs* (Chichester, 1976), n.p.
38. Horne, *Butler Winked*, p. 109; Margaret Powell, *My Mother and I* (London, 1972), p. 64.
39. Verse by Philip Yorke II at Erddig.
40. Roberts, "Mothers and babies," p. 291.
41. Ridley, *Cecilia*, p. 173.
42. Lanceley, *Hall-Boy*, pp. 167–8.
43. Bankes and Watkin, *Kingston Lacy Childhood*, p. 21.
44. Gorst, *Carriages and Kings*, p. 136; Northwick MS, 705:66 BA 4221/23.
45. Henley, *Rosalind Howard*, p. 87.
46. Jeune, *Lesser Questions*, p. 187.

47 Horne, *Butler Winked*, p. 153.
48 Mark Girouard, *A Country House Companion* (London, 1987; Leicester, 1992), p. 138; Dawes, *Not in Front*, p. 44; Thynne, *Sunset Fades*, p. 28.
49 Thomas in Streatfield, *Day Before Yesterday*, p. 94.
50 Thompson, *Lark Rise*, p. 167.
51 Gillis, "Illegitimacy in London," pp. 143, 158, 160.
52 Mary Clive (ed.), *Caroline Clive: From the Diary and Family Papers of Mrs Archer Clive (1801–1873)* (London, 1949), pp. 270–1; Horne, *More Winks*, p. 211.
53 Anna Clark, *Women's Silence, Men's Violence: Sexual Assault in England, 1770–1845* (London, 1987), pp. 107–8.
54 Henley, *Rosalind Howard*, pp. 87, 89; Charlton, *Northumbrian Lady*, p. 195.
55 Charlton, *Northumbrian Lady*, pp. 242, 246, 248, 250, 252; Walter R. Iley, *Corbridge* (Newcastle on Tyne, 1975), p. 141.
56 Iley, *Corbridge*, p. 138.
57 Quoted in Ronald Blythe, *The View in Winter: Reflections on Old Age* (London, 1979; paperback edn, Harmondsworth, 1981), pp. 80–1.
58 Powell, *My Mother and I*, pp. 65–6.
59 Badeau, *Aristocracy in England*, pp. 109–12; Le Lièvre, *Miss Wilmott*, p. 89; Everett, *Bricks and Flowers*, p. 50.
60 Tibble, *Greenhorn*, p. 12.
61 Harrison, *Rose*, pp. 2, 8.
62 Constable MS, Sir Clifford Constable to Ferdinand Ceroti, 16 Oct. 1827, DD CC/148/1.
63 Starkey MS, DDSN X/4; Burnett, *Destiny Obscure*, p. 237; Horne, *Butler Winked*, p. 191.
64 Northwick MSS, butlers' job applications, 705:66 BA 4331/35.
65 Estcourt MSS, correspondence between J.G. Bucknall Estcourt and T. Stiff, March and April 1833, D1571 F245, Gloucester Record Office; Packe MS, Lady Alice Packe to Edward Hussey Packe, 1913, DE 1749/8/19.
66 Trentham Parish Registers, Trentham Church; Geoffrey Markham, *Woolley Hall*, p. 60; Russell, *Amberley Papers*, I, p. 106.
67 Gillis, "Illegitimacy in London," p. 159.
68 Ibid, p. 154.
69 Arkwright MS, Joseph Yates's notebook; A. M. W. Stirling, *The Letter-Bag of Lady Elizabeth Spencer-Stanhope, compiled from the Cannon Hall Papers, 1806–1873*, 2 vols (London, 1913), II, pp. 99–102; Vulliamy, *Polderoy Papers*, p. 205.
70 Powell, *Margaret, Countess of Jersey*, pp. 111, 153.
71 Butler, *Domestic Service*, p. 39; see also Nicholas Cooper, *Aynho: a Northamptonshire Village* (London, 1964), pp. 284–5.

72. Thompson, *Lark Rise*, p. 207; Essex interview no. 84, p. 26; Allan Jobson, *Suffolk Remembered* (London, 1971), p. 18.
73. Badeau, *Aristocracy in England*, pp. 109–10; Sambrook, *Servant's Place*, p. 54.
74. Badeau, *Aristocracy in England*, p. 109; see also Thomas, *Wait & See*, p. 31.
75. Cooper, *Town and Country*, p. 163; John Bailey (ed.), *The Diary of Lady Frederick Cavendish*, 2 vols (London, 1927), I, p. 189; Halifax, *Fullness of Days*, p. 34.
76. Essex interview 372, pp. 23, 24.
77. Erddig MS, meals book 1850–1, D/E 2362.
78. Bankes and Watkins, *Kingston Lacy Childhood*, p. 67.
79. Beckwith, *When I Remember*, p. 72; Essex interview no. 18, pp. 30–2.
80. Tibble, *Greenhorn*, pp. 16–17, 23.
81. Powell, *My Mother and I*, p. 64.; Essex archives, interview 406, p. 34.
82. Gell, *Under Three Reigns*, pp. 73, 75; Waterson, *Servants' Hall*, p. 161; Morgan and Richards, *Paradise*, p. 221.

CHAPTER 10 RELATIONS BETWEEN EMPLOYERS AND SERVANTS

1. Howard Newby, "The deferential dialectic," *Comparative Studies in Society and History*, 17 (1975), pp. 139–64.
2. Lanceley, *Hall-Boy*, p. 153; King, *Green Baize Door*, pp. 132–3.
3. Harrison, *Gentlemen's Gentlemen*, p. 44.
4. Newby, "Deferential dialectic," pp. 150, 157.
5. Everett, *Bricks and Flowers*, p. 54.
6. Newby, "Deferential dialectic," pp. 155–8.
7. Fred Kitchen, *Brother to the Ox: the Autobiography of a Farm Labourer* (London, 1940; reprinted 1945), pp. 4–5, 17, 19; George Ewart Evans, *Where Beards Wag All: the Relevance of the Oral Tradition* (London, 1970), pp. 123–4.
8. Iley, *Corbridge*, p. 139.
9. Augustus Hare, *Story of My Life*, II, pp. 176–7; Dawes, *Not in Front*, p. 14.
10. Girouard, *English Country House*, p. 143.
11. Cissie Fairchilds, *Domestic Enemies: Servants and their Masters in Old Regime France* (Baltimore, 1984), pp. 143–4, 151.
12. Waterson, *Servants' Hall*, p. 10.
13. Edith Olivier, *Four Victorian Ladies of Wiltshire; with an Essay on Those Leisured Ladies* (London, 1945), p. 62; King, *Green Baize Door*, p.13.
14. Sneyd MSS, Ralph Sneyd to Henry Vincent, 7 May, 15–16 Oct. 1861, S/HWV/RS 421, S/HWV/RS 425.

NOTES, PAGES 242–9

15 Verses by Simon Yorke III and Philip Yorke II at Erddig; Waterson, *Servants' Hall*, pp. 10–11, 110–12.
16 "An Old Servant," *Domestic Service*, pp. 53–4, 69, 76, 101–2; Butler, *John Grey*, p. 323.
17 Badeau, *Aristocracy in England*, pp. 180–1; Allan Jobson, *Under a Suffolk Sky* (London, 1961), p. 161; Robert Wyndham Ketton-Kremer, *Felbrigg: the Story of a House* (London, 1962; paperback edn, 1982), p. 292; J. Gore (ed.), *The Creevey Papers* (London, 1848; revised edn, 1963), p. 228; Horne, *Butler Winked*, p. 99; Badeau, *Aristocracy in England*, p. 181.
18 Badeau, *Aristocracy in England*, p. 180.
19 James, *Our Servants*, p. 24.
20 See, for instance, Mrs Dow, *Hints to Mistresses* (London, 1856), pp. 12–13, 17; Mrs Henderson, *The Young Wife's Own Book: her Domestic Duties and Social Habits* (Glasgow, 1857), p. 7.
21 Northwick MSS, note in account book, 705:66 BA 4221/25; Englefield MS, D/E By A130.
22 Chadwick, *Victorian Miniature*, p. 61.
23 Northwick MSS, rules for servants, 705:66 BA 4221/23.
24 Thomson, *Clifton Lodge*, p. 163.
25 Sitwell, *Left Hand, Right Hand*, p. 74; Bankes and Watkin, *Kingston Lacy Childhood*, p. 35.
26 Horne, *More Winks*, pp. 125–6.
27 Caroline E. Stephen, "Mistress and servant," *Nineteenth Century*, 6 (1879), p. 1054.
28 Thomas in Streatfield, *Day Before Yesterday*, p. 91.
29 Gibbons interviews.
30 Wilson, *Rebel Daughter*, pp. 29, 77–8.
31 Horn, *Victorian Servant*, p. 38.
32 Verey, *Victorian Squire*, p. 84; King, *Green Baize Door*, pp. 25–6; Erddig MS, diary of Louisa Yorke, 17 July 1902, D/E 2816.
33 The Countess of Wemyss, *A Family Record* (London, 1932), p. 29; Charlton, *Northumbrian Lady*, p. 91; Sutherland MSS, Harriet Leveson-Gower, second Duchess of Sutherland to Mrs Ingram, (n.d.), D543/R/10/2; Henley, *Rosalind Howard*, p. 88; Betty Askwith, *A Victorian Young Lady* (Salisbury, 1978), p. 30.
34 Englefield MS, D/E By A130.
35 Ibid; Northwick MSS, memorandum book 1819–44, 705:66 BA 4221/35; agreements with servants, 705:66 BA 4221/23.
36 The best collection of letters concerning hiring of servants I found was in the Packe MSS: 105 letters 1873–87, DE/1346/437. The other major family collections I consulted also include varying numbers of letters, often for one position.

NOTES, PAGES 249–54

[37] Horne, *More Winks*, p. 79; Hare, *Story of My Life*, IV, p. 269.
[38] Packe MS, Augustus Birch to Hussey Packe, 16 June 1878, DE/1346/437.
[39] Cooper, *Town and Country*, p. 30; Willoughby de Broke, "Employer's Conclusion," p. 102.
[40] Cust and Pelham, *Earl of Darnley*, pp. 229–30; Chadwick, *Victorian Miniature*, pp. 70–1.
[41] Anon., *The English Matron* (London, 1846), pp. 50–1; Davidoff, *Best Circles*, p. 35; Hippolyte Taine, *Notes on England* (1872, tr. Edward Hyams, London, 1957), pp. 88–9.
[42] Chadwick, *Victorian Miniature*, p. 74.
[43] Englefield MS, D/E By A130.
[44] Dixon MS, rules for servants, Dixon 22/5/36; Cable in Evans, *From Mouths of Men*, p. 64.
[45] Vulliamy, *Polderoy Papers*, pp. 42–4.
[46] Françoise Barret-Ducrocq, *Love in the Time of Victoria: Sexuality and Desire Among Working-Class Men and Women in Nineteenth-Century London* (London, 1989, tr. John Howe, Harmondsworth, 1992), p. 174.
[47] Lewis, *In the Family Way*, pp. 36–7; Lambert, *Unquiet Souls*, p. 147; Essex archive, interview 38, pp. 11–12.
[48] Thomson, *Clifton Lodge*, p. 36; M. K. Ashby, *Joseph Ashby of Tysoe, 1859–1919: A Study of English Village Life* (Cambridge, 1961; 2nd edn, London, 1974), pp. 1–3; Walter Henry Barrett, *A Fenman's Story* (London, 1965), p. 27.
[49] John Colville, *Strange Inheritance* (London, 1983), pp. 78–91, 96–103.
[50] Lynne Haims found no evidence of this in her research for her dissertation on country house establishments 1850–70. Haims, "In their place," p. 309.
[51] Clark, *Women's Silence*, pp. 107–8.
[52] Vulliamy, *Polderoy Papers*, pp. 94, 98–9, 126–33.
[53] Margaret Meade-Featherstonehaugh and Oliver Warner, *Uppark and its People* (London, 1964), pp. 94–6.
[54] Anita Leslie, *Mr Frewen of England: a Victorian Adventurer* (London, 1966), p. 19.
[55] Marjorie Beach Telling, *Over My Shoulder* (London, 1962), p. 108.
[56] Badeau, *Aristocracy in England*, p. 182.
[57] Verily Anderson, The Northrepps Grandchildren (London, 1968; reprinted Lavenham, 1979), pp. 227–30, 234–5; see also Iley, *Corbridge*, pp.137–8.
[58] Northwick MS, 705:66 BA 4221/23; Ablett MS, rules of servants' hall 1829, DD/DM/87/3, Clwyd Record Office, Ruthin.
[59] Northwick MS, 705:66 BA 4221/23.

[60] Interview with Mrs Eleanor Claydon, Oral History Archives, Kent Public Library, p. 3.
[61] The Earl of Ilchester, *Elizabeth, Lady Holland to Her Son, 1821–1845* (London, 1946), p. 31.
[62] Horne, *Butler Winked*, pp. 62–4, 69, 136, 144–5.
[63] Blackwell, "Landed elite in decline," p. 47; Sneyd MS, Sneyd to Vincent, (n.d.), S/HWV/RS.
[64] Waterson, *Servants' Hall*, pp. 191–3; Bailey, *Diary of Lady Frederick Cavendish*, I, p. 117.
[65] Asquith in Streatfield, *Day Before Yesterday*, p. 119.
[66] Arkwright MS, Lucy Arkwright to John Hungerford Arkwright, 6 Nov. 1894, A63/IV/176.
[67] Sutherland MS, Anne, Duchess of Sutherland to Mrs Ingram, (n.d.), D593/R/10/2.
[68] Anson, *Book*, p. 360.
[69] Harrison, *Rose*, pp. 19–20.
[70] Quoted in Waterson, *Country House Remembered*, p. 194.
[71] Renton, *Tyrant or Victim*, pp. 103–4.
[72] Eric Gillett (ed.), *Elizabeth Ham, by Herself, 1783–1820* (London, 1945), pp. 224, 226, 230.
[73] Winifred Gérin, *Charlotte Brontë: the Evolution of Genius* (Oxford, 1967), p. 149; Spark, *Brontë Letters*, p. 77; Arkwright MS, Lucy Arkwright to John Hungerford Arkwright, 28 Sept. 1881, A63/IV/176.
[74] Winifred Gérin, *Anne Brontë*, p. 128; Spark, *Brontë Letters*, p. 77; Leconfield, *Three Howard Sisters*, pp. 243, 249–50; Poynder in Thompson, *Edwardian Childhoods*, pp. 223, 225.
[75] Hobhouse, *Margaret Hobhouse*, p. 115; Dixon MSS, Miss Robertson's accounts 1866–7, Dixon 10/14/5, Mary Ann Dixon's will, 31 Dec. 1875, Dixon 2/1/12; see also Anthony Glyn, *Elinor Glyn: a Biography* (London, 1955), p. 86.
[76] Vulliamy, *Polderoy Papers*, pp. 136–7, 205, 245, 274.
[77] Essex archives, interview 398, p. 3.
[78] *Servants' Practical Guide*, pp. 127–8.
[79] Carbery, *Happy World*, p. 185.
[80] Haims, "In their place," p. 302.
[81] Lubbock, *Earlham*, pp. 26–7.
[82] Gower, *My Reminiscences*, pp. 145–6.
[83] Thompson, *Lark Rise*, pp. 163–4.
[84] Sutherland MSS, Harriet, Duchess of Sutherland to George Fleming (n.d.), 1856, 1859, 1857–64, D593/K/3/8/4.
[85] Dixon MSS, Dixon 4/14/1–7; Mary Ann Dixon's personal accounts 1833–9, Dixon 10/12/11; household and personal accounts 1858–67, Dixon

10/12/13–14; 10/12/1–9; household accounts, Dixon 1881–1900, 4/18/7–9; diaries of Mrs Jameson Dixon 1895, 1902, 1903, Dixon 10/14/2–4; Gibbons interview.

[86] Firth, *Servant Problem*, p. 20.
[87] See, for instance, Harrison, *Rose*, pp. 1–2.
[88] Badeau, *Aristocracy in England*, pp. 173–4; Alsop, *Lady Sackville*, p. 94.
[89] Dorothy Devenish, *A Wiltshire Home: A Study of Little Dunford* (London, 1948), p. 110.
[90] H. G. Wells, *Tono-Bungay* (London, 1909; paperback edn, London, 1964), pp. 11–12.
[91] Butler, Domestic Service, p. 35; Essex oral history interview no. 59, p. 40; interview with Mrs Mayhew, Kent Oral History Archive, pp. 58–9; Slingsby Smith, *George*, p. 73.
[92] Interview with Miss B. Spier, Kent Oral History Archive, p. 5; see also Essex archive, interview 391, p. 70.
[93] Newby, "Deferential dialectic," p. 145.
[94] Alsop, *Lady Sackville*, p. 94.
[95] Harrison, *Rose*, p. 29.
[96] Booth, "Domestic service," p. 225.
[97] Essex archive, interview 59, pp. 1, 34, 40.
[98] Locker-Lampson, *Life in the Country*, p. 22.
[99] Mary Howard McClintock, *Portrait of a House: a Period Piece* (London, 1948), p. 51.
[100] Ann Estella, Countess Clare, *Odds and Ends of My Life* (London, 1929), p. 79.
[101] Fairfax-Lucy, *Mistress of Charlcote*, pp. 131–2.
[102] Locker-Lampson, *Life in the Country*, p. 123.
[103] "An Old Servant," *Domestic Service*, p. 30; Dixon MS, Mary Ann Dixon to Ann, 5 Feb. 1844, Dixon 10/3/6.
[104] Bankes and Watkins, *Kingston Lacy Childhood*, pp. 55–6.
[105] Lee, in Harrison, *Gentlemen's Gentlemen*, p. 133.
[106] Mary Lawton, *The Queen of Cooks – and Some Kings* (New York, 1925), p. 206.
[107] Elwes, *Fielding Album*, p. 82.
[108] Robert Roberts, *A Ragged Schooling* (Manchester, 1976; paperback edn, London, 1978), p. 82.
[109] Thompson, *Lark Rise*, pp. 108–9, 118; Arthur Barton, *Two Lamps in Our Street: a Time Remembered* (London, 1967), pp. 15, 34, 125, 179–80; Laurie Lee, *Cider With Rosie* (London, 1959; paperback edn, Harmondsworth, 1962), p.114.
[110] Virgoe and Yaxley, *Banville Diaries*, p. 108.

[111] Eliza Lynn Linton, "On the side of the maids," *Cornhill Magazine*, 29 (1874), p. 305.
[112] Lanceley, *Hall-Boy*, p. 152.
[113] Davidoff, "Mastered for life," p. 415; Haims, "In their place," p. 315.
[114] Prestwold MS, DE 1346/437.
[115] Haims, "In their place," p. 317.
[116] Gorst, *Carriages and Kings*, p. 96.
[117] King, *Green Baize Door*, p. 13.
[118] Horne, *Butler Winked*, pp. 110–11; Starkey MS, DDSN X/4.
[119] Charlton, *Northumbrian Lady*, p. 278; Lanceley, *Hall-Boy*, p. 163.
[120] Tweedsmuir, *Lilac and the Rose*, p. 94.
[121] Vulliamy, *Polderoy Papers*, p. 122.
[122] King, *Green Baize Door*, p. 20.
[123] Starkey MS, DDSN X/4; Dyott MS, D661/12/9.
[124] Haims, "In their place," pp. 315–16, 323.
[125] John Pearson, *Stags and Serpents: the Story of the House of Cavendish and the Dukes of Devonshire* (London, 1983), pp. 142–3; Hartcup, *Below Stairs*, p. 192.
[126] Charlton, *Northumbrian Lady*, pp. 195–6, 234, 242, 250, 257.
[127] Lanceley, *Hall-Boy*, p. 154.
[128] Taine, *Notes on England*, p. 90.
[129] Elizabeth Gaskell, *The Life of Charlotte Brontë*, 2 vols (New York, 1857), I, p. 190.
[130] Bailey, *Diary of Lady Frederick Cavendish*, I, p. 11; Asquith, *Haply I May Remember*, p. 208.
[131] Dolly Scannell, *Mother Knew Best: an East End Childhood* (1974; paperback edn, London, 1975), p. 21.
[132] See, for instance, Robin, *Elmdon*, p. 115.
[133] E.W. Martin, *The Shearers and the Shorn: a Study of Life in a Devon Community* (London, 1965), p. 99.
[134] Trevor Lummis and Jan Marsh, *The Woman's Domain: Women and the English Country House* (London, 1990), p. 138.
[135] Horne, *Butler Winked*, p. 46.
[136] Davidoff, "Mastered for life," pp. 406–9.
[137] Horne, *More Winks*, p. 215.
[138] Ibid, pp. 215–16.
[139] Horne, *Butler Winked*, pp. 166–7; Arkwright MS, Sarah Arkwright to John Hungerford Arkwright, Feb. 1864, A63/IV/63.
[140] *Supplement to the Sixty-Fifth Annual Report of the Registrar-General of Births, Deaths, and Marriages in England and Wales*, Part II, *Parliamentary Papers* 18, (1905), pp. xxxiv, clviii, cix.
[141] Vulliamy, *Polderoy Papers*, p. 45; Spencer Pickering (ed.), *Memoirs of Anna*

Maria Wilhemina Pickering (London, 1904), p. 317; Gore, *The Creevey Papers*, p. 243.
[142] Butler, *Domestic Service*, pp. 34–7.

CONCLUSION

[1] Lewis, *In the Family Way*, pp. 56, 223.
[2] This was a phrase coined by Thomas Carlyle in *Chartism* (London 1839), and used by Harold Perkin in discussing the decline of upper-class paternalism in *The Origins of Modern Society, 1780–1880* (London and Toronto, 1969; paperback edn, 1972), pp. 183–95.
[3] Stone, *Family, Sex and Marriage* (abridged edn, Harmondsworth, 1979), p. 426.
[4] Walter Besant, *Fifty Years Ago* (London, 1888), p. 111. For comments along similar lines see also *The English Gentlewoman* (London, 1861), pp. 77–9, and Charles Kingsley's preface to the 1862 edition of *Alton Locke*.
[5] Marshall, *The English Domestic Servant*, p. 28.
[6] "A Butler in a Gentleman's Family," *Hints to Domestic Servants, Addressed More Particularly to Male and Female Servants Connected with the Nobility, Gentry, and Clergy* (London, 2nd edn, 1854), pp. 87–8.
[7] Ralph Nevill (ed.), *My Own Times, by Lady Dorothy Nevill* (London, 1912), p. 244.
[8] Blackwell, "Landed elite in decline," pp. 6, 48, 70.
[9] Lee, in Harrison, *Gentlemen's Gentlemen*, p. 153.

Appendix

Servants' Wages Records

Amner Hall MS: maidservants' wages book 1873–96, MC 40/47.
Ashburnham MS: servants' wages books 1845–1900, ASH 2607, 2609–11.
Bradford MS: wages book 1827–44, 1878–94, D1287/20/1.
Bridehead MS: servants' wages book 1869–1908, D 289.
Brookes MSS: servants' wages 1887–1902, LL 17/278–9.
Davies-Cooke MS: servants' wages book 1863–86, DD. DC/H/4/1.
Chillington MSS: servants' wages books 1833–79, D590/650/1–2.
Davies-Cooke MS: servants' wages book 1863–86, DD. DC/H/4/2.
Derwydd MS: servants' wages book 1890–1913, CA 13.
Dixon MSS: ledger 1824–37, Dixon 4/10; cashbook 1831–4, Dixon 4/14/1; household accounts 1841–6, Dixon 4/14/4; servants' account book 1865–72, Dixon 4/18/10; ledger 1872–93, Dixon 22/4/9; cash book 1893–9, Dixon 22/4/13.
Dyott MS: notebook on servants 1816–41, D661/12/9.
Englefield MSS: servants' wage book 1854–94, D/E By A130; garden labour book 1858–96, D/E By A128.
Erddig MSS: household and personal accounts 1792–1821, D/E 428; household and personal accounts 1835–54, D/E 443; personal and estate accounts 1855–92, D/E 2363; household servants' wage book 1904–18, D/E 467; lists of servants 1907–18, D/E 1134; vouchers 1865–1913, D/E 509.
Frederick MS: wages book 1844–73, 183/36/6/9.
Giffard MS: servants' wages books 1832–79, D590/650/1–2.
Goodwood MSS: servants' wages books 1869–1900, Goodwood 1096, 1097.
Hardwicke Court MS: servants' wages book 1887–1928, D49/1/17.
Hussey MS: footmen's wages book 1874–1941, D49/1/17.
Margam MSS: servants' wages in estate accounts 1857–86, D/D L1/E 87–116.
North MSS: outdoor wages books 1872–85, U471 A170–1; household servants' wages, 1872–82, U471 A184.
Northwick MSS: bundle of servants' wages 1817–18; wages book 1819–44, 705:66 BA 4221/35; memorandum book 1837–58, 705:66 BA 4221/25;

wages book 1859–80, 705:66 BA 4221/23; memorandum book 1854–87, 705:66 BA 4221/17; household accounts 1907–12, 705:66 BA 4221/14.

Packe MSS: house payments books 1869–95, D/E 1346/366–8.

Petworth MSS: servants' wages books 1879–1912, Petworth 3112, 5111.

Pitt-Rivers MSS: household and estate accounts 1885–1901, D396 F79–80.

Radcliffe MS: servants' wages book 1897–1908, Rad I 414.

Shugborough MS: servants' wages book 1817–27, D16/E(H)38.

Sneyd MSS: cash books 1848–65, S2080–S2110.

Southampton MS: servants' wages book 1831–47, CR 1661/1223.

Starkey MS: menservants' wages book 1858–82, DDSN X/4.

Strachey MS: servants' wages book 1852–63, DD/SH 74/28.

Sutherland MSS: vouchers 1815–90, D593/R/2/2–95; undated wages list c 1817–18, D593 R/4/9; servants' wages lists 1840–52, D593 R/4/3–4; servants' wages lists 1875–8, D593 R/4/8.

Taplow Court MS: maidservants' wages book 1908–33, being catalogued.

Trollope-Bellew MS: wages book 1848–76, being catalogued.

Tuffnell MS: servants' wages book 1824–41, D/DTU 301.

Verulam MS: wages book 1895–1911, D/EV/F 271.

Wentworth Woodhouse MSS: voucher books 1809–38, WWM A1526–29; common cash books 1815–24, WWM A1026–1030.

Wynne-Edwards MSS: servants' wages book 1853–71, DD PN 29.

Wyville MS: menservants' wages book 1904–14, ZFW 4/4.

Bibliography

For books, the place of publication is London unless otherwise stated. The original hardback edition is given, rather than a later paperback edition.

PRIMARY SOURCES

Manuscript collections

Ablett MS, servants' rules, Clwyd Record Office (Ruthin).
Amner Hall MS, maidservants' wages book, Norfolk Record Office.
Arkwright MSS, family and household papers, Herefordshire Record Office.
Ashburnham MSS, servants' wages, East Sussex Record Office.
Beaudesert MSS, servants' accounts, Staffordshire Record Office.
Blackett MSS, personal accounts, agreements with servants, Northumberland Record Office.
Blagdon MSS, letters, Northumberland Record Office.
Bradford MSS, servants' wages, Staffordshire Record Office.
Bridehead MS, servants' wages, Dorset Record Office.
Brooks MSS, servants' wages, Bedfordshire Record Office.
Chichester-Constable MSS, servants' diaries and letters, East Riding Record Office.
Codrington MSS, household accounts, Gloucestershire Record Office.
Cornwallis MSS, servants' duties, characters, Kent Archives Office.
Davies-Cooke MS, servants' wages, Doncaster Library, Archives Department.
Derwydd MS, servants' wages, Dyfed County Record Office, Carmarthen.
Dixon MSS, family, household, and estate papers, Lincolnshire Archives Office.
Englefield MSS, servants' wages and rules, Berkshire Record Office.
Erddig MSS, family, household, and estate papers, Clwyd Record Office (Hawarden).
Frederick MS, servants' wages, Surrey Record Office.

Fremantle MSS, letters about servants, Buckinghamshire Record Office.
Giffard MS, servants' wages, Staffordshire Record Office.
Goodwood MSS, servants' wages, West Sussex Record Office.
Hatherton MSS, family and household papers, Staffordshire Record Office.
Heaton MSS, servants' duties, Clwyd Record Office (Ruthin).
Hussey MSS, family and household papers, Kent Archives Office.
Lloyd Baker MSS, servants' wages, Gloucestershire Record Office.
Margam MSS, servants' wages in estate accounts, Glamorgan Archive Service.
North MSS, servants' wages, Kent Archives Office.
Northwick MSS, family and household papers, Worcestershire Record Office.
Packe MSS, family and household papers, Leicestershire Record Office.
Petworth MSS, servants' wages, West Sussex Record Office.
Pitt-Rivers MSS, servants' wages in estate accounts, Dorset Record Office.
Radcliffe MS, servants' wages book, West Yorkshire Archive Service.
Ramsden MSS, letters about servants, Buckinghamshire Record Office.
Shiffner MS, servants' wages, East Sussex Record Office.
Shugborough MSS, servants' wages, job applications, Staffordshire Record Office.
Sneyd MSS, family and household papers, Keele University Library.
Sotherton-Estcourt MS, household accounts, Gloucestershire Record Office.
Southampton MS, servants' wages book 1831–47, Warwick County Record Office.
Strachey MS, wages book, Somerset Record Office.
Sutherland MSS, family, household, and estate papers, Staffordshire Record Office.
Taplow Court MS, maidservants' wages book, Buckinghamshire Record Office.
Tufnell MS, servants' wages, Essex Record Office.
Verulam MS, servants' wages, Hertfordshire Record Office.
Wentworth-Woodhouse MSS, servants' wages and rules, Sheffield City Library.
Wynne-Edwards MSS, servants' wages, Clwyd Record Office (Ruthin).
Wyvill MSS, menservants' wages, North Riding Record Office.

Oral history

Broadsheet IV, WEA, West Oxfordshire Oral History Group.
Kent Oral History Archive, Local History Room, Maidstone Public Library.
Oral History Archives, West Sussex Record Office.
Oral History Projects, "Family life and work before 1918," and "Upper and middle-class families," Sociology Department, University of Essex.
The First World War Memoirs of William Harrison, Oral History Transcript, Imperial War Museum.
Interviews with Misses Joan and Dora Gibbons, and Miss Hetty Stamp, 13–14 Jan. 1979.

BIBLIOGRAPHY

Parliamentary papers and public records

Census Returns, 1841–81, Public Record Office.
Collett, C. E., *Report on the Money Wages of Indoor Domestic Servants, Parliamentary Papers*, 1899, 92.
Parish Registers of Holton-Le-Moor, Holton-Le-Moor Anglican Church.
Parish Registers of Trentham, Trentham Anglican Church.
Parish Registers of Wrexham, Clwyd Record Office (Ruthin).
Register of Births, Deaths and Marriages, St. Catherine's House, London.
Register of Wills, Somerset House.
Return of Owners of Land, 1872–3 (England and Wales), *Parliamentary Papers*, 1874, 72.
Supplement to the Sixty-Fifth Annual Report of the Registrar-General of Births, Deaths and Marriages in England and Wales Part II, *Parliamentary Papers*, 1905, 18.

Principal sources of reference

Bateman, John, *The Great Landowners of Great Britain and Ireland* (final edn), 1883.
Burke's *Landed Gentry* and *Peerage, Baronetcy and Knightage*, all editions.
Cockayne, G. E., *The Complete Baronetage*, Exeter, 1900–9.
———, *The Complete Peerage*, 1910–65.
Kelley's *County Directories*.
Pevsner, Sir Nikolaus et al., *The Buildings of England*, 14 vols, 1951–74.
Walford's *County Families*, all editions.

Newspapers and periodicals

Domestic Gazette, Employer's Circular and Household Emporium, Sept. 1876.
Domestic Register, June–July 1900.
Domestic Servants' Advertiser, May–July 1913.
Domestic Servants' Journal 1875–95.
Field, the Farm, the Garden, the Country Gentleman's Newspaper, 1855–1914.
Hetheringon's Universal Register of Home, Colonial and Foreign Requirements, 1879–83.
Lady, 1885–1914.
Morning Post, 1815–1914.
Queen, the Lady's Newspaper and Court Chronicle, 1861–1914.
Servants' Magazine, 1838–66.
Servants' Register, March 1878.
The Times, 1815–1914.

Landed classes' diaries and letters

Bailey, John (ed.), *The Diary of Lady Frederick Cavendish*, 2 vols, 1927.

Bessborough, Earl of (ed.), *Lady Charlotte Guest: Extracts from her Journal, 1833–1852*, 1950.

——, *Lady Charlotte Schreiber: Extracts from her Journal*, 1952.

Cartwright, Julia (ed.), *The Journals of Lady Knightley of Fawsley*, 1915.

Clive, Mary (ed.), *Caroline Clive: from the Diary and Family Papers of Mrs Archer Clive (1800–1873)*, 1949.

Cust, Lady Elizabeth and Pelham, Evelyn Georgiana (eds), *Edward, Fifth Earl of Darnley and Emma Parnell his Wife: the Story of a Short and Happy Married Life Told in their Own Letters and Other Family Papers*, Leeds, 1913.

Dickinson, Violet (ed.), *Miss Eden's Letters*, 1919.

Gathorne-Hardy, Alfred E. (ed.), *Gathorne-Hardy, First Earl of Cranbrook: a Memoir with Extracts from his Diary and Correspondence*, 2 vols, 1910.

Gore, J. (ed.), *The Creevey Papers*, 1948; revised edn, 1963.

Hope-Nicholson, Jaqueline (ed.), *Life Amongst the Troubridges: Journals of a Young Victorian, 1873–1884, by Laura Troubridge*, 1966.

Ilchester, Earl of (ed.), *Elizabeth, Lady Holland to her Son, 1821–1845*, 1946.

Kennedy, A. L. (ed.), *"My Dear Duchess": Social and Political Letters to the Duchess of Manchester, 1858–1869*, 1956.

Leconfield, Lady (ed.), *Three Howard Sisters: Selections from the Writings of Lady Caroline Lascelles, Lady Dover and Countess Gower, 1825 to 1833*, revised and completed by John Gore, 1955.

Lever, Tresham (ed.), *The Letters of Lady Palmerston, Selected and Edited From the Originals at Broadlands and Elsewhere*, 1957.

Leveson-Gower, Hon. F. (ed.), *The Letters of Harriet Countess of Granville, 1810–1845*, 1894.

Lutyens, Lady Emily, *A Blessed Girl: Memoirs of a Victorian Girlhood Chronicled in an Exchange of Letters, 1887–1896*, 1953.

Mitford, Nancy (ed.), *The Ladies of Alderley: Being the Letters Between Maria Josepha Lady Stanley of Alderley, and her Daughter-in-law, Henrietta Maria Stanley during the Years 1841–1850*, 1938.

——, *The Stanleys of Alderley: Their Letters Between the Years 1851–1865*, 1937.

Oldfield, Susan H. (ed.), *Some Records of the Later Life of Harriet, Countess Granville*, 1901.

Ridley, Viscountess (ed.), *Cecilia: the Life and Letters of Cecilia Ridley, 1819–1845*, 1958.

Russell, Bertrand and Patricia (eds), *The Amberley Papers: the Letters and Diaries of Lord and Lady Amberley*, 2 vols, 1973.

Stirling, A. M. W. (ed.), *The Letter-Bag of Lady Elizabeth Spencer-Stanhope, compiled from the Cannon Hall Papers, 1806–1873*, 2 vols, 1913.

Verey, David (ed.), *The Diary of a Victorian Squire: Extracts from the Diaries and Letters of Dearman and Emily Birchall*, Gloucester, 1983.
Vulliamy, C. E. (ed.), *The Polderoy Papers*, 1943.
Wyndham, Hon. Mrs Hugh (ed.), *Correspondence of Sarah Spencer, Lady Lyttleton, 1787–1870*, New York, 1912.

Servants' diaries and letters

Howell-Thomas, Dorothy (ed.), *Goodwood: Letters from Below Stairs*, Goodwood, 1976.
Stanley, Liz (ed.), *The Diaries of Hannah Cullwick: Victorian Maidservant*, New Brunswick, 1984.
Virgoe, Norma and Yaxley, Susan (eds), *The Banville Diaries: Journals of a Norfolk Gamekeeper, 1822–1844*, 1986.

Domestic service

Adams, Samuel and Sarah, *The Complete Servant: Being a Practical Guide to the Peculiar Duties and Business of all Descriptions of Servants . . . with Useful Receipts and Table*, 1825.
Anderson, Nellie Lockhart, "A servant's view of the Servant Problem," *National Review*, 61, 1913.
Bayliss, T. Henry, *Rights, Duties and Relations of Domestic Servants and their Masters and Mistresses, With a Short Account of Servants' Institutions, and their Advantages*, 4th edn, 1873.
Beeton, Isabella, *The Book of Household Management: Comprising Information for the Mistress, Housekeeper, Cook, Kitchen-maid, Butler, Footman, Coachman, Valet, Upper and Under House-maids, Lady's-maid, Maid-of-all-work, Laundry-maid, Nurse and Nurse-maid, Monthly, Wet, and Sick Nurses, etc. etc. Also, Sanitary, Medical, & Legal Memoranda; With a History of the Origin, Properties, and Uses of All Things Connected with Home Life and Comfort*, 1861.
——, *How to Manage House, Servants, and Children*, 1871.
Benson, M. E., "In defence of domestic service: a reply," *Nineteenth Century*, 28, 1890.
Bird, M. Mostyn, *Woman at Work: a Study of the Different Ways of Earning a Living Open to Women*, 1911.
Black, Clementina, "The dislike to domestic service," *Nineteenth Century*, 33, 1893.
——, *Married Women's Work: Being the Report of an Inquiry Undertaken by the Women's Industrial Council*, 1915.
Booth, Charles, "Domestic service," in *Life and Labour of the People in London*, Series 2, Industry 4, 1903.

Broadhurst, S., "A plea for the domestic servant," *Macmillan's Magazine*, 80, 1899.
Bunting, M. H. L., "Mistress and maid," *Contemporary Review*, 108, 1910.
Butler, C. V., *Domestic Service: an Enquiry by the Women's Industrial Council*, 1916.
"A Butler in a Gentleman's Family," *Hints to Domestic Servants, Addressed More Particularly to Male and Female Servants Connected with the Nobility, Gentry and Clergy*, 2nd edn, 1854.
Capes, J. M., "On the side of the maids," *Cornhill Magazine*, 29, 1874.
Cassell's Household Guide; Being a Complete Encyclopaedia of Domestic and Social Economy, and Forming a Guide to Every Department of Practical Life, 3 vols, 1870.
Crawshay, Rose Mary, *Domestic Service for Gentlewomen*, 1877.
Darwin, Ellen W., "Domestic service," *Nineteenth Century*, 28, 1890.
"Domestic service – Nelly Armstrong," *North British Review*, 39, 1853–4.
Dow, Mrs, *Hints to Mistresses*, 1856.
——, *Hints to Young Women About to Enter Into Service*, 1855.
The Family Manual and Servants' Guide, 7th edn, 1856.
The Good Nurse; or, Hints on the Management of the Sick and Lying-in Chamber and the Nursery, 1825.
Greville, Lady Violet, "Men-servants in England," *National Review*, 18, 1892.
Haweis, Mrs Mary Eliza, *The Art of Housekeeping*, 1889.
"Internuncio," *Mistresses and Servants*, 1865.
James, Mrs Eliot, *Our Servants: their Duties to Us and Ours to Them*, 1883.
Jefferies, Richard, *The Gamekeeper at Home*, 1881.
Jeune, Lady, "The Servant Question," *Fortnightly Review*, 52, 1892.
Kitchener, William, *The Housekeeper's Oracle: or, Art of Domestic Management*, 1829.
"A Lady," *The Home Book, or Young Housekeeper's Assistant*, 1829.
Lady Servants – For and Against, 1906.
The Lady's Maid: her Duties, and How to Perform Them, 1877.
Layard, George S., "The doom of the domestic cook," *Nineteenth Century*, 33, 1893.
Layton, W. T., "Changes in the wages of domestic servants during fifty years," *Journal of the Royal Statistical Society*, 71, 1908.
Lewis, Elizabeth Alicia M., "A reformation of domestic service," *Nineteenth Century*, 33, 1893.
Linton, Eliza Lynn, "On the side of the maids," *Cornhill Magazine*, 29, 1874.
L. M. H. (ed.), *The Handbook of Women's Work*, 1876.
McCall, Mrs Dorothy Home, "Another aspect of the Servant Problem," *National Review*, 60, 1913.
"Maid Servants," *Fraser's Magazine for Town and Country*, 28, 1843.
Mann, T. G., *The Duties of an Experienced Servant*, 1847.

Martineau, Harriet, "Modern domestic service," *Nineteenth Century*, 115, 1862.
Massey, Mrs E. M., *Girls Entering Service*, Derby, 1914.
Maurice, Mary, *Governess Life: its Trials, Duties and Encouragements*, 1849.
"A Member of the Aristocracy," *The Servants' Practical Guide: a Handbook of Duties and Rules*, 1880.
A Mistress's Council: or, a Few Words to Servants, 1871.
A New System of Practical Domestic Economy, Founded on Modern Discoveries and the Private Communications of Persons of Experience (revised and enlarged edn), 1827.
"An old housekeeper," *Household Management*, 1877.
"An old servant," *Domestic Service*, Boston, 1917.
Oram, G., *Masters and Servants: their Relative Duties*, 1858.
Panton, J. E., *Leaves from a Housekeeper's Book*, 1914.
Parkes, Bessie Rayner, "The profession of the teacher. The Annual Reports of the Governesses Benevolent Institution, from 1843 to 1856," *English Woman's Journal*, 1, 1858.
"A plea for the domestic servant," *Macmillan's Magazine*, 80, 1899.
Rayner, John, *Employers and Their Female Domestics: their Respective Rights and Responsibilities*, 1895.
Reaney, Mrs G. S., *Woman's Sphere; or the Dignity of Domestic Work*, 1913.
Robinson, John, "A butler's view of men-service," *Nineteenth Century*, 31, 1892.
G. S., *The Governess* (n.d.).
Salmon, Edward, "Domestic service and democracy," *Fortnightly Review*, 49, 1888.
Stephen, Caroline E., "Mistress and servants," *Nineteenth Century*, 6, 1879.
Tytler, Elisabeth, "The eternal Servant Problem," *National Review*, 53, 1909.
"Vanity Fair and Jane Eyre," *Quarterly Review*, 84, 1848.
Waldemar-Leverton, Mrs, *Servants and their Duties: a Helpful Manual for Mistress and Servant*, 1912.
Walsh, J. H., *A Manual of Domestic Economy, Suited to Families Spending From £100 to £1000 a Year* (2nd edn), 1857.
Watkins, H. G., *Hints and Observations Seriously Addressed to Heads of Families In Reference, Chiefly, to Female Domestic Servants*, 1816.
Webb, Catharine, "An unpopular industry," *Nineteenth Century*, 53, 1903.
Webster, Thomas and Parkes, Mrs, *An Encyclopaedia of Domestic Economy, Comprising Such Subjects as are Most Immediately Connected with Housekeeping*, 1844.
Willoughby de Broke, Lady, "The pros and cons of domestic service," *National Review*, 60, 1912.

Other

Ansell, Charles, *Statistics of Families in the Upper and Professional Classes*, 1874.
Badeau, Adam, *Aristocracy in England*, New York, 1886.

Bancroft, Elisabeth Davis, *Letters from England, 1846–49*, 1904.
Baring-Gould, Sabine, *Old Country Life*, 1892.
Berkeley, Grantley F., *Anecdotes of the Upper Ten Thousand*, 2 vols, 1867.
Bosanquet, Helen, *The Family*, 1906.
Bourne, George, *Change in the Village*, 1912.
Braidwell, P. M., *Domestic Management of Children*, 1874.
Bull, Thomas, *Hints to Mothers for the Management of Health During the Period of Pregnancy, and in the Lying-in Room*, 1864.
Bulwer-Lytton, Edward, *England and the English*, 2 vols, 1833.
Burdett-Coutts, Baroness (ed.), *Woman's Mission*, 1893.
Burne, Mrs W. Pitt, *Social Hours with Celebrities*, 2 vols, 1898.
Butler, E. M. (ed.), *A Regency Visitor: the English Tour of Prince Pückler-Muskau Described in his Letters, 1826–28*, 1957.
Chavasse, Pye Henry, *Advice to a Mother on the Management of Her Children, and on the Treatment on the Moment of Some of Their More Pressing Illnesses and Accidents*, 1839.
Colton, Calvin, *Four Years in Great Britain*, New York, 1836.
Cox, Alfred, *The Landlord's and Tenant's Guide*, 1852.
Dana, Richard Henry, *Hospitable England in the Seventies: the Diary of a Young American, 1875–1876*, Boston, 1921.
Ditchfield, P. H., *The Old English Country Squire*, 1912.
Dow, Mrs, *Hints to Wives and Mothers*, 1856.
Early Influences (new edn), 1883.
Ellis, Sarah Stickney, *The Daughters of England: their Position in Society, Character and Responsibilities*, 1845.
——, *The Mothers of England: their Influence and Responsibility*, 1843.
——, *The Wives of England*, 1843.
——, *The Women of England* (2nd edn), 1839.
The English Gentlewoman: or, Hints to Young Ladies on their Entrance into Society, 1845.
The English Matron, 1846.
Escott, T. H. S., *England: its People, Polity, and Pursuits*, 2 vols, 1879.
Fay, Anna Maria, *Victorian Days in England: Letters of an American Girl, 1851–52*, Boston, 1923.
The Female Instructor: or, Young Woman's Friend and Companion, 1830.
Fletcher, Ronald (ed.), *The Biography of a Victorian Village: Richard Cobbold's Account of Wortham, Suffolk, 1860*, 1977.
Gaskell, C. M., "Women of to-day," *Nineteenth Century*, 26, 1889.
Greville, Lady Violet, *The Gentlewoman in Society*, 1892.
Hawthorne, Nathaniel, *English Notebooks*, 1894.
Hays, Frances, *Women of the Day*, 1885.
Henderson, Mrs, *The Young Wife's Own Book: Her Domestic Duties and Social Habits*, Glasgow, 1857.

Hill, Georgiana, *Women in English Life, From Medieval to Modern Times*, 2 vols, 1896.
Hoare, Louisa, *Hints for the Improvement of Early Education and Nursery Discipline*, 1819.
Howitt, W., *The Rural Life of England*, 2 vols, 1838.
Humphry, Mrs, *Manners for Women*, 1897.
Inglis, James, *Home, Marriage and Family Relations*, 1885.
Jameson, Anna B., *Memoirs and Essays Illustrative of Art, Literature and Social Morals*, 1946.
Jefferies, Richard, *Hodge and his Masters*, 2 vols, 1880.
——, *The Toilers of the Field*, 1892.
Jeune, Lady, *Lesser Questions*, 1894.
Kebbel, T. E., *The Old and the New English Country Life*, 1891.
Kerr, Robert, *The Gentleman's House: or, How to Plan English Residences from the Parsonage to the Palace*, 1864.
Kilvert, Adelaide Sophia, *Home Discipline*, 1851.
Kingsley, Charles, *Lectures to Ladies on Practical Subjects* (revised edn), 1857.
"A Lady in Society," *The New Book of Etiquette*, 1907.
Landels, William, *Woman: her Position and Power*, 1870.
Lewis, Sarah, *Woman's Mission*, 1839.
Linton, Eliza Lynn, *The Girl of the Period and Other Essays*, 1883.
Loudon, J. C., *Encyclopaedia of Cottage, Farm and Villa Architecture*, 1833.
Manners Makyth Men, 1887.
Manners of Modern Society, 1872.
Mitford, Mary Russell, *Our Village*, 1848.
"One of themselves," *The Manners of the Aristocracy*, 1881.
"One who is in it," "Society as it is," *Lady*, May, 1885.
Papworth, John B., *Rural Residences*, 1818.
Pedley, Mrs, *Infant Nursing and the Management of Young Children*, 1866.
Ponsonby, Arthur, *The Decline of Aristocracy*, 1912.
Robinson, P. F., *Rural Architecture; or, a Series of Designs for Ornamental Cottages* (5th edn), 1850.
Rowntree, B. Seebohm and Kendall, Mary, *How the Labourer Lives*, 1913.
Ruskin, John, *Sesame and Lilies*, 1882.
Sandford, Mrs John, *Woman, in her Social and Domestic Character*, 1831.
——, *Female Improvement*, 1836.
Scott, George Gilbert, *Remarks on Secular and Domestic Architecture, Present and Past*, 1857.
Sewell, Elizabeth Missing, *Principles of Education, Drawn From Nature and Revelation and Applied to Female Education in the Upper Classes*, 1866.
Starforth, J., *The Architecture of the Park*, 1890.
Stowe, Harriet Beecher, *Sunny Memories of Foreign Lands*, 1854.

Sumner, Mary Elizabeth, *Nursery Training*, 1892.
Taine, Hippolyte, *Notes on England*, 1872, trans. Edward Hyams, 1957.
Veblen, Thorstein, *The Theory of the Leisure Class*, New York, 1899.
Weaver, Lawrence, *The "Country Life" Book of Cottages*, 1913.
Whetham, Sir William C. Dampier and Catherine Durning, *The Family and the Nation: a Study in Natural Inheritance and Social Responsibility*, 1909.
Wilkinson, William, *English Country Houses*, 1870.
Willis, N. P., *Pencillings by the Way*, 3 vols, 1835.
Yonge, Charlotte M., *Womankind*, 1876.

SECONDARY SOURCES

Autobiographies of the landed classes

Acland, Eleanor, *Goodbye for the Present: the Story of Two Childhoods, Milly: 1878–88 & Ellen: 1913–24*, New York, 1935.
Amherst, Jeffrey, *Wandering Abroad*, 1976.
Anson, Lady Clodagh, *Another Book*, 1937.
———, *Book: Discreet Memoirs*, 1931.
Asquith, Cynthia, *Haply I May Remember*, 1950.
———, *Remember and Be Glad*, 1952.
Astor, Michael, *Tribal Feeling*, 1963.
Balfour, Lady Frances, *Ne Obliviscaris*, 2 vols, 1930.
Balsan, Consuelo Vanderbilt, *The Glitter and the Gold*, 1953.
Bankes, Viola and Watkin, Pamela, *A Kingston Lacy Childhood: Reminiscences of Viola Bankes*, Stanbridge, 1986.
Barrington, Charlotte, Viscountess, *Through Eighty Years (1855–1935)*, 1936.
Battersea, Constance, Lady, *Reminiscences*, 1922.
Beale, Erica (ed.), *Memories of Three Reigns by Ethel Raglan*, 1928.
Beckwith, Lady Muriel, *When I Remember*, 1936.
Bedford, Hastings, Duke of, *The Years of Transition*, 1949.
Bedford, John, Duke of, *A Silver-Plated Spoon*, 1959.
Berners, Lord, *First Childhood*, 1934.
Cadogan, The Hon. Sir Edward, *Before the Deluge: Memories and Reflections, 1880–1914*, 1961.
Carbery, Mary, *Happy World: the Story of a Victorian Childhood*, 1941.
Cardigan and Lancastre, The Countess of, *My Recollections*, 1909.
Carnarvon, Earl of, *No Regrets*, 1976.
Castlerosse, Viscount, *Valentine's Days*, 1934.
Chapman-Huston, Major Desmond (ed.), *Daisy, Princess of Pless, by Herself*, 1929.

Charlton, L. E. O. (ed.), *The Recollections of a Northumbrian Lady, 1815–1866; Being the Memoirs of Barbara Charlton (née Tasburgh), Wife of William Henry Charlton of Hesleyside, Northumberland*, 1949.
Clare, Ann Estella, Countess, *Odds and Ends of My Life*, 1929.
Clive, Mary, *The Day of Reckoning*, 1964.
Colville, Lady Cynthia, *Crowded Life: the Autobiography of Lady Cynthia Colville*, 1963.
Cooper, Diana, *The Rainbow Comes and Goes*, 1958.
Cornwallis-West, George G., *Edwardian Hey-Days; or, a Little About a Lot of Things*, 1930.
Cunliffe, Emma (ed.), *Pages from the Life of John Sparling of Petton, Edinburgh*, 1904.
Desart, Earl of and Lubbock, Lady Sybil, *A Page from the Past: Memories of the Earl of Desart*, 1936.
Devenish, Dorothy, *A Wiltshire Home: a Study of Little Durnford*, 1948.
Douglas, Lord Alfred, *The Autobiography of Lord Alfred Douglas*, 1929.
Dugdale, Blanche, *Family Homespun*, 1940.
Eden, Anthony, *Another World, 1897–1917*, 1968.
Egremont, Lord, *Wyndham and Children First*, 1968.
Ellis, Jennifer (ed.), *Thatched with Gold: the Memoirs of Mabell, Countess of Airlie*, 1962.
Elwes, Winefride, *The Fielding Album*, 1950.
Everett, Katherine, *Bricks and Flowers: Memoirs of Katherine Everett*, 1949.
Fairfax-Lucy, Alice (ed.), *Mistress of Charlecote: the Memoirs of Mary Elizabeth Lucy*, 1983.
Fane, Lady Augusta, *Chit-Chat*, 1926.
Fielden, Lionel, *The Natural Bent*, 1960.
Fielding, Daphne, *Mercury Presides*, 1954.
Forbes, Lady Angela, *Memories and Base Details*, 1921.
Fremantle, Anne, *Three-Cornered Heart*, 1948.
Gage, Lord, *Memories of Firle*, Tisbury, 1979.
Gell, the Hon. Mrs Edith Mary, *Under Three Reigns, 1860–1920*, 1927.
Gower, Lord Ronald, *My Reminiscences*, 1883.
Greville, Lady Violet, *Vignettes of Memory*, 1927.
Haggard, H. Rider, *The Days of my Life*, 2 vols, 1920.
Haldane, Elizabeth S., *From One Century to Another*, 1937.
—— (ed.), *Mary Elizabeth Haldane: a Record of a Hundred Years (1825–1925)*, 1925.
Halifax, Earl of, *Fullness of Days*, 1957.
Heber-Percy, Cyril, *Us Four*, 1963.
Horner, Lady Frances, *Time Remembered*, 1933.

Jalland, Pat (ed.), *Octavia Wilberforce: the Autobiography of a Pioneer Woman Doctor*, 1989.
Jersey, the Dowager Countess of, *Fifty-One Years of Victorian Life*, 1922.
Jones, E. E. Constance, *As I Remember: an Autobiographical Ramble*, 1922.
Jones, L. E., *A Victorian Boyhood*, 1955.
Leveson-Gower, Sir George, *Years of Content, 1858–1886*, 1940.
Lewis, Lesley, *The Private Life of a Country House, 1912–39*, 1980.
Londonderry, Marchioness of, *Retrospect*, 1938.
Lubbock, Percy, *Earlham*, 1922.
Malmesbury, Earl of, *Memoirs of an Ex-Minister*, 1884.
McClintock, Mary Howard, *Portrait of a House: a Period Piece*, 1948.
Meynell, Lady Mary, *Sunshine and Shadows Over a Long Life*, 1933.
Milner, Viscountess, *My Picture Gallery, 1886–1901*, 1951.
Munster, Countess of, *My Memories and Miscellanies*, 1904.
Nevill, Ralph (ed.), *Leaves from the Notebooks of Lady Dorothy Nevill*, 1907.
—— (ed.), *My Own Times by Lady Dorothy Nevill*, 1912.
—— (ed.), *The Reminiscences of Lady Dorothy Nevill*, 1907.
——, *Unconventional Memories*, 1923.
—— (ed.), *Under Five Reigns by Lady Dorothy Nevill*, 1910.
——, *Yesterday and Today*, 1922.
Onslow, the Earl of, *Sixty-Three Years: Diplomacy, the Great War and Politics, with Notes on Travel, Sport and Other Things*, 1944.
Peel, Ethel (ed.), *Recollections of Lady Georgiana Peel*, 1920.
Percy, Lord Eustace, *Some Memories*, 1958.
Pickering, Spencer (ed.), *Memoirs of Anna Maria Wilhemina Pickering*, 1904.
Picton-Turbervill, Edith, *Life is Good: an Autobiography*, 1939.
Powell, Violet, *Within the Family Circle: an Autobiography*, 1976.
Radnor, Helen, Dowager Countess of, *From a Great-Grandmother's Armchair*, 1927.
Ravensdale, Baroness, *In Many Rhythms: an Autobiography*, 1953.
Ribbesdale, Lord, *Impressions and Memories*, 1937.
Russell, Hon. George W. E., *Fifteen Chapters of Autobiography*, 1908.
St Helier, Lady, *Memories of Fifty Years*, 1908.
Sebright, Arthur, *A Glance into the Past*, 1922.
Sitwell, Edith, *Taken Care Of*, 1965.
Sitwell, Osbert, *Left Hand, Right Hand: an Autobiography*, 1946.
—— (ed.), *Two Generations*, 1940.
Stirling, A. M. W., *Life's Little Day*, 1924.
——, *A Scrapbook of Memories*, 1960.
Sutherland, Duke of, *Looking Back*, 1957.
Talbot, Matilda, *My Life and Lacock Abbey*, 1956.
Tallents, Sir Stephen, *Man and Boy*, 1943.

Tweedsmuir, Susan, *The Lilac and the Rose*, 1952.
Wake, Lucy (ed.), *The Reminiscences of Charlotte, Lady Wake*, 1909.
Warwick, Frances, Countess of, *Afterthoughts*, 1931.
——, *Life's Ebb and Flow*, New York, 1929.
Wemyss, Countess of, *A Family Record*, 1932.
Westminster, Loelia, Duchess of, *Grace and Favour*, 1961.
White, John Baker, *True Blue: an Autobiography, 1902–1939*, 1970.
Willoughby de Broke, Lord, *The Passing Years*, 1924.
Wood, Mary and Alan (eds), *Silver Spoon: Being Extracts From the Random Reminiscences of Lord Grantley*.
Yandell, Elizabeth, *Henry*, 1974.

Biographies and family histories of the landed classes

Acland, Arthur H. D., *Memoir and Letters of the Right Hon. Sir Thomas Dyke Acland*, 1902.
Adamson, Donald and Dewar, Peter Beauclerk, *The House of Nell Gwyn: the Fortunes of the Beauclerk Family, 1670–1974*, 1974.
Adelson, Roger, *Mark Sykes: Portrait of an Amateur*, 1975.
Alsop, Susan Mary, *Lady Sackville: a Biography*, New York, 1978.
Anderson, Verily, *The Northrepps Grandchildren*, 1968.
Askwith, Betty, *The Lyttletons: a Family Chronicle of the Nineteenth Century*, 1975.
——, *A Victorian Young Lady*, Salisbury, 1978.
Bagley, J. J., *The Earls of Derby*, 1985.
Battiscombe, Georgiana, *Mrs Gladstone: the Portrait of a Marriage*, 1956.
Beastell, T. W., *A North Country Estate: the Kinleys and Saundersons as Landowners, 1600–1900*, 1975.
Bermont, Chaim, *The Cousinhood: the Anglo-Jewish Gentry*, 1971.
Birkenhead, the Earl of, *Halifax: the Life of Lord Halifax*, 1965.
Blakiston, Georgiana, *Woburn and the Russells*, 1980.
Blyth, Henry, *The Pocket Venus: a Victorian Scandal*, 1966.
Buchan, Alice, *A Scrap Screen*, 1979.
Buchan, Susan, *John Buchan, by his Wife and Friends*, 1947.
Burnett, David, *Longleat: the Story of an English Country House*, 1978.
Butler, Evan, *The Cecils: the Story of a Great English Family Through Four Centuries*, 1964.
Butler, Josephine, *Memoir of John Grey of Dilston*, 1869.
Campbell, Barry, *The Badminton Tradition*, 1978.
Cartwright-Hignett, Elizabeth, *Lili at Aynhoe: Victorian Life in an English Country House*, 1989.
Cecil, David, *The Cecils of Hatfield House*, 1973.

Cecil, Lady Gwendoline, *The Life of Robert Marquis of Salisbury*, 4 vols, 1921–32.
Chadwick, Owen, *Victorian Miniature*, 1960.
Childe-Pemberton, William S., *Life of Lord Norton*, 1909.
Churchill, Randolph S., *Lord Derby, "King of Lancashire,"* 1959.
——, *Winston S. Churchill*, Vol. 1, *Youth, 1874–1900*, 1966.
Cohen, Lucy, *Lady de Rothschild and Her Daughters, 1821–1931*, 1935.
Cohen, Morton, *Rider Haggard: his Life and Work*, 1968.
Collis, Maurice, *Nancy Astor: an Informal Biography*, 1960.
Colville, John, *Strange Inheritance*, 1983.
Colvin, Howard, *Calke Abbey Derbyshire: a Hidden House Revealed*, 1985.
Devonshire, Duchess of, *The House*, 1982.
Dutton, Ralph, *Hinton Ampner: a Hampshire Manor*, 1969.
Fairfax-Lucy, Alice, *Charlcote and the Lucys: the Chronicle of an English Family*, 1958.
Fielding, Nancy, *Emerald and Nancy: Lady Cunard and her Daughter*, 1968.
Fitzpatrick, Kathleen, *Lady Henry Somerset*, 1923.
Fowler, Marian, *Blenheim: Biography of a Palace*, 1989.
Gathorne-Hardy, Alfred E., *Gathorne-Hardy, First Earl of Cranbrook: a Memoir, with Extracts from His Diary and Correspondence*, 2 vols, 1910.
Glyn, Antony, *Elinor Glyn: A Biography*, 1955.
Gurney, Samuel, *Isabel, Mrs Gurney, Afterwards the Lady Talbot de Malahide, 1851–1932*, Norwich, 1935.
Henley, Dorothy, *Rosalind Howard, Countess of Carlisle*, 1959.
Hobhouse, Stephen, *Margaret Hobhouse and her Family*, Rochester, 1934.
Hodder, Edwin, *The Life and Work of the Seventh Earl of Shaftesbury*, 3 vols, 1886.
Howell-Thomas, Dorothy, *Lord Melbourne's Susan*, 1978.
Huxley, Gervais, *Lady Elizabeth and the Grosvenors: Life in a Whig Family, 1822–1839*, 1965.
——, *Victorian Duke: The Life of Hugh Lupus Grosvenor, First Duke of Westminster*, 1967.
Hyde, H. Montgomery, *The Londonderrys: a Family Portrait*, 1979.
Ketton-Kremer, Robert Wyndham, *Felbrigg: The Story of a House*, 1962.
Kolbert, J. M., *The Sneyds & Keele Hall*, Keele University, 1967.
——, *The Sneyds: Squires of Keele Hall*, Keele University, 1976.
Leslie, Anita, *Mr Frewen of England: a Victorian Adventurer*, 1966.
Lever, Tresham, *The Herberts of Wilton*, 1967.
Londonderry, Edith, Marchioness of, *Frances Anne: the Life and Times of Frances Anne, Marchioness of Londonderry and her Husband Charles, Third Marquess of Londonderry*, 1958.
Longford, Elizabeth, *A Pilgrimage of Passion: the Life of Wilfrid Scawen Blunt*, 1979.

Markham, Geoffrey, *Woolley Hall: the Historical Development of a Country House*, Wakefield, 1979.
Marlow, Joyce, *Mr and Mrs Gladstone: An Intimate Biography*, 1977.
Martineau, John, *The Life of Sir Bartle Frere*, 1895.
——, *The Life of Henry Pelham, Fifth Duke of Newcastle, 1811–1864*, 1908.
Mauchline, Mary, *Harewood House*, Newton Abbot, 1974.
Meade-Featherstonehaugh, Margaret and Warner, Oliver, *Uppark and its People*, 1964.
More, Jasper, *A Tale of Two Houses*, Shrewsbury, 1978.
Munsell, F. Darrell, *The Unfortunate Duke: Henry Pelham, Fifth Duke of Newcastle, 1811–1864*, Columbia, 1985.
Nevill, Ralph, *The Life and Letters of Lady Dorothy Nevill*, 1919.
Newman, Aubrey, *The Stanhopes of Chevening, a Family Biography*, 1969.
Oldfield, Susan H., *Some Records of the Later Life of Harriet, Countess Granville*, 1901.
Oman, Carola, *The Gascoyne Heiress: The Life and Diaries of Frances Mary Gascoyne-Cecil*, 1968.
Pearson, John, *Façades: Edith, Osbert and Sacheverell Sitwell*, 1978.
——, *Stags & Serpents: the Story of the House of Cavendish and the Dukes of Devonshire*, 1983.
Powell, Violet, *Margaret, Countess of Jersey: a Biography*, 1978.
Roberts, Charles, *The Radical Countess: the History of the Life of Rosalind, Countess of Carlisle*, Carlisle, 1962.
Robinson, John Martin, *The Dukes of Norfolk: a Quincentennial History*, Oxford, 1982.
Rose, Kenneth, *Superior Person: a Portrait of Curzon and his Circle in Late Victorian England*, 1969.
Rothschild, Mrs James de, *The Rothschilds at Waddesdon Manor*, 1979.
Russell, George W. E., *Lady Victoria Buxton: a Memoir*, 1919.
——, *Portraits of the Seventies*, 1916.
——, *Sir Wilfrid Lawrence: a Memoir*, 1919.
Schmidt, Margaret Fox, *Passion's Child: the Extraordinary Life of Jane Digby*, 1976.
Stuart, Denis, *Dear Duchess: Millicent, Duchess of Sutherland, 1867–1955*, 1982
Stuart, Vivian, *The Beloved Admiral: the Life and Times of Admiral of the Fleet, the Hon. Sir Henry Keppel, 1809–1904*, 1967.
Surtees, Virginia, *A Beckford Inheritance: the Lady Lincoln Scandal*, 1977.
Sykes, Christopher, *Four Studies in Loyalty*, 1946.
Sykes, Christopher Simon, *The Visitors' Book: a Family Album*, New York, 1978.
Taylor, Fanny M., *The Inner Life of Lady Georgiana Fullerton*, 1899.
Trevelyan, G. M., *Grey of Falloden*, 1937.

Vulliamy, C. E., *The Onslow Family, 1528–1874, With Some Account of their Times,* 1953.
Wake, Joan, *The Brudenells of Deene* (revised edn), 1954.
Wavell, General Sir Archibald, *Allenby: a Study in Greatness,* 1940.
Weigall, Rachel, *Lady Rose Weigall,* New York, 1923.
Wilson, Francesca M., *Rebel Daughter of a Country House: the Life of Eglantyne Jebb, Founder of the Save the Children Fund,* 1967.
Wingfield-Stratford, Esmé, *The Lords of Cobham Hall,* 1959.
Winn, Colin G., *The Poulets of Hinton St George,* 1976.
Woodham-Smith, Cecil, *Florence Nightingale, 1820–1910,* 1950.
Ziegler, Philip, *Diana Cooper,* 1981.

Collected autobiographies

Barr, Pat (ed.), *I Remember: an Arrangement for Many Voices,* 1970.
Barry, Lady Margaret and Smith, Mrs Gertrude, *Lady Margaret Barry & Mrs Gertrude Smith,* Ipswich, 1976.
Blythe, Ronald, *Akenfield: Portrait of an English Village,* 1969.
———, *The View in Winter: Reflections on Old Age,* 1979.
Burnett, John (ed.), *Useful Toil: Autobiographies of Working People from the 1820s to the 1920s,* 1974.
———, *Destiny Obscure: Autobiographies of Childhood, Education and Family from the 1820s to the 1920s,* 1982.
Davies, Margaret Llewelyn (ed.), *Life as We Have Known It: by Co-operative Working Women,* 1931.
Harrison, Rosina (ed.), *Gentlemen's Gentlemen: My Friends in Service,* 1976.
Kightly, Charles (ed.), *Country Voices: Life and Lore in English Farm and Village,* 1984.
Oxford and Asquith, Countess of (ed.), *Myself When Young: by Famous Women of To-day,* 1938.
Pryce-Jones, Alan (ed.), *Little Innocents: Childhood Reminiscences,* 1932.
Streatfield, Noel (ed.), *The Day Before Yesterday: Firsthand Stories of Fifty Years Ago,* 1956.
Thompson, Thea (ed.), *Edwardian Childhoods,* 1981.
Waterson, Merlin (ed.), *The Country House Remembered: Recollections of Life Between the Wars,* 1985.

Servants' autobiographies and biographies

Anon, *The Memories of a Lady's Maid,* 1938.
Armstrong, Violet E., "In service at Wrest Park," *Bedfordshire Magazine,* 19, 1984.

Cooper, Charles, *Town and Country: or, Forty Years in Service with the Aristocracy*, 1937.
Field, Ernest, "Gardening memories at Halton," *Country Life*, 154, 11 Oct. 1973.
Gillet, Eric (ed.), *Elizabeth Ham, by Herself, 1783–1820*, 1945.
Gorst, Frederick John, with Beth Andrews, *Of Carriages and Kings*, 1956.
Harrison, Michael, *Rosa*, 1962.
Harrison, Rosina, *Rose: My Life in Service*, 1975.
Horne, Eric, *What the Butler Winked At: Being the Life and Adventures of Eric Horne (Butler), for Fifty-Seven Years in Service with the Nobility and Gentry*, 1923.
——, *More Winks: Being Further Notes from the Life and Adventures of Eric Horne (Butler), for Fifty-Seven Years in Service with the Nobility and Gentry*, 1923.
"Housekeeping at Shugborough," Information Sheet FL5, Staffordshire County Museum Service.
Humphis, Ted, *Garden Glory*, 1969.
In Service: Rose Gibbs Remembers, Cambridge, 1981.
James, John, *The Memoirs of a House Steward*, 1949.
Jones, Owen, *Ten Years of Gamekeeping*, 1910.
King, Ernest, *The Green Baize Door*, 1963.
Lanceley, William, *From Hall-Boy to House-Steward*, 1925.
Lawton, Mary, *The Queen of Cooks – and Some Kings*, New York, 1925.
"A laundrymaid's week 1910," Information sheet, Staffordshire County Museum Service.
Murphy, Clive (ed.) and Rogers, Evan, *A Funny Old Quist: the Memoirs of a Gamekeeper*, 1981.
Niall, Ian, *The Gamekeeper*, 1965.
Powell, Margaret, *My Mother and I*, 1972.
Rawlings, Leslie, *Gamekeeper*, Ipswich, 1977.
Rennie, Jean, *Every Other Sunday*, 1955.
Smith, Nina Slingsby, *George: Memoirs of a Gentleman's Gentleman*, 1984.
Thomas, Albert, *Wait & See*, 1944.
Wilkins, John, *The Autobiography of an English Gamekeeper* (2nd edn), 1892.

The landed classes

Beckett, J. V., *The Aristocracy in England, 1660–1914*, Oxford, 1977.
Bence-Jones, Mark and Montgomery-Massingberd, Hugh, *The British Aristocracy*, 1979.
Blackwell, Patricia, "The English landed elite in decline: a case study of five Sussex country houses," unpublished University of Sussex MA thesis, 1978.
Bush, M. L., *The English Aristocracy: a Comparative Synthesis*, Manchester, 1984.

Buxton, Meriel, *Ladies of the Chase*, 1987.
Cannadine, David, *The Decline and Fall of the British Aristocracy*, New Haven, 1990.
——, "The theory and practice of the English leisure classes," *Historical Journal*, 21, 1978.
Clemenson, Heather A., *English Country Houses and Landed Estates*, 1982.
Courtney, Nicholas, *"In Society": the Brideshead Years*, 1986.
Davies, John, "The end of the great estates and the rise of freehold farming in Wales," *Welsh History Review*, 7, 1974.
Gerard, Jessica, "Lady Bountiful: women of the landed classes and local philanthropy," *Victorian Studies*, 30, 1987.
Guttsman, W. L., *The English Political Elite*, 1963.
——, *The English Ruling Class*, 1969.
Hartcup, Adeline, *Children of the Great Country Houses*, 1982.
Hollingsworth, T. H., "The demography of the British peerage," supplement to *Population Studies*, 18, 1964.
Horn, Pamela, *High Society: the English Social Elite, 1880–1914*, Stroud, 1992.
——, *Ladies of the Manor: Wives and Daughters in Country-house Society, 1830–1918*, Stroud, 1991.
Howell, David W., *Patriarchs and Parasites: the Gentry of South-West Wales in the Eighteenth Century*, Cardiff, 1986.
Lambert, Angela, *Unquiet Souls: the Indian Summer of the British Aristocracy*, 1984.
Lewis, Judith Schneid, *In the Family Way: Childbearing in the British Aristocracy, 1760–1860*, New Brunswick, 1986.
Lumley, Trevor and Marsh, Jan, *The Woman's Domain: Women and the English Country House*, 1990.
MacColl, Gail and Wallace, Carol McD., *To Marry an English Lord: the Victorian and Edwardian Experience*, New York, 1989.
Margetson, Stella, *Victorian High Society*, 1980.
Mingay, G. E., *English Landed Society in the Eighteenth Century*, 1963.
——, *The Gentry: the Rise and Fall of a Ruling Class*, 1976.
Montgomery, Maureen E., *"Gilded Prostitution:" Status, Money, and Transatlantic Marriages, 1870–1914*, London and New York, 1989.
Moore, D. C., "The gentry," in G. E. Mingay (ed.), *The Victorian Countryside*, Vol. II, 1981.
——, "The landed aristocracy," in G. E. Mingay (ed.), *The Victorian Countryside*, Vol. II, 1981.
Nevill, Ralph, *English Country House Life*, 1925.
Phillips, Gregory D., *The Diehards: Aristocratic Society and Politics in Edwardian England*, Cambridge, Mass., 1979.
Roberts, Peter R., "The social history of the Merioneth gentry, 1660–1840," *Journal of the Merioneth Historical Society*, 4, 1961–4.

Robinson, John Martin, *The English Country Estate*, 1988.
Sinclair, Andrew, *The Last of the Best: the Aristocracy of Europe in the Twentieth Century*, 1969.
Spring, David, "Aristocracy, social structure and religion in the early Victorian period," *Victorian Studies*, 6, 1963.
——, *The English Landed Estate in the Nineteenth Century: its Administration*, Baltimore, 1963.
——, "The role of the aristocracy in the late nineteenth century," *Victorian Studies*, 4, 1960.
Stone, Lawrence and Fawtier, Jeanne C., *An Open Elite? England, 1540–1880*, Oxford, 1986.
Sykes, Christopher Simon, *The Golden Age of the Country House*, New York, 1980.
——, *The National Trust Country House Album*, 1989.
Thomas, David, "The social origins of marriage partners of the British peerage in the eighteenth and nineteenth centuries," *Population Studies*, 26, 1972.
Thompson, E. P., "Patrician society, plebian culture," *Journal of Social History*, 7, 1974.
Thompson, F. M. L., "Britain," in David Spring (ed.), *European Elites in the Nineteenth Century*, 1977.
——, *English Landed Society in the Nineteenth Century*, 1963.
——, "Landowners and the local community," in G. E. Mingay (ed.), *The Victorian Countryside*, Vol. II, 1981.
Trumbach, Randolph, *The Rise of the Egalitarian Family: Aristocratic Kinship and Domestic Relations in Eighteenth-Century England*, New York, 1978.
Vaughan, Herbert M., *The South Wales Squires*, 1926.

The country house

Bence-Jones, Mark, *Great English Homes: Ancestral Homes of England and Wales and the People Who Lived in Them*, New York, 1984.
Cannadine, David, "The stately homes of England," in *The Pleasures of the Past*, 1989.
Franklin, Jill, *The Gentleman's Country House and its Plan, 1835–1914*, 1981.
——, "The Victorian country house," in G. E. Mingay (ed.), *The Victorian Countryside*, Vol. II, 1981.
Girouard, Mark, *A Country House Companion*, 1987, Leicester, 1992.
——, *Historic Houses of Great Britain*, 1979.
——, *Life in the English Country House: a Social and Agricultural History*, London and New Haven, 1978.
——, "Living with the past: Victorian alterations to country houses," in Jane Fawcett (ed.), *The Future of the Past*, 1976.

Girouard, Mark, *The Victorian Country House* (revised and enlarged edn), New Haven and London, 1979.
Harling, Robert, *Historical Houses: Conversations in Stately Homes*, 1969.
Harris, John, "Gone to ground," in Roy Strong, Marcus Binney, and John Harris (eds), *The Destruction of the Country House, 1875–1975*, 1974.

Domestic service

Bloxham, Christine, *Domestic Service*, Information Sheet no. 19, Oxfordshire Museum Service, 1981.
Davidoff, Leonore, "Class and gender in Victorian England: The diaries of Arthur J. Munby and Hannah Cullwick," *Feminist Studies*, 5, 1979.
——, "Mastered for life: servant and wife in Victorian and Edwardian England," *Journal of Social History*, 7, 1974.
Dawes, Frank, *Not in Front of the Servants: Domestic Service in England, 1850–1939*, Newton Abbot, 1975.
Ebery, Mark and Preston, Brian, *Domestic Service in Late Victorian and Edwardian England, 1871–1914*, Geographical papers no. 42, University of Reading, 1976.
Fildes, Valerie, *Wet Nursing: a History from Antiquity to the Present*, Oxford, 1988.
Franklin, Jill, "Troops of servants: labour and planning in the country house, 1840–1914," *Victorian Studies*, 19, 1975.
Gathorne-Hardy, Jonathan, *The Rise and Fall of the British Nanny*, 1972.
Gerard, Jessica, "Invisible servants: the country house and the local community," *Bulletin of the Institute of Historical Research*, 57, 1984.
Gibbs, Mary Ann, *The Years of the Nannies*, 1960.
Gillis, John R., "Servants, sexual relations, and the risks of illegitimacy in London, 1801–1900," *Feminist Studies*, 5, 1979.
Green, J. A. S., "A survey of domestic service," *Lincolnshire History and Archaeology*, 17, 1982.
Haims, Lynne, "In their place: domestic servants in English country houses, 1850–1870," unpublished Johns Hopkins University PhD thesis, 1981.
Hartcup, Adeline, *Below Stairs in the Great Country Houses*, 1980.
Hecht, J. Jean, *The Domestic Servant in Eighteenth-Century England*, 1956 (repub. 1980).
Higgs, Edward, "Domestic service and households in Rochdale, 1851–1871," in Angela V. John (ed.), *Unequal Opportunities: Women's Employment in England, 1800–1918*, Oxford, 1986.
——, *Domestic Servants and Households in Rochdale, 1851–1871*, New York, 1986.

——, "Domestic service and households in Victorian England," *Social History*, 8, 1983.
Horn, Pamela, "Domestic service in Northamptonshire, 1830–1914," *Northamptonshire Past and Present*, 5, 1975.
——, *The Rise and Fall of the Victorian Servant*, Dublin, 1975.
Huggett, Frank E., *Life Below Stairs: Domestic Servants in England from Victorian Times*, 1977.
Hughes, Kathryn, *The Victorian Governess*, 1993.
King-Hall, Magdalen, *The Story of the Nursery*, 1958.
Lockwood, Leonore D., "Domestic service and the working-class life cycle," *Bulletin for the Study of Labour History*, 1, 1960.
McBride, Theresa M., "'As the Twig is Bent': the Victorian Nanny," in Anthony S. Wohl (ed.), *The Victorian Family: Structure and Stresses*, 1978.
——, *The Domestic Revolution: the Modernisation of Household Service in England and France 1820–1920*, 1976.
Marshall, Dorothy, *The English Domestic Servant in History*, Historical Association Pamphlet G 13, 1949.
Peterson, M. Jeanne, "The Victorian governess: status incongruence in family and society," in Martha Vicinus (ed.), *Suffer and Be Still: Women in the Victorian Age*, Bloomington, 1972.
Prochaska, F. K., "Female philanthropy and domestic service in Victorian England," *Bulletin of the Institute of Historical Research*, 54, 1981.
Renton, Alice, *Tyrant or Victim? A History of the British Governess*, 1991.
Richardson, Sheila, "The Servant Question: a study of the domestic labour market, 1851–1911," unpublished University of London M. Phil. thesis, 1967.
Roberts, Ann, "Mothers and babies: the wetnurse and her employer in mid-nineteenth-century England," *Women's Studies: an Interdisciplinary Journal*, 3, 1976.
Rollins, Judith, *Between Women: Domestics and Their Employers*, Philadelphia, 1985.
Sambrook, Pamela, *A Servants' Place: an Account of the Servants at Shugborough*, Stoke-on-Trent, 1989.
Stuart, Dorothy Margaret, *The English Abigail*, 1946.
Turner, E.S., *What the Butler Saw*, 1962.
Tyack, Geoffrey, "Service on the Cliveden estate between the wars," *Oral History*, 5, 1977.
Waterson, Merlin, *The Servants' Hall: a Domestic History of Erddig*, 1980.
Wilcox, Penelope, "Marriage, mobility, and domestic service in Victorian Cambridge," *Local Population Studies*, 29, 1982.

Other

Anderson, Michael, "Marriage patterns in Victorian Britain. An analysis based on registration district data for England and Wales 1861," *Journal of Family History*, I, 1976.
Anderson, Olive, *Suicide in Victorian and Edwardian England*, Oxford, 1987.
Archivists' Report, 22, Lincoln, 1970–1.
Ashby, M. K., *Joseph Ashby of Tysoe, 1859–1919: a Study of English Village Life*, Cambridge, 1961.
Athill, Diana, *Instead of a Letter: an Autobiography*, 1963.
Banks, Olive, *Becoming a Feminist: the Social Origins of "First Wave" Feminism*, Athens, Georgia, 1986.
Baring, Maurice, *The Puppet Show of Memory*, 1922.
Barret-Ducrocq, Françoise, *Love in the Time of Victoria: Sexuality and Desire Among Working-Class Men and Women in Nineteenth-Century London*, 1989, trans. John Howe, Harmondsworth, 1992.
Barrett, Walter Henry, *A Fenman's Story*, 1965.
Barton, Arthur, *Two Lamps in Our Street: a Time Remembered*, 1967.
Bell, Colin and Newby, Howard, *Community Studies: an Introduction to the Sociology of the Local Community*, 1971.
—— (eds), *The Sociology of Community: a Selection of Readings*, 1974.
Benson, E. F., *As We Were: a Victorian Peep Show*, 1930.
Bienefeld, M. A., *Working Hours in British Industry: an Economic History*, 1972.
Bovill, E. W., *English Country Life, 1780–1830*, 1962.
Bradley, Ian, *The Call to Seriousness: the Evangelical Impact on the Victorians*, 1976.
Bryant, Arthur, *The Age of Elegance, 1812–1822*, 1950.
Bossard, James H. S., *The Sociology of Child Development*, New York, 1948.
Booth, P. H. W., *Burton Manor: the Biography of a House*, Burton Manor, 1978.
Bullock, Jim, *Bowers Row: Recollections of a Mining Village*, Wakefield, 1976.
Bunsen, Victoria De, *Old and New in the Countryside*, 1920.
Burman, Sandra (ed.), *Fit Work for Women*, 1979.
Caine, Barbara, *Destined to be Wives: the Sisters of Beatrice Webb*, Oxford, 1986.
Clark, Anna, *Women's Silence, Men's Violence: Sexual Assault in England, 1770–1845*, 1987.
Clive, Mary, *The Day of Reckoning*, 1964.
Cooper, Nicholas, *Aynho: a Northamptonshire Village*, 1964.
Curtin, Michael, "Etiquette and society in Victorian England," unpublished University of California at Berkeley PhD thesis, 1974.
——, "A question of manners: status and gender in etiquette and courtesy," *Journal of Modern History*, 57, 1985.
Darely, Gillian, *Villages of Vision*, 1975.
Davidoff, Leonore, *The Best Circles: Society, Etiquette, and the Season* (1973).

—— and Hall, Catherine, *Family Fortunes: Men and Women of the English Middle Class, 1780–1850*, 1987.
Davidoff, Leonore, L'Esperance, Jean and Newby, Howard, "Landscape with figures: home and community in English Society," in J. Mitchell and A. Oakley (eds), *The Rights and Wrongs of Women*, Harmondsworth, 1976.
Davies, Mel, "Corsets and conception: fashion and demographic trends in the nineteenth century," *Comparative Studies in Society and History*, 24, 1982.
Ditchfield, P. H., *Country Folk*, 1923.
Dyhouse, Carol, *Girls Growing Up in Late Victorian and Edwardian England*, 1981.
——, "Mothers and daughters in the middle-class home," in Jane Lewis (ed.), *Labour and Love: Women's Experience of Home and Family, 1850–1940*, Oxford, 1986.
Earle, Mrs Charles William, *Memoirs and Memories*, 1911.
Erddig, 1978.
Evans, George Ewart, *From Mouths of Men*, 1976.
——, *Where Beards Wag All: the Relevance of the Oral Tradition*, 1970.
Fairchilds, Cissie, *Domestic Enemies: Servants and their Masters in Old Regime France*, Baltimore, 1984.
Ferguson, Michael Henry, "Land use, settlement and society in the Bagshot Sands region, 1840–1940," unpublished University of London PhD thesis, 1973.
Firth, Violet M., *The Psychology of the Servant Problem*, 1925.
Fletcher, Margaret, *O, Call Back Yesterday*, Oxford, 1939.
Flinn, M. W., "Trends in real wages 1750–1850," *Economic History Review*, 27, 1974.
Frankle, Barbara, "The genteel family: high Victorian conceptions of domesticity and good behaviour," unpublished University of Wisconsin PhD thesis, 1973.
Fulford, Roger (ed.), *The Greville Memoirs* (revised edn), 1963.
Fussell, G. E. and K. R., *The English Countrywoman: the Internal Aspect of Rural Life, 1500–1900*, 1953.
Gaskell, Elizabeth, *Life of Charlotte Brontë*, 2 vols, New York, 1857.
Gathorne-Hardy, Jonathan, *The Public School Phenomenon, 1597–1977*, 1977.
Gérin, Winifred, *Anne Brontë*, 1959.
——, *Charlotte Brontë: the Evolution of Genius*, Oxford, 1967.
Gorham, Deborah, *The Victorian Girl and the Feminine Ideal*, Bloomington, 1982.
Gras, Norman Scott Brien and Ethel Culbert, *The Economic and Social History of an English Village*, Cambridge, Mass., 1930.
Greenleaf, Barbara Kaye, *Children Through the Ages: a History of Childhood*, 1978.
Haldane, Louisa Kathleen, *Friends and Kindred: Memories*, 1961.

Hall, Catherine, "The early formation of Victorian domestic ideology," in Sandra Burman (ed.), *Fit Work for Women*, 1979.
Hall, Ruth (ed.), *Dear Dr Stopes: Sex in the 1920s*, 1978.
Hamilton, Lord Ernest, *Forty Years On*, 1922.
——, *Old Days and New*, 1924.
Hardy, Lady Violet, *As It Was*, 1958.
Hardyment, Christine, *Dream Babies*, 1983.
Hare, Augustus, *The Story of My Life*, 6 vols, 1896 and 1900.
Hareven, Tamara K., "The family as social process; the historical study of the family cycle," *Journal of Social History*, 7, 1974.
Harris, Mollie, *A Kind of Magic: an Oxfordshire Childhood in the 1920s*, 1969.
——, *Another Kind of Magic*, 1971.
Havinden, M. A., *Estate Villages: a Study of the Berkshire Villages of Ardington and Lockinge*, 1966.
Helterline, Marilyn, "The emergence of modern motherhood: motherhood in England 1899 to 1959," *International Journal of Women's Studies*, 3, 1980.
Hollis, Patricia, *Ladies Elect: Women in English Local Government, 1865–1914*, Oxford, 1987.
Honey, J. R. De Symons, *Tom Brown's Universe*, New York, 1977.
Horn, Pamela, *The Rural World, 1780–1850: Social Change in the English Countryside*, 1980.
——, *The Victorian Country Child*, Kineton, 1974.
——, *Victorian Countrywomen*, Oxford, 1991.
Horne, Michael, *Autumn Fields*, 1943.
——, *Spring Sowing*, 1946.
Horstman, Allen, *Victorian Divorce*, New York, 1985.
Houghton, Walter E., *The Victorian Frame of Mind, 1830–1870*, New Haven, 1957.
Howe, Bea, *Lady with Green Fingers: the Life of Jane Loudon*, 1961.
Howell, David W., *Land and People in Nineteenth-Century Wales*, 1978.
Howkins, Alun, *Reshaping Rural England: a Social History, 1850–1925*, 1991.
Hudson, W. H., *A Shepherd's Life*, 1910.
Iley, Walter R., *Corbridge*, Newcastle on Tyne, 1975.
Jalland, Pat, *Women, Marriage, and Politics, 1860–1914*, Oxford, 1986.
—— and Hooper, John (eds), *Women from Birth to Death: the Female Life Cycle in Britain, 1830–1914*, Brighton, 1986.
Jobson, Allan, *Suffolk Remembered*, 1969.
——, *Suffolk Yesterdays*, 1964.
——, *Under a Suffolk Sky*, 1961.
Kemble, Frances Anne, *Records of Later Life*, 3 vols, 1882.
Keppel, Sonia, *Edwardian Daughter*, 1958.
Kitchen, Fred, *Brother to the Ox: the Autobiography of a Farm Labourer*, 1940.

———, *Nettleworth Parva*, 1968.
Laslett, Peter, *Household and Family in Past Time*, Cambridge, 1972.
Le Lièvre, Audrey, *Miss Wilmott of Warley Place: her Life and her Gardens*, 1980.
Lee, Laurie, *Cider with Rosie*, 1959.
Lees-Milne, James, *Ancestral Voices*, 1975.
———, *Prophesying Peace*, 1977.
Leslie, Anita, *Edwardians in Love*, 1972.
———, *The Marlborough House Set*, New York, 1972.
Lewis, G. J., *Rural Communities*, 1979.
Lincolnshire Archives Committee, *Archivists' Report* 22, 1970–1.
Locker-Lampson, Godfrey, *Life in the Country*, 1948.
Lubbock, Lady Sybil *The Child in the Crystal*, 1939.
McCarthy, Desmond and Russell, Agatha (eds), *Lady John Russell: a Memoir*, 1912.
McGregor, O. R., *Divorce in England: a Centenary Study*, 1957.
Marcus, Stephen, *The Other Victorians*, 1964.
Martin, E. W., *The Shearers and the Shorn: a Study of Life in a Devon Community*, 1965.
Martin, Ralph G., *Jennie: the Life of Lady Randolph Churchill: the Romantic Years, 1854–1895*, New York, 1969.
Marshall, Sybil (ed.), *Fenland Chronicle: Recollections of William Henry and Kate Mary Edwards, Collected and Edited by their Daughter*, Cambridge, 1967.
Mason, Roger, *Granny's Village: Memories of the Yorkshire Dales in the 1880s*, 1977.
Mays, Spike, *Reuben's Corner: an English Country Boyhood*, 1969.
Meacham, Standish, *A Life Apart: the English Working Class, 1890–1914*, 1977.
Mingay, G. E., *Rural Life in Victorian England*, 1977.
Mitchell, B. R. and Deane, Phyllis, *Abstract of British Historical Statistics*, Cambridge, 1971.
Morgan, Joan and Richards, Alison, *A Paradise out of a Common Field: the Pleasures and Plenty of the Victorian Garden*, New York, 1990.
Neff, Wanda F., *Victorian Working Women: an Historical and Literary Study of Women in British Industries and Professions, 1832–1850*, 1929.
Newby, Howard, *Country Life: a Social History of Rural England*, Totowa, NJ, 1987.
———, "The deferential dialectic," *Comparative Studies in Society and History*, 17, 1975.
———, *The Deferential Worker: a Study of Farm Workers in East Anglia*, Madison, 1979.
Obelkevich, James, *Religion and Rural Society: South Lindsey, 1825–1875*, Oxford, 1976.

Olivier, Edith, *Four Victorian Ladies of Wiltshire; with an Essay on those Leisured Ladies*, 1945.
Parry-Jones, D., *Welsh Country Upbringing*, 1948.
Pearsall, Ronald, *The Worm in the Bud: the World of Victorian Sexuality*, 1969.
Pearson, Alexander, *The Doings of a Country Solicitor*, Kendal, 1947.
Peel, Dorothy Constance, *Life's Enchanted Cup: an Autobiography, 1872–1933*, 1933.
Perkin, Harold, *The Origins of Modern Society, 1780–1880*, 1969.
Perkin, Joan, *Women and Marriage in Nineteenth-Century England*, Chicago, 1989.
Peterson, M. Jeanne, *Family, Love, and Work in the Lives of Victorian Gentlewomen*, Bloomington, 1989.
Pinchbeck, Ivy, *Women Workers and the Industrial Revolution, 1750–1850*, 1930.
Plumb, J. H., *In the Light of History*, 1972.
Pollock, Linda A., *Forgotten Children: Parent–Child Relations from 1500 to 1900*, Cambridge, 1983.
Prochaska, F. K., *Women and Philanthropy in Nineteenth-Century England*, Oxford, 1980.
Pugh, Martin, *The Tories and the People*, Oxford, 1985.
Quinlan, Maurice J., *Victorian Prelude: a History of English Manners, 1700–1830*, 1965.
Reiss, Albert J. Jr, "The sociological study of communities," *Rural Sociology*, 24, 1959.
Richards, Eric, *The Leviathan of Wealth: the Sutherland Fortune in the Industrial Revolution*, 1973.
Roberts, Ann, "Mothers and babies: the wetnurse and her employer in mid-nineteenth-century England," *Women's Studies: an Interdisciplinary Journal*, 3, 1976.
Roberts, David, "The paterfamilias of the Victorian governing classes," in Anthony S. Wohl (ed.), *The Victorian Family; Structures and Stresses*, 1978.
——, *Paternalism in Early Victorian England*, 1979.
Roberts, Elizabeth, *A Woman's Place: an Oral History of Working-Class Women, 1890–1940*, Oxford, 1985.
Roberts, Robert, *A Ragged Schooling*, Manchester, 1976.
Robin, Jean, *Elmdon: Continuity and Change in a Northwest Essex Village, 1861–1964*, Cambridge, 1980.
Russell, George W. E., *Portraits of the Seventies*, 1916.
Sackville-West, Vita, *Country Notes*, 1939.
Scannell, Dolly, *Mother Knew Best: an East End Childhood*, 1974.
Scarr, Sandra, *Mother Care/Other Care*, New York, 1984.
Shears, Sarah, *Tapioca for Tea: Memoirs of a Kentish Childhood*, 1971.
Simon, Brian and Bradley, Ian (eds), *The Victorian Public School*, Dublin, 1975.

Smith, Daniel Blake, *Inside the Great House: Planter Family Life in Eighteenth-Century Chesapeake Society*, Ithaca, 1980.
Smith-Rosenberg, Carrol, "The female world of love and ritual: relations between women in nineteenth century America," *Signs*, 1, 1975.
Spark, Muriel (ed.), *The Letters of the Brontës: a Selection*, Norman, 1954.
Sproule, Anna, *The Social Calendar*, Poole, 1978.
Stacey, Margaret, "The myth of community studies," *British Journal of Sociology*, 20, 1969.
Stone, Lawrence, *The Family, Sex and Marriage in England, 1500–1800*, Oxford 1977. (Also abridged and revised edn, Harmondsworth, 1980.)
——, *Road to Divorce: England, 1530–1987*, 1990.
Stone, Michael H. and Kestenbaum, Clarice J., "Maternal deprivation in children of the wealthy: a paradox in socioeconomic vs. psychological class," *History of Childhood Quarterly*, 2, 1974.
Summers, Anne, "A home from home: women's philanthropic work in the nineteenth century," in Sandra Burman (ed.), *Fit Work for Women*, 1979.
Sutton, William A. Jr. and Kolaja, Jiri, "The concept of community," *Rural Sociology*, 25, 1960.
Telling, Marjorie Beach, *Over My Shoulder*, 1962.
Thompson, E. P., "Patrician society, plebian culture," *Journal of Social History*, 7, 1973–4.
Thompson, F. M. L., *The Rise of Respectable Society: a Social History of Victorian Britain, 1830–1900*, Cambridge, Mass., 1988.
Thompson, Flora, *Lark Rise to Candleford*, Oxford, 1945.
Thompson, Paul, *The Edwardians: the Remaking of British Society*, 1975.
Thomson, Lady Ethel, *Clifton Lodge*, 1955.
Thynne, D. W. L., *Before the Sunset Fades*, Warminster, 1951.
Tibble, Anne, *Greenhorn: a Twentieth-Century Childhood*, 1973.
Ticknor, G., *Life of William Hickling Prescott*, 1863.
Tranter, N. L., *Population and Society, 1750–1940: Contrasts in Population Growth*, 1985.
Trudgill, Eric, *Madonnas and Magdalens: the Origins and Development of Victorian Sexual Attitudes*, 1976.
Tweedsmuir, Susan, *The Edwardian Lady*, 1966.
Turner, Barry, *A Place in the Country*, 1972.
Vicinus, Martha (ed.), *Suffer and Be Still*, 1972.
——, *Independent Women: Work and Community for Single Women, 1850–1920*, 1985.
Vincent, David (ed.), *Testaments of Radicalism*, 1977.
Ward, Zoë, *Curtsy to the Lady: a Horringer Childhood*, Lavenham, 1985.
Wells, H. G., *An Experiment in Autobiography*, 1934.
——, *Tono-Bungay*, 1909.

Whitlock, Ralph, *Peasant's Heritage*, 1977.
Winstanley, Michael, *Life in Kent at the Turn of the Century*, Folkestone, 1978.
Wrigley, E. A. and Schofield, R. S., *The Population History of England, 1541–1871: a Reconstruction*, 1981.

Index

Acland, Eleanor (Cropper), 41, 44, 49, 58, 76
Acland, Sir Thomas Dyke, 80–1
Adams, Samuel and Sarah, 149, 150, 192, 222
adolescent girls in landed classes, 49–54, 57, 63, 85–7, 129, 162
Aldcliffe Hall, 152
Alnwick Castle, 180, 187
Amberley, Katherine Russell, Viscountess, 39, 75
Ampthill, 180, 217
Aqualate Hall, 194–5, 229
Arkwright family of Hampton Court, 16, 130
Arkwright, John, 30, 105, 208
Arkwright, John Hungerford, 67, 76–7, 85, 104, 107–8, 132
Arkwright, John Stanhope, 30, 36, 67, 76–7, 85
Arkwright, Lucy, 67, 76, 85, 105, 107–8, 126, 176, 205, 254
Arkwright, Sarah, 30, 125, 269
Ashburnham Place, 152, 182, 200, 201
Asquith, Lady Cynthia (Charteris), 41, 55, 59, 60, 62, 67, 72, 136
Astor, Nancy (Lady), 188, 227
authoritarian employer, 9, 239, 244, 246, 253, 258–60, 266, 270, 280
Aynhoe, 213

bachelor landowners, 23, 34, 151, 152

Badeau, Adam, 233, 235, 243, 253, 261
Balsan, Consuelo Vanderbilt (ninth Duchess of Marlborough), 112, 132, 133–4
Bankes, Henrietta, 113, 118
Bankes, Viola, 42, 59
Banville, Larry, 198, 208, 264
Barking Hall, 152
Barlborough Hall, 262
Beaulieu, 165 (plate 20), 228 (plate 29)
Beckett, J. V., 1, 6, 115
Bedford, Francis Russell, ninth Duke of, 208–9
Belgrave, Elizabeth, Lady, *see* Westminster
Bentley, 120
Benyon, Richard, 157, 182, 244, 247
Birchall, Dearman, 96–7, 98–9, 193, 216–7, 227, 247
Birchall, Emily (Jowitt), 98–9, 176, 216–7
Blackwell, Patricia, 135, 160, 282
Blagdon, 132, 188
Blake Hall, 175
Blankney, 33
Boileau, Caroline, 124, 140
Boileau, Lady Catherine, 102–4
Boileau, Sir John, first Baronet, 103–4, 131, 244, 250
Bowater, Louisa, *see* Knightley
Bowden Hall, 97, 193

Bowthorpe Hall, 92 (plate 11)
Bridehead, 179
Brontë, Anne, 175, 256
Brontë, Charlotte, 195, 255, 256, 267
Brougham Castle, 179
Bryn Myrddan, 60
Buckhurst Place 217
Burghwallis, 223
Burnett, John, 4, 149, 318
Burton Constable, 218
Burton Manor, 132
Burwood Park, 201
Butler, C. V., 199, 235, 261, 270

Cable, Annie, 187, 206
Cadogan, Honorable Sir Edward, 55, 60
Candybun, Martha, 167, 252–3, 257
Cannadine, David, 1, 6, 115–16
career servants
 attitudes towards family, 268; benefits, 209–11; definition, 11, 162, 164–5, 275; job mobility, 179–81; job satisfaction, 190, 197–99; marriage, 188–9, 233–4; motives, 12, 164; origins, 167–8; relations with family, 255–7; status, 235; training, 191, wages, 202–4
Carlisle, George Howard, ninth Earl of, 26 (plate 4), 79 (plate 9), 112, 121
Carlisle, Rosalind Howard, Countess of, 26 (plate 4), 112, 119 (plate 14), 121, 127, 247
Casewick, 155, 200, 201
cash nexus, 241–2, 245–6, 260, 270, 280
Ceroti, Ferdinand, 218, 233
Chaplin family of Blankney, 48, 56–7
Chaplin, Helen, *see* Radnor
character (servant's letter of reference), 248–9
Charlton, Barbara (Tasburgh), 81, 86

child-rearing in country house
 artificial feeding of infants, 39, 74; austerity in the nursery, 46, 68, 276, 279; breastfeeding, 38, 68, 73–4, 276, 283; change over century, 65–6, 276–8, 280, 282; children's hour, 78; code of conduct, 45, 65, 69–70, 88; diet, 46–7, 58; discipline, 38, 44–6, 58, 60, 63, 65–6, 81–4, 88–9, 277, 279, 283; distinctive features, 8, 65–7, 69–70, 88–9, 276, 279; gender, 48–9, 70, 72, 273–4; nursery, 38, 43–4, 45–7, 57, 63–4, 67; outdoor activities, 55–7; playthings, 46–7, 55–6, 79–80; religious instruction, 40, 47–8, 63, 80–1; routines, 38, 43–4, 78; schoolroom education, 43–4, 49–54, 63, 279; *see also* childhood, fatherhood, motherhood
childhood in the country house
 distinctive features, 54, 38, 63–4; distinctive goals and values, 69, environment, 54–5, 57; isolation, 57, sociability, 57–8; *see also* child-rearing
Childwickbury, 29, 36
Chillington, 152, 181, 200, 201
Clandon Park, 147
class-consciousness
 among children, 61–3; among former servants, 264; among nurses, 62; in landed classes towards servants, 2, 9, 221, 244–6, 250, 260, 263, 280; in middle classes, 10, 221; in nineteenth century, 1, 241, 246; in working classes, 271
Clifton, Edward Bligh, Baron Clifton (5th Earl of Darnley), 76, 95
Clifton, Emma, Lady (Parnell), 76, 95, 250

INDEX

Cliveden, 31, 35, 120, 202, 227
code of conduct
among servants, 3, 141, 241, 262, 271; between family and servants, 3, 9, 239–41, 244–5, 254–5, 262, 271–3, 275, 280; in marriage, 90, 110, 113; taught to landed children, 45, 65, 69–70, 88; within landed family over century, 3, 17, 140–1, 272–3, 277–9, 280, 282
Colville, Lady Cynthia (Milne), 43, 55
coming out (debut into Society), 54, 86–7, 129, 162
community of family and staff, 2–4, 158, 240–1, 244, 250, 261, 271, 273–4, 285
companionate marriage, 8, 90, 93, 104–9, 114–15, 118, 131–2, 140, 276, 279–80
Cooper, Charles, 168, 179–80, 191, 197, 229
Cooper, Lady Diana (Manners), 45, 52, 111
Cooper, Mr (butler at Kingston Lacy), 218, 237
Coton Hall, 194
country house
children's attitudes towards, 54, definition, 6–7; functions, 4–6; elite welfare institution, 33; labour required to maintain, 142; late nineteenth century, 19, 159; occupancy rates, 34–7; rebuilding, 158; role in defining staff numbers, 157–8; venue for matchmaking, 93
country house servants
age at entry, 162, 183–5; attitudes towards employers, 260–70, 274–5; geographical mobility, 177–8; geographical origins, 168–9, 170, 182, 178, 312; job mobility, 44, 162, 178–81, 259; length of service, 178–82, 314; motives for entering country houseservice, 162–6; resistance and insubordination, 261, 264–70; social origins, 162, 167–8; social status in rural community, 235–7; suicide among menservants, 269; *see also* career servants, distressed gentlewomen, labourers and life-cycle servants
country house service
accommodation, 58, 158, 205, 208, 212–15, 219, 243, 271, 275, 283; allowances, 205–6, 208–9, 274; annuities, 208–9, 219; attractions, 275; board wages, 205–6; Christmas gifts, 207; dances for servants, 215–6; deference of servants, 221, 225, 237, 239–40, 250, 260–1, 268, 274–5, 279–80, depersonalization and dehumanization, 220–1, 245, 260–2, 270; diet 58, 211, 219, 275, 283; dress, 206–7, 209, 220, 225, 242, 244, 250, 264, 268; elite sector of occupation, 10–12, 190, 240, 275; functions of servants, 3, 144, 239, 275; hierarchy below stairs, 67, 220–7, 237, 262, 271, 274; hours of work, 195–6; impact of environment, 197, 218; job demarcation, 154, 192, 215, 278, 280; job satisfaction, 190, 196–9, 219; labour markets, 169–77; legacies 208–9, 219, 243–5, 260; medical care 207–9, 245, 259, 275; pensions 208–9, 210, 243–5, 257; perquisites, 206–7, 219, 242, 275; promotion 162, 181–2, 183–5, 219, 227; recreation 215–18, 260; retirement, 162, 163–4, 184–6; social mobility, 234–5, 275; time off, 215, 217–8, 247, 270, 278; training, 190–1, 219; transfer,

181, 190; workload, 194–5; vails (tips), 207, 209, 219, 242, 275; wages, 219, 199–205, 209, 219, 277, 283, 318

courtship in landed classes
differences in motives over time and between ranks, 100–1, 276–7, 280; male role in courtship, 95; motives in spouse selection, 91–2, 94–7, 100, 101, 104, 114, 273; parents forcing marriage, 95–6; parents' role in courtship, 91–5, 114, 273

Cowper, Amelia, fifth Countess, 91, 100, 113
Cowper, Lady Emily, 97–8
Cox, Alfred, 149–50
Cramner Hall, 62, 159, 218
Cranborne, Viscount (second Marquess of Salisbury), 94, 97–8
Crawley Court, 170
Crawshay, Lady, 166, 175
Cropper, Edith, 78, 122
Crosby Hall, 177
Cuerdon Hall, 177
Cullwick, Hannah, 164, 183, 194–5, 222, 229
cult of true womanhood, 68–9, 71, 123, 244, 279, 280
Curzon, George Nathaniel (Marquess), 71, 132
Curzon, Mary, 40, 71

Davidoff, Leonore, 86, 98, 115, 130, 197, 265, 269
day and casual labour, 143, 153–7, 168, 184, 187–8, 190, 194, 201–2, 230, 259, 268, 283
demography of country house servants
family size of menservants, 188; life expectancy, 186; nuptiality, 162, 167, 185–9.
demography of landed classes
duration of owners' marriage, 24, 287; effects of tight corsets on fertility, 25; family size, 25–6, 37, 276, 280, 283; infant and child mortality, 27, 288; heirs' ages at marriage, 23, 36; infertility, 24–5, 288; life expectancy, 27; nuptiality of heirs, 23, 36, 287; remarriage, 24; wives' age at marriage, 24, 98; younger sons' nuptiality, 289

Derwydd, 182
distressed gentlewomen
age at entry 185, 189; attitudes towards family, 267–8; benefits, 209; definition, 11–12, 162, 167, 275–6; geographical origins, 178; hours of work, 195; job mobility, 179; labour market, 172, 175–6; motives, 12, 42, 48, 165–6; nuptiality, 164, 189, 235; qualifications, 42, 166, 175–6, 187; relations with family, 42–3, 255–7; social status, 167; wages, 203, 209; 255–7, 267–8, 275–6

divorce in landed classes, 24, 43, 111–13, 281
Dixon family of Holton, 130, 152–3, 200–1, 215
Dixon, Amelia Margaretta (Mrs Jameson Dixon), 15, 34, 78, 153, 154 (plate 19), 156–7, 260
Dixon, Ann, 15, 31, 34, 51, 78–9, 120, 153, 263
Dixon, Mary Ann, 14, 30–1, 34, 105, 124, 125 (plate 15), 127, 130, 153, 156, 251, 257, 259–60, 263,
Dixon, Richard Roadley, 15, 28, 79
Dixon, Thomas (Gibbons), 15, 34, 84, 153, 182, 246
Dixon, Thomas John, 14–15, 28, 30, 34, 77, 78–9, 153, 260
domestic servants
discontent, 221, 270; life expectancy, 186; mobility, 177–8; origins, 168–9; relationship between employer

and servant, 239–40; types of
servant, 162
domestic service
 characteristics of occupation,
 10–11; dissatisfaction of servants,
 221, 270; developments in
 nineteenth century, 241; hours of
 work, 195; time off, 215
domesticity, 2, 8, 18–19, 30, 65,
 104, 107, 136, 276, 280, 282–3
dowagers, *see* widows
Drew, Mary (Gladstone), 27, 52
drink and servants
 beer at meals, 211; beer money,
 206; brewing at country houses,
 156, 160; butlers retiring to run
 public houses, 163, 208;
 drunkenness, 249, 253, 265, 268,
 281
Dunrobin Castle, 14, 35, 120, 145
Dynes Hall, 106 (plate 13), 134
 (plate 16)
Dyott family of Freeford Hall, 182,
 266

Earlham Hall, 257–8 (plate 33)
Eaton Hall, 180
Eden Hall, 152, 179, 229
education
 boarding schools for girls, 51,
 276–7, 282; by parents, 80–1;
 public schools for boys, 7, 17–18,
 38, 49, 63, 84–5, 276, 279, 282;
 schoolroom education, 42–5,
 48–54, 63, 199, 279
Elcho, Mary, Lady, 160, 268
Ellenborough, Edward Law, second
 Baron, 98, 100
Ellenborough, Jane Law (Digby),
 Lady, 98, 100
Elwes, Lady Winifride (Fielding),
 42, 62
Englefield House, 155, 157, 201
entail, 28, 30
equity law, 105–6, 117
Erddig, 15, 75, 152–3, 155, 157,
 160, 168, 181, 187, 201, 212–13,
 226, 229, 236–7, 242, 259.
Ewenny Priory, 30

family life cycle, 23, 37
Fane, Lady Rose, *see* Weigall
fatherhood in landed classes
 authority, 70–1, 273; at births,
 77; in courtship of child, 91–6,
 98–100; educating children,
 80–1; generosity with toys and
 treats, 79–80; involvement with
 children, 72, 76–9, 85; marriage
 settlement for child, 99–100,
 105–6; religious and moral
 training, 80; roles, 88, 279;
 stereotypes, 8, 65–6; values, 71;
 Victorian views of father's roles,
 66–7, 68–9, 70, 278–9; *see also*
 child-rearing.
Ferrers, Sewallis Shirley, tenth Earl,
 96, 233, 240
Fetcham Park, 179
Finborough Hall, 151
Forbes, Lady Angela (St Claire
 Erskine), 61, 72
Franklin, Jill, 1, 6, 148, 157,
 159–60, 204, 212
Freeford Hall, 182, 187
Frewen, Anne, 76, 254

Gardener's Chronicle, 174
Gascoyne family, 97–8
Gaskell, Catherine Milnes, 135–6
Gathorne-Hardy, Jonathan, 41, 66,
 76, 85
gender
 in gentleman's service, 199, 203,
 205–6, 269; in upbringing of
 landed children, 48–9, 70, 72,
 273–4; *see also* separate spheres
gentleman's service
 definition, 11–12, 190; treatment
 by historians, 12
Gibbons family of Holton Hall, 43
Gibbons, Dora, 15, 44

Gibbons, Joan, 15, 44
Gillis, John, 167, 231
Girouard, Mark, 1, 3, 5–7, 157
Gladstone, Catherine, 69, 73, 75, 82, 85, 126
Gladstone, Mary, *see* Drew
Gladstone, William, 73, 75, 81–2
Glenliven, 217–18
Goodwood, 160, 181, 229
Gorhambury, 178, 182
Gorst, Frederick, 166, 218, 226
governesses, 33, 42–5, 47–53, 55, 63, 72, 80–1, 151, 153, 165–6, 179, 189, 195, 199, 203, 209, 223, 253; *see also* distressed gentlewomen
Governesses' Benevolent Institution, 175, 185
Granby, Violet Manners, Lady, 52, 111
Greville, Lady Violet, 111, 123, 133
Grey, John, 87, 251, 243
Grimmett, Gordon, 218, 240
Guest, Lady Charlotte, *see* Schreiber

Hadspen House, 96
Hagley Hall, 47 (plate 5), 50 (plate 6), 132, 199, 234, 268
Haims, Lynne, 146, 265, 326
Halifax, Edward Woods, first Earl, 49, 71
Hall, 170, 265
Halton House, 217
Hampton Court, Herefordshire, 15 (plate 2), 16, 143, 156, 178, 214, 216, 235, 259, 269
Hardwicke Court, 217
Harrison, Rosina, 255, 262
Harrison, William, 172, 217–8
Henham Hall, 58, 160
Hesleyside, 31, 232, 266–7
Hickleton Hall, 156, 160
Higgs, Edward, 149, 308
Hinchingbroke, 147 (plate 18)
Hoare, Louisa, 69, 82

Hobhouse, Margaret (Potter), 96, 109, 135
Hodnet Hall, 135
Holkham Hall, 229
Holton, 14–15, 125 (plate 15), 154 (plate 19), 155–6, 160, 168, 170, 181–2, 192, 200–2, 209, 214, 259 (plate 34)
Horne, Eric, 164, 217, 228–9, 233–4, 245, 269
household management in country house
  conspicuous consumption, 143–4, 190, 274, 277, 281, 283; ritual and ceremony, 3, 190, 244–5, 275, 280; segregation, 3, 30, 67–8, 112, 143, 157, 192, 195, 231, 280; self-sufficiency, 143, 155–6, 159, 190; timetables and strict routines, 9, 38, 43–4, 63–4, 67–8, 178, 108, 190, 192–4, 196, 215, 277–8, 280
household structure in country house
  family types, 30, 33–4, 37, 152; live-in servants 158–9; staff turnover, promotion, transfer, 178–182; *see also* country house servants, demography, staff size

Ingram, Jane, 41, 257
inheritance, 28–9, 30, 37, 288–9
Inkley (butler at Hesleyside), 232, 267

Jalland, Pat, 73, 90, 98, 100, 116, 121
Jebb, Eglantyne, 78, 140
Jebb, Eglantyne (wife of Arthur Jebb), 135, 246
Jeune, Lady, 4, 86–7
Jones, E. E. Constance, 42–3
Jones, Sir Lawrence, fourth Baronet, 79, 81
Juniper Hill, maids from, 163, 167–8, 183, 186, 213, 231, 235, 258, 264

Keele Hall, 23, 30, 35, 155, 157–8, 214 (plate 26)
Ketteringham Hall, 244, 250
King's Bromley Manor, 236 (plate 30)
Kingston Hall, 180
Kingston Lacy, 59, 168, 230
kinship in landed classes
  heirs living with parents, 29; kin living with landowner, 32–4, 37; parents' ties to married children, 87, 107–8, 276, 280; visits to relatives, 57–8
Knebworth, 227
Knightley, Lady Louisa (Bowater), 95, 126
Knole, 97, 198

labourers
  attitudes towards family, 268; benefits, 209; definition, 12, 162, 189, 276; job mobility, 177–9; job satisfaction, 196; marriage, 188, 233; motives, 12, 166–7; relations with family, 255; social status, 235; wages, 201, 317–18; working conditions, 194
Lanceley, William, 207, 218, 266–7.
landed classes
  changes over time, 16–19, 272, 276–82; characteristics of landed family, 273–4; definition, 6–7; income, 4–5; *see also* code of conduct, reform of landed classes, values
Lee, Edwin, 164, 218, 264, 284
Leveson–Gower family, Dukes of Sutherland, 13–14, 31, 35, 191, 203–4, 223
Lewis, Judith Schneid, 25, 73, 92, 107, 116
liberal employer, 9, 239, 242–3, 246, 258–60, 266, 270, 280, 283
life-cycle servants
  attitude towards employers, 268; benefits, 209; definition, 11, 162, 164–5, 167, 188–9, 275; geographical mobility, 178; job mobility, 179; in laundry, 184; marriage, 186–7, 189; motives, 12, 163–4; origins, 168, 188; relationship with employers, 255; in stables, 186; wages, 202
Lilleshall, 29, 35, 120, 145, 217
Linton Park, 195, 210 (plate 25), 237
Llangoedmor, 59
Longleat, 30, 160, 216, 231, 240
Lucy, George, 87, 95–6
Lucy, Mary Elizabeth (Williams), 87, 95–6, 110, 113, 117, 120, 262
Lyme Park, 160
Lythe, The, 32
Lyttleton family, 47 (plate 5), 50 (plate 6), 132, 254
Lyttleton, George, fourth Baron, 71, 113–4
Lyttleton, Mary (Glynne), Lady, 82–3, 97, 100, 108, 268
Lyttleton, Sarah, Lady, 32, 199
Lytton, Lady Emily, 61, 69, 82

McBride, Theresa, 10, 163, 318
Macclesfield, Louisa, Countess of, 123, 244
Maddison, Jane, 156, 259–60
Marlborough, Consuelo Spencer–Churchill, ninth Duchess, *see* Balsan
marriage between landed classes and servants, 253
marriage in domestic service, 164, 233–4, 247, 262, 268, 315; *see also* demography of country house servants
marriage in landed family
  before inheriting, 29; demographics, 24, 36, 98; functions, 91; historians' views, 90; husbands' dominance, 103,

273; impact of servants, 108; marriage breakdown 109–12; as partnership, 105, 107, 274; remarriage, 113–14; separation of husband and wife, 109; sense of duty, 110; support from family and friends, 107–8; wives' responsibilities, 101–4; as women's career, 98; *see also* companionate marriage, divorce
marriage portion, 105–6
marriage settlement, 99, 105–6, 273
Massey, Mrs, 185, 205; registry office, 172, 247
master and mistress, role of annuities, legacies, and pensions, 208–9, 275; changes over time, 278–82; controlling servants' sexuality, 230–1; discipline and punishment, 10, 254, hiring and firing, 171–2, 178–9, 182, 246–9; medical care, 207–8, 275; paying wages, 199–205; personnel management, 249–51, 253–55; providing accommodation, 212–5; providing recreation, 215–6, 237; *see also* authoritarian employer, liberal employer, remote employer
Matfen Hall, 156
men and housekeeping in country house, 105, 107, 131–2, 193, 267
middle-class domestic service class-consciousness of employers, 10, 221; food and accommodation, 211–13, inefficiency, 192; isolation of maid-of-all-work, 211–12, labour market, 172, 283; lack of recreation, 215; lack of upper servants, 223–4, 271; lack of upward mobility, 197; lower remuneration, 199, 209; petty place, 168, servants' dissatisfaction, 190–1, 270

migration, landed classes' annual cycle of, 34–5, 57, 132–3, 154, 176
Milne, Cynthia, *see* Colville
modernization, 10, 274
Moor Park, 32, 54
More, Hannah, 48, 104
Morpeth, 121
motherhood in landed classes breastfeeding, 38–9, 68, 73–4, 88, 283; bringing out teenage daughters, 85–6; change over century, 68–9, 72, 83–4, 276, 279, 282; childbearing, 24–5; 72–3; discipline, 81–3; educating children, 80, 89; matchmaking, 91, 93–9; raising heir, 30, 118; religious and moral training, 80, 89; roles, 8, 140, 276; sleeping with newborn, 73; stereotypes, 8, 65–6; time with children, 78, 80, 89; Victorian views of mother's roles, 66–7, 69, 70–1, 74–5
Mumby, Amelia, 154 (plate 19), 260
Mumby, Sarah, 156–7, 260
Naworth Castle, 112, 121, 232
Newby, Howard, 128, 239
Newnham Paddox, 264
Nightingale, Florence, 52, 87
Norland Nursing School, 45, 166, 176
Northwick Park, 150, 160, 181, 188, 195, 200–2, 206, 212–4, 231, 234, 244, 248 (plate 31), 254, 259
Northwick, Elizabeth Rushout, Lady, 34, 150, 160
Northwick, George Rushout, third Baron, 31, 34, 132, 152, 200–2, 208, 253
Northwick, John Rushout, second Baron, 34, 150, 244
Norwood, 202
Nunwell Park, 34, 152
nurses (nannies), 22–5, 38–42, 47–8, 62–63, 66–7, 72, 184–5,

204, 206, 213, 227, 257, 262–3, 279, 283

organic community, 4, 18, 221, 240, 243–4, 273
Osberton Hall, 229
Otterburn, 121

Packe family of Prestwold, 150, 172, 207
Parnell, Emma, *see* Clifton
paternalism, 9, 18, 103, 123, 128, 131, 208, 241, 243–4, 268, 279, 273, 278–9.
paternalistic employer, *see* authoritarian employer
patriarchal employer, *see* authoritarian employer
patriarchy, 2, 5, 65–6, 69, 88, 90, 104, 114, 131, 241–2, 269, 277–9
Peper Harrow, 58, 237
Perkin, Joan, 90, 106, 117
Peterson, M. Jeanne, 51–2, 104, 107, 116, 118
Petworth House, 155, 156, 160, 184 (plate 22), 206, 270
philanthropy
children's role, 62–3, 86; men's role, 7, 118, 122, 277, 282; towards servants, 207–9, 244; women's role, 1, 8, 105, 115–7, 122–8, 134–8, 277–8, 280, 282
Picton Castle, 99 (plate 12).
Picton–Turvervill, Edith, 42, 84
Picton–Turbervill, Colonel John, 30, 84
pin money, 100, 105
Polderoy, Henry, 112, 167, 201, 228, 251–3, 257, 269–70
Pollock, Linda, 81–2
Port Eliot, 199
Powderham Castle, 33
Pre, The, 36
Prestwold Hall, 150, 155, 201–2, 206, 216–17 (plate 27)

primogeniture, 21, 28, 30–1, 36–7, 95, 117, 273
Primrose League, 121–2, 139
Princess Christian Nursery Training College, 45, 166, 176

Radnor, Helen Bouverie (Chaplin), Countess of, 55, 87
reform of landed classes, 17–18, 44, 65, 68, 123, 147, 278–9
registry offices, 172, 174–7
relationships between family and servants
children and governesses, 9, 42–3, 45; children and nurse, 9, 39–42, 61, 63, 257; children and servants, 9, 58–62, 263–4; distressed gentlewomen and employers, 199, 255–7, 253; family and nurses, 257; family and servants, 8–9, 10, 27, 108, 221, 233–4, 239–43, 251–3, 260–70; family and upper servants, 257; mistresses and ladies' maids, 258; mothers and governesses, 80, 276; mothers and nurses, 67, 75–6, 276, 283
relationships between parents and children
children's love for parents, 72–3, 76, 85, 89, 91–2; *see also* fatherhood and motherhood (in landed classes)
relationships between servants
conflict between servants, 220, 227–9, 254; courtship and liaisons among servants, 230–1, 237, 264–5, 268, 270; distressed gentlewomen and other servants, 223; friendship between servants, 220, 229–30, 237; hierarchy below stairs, 211, 220–7, 229, 237, 262, 271, 274; hierarchy within nursery, 38–9, 67; segregation of men and women servants, 223, 226–7; servants'

solidarity, 230, 237; upper and lower servants, 191, 197–98, 223–7.
relationships between servants and rural community, 220, 235–37
religion
  affecting servants, 220–1, 241, 247, 250, 280–2; as career for single women, 140; in child-rearing, 44, 46, 47–8, 63, 78–80, 279; declined in 18th century, 241–2; discouraging birth control, 25; discouraging divorce, 111; in philanthropy, 123–4; revival in nineteenth century, 9, 17–18, 214, 243, 221, 278; religious families, 2, 282
remote employer, 239, 245–6, 259–60, 266–7, 270, 278, 280, 283
Rendlesham Hall, 216, 251
Renishaw, 40
Ridley, Cecilia, Lady, 69, 74–5, 78, 105, 126, 132, 150, 201, 230
Ridley, Sir Matthew, fourth Baronet, 77, 132
Ridley Hall, 121
Roberts, David, 60, 66, 70, 80–1, 88, 122
Roberts, George, 237, 242
Robertson, Miss, 43, 257
Rogers, Fanny, 40, 45
Rougham, 177
Rounton Grange, 237
Rousseau, Jean-Jacques, 68, 73, 276
Rudding Park, 204
Rufford Abbey, 192, 226
Runcton, 33
Rushmere, 156
Rushout family of Northwick, 16, 181

Sackville, Lionel Sackville-West, third Baron, 27, 73, 97
Sackville, Victoria Sackville-West, Lady, 27, 73, 97, 108

Schreiber, Lady Charlotte, 87, 96, 113–14
Scotney Castle, 201
Season, the, 1, 34, 51, 64, 86, 93, 98, 127, 176
Sedgwick, Sarah, 43–5, 227
separate spheres, 8, 91, 104–5, 114, 116–18, 131, 139, 273–4, 279–81
sexuality in landed classes
  adultery, 110–11, 278, 281; boys' initiation with maidservants, 61, 84; in marriage, 108; liaisons with servants, 251–3; repressed, 61, 66
sexuality of servants
  courtship and liaisons among servants, 230–1, 237, 264–5, 268, 270; employers' attitudes, 220, 228, 230–1, 250–1; 260, 280; liaisons with employers, 251–3; rape of maidservants, 232, 252; repression, 228; unwed mothers, 232, 250–2
Shirburn Castle, 160, 216
Shugborough, 160, 173 (plate 21), 174, 210, 235, 263 (plate 35)
Sitwell, Ida, Lady, 110, 135
Sitwell, Louisa, Lady, 118, 126
Sitwell, Sir Osbert, fifth Baronet, 54–5, 58
Slingsby, George, 185, 192, 226, 229
Sneyd, Ralph, 22–3 (plate 3), 30, 145, 157, 181, 208–9, 242, 254
Southill Park, 177
St Claire Erskine, Lady Angela, *see* Forbes
staff size
  decline from 1870s, 158–60, 283; historians' estimates, 148–9, 308; mid-century, 281; motives for hiring servants, 142–4; Regency, 277; role of family life cycle, 160; role of income, 149–51, 160–1; role of rank, 151, 160–1, 308

Stafford House, 14, 35, 139, 145
Stanway, 59, 160
Stanley, Henrietta Maria, Lady, 27, 29, 96, 117
Stanley, Maria Josepha, Lady, 29, 72, 97
Staunton Harold, 170, 192, 240
Stone, Lawrence, 1, 6, 65–6, 81, 83, 88, 90, 98, 107, 122, 221, 277
Stoneleigh, 55, 235
Street End, 206
strict settlement, 28, 30
Suffolk census sample, 36
Sutherland, Anne Leveson-Gower, third Duchess of, 35, 94, 145, 207–8, 254, 258
Sutherland, Cromartie Leveson-Gower, fourth Duke of, 33, 94, 109, 132
Sutherland, Elizabeth Leveson–Gower, first Duchess of, 13–14
Sutherland, George Granville Leveson-Gower, first Duke of, 13, 29
Sutherland, George Granville Leveson-Gower, second Duke of, 29, 145, 150, 207–8.
Sutherland, George Granville Leveson-Gower, third Duke of, 113, 145
Sutherland, Harriet Leveson-Gower, second Duchess of, 67, 74, 80, 120, 126, 130, 247, 256, 259
Sutherland, Millicent Leveson-Gower, fourth Duchess of, 33, 72, 94, 109, 130, 139

Taine, Hippolyte, 192–3, 267
Tallents, Sir Stephen, 54, 61
Thomas, Margaret, 190–1, 194, 226, 246
Thompson, F. M. L., 5–7, 122, 148, 150
Tolson Hall, 49, 58–9

Toulmin family of the Pre and Childwickbury, 40, 44–5, 72, 257
Toulmin, Emma, 29, 36
Toulmin, Harry, 29, 36.
Tregyb, 99 (plate 12).
Trentham Hall, 14 (plate 1), 35, 120, 139, 145, 155, 174, 180, 187, 191, 202, 208–9, 214–5, 222 (plate 28), 234, 259
Trevelyan, Molly (Bell), 103, 108
Trollope–Bellew family of Casewick, 200, 203
Troubridge family at Runcton, 33, 43, 51, 53
tutors, 8, 49, 81, 166, 276
Tweedsmuir, Lady Susan (Grosvenor), 54, 58

unmarried women in landed classes, 5, 32–4, 37, 93, 95–8, 117, 123–4, 129, 132, 140, 152, 282

values of landed classes
adopted by servants, 240, 264; in behaviour towards kin, 37; in child-rearing, 8, 45, 49, 65–6, 68–71, 85, 88–9; in courtship, 91; duty, 8, 19, 69–71, 83, 113, 123, 244, 273, 277, 279; dynasty, 4, 8, 27–8, 69, 240, 273–4; noblesse oblige, 69, 123, 244, 277, 281; 242, 281; reform, 17–18, 44, 65, 68, 123, 147, 278–9; subordination of individual's interests, 8, 91, 94, 273.
Vanderbilt, Consuelo, *see* Balsan

Waddesdon Manor, 120
Waldershare Park, 200 (plate 24)
Wales, 15, 272; recruitment of servants, 176–7, 182; staff size, 151; wages, 201
Walsh, J. H., 149–50, 205
Weigall, Lady Rose (Fane), 87, 124

Welbeck Abbey, 181, 211, 216, 224, 231
Wells (nurse at Blagdon), 75, 196, 230
Wentworth Woodhouse, 56 (plate 7), 270
Westhill Park, 35
Westminster, Elizabeth Grosvenor, Marchioness of, 31, 39, 105, 108
Westminster, Richard Grosvenor, second Marquess of, 31, 108
wet-nurses, 38–9, 187–8, 202, 230
White, John Baker, 43, 61, 167
widowers in landed classes, 32–3, 152
widows in landed classes, 5, 30–1, 33–4, 37, 113, 117, 123, 129
Williams, Sir John, 87, 95, 96
Wilton House, 120
Winnington, 29
Wollaton Hall, 265
women in landed classes
  as authors, 13, 137, 139; changes in roles over century, 136–7, 139; in estate management, 115, 118, 120–1; historians' views, 115–16; as hostess, in Society, 8, 115, 117–18, 121–3, 128–30, 133–5, 140, 277, 280–1; as housekeeper, 8, 117, 123, 130–5, 140, 280; as landowner, 105, 115, 118, 120, 123; in local government, 122, 139; in philanthropy, 1, 8, 105, 115–7, 122–8, 134–8, 277–8, 280, 282; in politics, 105, 107, 118, 121–22; restrictions in London, 303; *see also* marriage, master and mistress of servants, unmarried women
women's rights movement, 122, 128, 139–40
Wood family of Hickleton, 58–9, 71
Woodcote, 194, 222
Woodhouse, 233
Woolley Hall, 234
Worth Park, 217
Wrest Park, 218
Wynn, Honorable Frederick, 150, 217

Yandell, Elizabeth, 51, 52, 59
Yarborough, Countess of, 118, 120
Yonge, Charlotte M., 102, 124
Yorke family of Erddig, 130, 152–3, 180–1, 208, 242, 254
Yorke, Jock, 60, 62, 63
Yorke, Louisa, 74, 75–6, 83 (plate 10), 215, 242, 247.
Yorke, Philip II, 15, 153, 215, 230, 242
Yorke, Philip III, 16, 83 (plate 10)
Yorke, Simon II, 15, 153
Yorke, Simon III, 15, 153, 207, 242
Yorke, Simon IV, 15–16, 83 (plate 10)
Yorke, Victoria, 130, 201
younger sons in landed classes, 25, 31–2, 37, 279, 289